The Resilience of Religion in American Higher Education

John Schmalzbauer and Kathleen A. Mahoney

BAYLOR UNIVERSITY PRESS

Waco, Texas 76798

Cover Design by *the*BookDesigners
Cover art created from stock art images © Shutterstock/Marijus Auruskevicius, Evgenyi

The Library of Congress has cataloged this book under ISBN
978-1-4813-0871-7

Printed in the United States of America on acid-free paper with a minimum of 30 percent post-consumer waste recycled content.

To our spouses,
John Brophy and Susan Schmalzbauer

CONTENTS

ACKNOWLEDGMENTS

We have accumulated many debts during the research and writing of this book. The early stages of the project were made possible by an evaluation grant from Lilly Endowment, Inc. We are grateful for the support of Religion Division Vice President Craig Dykstra and program officer Jeanne Knoerle, S.P., as well as Lilly evaluation coordinator Kathleen Cahalan.

Special thanks to our coevaluator, James Youniss of the Catholic University of America, who brought his expertise on religion and education to the Lilly evaluation project. Boston College graduate students Andrew Simmons, Lisabeth Timothy, Kristin Hunt, Kevin Sayers, and Mandy Savitz were integral members of the research team.

When this project began, we were both employed at Jesuit institutions. Though our circumstances have changed, we are grateful for our colleagues at Boston College and the College of the Holy Cross, especially David O'Brien, David Hummon, Susan Rodgers, Mathew Schmalz, Royce Singleton, Stephen Ainlay, Thomas Landy, Joseph Appleyard, S.J., Karen Arnold, Philip Altbach, Joseph O'Keefe, S.J., and Alan Wolfe.

John Schmalzbauer is thankful to Betty DeBerg and Lilly Endowment for his involvement with the National Study of Campus Ministries. Schmalzbauer's work at Missouri State University was made possible by the generosity of the Thomas G. Strong family. His understanding of religion and higher education was enriched by conversations with colleagues in the Department of Religious Studies, in particular Martha Finch, Kathy Pulley, Robert Jones, LaMoine

DeVries, Amy Artman, Victor Matthews, David Embree, Micki Pulleyking, Leslie Baynes, John Strong, Austra Reinis, Julia Watts Belser, Vadim Putzu, Mark Given, and Philippa Koch. While James Moyer, Jack Llewellyn, and Stephen Berkwitz created a supportive environment for faculty growth, administrative assistants JoAnne Brown, Carolyn Mayer, and especially Jane Terry helped in countless ways. Graduate assistants Marguerite Langille-Hoppe, Jane Terry, Travis Cooper, Adam Park, Michael Bohlen, Adam Blaney, Steven Fouse, Logan Burke, and Jade Callaway provided valuable research support.

Portions of the project were presented at the Life Cycle Institute at the Catholic University of America, the Social Science and Religion Network at Boston University, the Social Science Research Council in New York City, the MacMillan Center at Yale University, Michigan State University, Virginia Wesleyan University, the College of the Holy Cross, the Danforth Center at Washington University, the Radcliffe Institute at Harvard University, and the University of Missouri. The 2004–2005 class of the Young Scholars in American Religion offered useful feedback on an early chapter, along with seminar leaders Catherine Brekus and Peter Williams. In 2011 the project was the focus of a Books in Public Scholarship Workshop sponsored by Rice University's Religion and Public Life Program. Special thanks to program director Elaine Howard Ecklund for hosting this gathering and to Julie Reuben, George Marsden, and Amy Binder for preparing detailed comments.

Many colleagues provided helpful feedback on our research, including John DiIulio, Nancy Ammerman, Peter Steinfels, Amy DeRogatis, Arthur Versluis, Timothy Larsen, David Nichols, Michael Emerson, Helen Rose Ebaugh, Perry Glanzer, Thomas Landy, Jonathan Imber, Jonathan VanAntwerpen, Courtney Bender, Thomas Banchoff, John Torpey, R. Marie Griffith, Leigh Schmidt, James Bielo, Eric Michael Mazur, James Jasper, Jonathan Hill, Michael Lindsay, Wendy Cadge, Christian Smith, Richard Callahan, John Giggie, Sarah McFarland Taylor, Thomas Kidd, and Amy Koehlinger. Others furnished encouragement and moral support, including Gerardo Marti, Penny Edgell, Brian Steensland, Grant Wacker, Mark Noll, John Wilson, James Mathisen, Lyman Kellstedt, Shirley Roels, Michael Cartwright, Robert Jones, Michèle Lamont, and Robert Wuthnow.

Special thanks to the anonymous readers at Baylor University Press. Editor Carey Newman's enthusiastic support of the project gave us the energy to finish the job. His wisdom and humor make the press a nurturing environment for its authors. While Cade Jarrell helped us prepare the manuscript, Madeline Wieters walked us through the final steps, and Diane Smith is to thank for her masterful design work. The expert copyediting of John Morris and proofreading of Susan Matheson made this a better book.

Though we are grateful to all those we have mentioned, our deepest debts are to our families. When we were still young, Neil and Dorothy Mahoney and Arnold and Norma Schmalzbauer taught us to care about books and learning. John Brophy, a graduate of a religiously sponsored university, has been unflagging in his encouragement. His patience, keen questions, and good humor buoyed his wife during this project and made it more enjoyable. A constant source of love and support, Susan Schmalzbauer has never stopped believing in this project. A product of church-related higher education, she has found her calling in faith-based social activism. Striving daily to do justice, she exemplifies the best traditions of religion in public life. John Henry, Max, and Martin Schmalzbauer have never known a time when Dad wasn't working on this book. Their efforts to find joy and purpose in life have enriched his own sense of vocation. May all of us honor such quests.

1

THE COMEBACK

As the twenty-first century opened, religion staged an unexpected comeback in American higher education. Its return contravened long-accepted theories that held society would become less religious as it became more modern. Portrayed as a carrier of secularization, higher education was its chief exemplar.[1] Historical studies also supported the view that the academy had or was about to become thoroughly secular.[2]

There is much to commend in this interpretation, but recent developments suggest the secularization narrative seriously underestimates the resilience of religion in the American academy. A closer reading of history and contemporary sources demands an alternative assessment and a more complex explanation.

Despite the undeniable impact of secularization, the sacred did not disappear from higher education. Coexisting with the secular, religious frameworks and concepts continued to influence American intellectual life. Most visible in church-related colleges, divinity schools, and campus ministries, the teaching and the practice of religion persisted in a wide variety of institutions, waxing and waning over the course of the past century. Sometimes this presence was more overt. For example, in the years following World War II through the late 1960s, colleges and universities experienced a resurgence of piety that found expression in a Protestant theological renaissance on campus. By nurturing the nascent field of religious studies, it laid the foundation for future scholarship. Though the postwar revival ended, it showed that the academy need not follow a straight and inevitable path toward secularization.[3]

As in the postwar era, religion is making a comeback in American higher education. Unlike the postwar revival, it is not led by Protestant theologians. Reflecting the pluralistic character of the contemporary university, today's resurgence is the work of diverse groups of faculty and students, including people of faith and the religiously unaffiliated, engaged practitioners and detached scholars. While some have treated religion as an object of study, others favor more confessional approaches. Still others have challenged the binary between the religious and the secular.

Over the past three decades, religious activity in higher education has increased rather remarkably. There is more interest in religion in the academy and more commitment to the project of religious higher education. There are growing campus ministries and unprecedented diversity in student religious life. Claims that higher education is wholly secular are no longer credible, if they ever were. Instead, the academy is better described as post-secular, a set of intellectual and social institutions where the sacred and secular coexist.[4]

In the post-secular academy, faculty blur the boundary between religion and knowledge. While some emphasize religiously grounded scholarship, others engage in the nonconfessional study of religion. Though definitions of religion vary widely, both theological and nontheological approaches are on the rise. So is attention to spirituality. Membership in religiously oriented scholarly societies has soared, specialization in religious topics has increased, and articles on religion have proliferated. Reflecting targeted investments by philanthropists, religiously oriented centers and institutes can be found at America's leading universities, part of a surge in the interdisciplinary study of religion.[5]

At the institutional level, churches and denominational colleges have reassessed their often less than robust relationships and fostered closer ties. Through several foundation-supported initiatives, hundreds of representatives from religious colleges have gathered at conferences, seminars, and consultations to talk about the religious identities of their institutions. On individual campuses, dozens of religion-oriented centers and institutes, faculty mentoring programs, and new mission statements have signaled a renewed commitment to the cause of church-related higher education.[6]

Finally, voluntary religious expression is thriving and increasingly visible. Membership in evangelical parachurch groups has risen dramatically, while student religious life is now remarkably diverse. Reflecting the rise of a new religious pluralism, Hindu Students Councils and Muslim Students' Associations continue to proliferate, while a campus interfaith movement brings many voices to the table. Experimenting with new forms of ministry and new development strategies, some Catholic and mainline Protestant ministries are showing signs of revitalization.[7] Responding to the vitality of undergraduate religion, national leaders in the student affairs field have called for the integration of spirituality into campus life.[8]

In the late 1990s, commentators began to notice religion on campus, describing its presence as a resurgence, a rediscovery, a revival, or a revitalization. In the year 2000, George Marsden, whose *The Soul of the American University* chronicled the secularization of higher education, acknowledged the potential for reversal. As he told the *Chronicle of Higher Education*, "The general consensus is that there's no reason to have to continue along the slippery slope toward secularism." The very next year, an ethnographic study reported that the teaching and the practice of religion was "alive and well in the institutions of higher education." A decade later, another study concluded that religion was "no longer invisible."[9]

Going beyond previous accounts, this book comprehensively documents the return of religion in American colleges and universities at the turn of the twenty-first century. It takes up the history of religion in higher education where the historians left off: in the early seventies, when religion's presence was less conspicuous. Chronicling multiple movements, it examines how the sacred moved back toward the mainstream of academic life *intellectually*, *institutionally*, and *socially* over the past three decades. It documents growing interest in the study of religion, as well as greater willingness on the part of some scholars to recognize the intellectual relevance of religious convictions. It recounts how church-related colleges are taking their religious identities more seriously. And finally, it describes the vitality of student religious life in all its diversity.

Over the course of four centuries, the history of higher education and the history of American religion have frequently intersected. The United States remains among the most religious of the industrialized nations. While episodes of disestablishment have loosened the authoritative claims of religion over government, they have set the stage for religious mobilization in civil society.[10] Disestablishment found formal political expression in the First Amendment of the Constitution as early citizens rejected European patterns of church-state relations: no religion would enjoy the legal privilege of state sanction, nor would the state interfere with the free exercise of religion by its citizens. Remarkable for its mixture of deists and Christians, Catholics and Protestants, Europeans and Africans, newcomers and natives, colonial America was far from religiously monolithic. Amidst this diversity, religion remained vital.[11] And though legislation prohibited the government from establishing a national church, it did not deter some early nineteenth-century Americans from proclaiming Protestantism the national religion. They unambiguously claimed America for the Protestant faith and invented a national mythology, bestowing upon their new country a pivotal role in salvation history as a light to the nations. The press, voluntary associations, schools, and colleges stood with the churches as essential agents in the cause of a Protestant America.[12]

Cast as the national religion in the nineteenth century, and once at the very center of American life, Protestantism saw its cultural hold weakened in time, culminating in a second disestablishment during the 1920s. Its influence diminished as scientific discoveries, technological advances, and the emergence of strong nonecclesial forces such as unions, corporations, organized sports, and popular entertainment successfully vied for men's and women's attention. Under the weight of demographic shifts, Catholic and Jewish immigration, and intellectual advances, Protestantism's identity as the "soul of the nation" waned, and with it much of its capacity to shape society and culture through the press, schools, and other agencies.[13]

Religion's increasingly marginal role in higher education constituted one of the clearest signs of the cultural disestablishment of Protestantism. Once taken for granted as a part of academic life, Christianity lost its central place in the academy toward the end of the nineteenth century. This marked nothing less than a sea change.[14] From the earliest days of colonial history, Protestantism exerted considerable influence by educating men of standing in denominationally sponsored colleges. Its sway grew in the antebellum years as the evangelical fervor of the Second Great Awakening led to the creation of hundreds of denominationally affiliated colleges.[15]

The era of the denominational college closed rather quickly at the end of the nineteenth century as an academic revolution fueled by the forces of modernity swept through higher education. Reform, innovation, and significant structural change remade the academy. The signal event in this revolution was the emergence of the modern, nonsectarian university in the second half of the nineteenth century. It quickly came of age, and by the early twentieth century the nonsectarian university, rather than the denominational college, stood at the head of the new academic order.[16]

The revolution that produced the modern university and a new academic order at the end of the nineteenth century helped disestablish Protestant Christianity in higher education. This process of de-Christianization led to three boundaries constraining the religious, separating *religion and knowledge*, *churches and colleges*, and *spirituality and student life*. Though never airtight, these boundaries often segregated religious and educational activities.

One boundary differentiated faith and knowledge, separating what was known through religious sources from what was known through reason and empirical study. The growing divide between faith and knowledge undermined earlier assumptions about the nature of truth. At one time, all truth, whether religious, moral, or scientific, was considered part of one greater, seamless whole.

But this conception of truth fragmented with the vast expansion of science in the eighteenth and nineteenth centuries and concomitant development of specialized inquiry. An unintended consequence of professionalization, the rise of specialized disciplines rendered theological and religious questions less germane to academic research. Knowledge derived through focused investigation gained primacy over the knowledge obtained from the Bible, revelation, creeds, and pronouncements of the clergy.[17]

The disestablishment of religion also created an institutional boundary between the churches and the colleges. From the earliest years of the colonial period, the churches had exercised a central role in the field of higher education; hundreds of colleges were established under the auspices of particular denominations or, in the case of Catholic colleges, under the sponsorship of dioceses or religious orders. But the traditional sponsorship pattern changed significantly during the second half of the nineteenth century as the state matured and entered the arena of higher education. Though established as nonsectarian institutions, nineteenth-century state universities were still considered Christian institutions and partners with the churches in the cause of a Protestant America. But over time, the logic of nonsectarian education in a pluralistic nation undermined even a loosely construed sense of religious identity.[18]

Of course, the state did not capture the complete field of higher education from the churches. Hundreds of colleges remained church affiliated, and many were established with religious sponsorship. Yet more than a few, such as Duke and Princeton, severed their church ties. Even among those retaining their religious affiliation, distance grew between the churches and the colleges. The colleges abjured direct control by the churches, while the churches manifested growing disinterest in the colleges. On the part of the colleges, greater autonomy took the form of independent boards of trustees and the appointment of nonclerical presidents. On the part of the churches, growing disinterest in the colleges led to cutbacks in financial support.[19]

The academic disestablishment of religion found expression in a third boundary constraining the free exercise of religion on campus. Once at the center, functioning publicly and normatively, religion moved to the margins, where it became more private and voluntary. Through much of the nineteenth century, colleges and universities, even nonsectarian state universities, publicly witnessed to their Christian commitments. It was carved into the granite of academic buildings, found in the curriculum, and heard in prayers and hymns when faculty and students gathered for mandatory daily chapel exercises. But during the first half of the twentieth century, most institutions of higher education abandoned public commitments to Christianity. Colleges and universities did not become antireligious per se; they simply declared themselves religiously neutral. Colleges and universities allowed for and even encouraged the free exercise of religion among students, provided it was private and voluntary.[20]

During the twentieth century, religion's presence on campus waxed and waned. And though Protestantism gradually relinquished control, it left its intellectual fingerprints on American higher education. From the post-Protestant thinkers of the Metaphysical Club to the Social Gospelers who became sociologists, early twentieth-century scholars confirmed Nietzsche's observation that the "Protestant parson is the grandfather of German philosophy." Increasingly devoid of religious substance, a cultural Protestantism continued to shape undergraduate life on campus. Reflecting the intolerance of the Protestant establishment, Ivy League universities enforced quotas against Jewish applicants while harboring deep-seated prejudices against Roman Catholics. By the election of John F. Kennedy, this establishment was fading away as the campus witnessed the emergence of a "tri-faith America."[21]

In many respects, the early 1970s marked a nadir for religion on campus as Protestant influence waned. Although evangelical parachurch groups were beginning to grow, campus religious life was still recovering from the collapse of the massive ecumenical student Christian movement in 1969. Though the nascent field of religious studies showed signs of vitality, it was one discipline among many. With some important exceptions, scholarship on religion remained concentrated in religious studies departments and divinity schools, as most disciplines paid little attention to the sacred. Across much of the humanities and social sciences, there was little scholarly interest in religion and relatively little religious activity.[22]

An earlier generation of historians emphasized the secularization of American higher education.[23] This well-accepted historical narrative neatly complemented leading theories of secularization which held that societies became more secular as they became more modern. *Differentiation* and *privatization*, the two main drivers of secularization, had weakened religion's place. Higher education became more secular through differentiation as colleges and universities distanced themselves from the institutional control of organized religion. So, too, with the academic disciplines that embraced the scientific method while eschewing religious thought. Privatization also played a critical role in the secularization of higher education. Faculty and students were trained to keep their religious beliefs out of the classroom, as religious practice became voluntary and private.[24]

But once-popular theories of secularization are now critically scrutinized. Indeed, religion's staying power in modern societies and public institutions has demonstrated the need to rethink theories that equated modernization with religious decline. The sacred, secular, and modern can and do coexist.

Sociologist Peter Berger, known as a founding father of postwar secularization theory, has since recanted, observing that "[m]ost of the world today is as religious as it ever was and, in a good many locales, more religious than ever." Likewise, Harvey Cox, whose 1965 *The Secular City* sold nearly one million copies in fourteen languages, now believes that "secularity, not spirituality . . . may be headed for extinction."[25]

In the field of sociology, secularization is now understood as partially reversible; the boundaries between the religious and other sectors are seen as semipermeable. According to sociologist José Casanova, "we are witnessing the 'deprivatization' of religion" as "religious traditions throughout the world are refusing to accept the marginal and privatized role which theories of modernity as well as theories of secularization had reserved for them." Others herald an era of *dedifferentiation* in which the boundaries separating religion from other social institutions are starting to dissolve.[26]

Over the past three decades, higher education has experienced both the *deprivatization* and *dedifferentiation* of religion. The walls that segregated faith and knowledge, separated churches and colleges, and delimited religious expression have become more porous. Scholarship on religion extends far beyond divinity schools and religious studies departments. Talk about religious beliefs and visible religious practices are more accepted. Scholars from a variety of disciplines—from psychology to political science to medicine—are studying the "religious factor," often with philanthropic support. Many faculty and staff are more open about their religious commitments. Growing numbers of students are taking religion courses, while some campus religious groups are enjoying a period of unusual vitality.

To be sure, the desecularization of the academy is not a return to a religious university; it is a partial reversal. The gains made by religion in higher education are quite noticeable but limited; on balance, the academy remains religiously unmusical, with large portions still indifferent to the sacred. While some campus ministries have grown, others have declined. Much of the religious discourse in higher education focuses on religion as an object of study, not as an object of faith. For the most part, religion's return to campus is not a restoration project. Religion on today's campus is as vital and complex as it is in society at large. While some have evinced a strong propensity for traditional religious expression, "spirituality," with all its diverse meanings and forms, has made strong headway on campus and sometimes vies with religion. Today's campuses are diverse, with Baha'is, Buddhists, Muslims, and Wiccans joining Protestants, Catholics, Jews, and the religiously unaffiliated. In its mixture of religious and secular, the contemporary academy mirrors the hybrid state of American culture as a whole.[27]

The Wider Context

Far from an isolated development, the return of religion reflects wider shifts in American culture. It is part of a much broader phenomenon, in which the sacred has secured a more prominent place in the public square.[28] The public face of religion has been especially visible in American politics, but can also be seen in the workplace and popular culture.

Several groups have contributed to the return of religion in public life. From the civil rights movement to Black Lives Matter, African American leaders have drawn on a deep reservoir of prophetic discourse. Shaped by this tradition, some of America's most prominent intellectuals echo the cadences of the black church.[29] Often found on the other end of the political spectrum, white evangelicals have played an equally important role in American public life. Once concentrated near the bottom of the social ladder in the South and the Midwest, a growing number have joined the college-educated professions, embracing a more cosmopolitan faith and a new engagement with contemporary issues.[30] So too with American Catholics. Buoyed by the mobility of the postwar years, they have witnessed the emergence of a Catholic cultural and intellectual elite, and resources sufficient to support more than 200 colleges and universities.[31] And mainline Protestantism's emphasis on tolerance and diversity has paved the way for a more diverse society.[32]

The religious diversity of today's campuses reflects wider societal trends. In the years following World War II, American Jews participated in the "triple melting pot."[33] As America moved from a tri-faith to a multireligious society, immigration has permanently altered the religious landscape. In the suburbs of Houston and Atlanta, Hindu temples have appeared alongside Baptist megachurches, while Buddhist centers have proliferated across the land.[34] The new diversity has sparked a fresh era of spiritual experimentation. A spirituality of seeking is especially prevalent on campus, where some student unions are as diverse as the World Parliament of Religions.[35]

In unsettled times, Americans turn to new cultural styles. Paralleling the return of the sacred in politics and higher education, religion has staked a larger claim in the world of business, where employers have built the spiritual into day-to-day operations and employees have brought their religious commitments to work.[36] The sacred can also be found in American popular culture. In the early years of the twenty-first century, religion returned to the suburban multiplex, demonstrating a ready market for faith and celluloid. Reflecting the American hunger for religious material culture, Christian kitsch and new-age fare continue to fascinate consumers. Surveying the media landscape, Martin

Marty writes that religion "for better and for worse—often for worse—gets more space and time in media than at any time in memory."[37]

The return of religion has extended to America's public intellectuals. In the 1990s, journalist Cullen Murphy attributed a "new prominence and legitimacy to the discussion of religion," a trend that accelerated during his tenure as managing editor of the *Atlantic*. Other leading journals of opinion have paid more attention to the sacred, including *Dissent*, the *New Republic*, and the *Nation*.[38] People of faith have carved out intellectual niches at venerable magazines like *Commonweal* and the *Christian Century*, as well as newcomers such as *First Things*. Like *Commonweal*, the *Jewish Review of Books* (founded in 2010) is a place where religion and intellectual life converge.[39] The growing openness of America's cultural gatekeepers to the sacred is reflected in the number of leading thinkers who address religious concerns. University of Chicago law professor Richard Posner's list of the top one hundred public intellectuals included many individuals who are religiously attuned, such as E. J. Dionne Jr., Alan Wolfe, Garry Wills, and Bill Moyers. More recent rankings of global thinkers by *Foreign Policy* and *Prospect* magazines have listed Pope Francis, Slavoj Žižek, Jürgen Habermas, Martha Nussbaum, John Gray, Tariq Ramadan, Reza Aslan, Michael Sandel, and Marilynne Robinson, among others.[40]

The rise of global religious public intellectuals underscores an important reality. Far from a product of American exceptionalism, the return of religion is a worldwide phenomenon. For decades, the received view of international relations stressed the emergence of the secular state. As it had in the West, the modernization of developing countries would result in secularization. In the postwar era, events seemed to confirm this prediction. Articulating a secular conception of nationalism, governments from Turkey to India deemphasized the sacred. In the bipolar world of the Cold War, the United States and the Soviet Union promoted competing versions of modernization. Slowly but surely, this secular consensus came undone, beginning with the Iranian Revolution of 1979 and culminating with the events of September 11, 2001. Instead of secularization, scholars began to speak of a crisis of modern secularism. Belatedly recognizing the importance of religion, former secretary of state Madeleine Albright penned *The Mighty and the Almighty: Reflections on America, God, and World Affairs* (2006).[41]

Challenging the myths of modernity, the religious resurgence has accompanied wider shifts in contemporary intellectual life. The fall of communism and the trials of advanced capitalism have led some to declare the exhaustion of modern culture. Science and technology have come under greater scrutiny. So have empiricism and positivism.[42] Criticizing entrenched notions of academic neutrality, feminists and multiculturalists have focused on the experiences of oppressed groups. Evaluating these shifts, Cornel West wrote that Americans have "witnessed the shattering of male WASP cultural homogeneity and the collapse of the short-lived liberal consensus."[43] At the height of the Cold War, sociologist Daniel Bell announced the "end of ideology." Like Bell, many American social scientists linked their faith in liberal democracy to a belief in objectivity. In recent decades, such confidence has vanished. Surveying the intellectual landscape in the early 1990s, Bell concluded, "There is no longer any intellectual center in the United States." Such shifts have made room for the sacred.[44]

Compared to Europe, the United States continues to enjoy remarkably high rates of religious affiliation and participation. Despite the rise of the "nones," 77 percent of Americans continue to identify with a religious tradition. Though religious attendance is "softening," 53 percent attend services at least monthly.[45] And yet there has been no turn-of-the-century increase in personal religiosity to match the increased visibility of religion in American public life. In reality, many indicators point in the opposite direction (see chapter 6 for a discussion of these developments).[46] Still, the comparative strength of American piety, coupled with the visibility of religion in the public square, has led many to challenge the secularization thesis.

Religious Revitalization on Campus: A Social Movements Approach

Newer approaches to the study of religion and modernity recognize the historical contingency of social change. In *The Secular Revolution*, sociologist Christian Smith argues that the secularization of major public institutions in the late nineteenth and early twentieth centuries did not follow inevitably from modernization. Rather, secularization resulted from the purposeful activity of individuals and organizations seeking to limit religion's influence.[47] The product of an organized movement, the academic revolution that transformed higher education in the late nineteenth and early twentieth centuries was, in large measure, a contest won by those who considered religion an impediment to intellectual progress. Underwritten by the fortunes of John D. Rockefeller, Andrew Carnegie, Andrew Mellon, Cornelius Vanderbilt, and Ezra Cornell, they constructed institutions that kept the sacred at arm's length. Taken together, liberal Protestant and secular efforts to transform higher education constituted a social movement with its own leaders, frameworks, networks, organizations, and resources. Part of the larger "secular revolution" sweeping American public life, it had as its primary goal to free the university from ecclesial constraint at the intellectual level and denominational affiliation at the institutional.[48]

Following Smith's lead, this book interprets the return of religion through the lens of social movement theory. In *The Secular Revolution*, Smith focuses on the leaders and networks behind the movement to secularize American public life.[49] By contrast, this study focuses on efforts to raise religion's academic profile, partially reversing the effects of the secular revolution. While far less sweeping than its nineteenth-century predecessor, the religious turn has changed the way American higher education encounters the sacred.

Part of the wider resurgence of faith in American public life, the return of religion is the work of competing movements with different aims and grievances. Far from unified, the comeback of religion on campus has been led by diverse networks of faculty and administrators who do not always share the same goals. Some have focused on strengthening the academic study of religion. Some have emphasized the integration of faith and learning. Another group of educators has worked to revitalize church-related colleges and universities. Still others have focused on campus religious life and student spirituality. Advancing competing, conflicting, and complementary agendas, these critics have played a key role in the return of religion. Through their books, articles, and speeches, they have produced passionate critiques of American higher education.

Framing Religion and Higher Education

During the past three decades a diverse group of commentators and activists has surfaced, arguing that *religion's absence* diminishes higher education. Given diversity in their views on the purposes of higher education, they have described the problem of religion and higher education in different ways, *diagnostic* and *prognostic*. Frequently, diagnoses have assumed a narrative form, tracing the history of higher education. Along the same lines, prognoses have envisioned a new future for American colleges and universities. Over time several competing frameworks and narratives have emerged.[50]

One group of critics (profiled in chapter 2) has framed the problem as an *intellectual* issue, arguing that it is impossible to understand America and its global context without understanding religion. From this angle, there is a mismatch between religion's public resurgence and its absence from classrooms and journals. Although there is wide agreement on the goal of religious literacy, scholars have taken conflicting approaches to the study of religion. Such differences have resulted in *frame disputes*. While most have focused on religion as an object of study, some have argued for the validity of knowledge grounded in religious traditions. Chronicling the secularization of higher education (a *master frame* for some people of faith), they have criticized the exclusion of religious viewpoints from academic discourse. A somewhat broader group of scholars has lamented the loss of meaning and purpose in the lives of students and faculty, and proposed a spiritual vision of higher education. Others have linked these issues to civic engagement and moral reflection.[51]

Another group (discussed in chapter 3) has defined the problem of religion in the academy as an *institutional* issue, highlighting the attenuation of denominational identity in American colleges and universities. Sometimes this frame is combined with the story of secularization ("Our college is losing its religious identity"). Sometimes it is linked to the topic of denominational survival. Although found in all sectors of higher education, discussion about the institutionalized presence of religion has been most lively among representatives of church-related schools, with proponents arguing for the value of a revitalized religious identity and mission.[52]

A third group of commentators (described in chapter 4) has defined the problem of campus religion as a *student development* issue. Concerned about the spiritual lives of emerging adults, they have criticized colleges and universities for neglecting the religious needs of students. Some campus ministers have framed this problem in terms of personal faith, arguing that undergraduates are losing their religion. Whether or not this claim is true, it has motivated outreach to students. From Catholic campus ministries to Muslim Students' Associations, student religious groups have emphasized the precariousness of religious identity. Others have focused on spiritual exploration, faulting colleges for ignoring life's big questions. Such critics have urged student affairs professionals to pay more attention to spirituality. Last but not least, advocates of interfaith dialogue have celebrated America's religious diversity. Mediating between the one and the many, they have emphasized the values of tolerance and mutual respect.[53]

Building Organizations and Networks

More than a set of disembodied ideas, such concerns have required institutional expression. When they are effective, social movements mobilize through organizations and networks.[54] Toward this end, new and extant organizations have become vital platforms from which to advocate for the academic study of religion, strengthen church-related colleges, and engage in religious activity. Through different organizational channels, scholars and practitioners of religion have realized significant results: hundreds of centers, thousands of conferences and seminars, multiplying campus ministries, and innumerable newsletters, journals, and books—all focused on the sacred.

Depending on the problems being addressed, these organizations and networks have taken different forms. In the *intellectual domain* (discussed in chapter 2), religious scholarly societies, centers and institutes, networks of mentors and students (what sociologists call master-pupil chains), and disciplinary professional associations have raised the profile of religion. These include the American Academy of Religion, the Center for the Study of Religion, the Society of Christian Philosophers, the Association for Jewish Studies, the International Qur'anic Studies Association, the Society for Spirituality and Social Work, and the International Association for the Cognitive Science of Religion. While most focus on religion as an object of study, others promote scholarship grounded in religious commitments.[55]

Within the realm of *church-related higher education* (the focus of chapter 3), associations of denominational colleges, interdenominational networks, and foundation-sponsored programs have fostered religious revitalization. Connecting institutions from across the country, organizations like the Association of Jesuit Colleges and Universities, Collegium, the Lilly Fellows Program, and the Lutheran Educational Conference of North America have disseminated new strategies for strengthening religious identity. Taking different approaches to the topic of church-related higher education, they have raised the visibility of religion on campus.

A third set of organizations has fueled the renewal of *student religious life* (explored in chapter 4), including denominational campus ministries, evangelical parachurch groups, interfaith networks, and student affairs organizations. Bringing the religions of the world into the student union, they have included the Fellowship of Christian Athletes, the Catholic Campus Ministry Association, Hillel, the Orthodox Christian Fellowship, the Hindu Students Council, and Interfaith Youth Core. Though many of these groups are new, they have recycled older forms. Dating back to the collegiate YMCA and YWCA, these organizational technologies have served as a template for a host of student religious groups. Representing the diversity of American religions, they have turned the campus into a lively religious marketplace.[56]

Like many social movements, efforts to revitalize religion have built on preexisting networks and organizations.[57] Some were founded in the early decades of the twentieth century. Others are the offspring of midcentury mainline Protestantism, as well as Catholicism and Judaism. Without preexisting structures, the return of religion would not have happened. At the same time, new organizations have proven critical for its success, engaging the campus with fresh expressions of religious diversity.

Mobilizing Religious Philanthropy

Timing has mattered, for there have been new resource streams for the teaching and the practice of religion. A strong stock market through most of the 1990s and early 2000s enlarged the philanthropic coffers that underwrote hundreds of large and small initiatives. Though these coffers shrank in the wake of the recent recession, the return of a bull market may lead to a rebound in religious giving.

Historically, campus philanthropy has been religion-friendly and religion-averse. On the one hand, eighteenth-century divinity students relied heavily on scholarships collected from congregations and bequests. On the other, philanthropist Andrew Carnegie helped fuel the secular revolution through his collegiate pension plan. Though secularization made significant inroads during the twentieth century, religion did not completely disappear from American philanthropy. In 1921, John D. Rockefeller Jr. created the Institute of Social and Religious Research, the predecessor of the Religious Research Association. In the 1950s and 1960s, discussions of faith and knowledge often depended on religion-friendly funders such as the Danforth Foundation.[58]

More recent efforts to strengthen religious higher education have also benefited from sympathetic foundations and donors. A fruitful time for religion on campus, the period of 1999 to 2003 may have set a record for religious philanthropy. For a generation, Lilly Endowment and the Pew Charitable Trusts have consistently ranked among the largest American foundations (in 2014 Lilly ranked fifth), while the assets of the John Templeton Foundation have now passed the 3 billion dollar mark. Together with a number of smaller foundations and individual donors, these three philanthropic giants played a central role in supporting the revitalization of religion in American higher education.[59]

Once a supporter of conservative political causes, Pew refocused its attention on evangelical scholarship in the 1980s. All told, Pew spent $24 million on the Pew Christian Scholars Program. Over 450 individuals participated in programs at the undergraduate, graduate, and faculty levels.[60] Complementing these efforts, Pew funded the creation of ten centers at American universities, fostering the academic study of religion. Though the foundation's funding is now focused on opinion surveys, its earlier initiatives helped institutionalize several areas of religious scholarship.[61]

Established in 1937, Lilly Endowment has made its mark in religious philanthropy, drawing on the profits from the family pharmaceutical business. In the 1970s, Lilly sponsored initiatives on campus ministry, American religious history, and Protestant colleges. Under program officer Robert Wood Lynn, who faulted foundations for overlooking religion, the Endowment expanded its religious activity, awarding 1,895 grants totaling $100 million. Noting the foundation's impact on the academic study of religion, *Newsweek* dubbed Lynn the "high priest of scholarship."[62] Over the next two decades, Lilly remained committed to religious scholarship and church-related colleges. Beginning in 1989, the endowment invested almost $16 million in a ten-year religion and higher education initiative. Lilly's most significant initiative in higher education was the Programs for the Theological Exploration of Vocation (PTEV), which awarded $225 million in grants to eighty-eight church-related colleges between 2000 and 2007. More recently, the endowment has turned its attention to campus ministry and theological education.[63]

Rounding out the big three, the John Templeton Foundation has pursued a narrower focus on religion, values, and science. Established in 1987, it is the creation of the late John Marks Templeton, a billionaire investor who sat on the board of Princeton Theological Seminary. A practicing Presbyterian, Templeton was also shaped by the metaphysical traditions of Christian Science and Unity.[64] Since the 1990s, Templeton has awarded hundreds of grants for new religion and science courses, established a high-profile religion prize, and sponsored a series of dialogues by groups such as the American Association for the Advancement of Science. It has also become a major supporter of research in the philosophy of religion. In 2009 alone, Templeton devoted nearly $32 million to its initiative on "science and the big questions."[65]

Beyond the big three, a host of religion-oriented foundations and donors have shaped higher education. The proliferation of Catholic and evangelical philanthropists reflects the upward mobility of their constituencies. As both groups have grown in wealth and social status, their ability to fund initiatives in higher education has increased. Within the realm of Catholic higher education, alumni have played a key role in religious philanthropy. Possessing the twelfth-largest educational endowment in the country, the University of Notre Dame has served as an incubator for religious scholarship.[66] In the evangelical world, donors and foundations have established an umbrella organization which sponsors an annual conference on Christian philanthropy. Called the Gathering, it requires members to donate at least $200,000 annually.[67]

Outside the orbit of Christian philanthropy, other groups have benefited from the generosity of private foundations. During the 1990s, Hillel raised over $70 million in its Campaign for a Jewish Renaissance. Chabad has also cultivated a loyal donor base.[68] Connecting Judaism and the classroom, philanthropists have created over 150 Jewish studies positions. In a similar way, the Posen Foundation has underwritten the production of an international fellowship program for junior scholars.[69] While the Nathan Cummings Foundation has funded more than one hundred contemplative practice fellowships, the Muslim Students' Association maintains an annual Ramadan fundraising campaign. The impact of private donations can be seen in the proliferation of endowed chairs in Buddhist, Islamic, Sikh, and Hindu studies. The largest gift of this kind came in 2005 when a Saudi prince provided $40 million for Islamic studies at Harvard and Georgetown universities.[70]

The return of religion would not have happened without philanthropy. Increasing the amount of resources in the social movement sector of religion and higher education allowed a wide variety of movements to mobilize.[71] Underwriting a host of new initiatives, religious philanthropy reshaped the academic study of religion (chapter 2), church-related colleges (chapter 3), and student religious life (chapter 4).

Cultural Opportunities

In analyzing the comeback of religion on campus, this chapter has examined the rhetorical frameworks, organizational contexts, and philanthropic resources behind higher education's religious turn. A comprehensive account of religion's comeback must also include a discussion of the *cultural opportunities* facilitating these intellectual and cultural movements. By removing social and cultural barriers, such opportunities make it easier for movements to mobilize.[72] In recent decades, several historical developments have made the campus more receptive to religious concerns. A perfect storm of factors, they have created a more conducive environment for religion in higher education.

As noted above, faith has become more visible in American politics, an external development that has led academics to rediscover religion. Inside the university, changes in academic culture have also proved propitious for religious scholarship. The decline of positivism and the rise of postmodernism have lent some legitimacy to religious understandings of reality. Questioning the notion of value-free objectivity, faculty have acknowledged the ways in which personal convictions shape scholarly inquiry. Though many disciplines remain committed to scientific detachment, other fields have opened themselves up to more interpretive approaches. On the qualitative end of the social sciences, ethnographers have become more aware of their privileged positions. Engaging the epistemologies of their informants, they have viewed them as collaborators in the production of knowledge. Such approaches have fostered a new openness to religious experience.[73]

The past few decades have witnessed the breakdown of disciplinary boundaries. As early as 1973, sociologist Peter Berger noted an "aversion to disciplinary specialization" among college students. In the 1980s, anthropologist Clifford Geertz wrote about "blurred genres," observing "an enormous amount of genre mixing in the humanities and social sciences."[74] Since then the lines between disciplines have become even more porous.[75] Such developments have paved the way for the rise of interdisciplinary centers and institutes, including centers for the study of religion. With interdisciplinarity in vogue, religious scholarship is less likely to be perceived as a form of intellectual trespassing.[76]

The religious resurgence has also been aided by the diversification of the American campus. The UCLA survey on faculty spirituality found that women and African Americans were more likely to describe themselves as religious or spiritual. While Asian Americans have revitalized evangelical parachurch groups, the children of Hindu and Muslim immigrants helped create a multireligious campus.[77] Responding to the new diversity, the field of student affairs has expanded its mission. Since the 1970s, the student life portfolio has come to include multicultural education, campus wellness, and life skills training. Student spirituality is a recent addition to the list. During the same period, universities have reported a corresponding increase in the number of clubs and organizations. Several recent Supreme Court decisions have given campus ministries access to student activity budgets. With more money and space being devoted to student life, campus religious groups have flourished.[78]

From Baptists to Buddhists, higher education has become a haven for religious diversity. Far from uniform, the place of religion on campus varies widely by context and setting. While emerging at the same historical moment, the various strands of religion's academic resurgence have not formed a single tapestry. Animated by competing approaches to American higher education, the return of religion has taken many forms.[79]

Sometimes this diversity can be found in a single institution. Such cultural pluralism is on display at Princeton University, where the study and practice of religion are embraced by a wide range of constituencies and organizations. For decades some of the country's leading African American scholars have called Princeton home, including Toni Morrison, Cornel West, and Nell Irvin Painter. Most have discussed religion in their work. Focusing on race, politics, and American democracy, religion scholar Eddie Glaude Jr. currently serves as the chair of Department of African American Studies. Across campus the James Madison Program has advanced a conservative vision of ordered liberty and limited government. Led by the Catholic political philosopher Robert George, it is concerned with the role of religion and morality in public life. For several years, George taught a great books seminar with West, who has returned to Harvard University. An ideological odd couple, they shared a commitment to the importance of religion and the liberal arts. From 2003 to 2011, Paul Raushenbush served as Associate Dean of Religious Life and the Chapel. The great-grandson of Social Gospel pioneer Walter Rauschenbusch, he connected the university to its mainline Protestant heritage. In a post-Protestant Princeton, the Office of Religious Life functions as a spiritual clearinghouse, overseeing more than thirty religious groups, including Athletes in Action, the Aquinas Institute, Hindu Life, and the Sikhs of Princeton. Once the headquarters for Princeton's YMCA, Murray-Dodge Hall is home to the Interfaith Prayer

Room, the Muslim Prayer Room, a café, and several meeting spaces. Standing at arm's length from these religious and political visions, Princeton's Center for the Study of Religion promotes academic research in the humanities and social sciences. Under the direction of sociologist Robert Wuthnow, the Center has engaged faculty from more than a dozen disciplines. As the case of Princeton makes clear, the comeback of religion has manifested itself in multiple ways, extending far beyond one tradition or approach. When journalists and scholars take stock of the religious resurgence, they should remember this diversity.[80]

The Story of the Project and this Book

Beginning with a narrower focus on religious institutions, this project slowly grew to encompass the full diversity of campus religion. Emerging out of an evaluation of Lilly Endowment's $15.6 million religion and higher education initiative, it initially examined the revitalization of church-related colleges and universities. It documented heightened attention to religious mission and identity in Protestant and Catholic schools. In a survey sent to 1,100 participants in five Lilly programs, 60 percent of respondents perceived a "growing openness toward religious perspectives in American higher education," while 58 percent reported "more discussion of religion on my campus." Conversations with key grantees confirmed these findings. People interviewed as part of the evaluation often commented on the surge of interest in religion; it was "really sort of stunning," remarked one faculty member, since the issue of religion "wasn't even on the table" ten years ago.[81]

The project soon expanded beyond the sphere of religious colleges, charting the place of religion in American higher education. Initially, this involved tracking the initiatives funded by other religion-oriented foundations, especially the Pew Charitable Trusts and the John Templeton Foundation. This led to a broader examination of the landscape of religion scholarship across the disciplines. It soon became clear that the heightened focus on religion was not confined to church-related colleges, but could be found in all types of institutions. Though other studies had noted academia's growing interest in the sacred, none had systematically documented the religious turn across the humanities, the social sciences, and other fields. The magnitude and diversity of the student religious marketplace were also understudied.

The book that emerged from this research focuses on three central aspects of the religious turn: the growth of the academic study of religion (covered in chapter 2), the revitalization of church-related colleges (the focus of chapter 3), and the renewal of student religious life (discussed in chapter 4). Each begins with a brief history of the role of religion in a particular sector (academic research and teaching, church-related colleges, and student life), describes the partial impact of secularization, and chronicles the return of religion.

After documenting the return of religion on campus, the book considers its wider significance and future sustainability. Looking beyond the campus gates to the larger culture, chapter 5 discusses the importance of religion and higher education for civic engagement, the arts, and intellectual life. Exploring the future of religious initiatives on campus, chapter 6 examines the recent fiscal challenges in higher education (including the "crisis of the humanities" and the rise of online education), the growth of the religiously unaffiliated, and the globalization of campus religion. Noting the continuing salience of religion in public life, it sees a future for the religious turn.

For decades scholars have told a tale of decline and fall, chronicling the exclusion of the sacred from American higher education. In the academy and the media, the secularization storyline remains the dominant narrative for describing the place of religion in American colleges and universities. Despite its widespread acceptance, there is strong evidence that a new story needs to be told about religion in the academy, one that recognizes the resilience of the sacred in a secular institution.

2

RELIGION AND KNOWLEDGE IN THE POST-SECULAR ACADEMY

The college campus has long been perceived as one of the most secular precincts of American society.[1] Yet recent scholarship suggests that the secularization narrative has exaggerated the extent to which colleges and universities have marginalized the teaching of religion. Such scholarship points to the survival and growth of the academic study of religion, as well as an increase in religious and intellectual diversity.[2]

At the same time, there is strong evidence that something like the secularization of knowledge did occur. Until the late nineteenth century, religion exerted considerable influence over American intellectual life. Intertwined with the rise of the modern research university, an intellectual transformation overtook most fields in the first decades of the twentieth century. In the process, religion's place in the modern university was gradually redefined. Across the academy, the influence of Freud, Nietzsche, and Spencer cast doubt on religious understandings of reality. As the academic disciplines matured, scholarly inquiry became increasingly specialized and empirical, while moral and theological questions became less important. Though the academic study of religion continued in religious studies departments and divinity schools, it was no longer at the center of the academic enterprise.[3]

As noted in chapter 1, the transformation of the university was not a faceless process unfolding over time, but an organized movement with clearly identifiable leaders, organizations, networks, and resources. Social scientists such as Lester Ward, organizations such as the American Sociological Society, and philanthropists such as Andrew Carnegie helped move religion to the margins of academic life. Motivated by cultural grievances about the restriction of academic freedom, scholars distanced themselves from sectarian religious traditions, embracing a more inclusive liberal Protestantism. Eventually, this nonsectarian Christianity yielded to a more secular identity.[4]

Despite the success of the secular revolution, it was not irreversible or complete.[5] Instead of a linear story of decline and fall, the relationship between religion and higher education is better conceptualized as a mixture of linear and cyclical elements. While often on the sidelines, religious concepts and frameworks continued to influence American intellectual life throughout the last century. So did the academic study of religion. In the years following World War II, religious scholarship staged a comeback.

More recently, religion has returned again in what has been called a postsecular moment.[6] Articles on the return of religion have appeared in a dozen disciplines, including art, English, philosophy, music, political science, social work, medicine, history, and sociology. Over fifty religious scholarly associations foster the integration of faith and learning, while centers for the study of religion can be found at Columbia, Virginia, Chicago, Emory, Princeton, New York University, and a host of other institutions.[7] While some focus on religion as an object of study, others promote overtly religious scholarship. In a postmodern era, more and more scholars are challenging the boundary between faith and knowledge, acknowledging the importance of religion as a human phenomenon and as a way of knowing.

Far from inevitable, the comeback of religion has been realized by organized networks of scholars. Their efforts have found expression in and support from religious professional associations, centers and institutes, journals, and philanthropic foundations.[8] The return of religion has also been assisted by the rise of multiculturalism and postmodernism, the heightened place of religion in international relations, and the increasing visibility of faith in the American public square.

Some have gone so far as to call the return of religion a "movement." A closer look reveals not one movement but many. Unlike the secular revolution, it has proceeded incrementally and without a unified agenda. Like most shifts in academic culture, it has been achieved by heterogeneous groups of scholars with competing views of religion and the role it should play in higher education. Reflecting this diversity, the revival of religious scholarship has included believers and skeptics, insiders and outsiders, those who integrate faith and scholarship and those who emphasize the separation of religious convictions from their academic work. Sometimes they have worked together. Sometimes they have pursued conflicting agendas. While securing a more prominent place for religion in the academy, their influence has been uneven.[9]

Before exploring the resurgence of religion, this chapter briefly recounts the changes that overtook academic scholarship during the late nineteenth and early twentieth centuries. This historical overview includes a short discussion of the post–World War II revival of religion in the academy. After describing the end of this revival in the late 1960s, it explores the return of religion on both the disciplinary and interdisciplinary level, examining the competing visions that animate today's religious scholarship. It concludes with a discussion of the faculty response to the comeback of religion.

The Changing Place of Religion in Higher Education

From the founding of Harvard College in 1636, the relationship between faith and knowledge has been a source of tension in American higher education. Formed for the training of Christian gentlemen, the earliest American colleges offered a classical curriculum inherited from English Puritan and medieval Catholic models. A high proportion of graduates became clergy, though many pursued other occupations. Although much of the instruction focused on Greek and Roman texts, the Hebrew and Christian scriptures were a regular part of the curriculum. In Puritan New England, a distinction was made between the book of nature and the Bible, reflecting an ongoing dialectic between Athens and Jerusalem in the history of Western Christianity.[10]

In the eighteenth and nineteenth centuries, American colleges and universities were transformed by the multiple strains of the European Enlightenment. Classic treatments of academic freedom have depicted these intellectual movements as liberating influences. More recently, historians have emphasized the ways Americans reconciled the moderate Enlightenment with Christian theology, often with ironic results. At the College of New Jersey, the Reverend John Witherspoon attempted to combine Scotch-Presbyterian Calvinism with republicanism and the Scottish Enlightenment. Thanks to Witherspoon's successors, Scottish common-sense realism came to exercise a strong influence over Protestant colleges. Nowhere was this more apparent than in the senior moral philosophy course taught by many college presidents. While sometimes reactionary and authoritarian, the antebellum colleges created an American *paideia*, fostering civic engagement. Whatever their strengths and weaknesses, they were overshadowed by the coming of the research university.[11]

During the formative period of modern higher education, American research universities were a mixture of nonsectarian piety, character formation, and technocratic pragmatism. Virtually all of the important university builders advanced a generically Protestant vision for their institutions. While rejecting denominational control, they were far from secular. At the University of Chicago, William Rainey Harper put a strong emphasis on the academic study of religion, giving pride of place to the divinity school. Harper and his contemporaries affirmed the unity of truth, seeing no conflict between the progress of science and Christian morality. Speaking at the inauguration of Johns Hopkins University's first president, Harvard's Charles Eliot noted that "the absence of sectarian control should not be confounded with lack of piety," adding that "the whole work of a university is uplifting, refining, and spiritualizing."[12]

Despite its overwhelmingly Protestant leadership, historians have portrayed the academic revolution as a prelude to secularization. In one version of the story, the rise of the modern university led to the repudiation of religious authority and the rise of academic freedom. In another, liberal Protestant educators adopted a stance of "methodological secularization," excluding religious and metaphysical presuppositions.[13] Other accounts emphasize the role of the emerging disciplines, arguing that the marginalization of religion was an unintended consequence of departmental specialization. In both the social sciences and humanities, an emphasis on specialized research led scholars to "think small," ignoring religious and metaphysical questions.[14]

By the early twentieth century, the impact of secularization could be seen across the university. With roots in the older moral philosophy, the nascent social sciences were influenced by the Protestant Social Gospel and European social theory. In the beginning, liberal Protestant social scientists played a central role in debates over "Christian sociology." Yet these scholars embraced a functional approach to religion, melding positivist scholarship with social reform. While not wholly secular, their writings were a departure from Protestant orthodoxy. By the 1920s, the ethical thrust of American social science had been replaced with an emphasis on the separation of facts from values. Although humanities faculty continued to see themselves as guardians of morality, they were not untouched by the intellectual shifts of the early twentieth century. Gradually, fields like philosophy secularized. This transformation could be seen in the career of philosopher John Dewey. Once a churchgoing Protestant with roots in the metaphysical tradition, he became a naturalist with a spiritual conception of America's common faith. Such thinkers combined secular and religious impulses.[15]

Participants in the secular revolution were motivated by longstanding cultural grievances. In many fields, the de-Christianization of American higher education was accomplished by a coalition of liberal Protestants, ex-Protestants, and Jews. From the founding of the first American colleges, Jewish faculty and students faced significant discrimination. Until the postwar era, American

Jews were not a major presence in the academy. While restrictive admissions quotas kept the Jewish student body small, Jewish learning was excluded from the academic study of religion. Both victims and agents of transformation, Jewish scholars overcame significant obstacles, developing distinctively American forms of social criticism.[16]

In most fields, the secular revolution was accompanied by a decline in the academic study of religion. Concentrated in seminaries, divinity schools, and a handful of religion departments, there was less focus on religion as an object of study.[17] This trend could also be observed in the social sciences. In American sociology's top journals, the percentage of articles focusing on religion reached a record low in the 1930s.[18] Under the influence of materialist views of history, American historians increasingly ignored the religious dimensions of the past, believing that "economics explains the mostest." In a similar way, political scientists paid little attention to religious factors, favoring economic and psychological theories. Across the disciplines, religion had gone out of fashion as an object of study and as a way of knowing.[19]

Though the academy was secularizing, the boundary between religion and knowledge was not impermeable. In the humanities, many saw their fields as the carriers of spiritual truth. In the social sciences, traces of religious thought survived in several disciplines, albeit in secular forms. Pockets of religious intellectual life could be found in mainline Protestant divinity schools, church-related colleges, Bible chairs in public universities, and a small number of religion departments. Despite these islands of religious scholarship, religion had moved to the margins in most institutions.[20]

The Postwar Religious Revival and Its Collapse

Though quite pervasive, the secularization of intellectual life was never absolute. On campus and off, the late 1940s and 1950s were a time of religious curiosity, as neo-orthodox theologians made the cover of *Time* magazine. In higher education, the revival could be seen in the increasing attention to religion. In his 1947 book *The College Seeks Religion*, Merrimon Cuninggim wrote that religious faith held "a larger place in the college's thinking and practice than at any time in the twentieth century." Along the same lines, Will Herberg described the "intellectual rehabilitation of religion," noting that "[r]eligious ideas, concepts, and teachings have become familiar in the pages of the 'vanguard' journals of literature, politics, and art."[21]

Religious scholarship was moving back toward the center of academic life.[22] Between 1945 and 1960, there was a 100 percent increase in the number of undergraduate religious studies programs. Students flocked to religion classes, making them the most popular courses in the postwar years.[23] During the same period, faculty interest in religious questions increased across the disciplines, resulting in the creation of the Society for the Scientific Study of Religion (1949), the Religious Research Association (1951), the Institute on Religion in an Age of Science (1954), and the Faculty Christian Fellowship (1952).[24] The last group served as a clearinghouse for mainline Protestant efforts to reunite faith and knowledge, forming chapters on over half of American college and university campuses. By the early 1960s it reached over 37,000 scholars through its *Faculty Forum* newsletter. Underwritten by the Danforth Foundation, the Edward W. Hazen Foundation, and John D. Rockefeller Jr., efforts to integrate faith and knowledge relied on private philanthropy.[25]

With the exception of the Faculty Christian Fellowship, most of these organizations focused on religion as an object of study. At the same time, the lines between religious advocacy and religious research were often blurred in an academy still under the influence of the mainline Protestant establishment. During the early years of religious studies, it was difficult to distinguish a typical religion department curriculum from that of an oldline Protestant divinity school.[26] For a season, the postwar revival attracted the attention of some of America's leading intellectuals, including the famous "atheists for Niebuhr" (Arthur Schlesinger Jr., Perry Miller, and Morton White).[27] Yet when all was said and done, its impact was surprisingly limited. A few scholars openly criticized the religious revival, defending the modern university against the new medievalism. Most, however, simply went about their business, unaware of religion's bid for intellectual legitimacy.[28]

Tied as it was to mainline Protestantism, the postwar religious resurgence was as lasting as its chief sponsor's hegemony over American culture. When the Protestant establishment declined in the turbulent sixties, efforts to reconcile faith and knowledge faltered. In the face of student radicalism and widespread social unrest, organizations like the Faculty Christian Fellowship underwent a collective identity crisis.[29] Explaining its transformation from the *Christian Scholar* to *Soundings* in 1968, the postwar revival's house organ noted that few "now see Christianity or any other religious tradition as the necessary foundation of the various academic disciplines," adding that to "forgo the word 'religion' in preference for 'common human concerns' is not to put on the armor of contemporary atheism or secularism."[30] Consistent with this sentiment, the Society for Religion in Higher Education (the journal's sponsoring organization) became the Society for Values in Higher Education in 1975. About the same time, the Danforth Foundation shifted its focus from religion scholarship to the state of Missouri, bringing to a close a remarkable period of religious philanthropy. By the mid-1970s, mainline Protestants were reducing their presence in higher education.[31]

In some disciplines, religion's place in the academy seemed more tenuous than ever. Among historians, the study of "American church history" was concentrated in seminaries and divinity schools. As the new social history replaced the intellectual history of Perry Miller, the fate of religious scholarship remained uncertain. Describing the situation in sociology, Nancy Ammerman writes that in the "pervasively secular" culture of the seventies, the topic of religion "had simply passed off [the] radar screens" of many scholars. In other fields, reductionist approaches to knowledge further marginalized religion. In political science, the leaders of the behavioral revolution called for the exclusion of political and moral values from empirical research.[32]

To be sure, religious studies was enjoying steady growth. During the 1960s, sixty-one state universities created new religion programs. While some church-related schools reduced religion requirements, enrollments swelled in public institutions. Despite these developments, the field seemed to be moving in a secular direction. Once dominated by mainline Protestant concerns, it underwent a significant transformation. In 1964, the National Association of Biblical Instructors became the American Academy of Religion (AAR). Distancing themselves from the Bible and theology curriculum of the Protestant divinity schools, a new generation of scholars worked to professionalize the field. Modeling themselves after social scientists and historians, rather than theologians, many scholars articulated a secular rationale for studying religion. Widening their focus to include non-Western religions, they ushered in a "post-Protestant" phase of religious studies. Using the 1963 Supreme Court decision *Abington School District v. Schempp* to justify these developments, faculty drew an increasingly sharp boundary between religion scholarship and religious belief. Like the end of state-sanctioned prayers and Bible reading in the public schools, the de-Protestantization of religious studies could be described as yet another instance of disestablishment. Whether or not it amounted to secularization was in the eye of the beholder.[33]

The Return of Religion across the Disciplines

In light of these historical developments, some might predict that religion would remain on the margins of academic life. But such an interpretation would ignore a growing interest in the sacred over the past three decades, a development that has touched most disciplines in the humanities and social sciences.

Like most academic developments, the rebirth of religion scholarship did not start from scratch but built on the cultural and organizational legacies of the past, in this case the declining mainline Protestant establishment. The decline of mainline Protestant denominations should not blind us to their cultural influence on American society.[34] In a similar way, the organizational decline of mainline Protestant higher education has not led to the secularization of academic life. Though institutions originally associated with mainline denominations have distanced themselves from their Protestant roots, the cultural and organizational influence of liberal Protestantism lives on in the academic study of religion. Instead of secularization, the de-Protestantization of religious studies has opened the academy to a host of competing approaches.

While often portrayed as secular, the field of religious studies is the cultural and institutional offspring of liberal Protestantism.[35] Given this Protestant lineage, it is not surprising that formerly Protestant schools should devote significant resources to the academic study of religion. In 2017, Harvard's Committee on the Study of Religion listed more than sixty faculty from across the university, while Harvard Divinity School had over forty professors and instructors. Together with the University of Chicago, Emory, Vanderbilt, Princeton, and Duke, Harvard remains one of the more vital centers for the study of religion in America. While modest in size compared to programs in the natural and social sciences, divinity schools and religious studies departments preserve an institutional home for religion in America's elite colleges and universities.[36]

Moving beyond its origins in Protestant divinity schools, the field has slowly diversified. Reflecting the growth of religious studies in state universities, 28 percent of undergraduate religion programs can be found in public institutions. During the first five years of the twenty-first century, enrollment in state university religious studies programs increased by 40 percent. Religious studies programs are also diversifying their course offerings. An American Academy of Religion survey found that 49 percent of religious studies programs offered an introductory world religions class, with the number of Islam and Hinduism sections nearly doubling between 1999–2000 and 2004–2005. In particular, the events of September 11, 2001, expanded the number of positions and funding sources in Islamic studies.[37] Despite the growing attention to world religions, religion departments have continued to take theology quite seriously. In 2004–2005, 48 percent of programs offered classes in Christian theology, while 38 percent had a Christian ethics course. The same year a majority of papers at the organization's annual meetings were on theological topics.[38] Many of the AAR's presidents have remained open to theological concerns. During Hans Hillerbrand's term, the AAR sponsored a new initiative on theological programs. More recently, Christian ethicist Charles T. Mathewes edited the *Journal of the American Academy of Religion*, while theologians Serene Jones and David Gushee served neighboring terms as AAR president.[39]

So seriously have theological perspectives been taken that some prominent scholars have criticized the American Academy of Religion for its proreligious outlook, founding the North American Association for the Study of Religion

(NAASR). Rejecting the "hegemonic liberal Protestant framework" of religious studies, they argue that scholars should be "critics not caretakers." As in the AAR, some in the Society of Biblical Literature have worried about the influence of religious biases, including the growing presence of evangelical Protestants. While some in the AAR and SBL have called for a more detached approach to religious studies, others have rejected a perceived dichotomy between advocacy and objectivity.[40] Because the conflict between theology and religious studies has never been resolved, normative religious perspectives continue to have a place in both the AAR and the SBL.[41]

Whether critics or caretakers, religious studies scholars work in a field that has grown. Between 1990 and 2007, the membership of the American Academy of Religion increased from 5,500 to 11,400 members. Though the recent recession has cut into its numbers, the AAR's current membership of 9,000 scholars is more than it has had for most of its history. The Society of Biblical Literature is nearly as large, and grew by 30 percent during the first decade of the twenty-first century.[42] Reflecting heightened student interest, enrollments in undergraduate religion courses rose by 23 percent between 1996 and 2005, while the number of majors increased 31 percent. During the same period, U.S. postsecondary enrollment grew by 22 percent. Other data sources tell a similar story. Between 1991 and 2011, the number of philosophy and religious studies graduates rose by 75 percent, surpassing the overall growth in bachelor's degrees by 18 percent. As *Newsweek* noted in 2010, higher education was experiencing a "religious studies revival."[43]

A quick tour of the disciplines documents the return of religion across the humanities and social sciences. As in religious studies, this comeback has been led by scholars with competing approaches to the sacred. While some faculty bracket their own religious and metaphysical commitments, others bring their personal commitments into teaching and research. Still others come down somewhere in between. In most disciplines, scholars in all three categories have raised the profile of religion. Of course, these categories do not begin to exhaust the ways that religion and scholarship intersect in the contemporary academy. In many traditions, embodied practices and collective rituals may be more important than religious beliefs. Some scholars may integrate a diffuse spirituality with their research. Many enter empathetically into the religious worlds of their subjects, whether they agree with them or not. Still others draw on their own religious autobiographies.

Nowhere has the return of religion been more dramatic than in philosophy, a trend that has been led largely by religious philosophers. Chronicling this resurgence in the journal *Philo*, the philosopher Quentin Smith explored what he called the "desecularization" of American philosophy. According to Smith, "it became, almost overnight, 'academically respectable' to argue for theism, making philosophy a favored field of entry for the most intelligent and talented theists entering academia today."[44] The publication of Alvin Plantinga's *God and Other Minds* (1967) marked the beginning of theism's modest resurgence. Thirteen years later, *Time* magazine announced that "God is making a comeback" in American philosophy. In the early eighties, Plantinga served as president of the American Philosophical Association's central division and the Society of Christian Philosophers. Founded in 1978, the Society grew to over 1,000 members by 1993. Writing in the Society's journal, Plantinga argued that "we who are Christians and propose to be philosophers must not rest content with being philosophers who happen, incidentally, to be Christians."[45] Together with William Alston (Plantinga's mentor at Michigan), Nicholas Wolterstorff (recently retired from Yale), and Richard Swinburne (professor emeritus at Oxford), he helped theism return to mainstream philosophy. Between 1982 and 2002, Plantinga directed the Center for Philosophy of Religion at Notre Dame. Supported by the Pew Charitable Trusts and several other foundations, the Center has awarded over 170 fellowships since 1984. Plantinga's intellectual family tree (his *master-pupil chain*) also includes some two dozen doctoral students. While most work in church-affiliated institutions, some have found employment at nonsectarian colleges and universities. Plantinga has also influenced Muslim and Jewish scholars, including Harvard's Hilary Putnam.[46] Currently a Plantinga student serves as a senior vice president at the John Templeton Foundation, which awarded Plantinga its $1.4 million religion prize in 2017. Tracing Templeton's impact on the discipline of philosophy, the *Chronicle of Higher Education* notes its "potential to transform the whole field."[47]

Despite these shifts, theists remain a minority in American philosophy. According to a 2009 survey, just 15 percent of philosophers "accept or lean toward theism," compared to 72 percent of those who specialize in the philosophy of religion.[48] Rather than transforming the field, religious scholars have constructed their own disciplinary subculture, complete with its own journals (*Faith and Philosophy*, the *American Catholic Philosophical Quarterly*, *Philosophia Christi*) and professional associations (the Society of Christian Philosophers, the Evangelical Philosophical Society, the American Catholic Philosophical Association).[49]

Though less visible than in philosophy, the field of literary studies is also experiencing a post-secular moment.[50] As early as 1983, Edward Said noted the rebirth of religious criticism, writing that "when you see influential critics publishing major books with titles like *The Genesis of Secrecy*, *The Great Code*, *Kabbalah and Criticism*, *Violence and the Sacred*, *Deconstruction and Theology*, you know you are in the presence of a significant trend."[51] In *Real Presences* (1989), the polymath George Steiner argued that "any coherent account of the capacity of human speech to communicate meaning and feeling is, in the final analysis, underwritten by the assumption of God's presence."[52] In 1997, the legendary New York critic Alfred Kazin published *God and the American Writer*, tracing the influence of faith, lost and found, on Walt Whitman, Herman Melville, and Emily Dickinson. The same year John McClure wrote of the "return of religion in contemporary theory and literature," noting that "over the last twenty years, a growing number of influential secular intellectuals . . . have begun to reopen negotiations with the religious."[53] In 2006, the journal *English Language Notes* devoted an issue to the religious turn in literary studies. Turning their attention to the sacred, several postmodern and Marxist thinkers have expressed an interest in religious thought, including Terry Eagleton, Frank Lentricchia, and Stanley Fish.[54] Paralleling these developments, the Modern Language Association and the American Academy of Religion have devoted more sessions to literary studies, while the 1,300-member Conference on Christianity and Literature has welcomed such luminaries as René Girard, Denis Donoghue, Wayne Booth, and Robert Alter to its annual meeting.[55]

Even more so than English literature, the discipline of history has seen a return of religion. In recent years, religious history has been the most popular specialization in the American Historical Association. Between 1992 and 2011, the proportion of historians specializing in religion rose from 4.6 to 7.8 percent. At the 2011 meeting of the Organization of American Historians, David Hollinger devoted his presidential address to ecumenical Protestantism's influence on American pluralism. The same year the American Historical Association awarded its John H. Dunning Prize for best book in U.S. history to Darren Dochuk's *From Bible Belt to Sun Belt*. Summarizing these developments, one historian concluded "there has been a 'turn' toward or, perhaps better, a 'tsunami' of scholarship on religion."[56] For decades the study of American religion was dominated by people of faith. The current interest is something altogether different, attracting scholars with a variety of motivations. While some worry about the Christian Right, others explore the religious roots of American progressivism.[57]

In 1964, Henry May wrote hopefully of the "recovery of American religious history." At that time, the study of American religion was still the property of "church historians" in mainline Protestant divinity schools. Following in the footsteps of Perry Miller, many scholars focused on the history of religious ideas. Reflecting this legacy, respondents to a 1993 survey of the field identified Martin Marty (University of Chicago Divinity School) and Sydney Ahlstrom (Yale Divinity School) as very important influences on their own work. Though dozens of American religious historians traced their academic family trees back to Ahlstrom and Marty (together they advised approximately 150 doctoral students), the next generation took the field in new directions. While some applied the methods of intellectual history to a broader range of groups, others embraced new forms of social and cultural history. These shifts reflected the changing demographics of the field. In 1993, over half of the American religion scholars surveyed identified as Catholics (26 percent) or evangelicals (32 percent), with just 18 percent coming from the mainline Protestant tradition. Slowly, the field's center of gravity moved from Protestant divinity schools to departments of religious studies and interdisciplinary centers. By the year 2000, centers and institutes dedicated to the study of American religion had been established at Princeton University, Indiana University–Purdue University Indianapolis, the University of Virginia, and the University of Southern California. Many were created with the support of religion-oriented foundations, including Lilly Endowment and the Pew Charitable Trusts. Supported by Lilly, the Young Scholars in American Religion program has mentored over 150 fellows. Because of such initiatives, American religious history now thrives in the American Academy of Religion, where 4,771 scholars name "North American Religion" as one of their research interests.[58]

Some have interpreted the shift from American church history to American religious history as a sign of secularization. Far from secular, the "new evangelical historiography" has been a major force in the mainstreaming of American religious history.[59] During the 1980s and 1990s, Pew spent millions of dollars strengthening Christian scholarship, much of it through the Institute for the Study of American Evangelicals at Wheaton College.[60] By 1991, Jon Butler could describe the "evangelical paradigm" as "the *single* most powerful explanatory device adopted by academic historians to account for the distinctive features of American society, culture, and identity."[61] Despite its visibility, the evangelical paradigm remains one approach among many. In recent years, scholars from diverse backgrounds have challenged the field's white Protestant narratives. Since the 1960s, historians have shifted their focus from liberal Protestant churchmen to Italian American Catholics, African American Baptists, Orthodox Jews, and Japanese American Buddhists. Founded in 1975 by historian Jay Dolan, Notre Dame's Cushwa Center has served as a clearinghouse for scholarship in American Catholic studies. The beneficiary of grants from Lilly and Pew, it has sponsored dozens of conferences and research projects. The same is true in Jewish studies, where scholars like Deborah Dash Moore have challenged American historians to "rewrite their narratives of the past."[62]

Along the same lines, African American studies has embraced the academic study of religion. Looking back on the early 1990s, one scholar proclaimed it "a golden age for literature on black churches and African-American religion."

Since then scholars like Jonathan Walton (Harvard), Wallace Best (Princeton), and Anthea Butler (University of Pennsylvania) have brought fresh perspectives to the study of African American religion. This same is true in women's history. According to Ann Braude, who directs the Women's Studies in Religion Program at Harvard Divinity School, "Women's history *is* American religious history." Founded in 1973, Harvard's program has welcomed over 180 research associates from around the world, including Karen McCarthy Brown, Evelyn Brooks Higginbotham, and Emilie Townes. Cultivating a national network of donors, it has received grants from Ford, Lilly, and Rockefeller.[63]

Like historians, social scientists have rediscovered the power of religion. Heralding "the return of the sacred," Harvard sociologist Daniel Bell gave a widely reported lecture at the London School of Economics in 1977, arguing that the exhaustion of secular ideologies had led to a new hunger for meaning and transcendence.[64] During the 1980s and 1990s, quantitative researchers in sociology and political science produced reams of computer printouts documenting the continuing influence of religion in American society. Such research helped debunk theories predicting the complete secularization of modern societies. Chronicling the "desecularization of the world," scholars envisioned a post-secular era.[65]

Responding to the religious resurgence in American politics, the study of religion has achieved what Kenneth Wald and his colleagues describe as a "new prominence in political science." In the 1980s, the Caucus for Faith and Politics (reorganized as the Christians in Political Science) paved the way for the religion and politics section of the American Political Science Association (founded in 1986). With 433 members, it is larger than the APSA sections on public administration, the presidency, urban politics, and political communication. In 1993, Lyman Kellstedt and David Leege published *Rediscovering the Religious Factor in American Politics*, documenting the influence of religion on ordinary voters.[66] In 2005, the APSA established a task force on religion and democracy, declaring that there is "perhaps no subject more important to the future of American democracy that has received so little scholarly attention."[67] The journal *Politics and Religion* was established in 2008. In the past, many graduate students in comparative politics were not exposed to religious topics. In *God's Century: Resurgent Religion and Global Politics* (2011), a trio of young political scientists called attention to this oversight, tracing "the fall and rise of religion" in international relations theory. Much of this work has been supported by the Henry Luce Foundation. Since 2005 the Henry R. Luce Initiative on Religion and International Affairs has made over seventy grants to colleges, universities, and scholarly societies.[68]

Reflecting similar developments in the American Sociological Association (ASA), the top three sociology journals are paying more attention to religion. Tracking articles between 1978 and 2007, a recent study found a modest increase in religion-oriented articles.[69] Created in 1994, the religion section of the ASA had 605 members in 2015, making it larger than thirty-one of the organization's fifty-two sections. Future faculty are also interested the sacred. In a 2013 ranking of graduate student interests, religion ranked seventeenth out of seventy specializations.[70]

Tapping into this curiosity, the Social Science Research Council (created by the Rockefeller family in 1923) recently established a program on religion and the public sphere, underwriting university press books, academic conferences, and scholarly working papers. On the SSRC's Immanent Frame blog, theologians and philosophers have exchanged ideas with sociologists, anthropologists, and literary theorists, blurring the boundaries between normative and empirical approaches. Participants have included Talal Asad, Robert Bellah, Tomoko Masuzawa, John Milbank, Charles Taylor, and Nicholas Wolterstorff.[71] Such conversations can also be found at the University of California's Berkeley Center for the Study of Religion. Founded in 2015, the Berkeley Public Theology Program received a three-year grant from the Henry Luce Foundation (where Immanent Frame founder Jonathan VanAntwerpen now serves as a program officer). Invoking theology in the *New York Times*, Center codirector Jonathan Sheehan described "teaching Calvin in California," arguing that "theology spurs secular and religious students to discuss issues of common concern."[72]

Over the past century, attention to religious thought has fluctuated in the social sciences. As noted earlier, the Society for the Scientific Study of Religion had its origins in the postwar religious revival. Descended from a Harvard seminar that included Talcott Parsons, Pitirim Sorokin, and Paul Tillich, it was founded to bring "together the social scientist and the religious person." Though the SSSR moved away from this mission, many of its members remained preoccupied by religious questions. In the 1960s and 1970s, these concerns found new expression in the works of Peter Berger and Robert Bellah. Influenced by Tillich, Bellah argued that religion is true insofar as its symbols orient human beings to the ultimate problems of life. In *A Rumor of Angels* (1969), Berger drew on the inductive tradition in Protestant theology.[73] While outside the disciplinary mainstream, the works of Bellah and Berger are among the sociological best sellers of all time. They also influenced scores of graduate students. Over forty sociologists of religion studied at the University of California under Robert Bellah and and his colleague Charles Glock. They went on to train a subsequent generation of sociologists. Through its progeny, the "Berkeley Circle" helped to shape the future of the discipline. A 2007 study identified 77 distinct branches of Bellah's family tree, with 212 direct descendants. According to Bellah student Jeffrey Alexander, "There is a sense in which every contemporary sociologist is Bellah's child, niece, or nephew."[74]

Like his mentor Robert Bellah, Princeton sociologist Robert Wuthnow has lived on the boundary between religion and social science. In over forty books and edited volumes, Wuthnow has pursued a research agenda informed by religious questions. Likewise, sociologist Christian Smith has explored the religious and philosophical dimensions of sociology. In *What Is a Person?* (2010), Smith presents a nonreductionist account of human social life, invoking the "Polish phenomenologist Karol Wojtyla" (Pope John Paul II). Smith discussed these topics at length in an Andrew W. Mellon Working Group that included Nancy Ammerman, José Casanova, Elaine Howard Ecklund, John H. Evans, and Philip Gorski. Proposing twenty-three theses on sociology and religion, they urged social scientists to learn from theology.[75]

Developing separately from its sociological counterpart, the anthropology of religion has long enjoyed pride of place in the Anglo-American world. Boasting such leading lights as Edith and Victor Turner, Clifford Geertz, Mary Douglas, and Talal Asad, it has been a staple for many departments. Despite this tradition, the Society for the Anthropology of Religion (established in 1997) represents a new wave of interest in the sacred. Building on this interest, the University of California Press has inaugurated a new series on the Anthropology of Christianity, edited by Joel Robbins. Like their colleagues in sociology, anthropologists have explored the discipline's complicated relationship with theology. In a special issue of the *South Atlantic Quarterly*, Robbins and Matthew Engelke convened a dialogue between anthropologists and theologians, including Stanley Hauerwas and Catherine Pickstock.[76]

In a similar way, the discipline of psychology has become more open to the sacred. In a 2003 essay in the *Annual Review of Psychology*, Robert Emmons and Raymond Paloutzian argued that the psychology of religion had "re-emerged as a full-force, leading edge research area."[77] Emerging out of the American Catholic Psychological Association (which reorganized in the early 1970s), Division 36 of the American Psychological Association gradually diversified its membership. Reflecting this wider focus, it includes both secular and religious scholars. Founded in 1975, Division 36 had 974 members in 2010, making it larger than twenty-six of the APA's fifty-six sections. Now known as the Society for the Psychology of Religion and Spirituality, the division publishes a journal bearing the same name.[78] Like sociology, the modern psychology of religion traces its lineage back to postwar Harvard, where Gordon Allport participated in sessions with Parsons and Tillich. The more recent upsurge of interest in religion dates back to a 1980 debate between the noted psychologist

Albert Ellis and Allen Bergin, a practicing Mormon who taught at Brigham Young University. In 1997, the APA published Bergin's *A Spiritual Strategy for Counseling and Psychotherapy*. By 2014 the APA's psychology of religion index contained over 74,000 bibliographic entries.[79]

Social workers are also rediscovering the importance of religion and spirituality. While the North American Association of Christians in Social Work (established in 1954) focuses on "Christian faith and professional social work practice," the Society for Spirituality and Social Work (founded in 1990) serves "social workers of many contrasting spiritual perspectives." Between 1995 and 2001, the number of accredited social work programs with courses on religion and spirituality rose from seventeen to fifty. In 2005 alone, the flagship journal *Social Work* featured a half dozen articles on religion. Reflecting the same trend, the Council on Social Work Education produced *Spirituality and Religion in Social Work Practice*, establishing a work group on Religion and Spirituality in 2011. Part of the discourse of the profession, such approaches are becoming mainstream.[80]

Paralleling the return of religion in psychology and social work, the field of medicine is exploring the nexus between spirituality and health. The number of medical schools offering religion-related courses grew from 5 in 1992 to 101 in 2005. According to a recent literature review, the amount of research on religion, spirituality, and health has increased dramatically since the mid-1990s. Between 1982 and 2011, over 15,000 MEDLINE articles were published on the topic of religion, spirituality, and medicine. At Duke University's Center for Spirituality, Theology, and Health (supported by the John Templeton Foundation), scholars are exploring the impact of spirituality on blood pressure, depression, and alcoholism. Part of the federal National Institutes of Health, the National Center for Complementary and Integrative Health has sponsored research on Ayurvedic healing, prayer, and mind-body medicine. According to psychologist David Myers, the "wall between faith and medicine is now breaking down."[81] Not surprisingly, such research is extremely controversial. In *Blind Faith: The Unholy Alliance of Religion and Medicine*, Columbia University's Richard Sloan writes that the field of religion and health is based on shoddy scholarship, arguing that there are very few high-quality studies of spirituality and medicine.[82] Such critiques have not slowed the pace of new research. In 2013, the University of Michigan received an $8 million grant to conduct a landmark survey on religion and health.[83]

The relationship between religion and the natural sciences has also received more scrutiny. In *Why Religion Matters*, Huston Smith noted that "God-and-science talk seems to be everywhere," citing the profusion of science and religion centers (Columbia's Center for the Study of Science and Religion), journals

(*Science and Spirit, Zygon, Theology and Science*), and hundreds of science and religion courses (including 800 funded by the John Templeton Foundation's course-development program). Like the research on spirituality and health, many of these initiatives have been sponsored by Templeton, including the American Association for the Advancement of Science's Dialogue on Science, Ethics, and Religion.[84] In large part because of Templeton, there are now over 150,000 citations in the literature on religion and science.[85] Though most of this scholarship is oriented toward Christianity, Hinduism and Buddhism have entered the conversation. While the Templeton-funded Metanexus Institute sponsored a lecture series on "Indic Religions in an Age of Science" (later published as a book), the Dalai Lama was a featured speaker at the 2005 meeting of the international Society for Neuroscience. Through its Local Societies Initiative, Metanexus created 250 religion and science discussion groups around the world, in countries such as Iran, India, Armenia, and Nigeria. Between 1999 and 2009, over 11,000 individuals participated in the program.[86]

Across the university, religion has made a comeback. In dozens of disciplines, scholars have argued that it is impossible to understand their subject areas without understanding religion. Many have written articles lamenting the *neglect* of religious topics. Others have discussed the *return* of religion. In most fields, faculty interested in religion can point to the existence of new professional associations, journals, and scholarly networks.

Religion across the Disciplines: Multiple Movements, Conflicting Agendas

In the past three decades, scholars have uncovered new connections between religion and disciplinary knowledge. Now many of them are speaking and writing *across* departmental lines, addressing the sorts of *meta*-questions that concern the entire university. By practicing interdisciplinarity, scholars are resisting a key feature of the modern American academy: the institutional *differentiation* of knowledge into specialized disciplines and subdisciplines. If the rise of specialized, departmentalized knowledge led faculty away from questions of ultimate meaning, the emergence of *interdisciplinary* discussions has helped to bring those questions back into the spotlight.[87] In her presidential address to the American Academy of Religion, Rebecca Chopp described the emergence of a postmodern, networked multiversity with interdisciplinary centers and cross-disciplinary concentrations. While the modern university drew sharp boundaries between disciplines, in the multiversity flexible boundaries prevail. Though departments still have the power to hire and tenure, the blurring of disciplinary boundaries has changed the *kinds* of knowledge that they produce.[88]

Focusing on the heightened visibility of religion *within* and *across* the disciplines, some have spoken of an *interdisciplinary* movement to reshape American universities. Back in 1999, education researchers Alexander and Helen Astin noted that a "movement is emerging in higher education in which many academics find themselves actively searching for meaning and trying to discover ways to make their lives and their institutions more whole."[89] Because today's religious and spiritual initiatives assume so many forms, it is more accurate to speak of *multiple movements*. Several academic movements (with many variations) have heightened the place of religion in higher education. Though they sometimes intersect, each has a distinct way of framing the academic study of religion, as well as its own leaders, organizations, and sources of funding. The following section describes efforts to promote *religion as an object of study, scholarship grounded in religious commitments, spirituality and education, civic and moral education,* and the *new religious pluralism.*[90]

Most visible are initiatives that promote *religion as an object of study*. While far from a coordinated movement, such efforts have a family resemblance to each other. In many cases, they employ similar rhetoric, urging colleagues to pay attention to the "religious factor" in human affairs. Often such appeals are framed in spatial terms. Calling attention to the "holes" and "gaps" in the literature, scholars of religion attempt to fill in the missing pieces. As noted above, they can be found in individual disciplines, in groups like the religion and politics section of the American Political Science Association, Division 36 of the American Psychological Association, and in the American Academy of Religion. While often interdisciplinary, such organizations may not be connected to developments outside of a particular field.

In other cases, attempts to promote religious scholarship have transcended departmental boundaries, involving university-wide efforts to shape curricula and research. Nowhere has this effort been more visible than in the creation of religion-oriented centers and institutes. Currently, several centers specialize in the intersection of religion and science, and over thirty focus on some aspect of North American religions.[91] Ten of the most prominent centers and institutes were funded under Pew's "centers of excellence" program, a $23 million initiative that began in 1997. The goal of this program was to establish an academic foothold for the study of religion at America's most elite universities, including Princeton, Boston University, NYU, Virginia, Emory, USC, Missouri, and Penn. Twenty years after Pew's initiative began, several continue to operate.[92] At Princeton's Center for the Study of Religion, faculty members from across the university have participated in seminars, conferences, and thematic projects. Since its creation in 1999, the Center has sponsored courses in history, sociology, philosophy, English, art, theater and dance, anthropology, and East

Asian studies. At the time of its founding, it received the endorsement of the university's president, who said he knew of "no other institution in the United States pursuing efforts as interdisciplinary and wide-ranging."[93]

Nearly sixty years ago, physicist and novelist C. P. Snow described the widening gap between the humanities and the natural sciences. Bridging Snow's "two cultures," the cognitive science of religion is experimenting with interdisciplinarity. While some of its work takes place in disciplinary venues, such as the American Psychological Association's Division 36, it has spawned a host of new associations, journals, and centers. These include the journal *Religion, Brain, and Behavior* (2011), the Centre for Religion and Cognition (2005), and the International Association for the Cognitive Science of Religion (2006). A leader in the field, historian Ann Taves recently served as president of the American Academy of Religion. In one of the few presidential addresses to invoke the natural sciences, Taves noted that her "goal is not to reject the humanities for the sciences but to build bridges and make connections," calling religious studies "intercultural, comparative, and multi-disciplinary."[94]

Focusing more on undergraduate education, others have made a public case for the academic study of religion. In *Religion and American Education* (1995), the philosopher Warren Nord emphasized the centrality of religious studies to the liberal arts.[95] Directing a similar message to the academy, the authors of the *Wingspread Declaration on Religion and Public Life* (2005) concluded that the "study of religion and its public relevance is a crucial dimension to liberal education." Sponsored by the Society for Values in Higher Education (the successor to the Society for Religion in Higher Education), it was drafted by twenty scholars, including the editor of the *Journal of American History* and the president of the Association of American Colleges and Universities.[96]

In recent years, the trope of religious literacy has become the master frame for many religion scholars. In a 2007 best seller, Boston University's Stephen Prothero outlined what Americans should know about the world's religions. Documenting the public's religious illiteracy, the U.S. Religious Knowledge Survey revealed that the average American missed half the questions. Arguing that "social and individual life everywhere is inextricably tied up with religious issues," the Dean of Harvard Divinity School called for the "study of religion globally in every liberal arts or general education curriculum." Putting the issue more baldly, anthropologist Scott Atran argued that "what we don't understand about religion just might kill us." Far more than an academic pursuit, religious studies has become a way of forming global citizens. In a 2006 speech to the AAR, former secretary of state Madeleine Albright noted that "diplomats need to be trained to know the religions of the countries where they're going."[97]

The same year as Albright's speech, a Harvard University committee recommended adding a requirement in "Reason and Faith" to the undergraduate core. In the judgment of committee chair Louis Menand, "It's noncontroversial that there is this thing called religion out there and that it has an enormous impact on the world we live in. Scholars should be able to study and teach it without getting cooties." Though the proposal was later withdrawn, the fact that it was on the table is significant. Given Harvard's historic role as an opinion leader for American higher education, the possibility of a required religion course was widely reported. If nothing else, the controversy helped raise the profile of religion at Harvard. While the committee's final report omitted a religion requirement, it included twenty mentions of the words "religion" and "religious" in the space of thirty-four pages (the 1945 Harvard report *General Education in a Free Society* made only twenty-four references to religion and its cognates in over 260 pages).[98]

Many calls for religion in the academy have focused on nonsectarian approaches, taking their epistemological cues from a tradition that has prized scholarly objectivity and the separation of facts from values. As noted above, this tradition was affirmed in the 1963 Supreme Court decision *Abington School District v. Schempp*, which recognized the nonconfessional study of religion in taxpayer-supported universities (something that was already growing before the court's ruling). Writing for the majority, Justice Tom C. Clark affirmed the "study of the Bible or of religion, when presented objectively as part of a secular program of education." In a concurring opinion, Justice Arthur Goldberg recognized the propriety of teaching *about* religion.[99]

While *Abington v. Schempp* was used to justify the emerging field of religious studies, it tied the field to an epistemology that few would accept without qualifications. By the late 1960s, objectivity had become "a very bad word and a totally unacceptable notion," according to AAR president Robert Michaelsen. Recounting a conversation with Danforth and Kent Fellows, Michaelsen noted their contempt for the concept. Such critiques multiplied with the advent of feminism and multiculturalism. Many of the field's leading figures remain critical of objectivity. While Martin Marty has criticized "artificial and militant distancing," Stephen Prothero urges scholars to "move beyond bracketing to moral inquiry." Reflecting these tensions, there is no dominant epistemology in religious studies.[100]

Some of the most sophisticated critiques of religious studies have traced the genealogy of "religion" in the modern West, arguing that the concept is fraught with political and cultural assumptions. In 2009, the *Journal of the American Academy of Religion* commissioned a special issue on "The Return of Religion after 'Religion,'" noting that "public talk about the return of religion is taking place at precisely the same time as we see within the academic study of religion a sharp genealogical critique of the category 'religion.'" In a similar way, a Syracuse University conference asked, "What new openings for feminism and gender theory are being made by the renewed interest of intellectuals in religion?"[101]

Influenced by postcolonial theory, some have questioned the epistemological assumptions of modern scholarship. Writing in the *American Scholar*, historian Robert Orsi discussed the relationships believers have with supernatural beings. Calling such encounters abundant events, he urged scholars to "think about unexplained religious experiences in ways that acknowledge their existence." Endorsing Orsi's proposal, Columbia University historian Richard Bushman called abundant history a promising way to think about figures like Joseph Smith, the subject of Bushman's magnum opus. In a 2011 conversation published in the Mormon journal *Dialogue*, Orsi and Bushman talked about the difficulty of interpreting religious phenomena. Historian Ann Taves has compared Orsi's "attitude of open, disciplined, and engaged attentiveness" to the Spiritual Exercises of St. Ignatius of Loyola. While distancing himself from theology, Orsi has challenged the reductionism of modernist historiography.[102]

Crossing the line between confessional and nonconfessional approaches, another group of scholars has promoted *scholarship grounded in religious commitments*. Conceiving of religion as a way of knowing, rather than an object of study, they have incorporated normative religious convictions into the content of their scholarship and teaching. In the 1990s, the evangelical historian George Marsden was the most visible advocate of this point of view. In books such as *The Soul of the American University* (a project funded by the Pew Charitable Trusts), he criticized the exclusion of religious viewpoints from academic discourse. Addressing a wider public, Marsden's plenary address at the American Academy of Religion, a cover story in the *Chronicle of Higher Education*, and op-ed pieces in the *New York Times* and the *Wall Street Journal* gave new visibility to his critique. Echoing the rhetoric of postmodernism and multiculturalism, he asked why Christian perspectives cannot be welcome at the table.[103]

Much of Marsden's argument comes down to epistemology. In his view, all knowledge is *perspectival*, that is, filtered through worldviews, perspectives, and paradigms. In this respect, he has much in common with his Notre Dame colleague Alvin Plantinga (also emeritus), one of the architects of religion's comeback in American philosophy. For four decades, Plantinga advanced a philosophical defense of Christian theism, arguing that belief and unbelief rest on assumptions that cannot be proven. Like Marsden, Plantinga was influenced by the turn-of-the-century Dutch Calvinist Abraham Kuyper, a thinker who stressed the role of presuppositions in the making of knowledge. Anticipating

Thomas Kuhn's discussion of paradigms, "Kuyperian presuppositionalism" has a great deal in common with postpositivist critiques of value-free knowledge.[104] Not all evangelical faculty have adopted the Kuyperian model. Rejecting its cognitive approach, a younger generation has developed an alternative vision rooted in Christian praxis, drawing on the Pietist, Anabaptist, and mystical strains in Christian history. In place of worldviews and presuppositions, they have focused on the practices of worship, hospitality, and spiritual formation.[105]

Whether cognitive or liturgical, the case for Christian scholarship has often been articulated by historians and philosophers. Given the central role of these disciplines in discussions of faith and knowledge, it is fitting that the Lilly Seminar on Religion and Higher Education was codirected by historian James Turner and philosopher Nicholas Wolterstorff. Paying special attention to confessional approaches, the Lilly Seminar explored the epistemological implications of faith and knowledge. Located at the University of Notre Dame (then home to Marsden, Turner, and Plantinga), the seminar met six times between 1997 and 1999. By bringing religious academics (Turner, Wolterstorff, Mark Noll, Douglas Sloan) into conversation with other scholars (David Hollinger, Richard Bernstein, Alan Wolfe), it helped raise the profile of religion in American scholarship.[106]

Predating the Lilly Seminar, some fifty Christian scholarly societies have worked to bring confessional scholarship into the mainstream academy. From the Society of Christian Philosophers to the Conference on Faith and History to the North American Association of Christians in Social Work, such organizations have helped nurture the scholarship of both evangelical and nonevangelical Christians. Several Christian scholarly associations publish journals, including *Faith and Philosophy* and *Christianity and Literature*.[107] The recent growth of these Christian scholarly organizations reflects the increasing number of evangelicals in American higher education. It is also the result of strategic philanthropy. During the 1990s, the Pew Charitable Trusts spent $24 million on its Christian Scholars Program (formerly known as the Evangelical Scholar's Program). Chronicling the growth of evangelical academia, Boston University's Institute on Culture, Religion, and World Affairs launched the Emerging Evangelical Intelligentsia Project in 2007. A 2006 survey found that 19 percent of American faculty identified as born-again Christians.[108]

Boasting higher educational levels and larger universities than evangelicals, American Catholics have also played a key role in revitalizing religious scholarship. Like evangelicals, they have acknowledged the influence of religious commitments on their work. In *Faith and the Historian: Catholic Perspectives* (2007), eight scholars describe the role of religion in their research. While one contributor recounts his search for a "Catholic hermeneutic," another describes the process of "becoming (and being) a Catholic historian." Like historian John McGreevy, now an administrator at Notre Dame, many accept the norms of scholarly objectivity. Launching a more radical critique of the American historical profession, Christopher Shannon questions the underlying presuppositions of mainstream historiography, urging scholars to craft narratives grounded in religious traditions. Though such critiques were more common in the decades before Vatican II, several organizations have continued to emphasize distinctively Catholic perspectives. These include the American Catholic Philosophical Association and the Society of Catholic Social Scientists. While the former includes Catholics from across the theological spectrum, the latter emphasizes loyalty to the church's teaching authority.[109]

Paralleling efforts to strengthen Christian scholarship, a very different group of scholars has called for the *integration of spirituality and higher education*. If George Marsden and Alvin Plantinga have inspired efforts to integrate faith and learning, the educational consultant Parker Palmer has been a central figure in the movement to bring spirituality into academic life. A 1997 survey of 11,000 faculty and administrators identified Palmer as one of the thirty most important leaders in American higher education, along with Alexander Astin, Arthur Levine, and Bill Gates. In 2010, he received the William Rainey Harper Award from the Religious Education Association.[110] In works such as *To Know as We Are Known* (1983), *The Courage to Teach* (1997), and *The Heart of Higher Education* (2010), he has laid out a vision of education as spiritual journey, criticizing the separation of the knower from the known, the objective from the subjective, and the spiritual from the academic.[111]

Reflecting this interest in all things spiritual, the Education as Transformation Project at Wellesley College drew 800 faculty, students, staff, and administrators, including 28 college presidents, to a 1998 conference on "religious pluralism, spirituality, and higher education." At the 1998 gathering, attendees witnessed presentations on classical Indian dance, spirituality and jazz, and Tibetan Buddhism, as well as talks by Parker Palmer and Diana Eck. The project also produced a ten-volume book series for Peter Lang Publishing on spirituality and higher education. In 2000, Education as Transformation cosponsored a meeting with the University of Massachusetts on "Going Public with Spirituality in Work and Higher Education." Organized by the university's chancellor, David Scott, a nuclear physicist, it featured presentations on "Science and Spirituality," "Spiritual Intelligence," and "Going Public with Spirituality in the Course Catalogue."[112] At both UMass and Wellesley, efforts to bring spirituality into the classroom were supported by high-level administrators. Using the chancellor's office as a bully pulpit, Scott wrote hopefully of an "integrative university" where questions of ultimate meaning could be brought "into every one of the majors." Reflecting on the themes of the Education as Transformation Project, Wellesley President Diana Chapman Walsh said that colleges should "envision a whole new place for spirituality in education."[113]

Beyond New England, the quest for the spiritual has made inroads into national higher education leadership circles. Over the past two decades, stories in *Liberal Education, Academe,* and *Change* have explored the topics of religion and spirituality.[114] In 2002, the Association of American Colleges and Universities sponsored a conference on spirituality and learning. The keynote speaker was UCLA's Alexander Astin, the most-cited higher education researcher in America.[115] According to a 1999 study Astin coauthored with his wife Helen, there is a "growing concern with recovering spirituality and meaning."[116] As leaders in this movement, the Astins signed a 2002 position statement critiquing the exclusion of spiritual and religious concerns from American colleges and universities. In this document and others, they have framed the problem of religion and higher education in the language of spirituality.[117]

From 2003 to 2011, the Astins served as coinvestigators on a massive Templeton-funded project on spirituality in the academy. In a national survey of 112,000 undergraduates, the project documented strong student interest in spirituality and religion. Its findings have been used to legitimate the goal of integrating spirituality into college and university classrooms. Consistent with this goal, UCLA held a National Institute on Spirituality in Higher Education in the fall of 2006 focused on "integrating spirituality into the campus curriculum and co-curriculum." In 2011, the Astins and coinvestigator Jennifer Lindholm released *Cultivating the Spirit: How College Can Enhance Students' Inner Lives.* Endorsed by former Harvard president Derek Bok, it focuses on higher education and spirituality. Published in 2014, Lindholm's *The Quest for Meaning and Wholeness* explores the role of spirituality among the faculty.[118]

The influence of the metaphysical tradition can also be seen in the late John Templeton's support for the dialogue between spirituality and science. A lifelong Presbyterian, Templeton was influenced by Christian Science, Unity, and Religious Science.[119] New Thought influences can also be seen in the life of philanthropist John Earl Fetzer (1901–1991), whose foundation funded Alexander and Helen Astin's *Meaning and Spirituality in the Lives of College Faculty* (1999). The founding donor of the Fetzer Institute, he experimented with spiritualism and *A Course in Miracles,* while also attending a Presbyterian church.[120]

Many of the advocates of spirituality in higher education could be described as spiritual, but not religious. In their Fetzer Institute study on faculty spirituality, the Astins defined the spiritual as "the individual's sense of self, sense of mission and purpose in life, and the personal meaning that one makes out of one's work."[121] These approaches grow out of the American metaphysical tradition, a family of movements constituting a third component of U.S. religious history.[122] Along these lines, the Fetzer Institute and the California Institute of Integral Studies drew 600 attendees to a conference on "integrative learning for compassionate action in an interconnected world" at San Francisco's Hotel Nikko.[123]

Closely related to the quest for spirituality are recent efforts to revitalize *moral and civic education*, a movement that Templeton has also backed. Published in 1999, *The Templeton Guide: Colleges That Encourage Character Development* profiled 405 programs. Since the 1990s, the foundation has funded a variety of college-level character initiatives, including the Jon C. Dalton Institute on College Student Values, *In Character* magazine, Big Questions Online, the *Journal of College and Character*, the Character Clearinghouse, and the Center for the Study of Values in College Student Development (now known as the Hardee Center for Leadership and Ethics in Higher Education).[124]

These initiatives are part of a larger shift in higher education that Alan Wolfe has called the "revival of moral inquiry."[125] Like so much of contemporary academic culture, today's renewed emphasis on moral education has its roots in the upheavals of the 1960s. Influenced by the social activism of the students, faculty brought morality back into the classroom.[126] In the 1970s, concern over the Watergate scandal and the Vietnam War helped fuel increased interest in the field of ethics. In 1980, the *Christian Science Monitor* reported that "ethics are back in fashion," recognizing some 12,000 new courses. Though many classes focused on narrow topics, they often made room for religious questions.[127] While the field of bioethics later secularized, theology was once the leading discipline.[128] Beyond applied ethics, the moral revival has included the rediscovery of moral development by psychologists (following Lawrence Kohlberg), James Q. Wilson's work on the moral sense, and the rise of communitarianism.[129]

Of these movements, communitarianism has done the most for the academic study of religion. Framing the problem of community in ethical terms, it combines social science with public philosophy. In *Habits of the Heart* (1985), Robert Bellah and his colleagues articulated a critique of American individualism, drawing on the biblical tradition and civic republicanism. One of the most popular sociological works of all time, *Habits* sold over 400,000 copies.[130] Along the same lines, Robert Putnam's *Bowling Alone* has spurred a lively debate on religion and civic engagement. Housed at Harvard University from 1995 to 2000, Putnam's Saguaro Seminar included several participants with an interest in religion and public life, such as John DiIulio, Glenn Loury, Martha Minow, Jim Wallis, Stephen Goldsmith, and a young Barack Obama.[131]

Across campus, political philosopher Michael Sandel's "Justice" course has become one of the most popular undergraduate offerings at Harvard. Since 1981 it has been attended by over 15,000 students at Harvard.[132]

Moral issues have also been at the forefront of debates about higher education. In *College: The Undergraduate Experience* (1987), the late Ernest Boyer argued that "students should become personally empowered and also committed to the common good." Citing *Habits of the Heart,* he criticized the lack of a "coherent view of the human condition." A product of church-related colleges (Greenville and Messiah), Boyer drew on his religious background during his years at the Carnegie Foundation for the Advancement of Teaching. In the words of his widow, he believed in "putting Christian principles into action for everybody."[133] Continuing where Boyer left off, Carnegie sponsored a major study of moral and civic learning directed by Anne Colby and Tom Ehrlich. Entitled *Educating Citizens: Preparing America's Undergraduates for Lives of Moral and Civic Responsibility* (2003), it profiled twelve colleges and universities. A disproportionate number were church-related.[134] Adding his voice to the moral revival, former Harvard president Derek Bok included character building on a list of key educational goals. In *Education's End* (2007), Yale Law School professor Anthony Kronman makes a similar case for the exploration of meaning and purpose, highlighting the "spiritual crisis in which we find ourselves today." According to Kronman, today's students "hunger for a serious spirituality of a non-fundamentalist kind." Advocating a return to the great books, he teaches in a Yale program that assigns works by Augustine, Dante, Luther, and Kierkegaard. More recently, Columbia University professor Andrew Delbanco has discussed the "growing movement promoting education for citizenship," praising both the Enlightenment and the age of faith.[135]

A by-product of this focus on citizenship, the pedagogy of service learning has spread across American higher education. Established in 1985, Campus Compact has played a key role in its diffusion. A national network of college presidents committed to civic engagement, Campus Compact has a presence at over 1,100 institutions, many of them church-related. In 2014, students at member institutions logged over 154 million hours of community service.[136] Committed to making "civic and community engagement an institutional priority," service-learning advocates have blurred the boundaries between morality and knowledge. For much of the past century, ethical concerns have been consigned to the extracurricular world of student development. With the rise of service learning and civic education, this is beginning to change.[137]

In the judgment of former AAR president Rebecca Chopp, the "movement of civic education in this country is vast and sustained." She adds that "in recent years educators, educational associations, and students have returned to the long and deep American tradition to educate citizens."[138] To the extent that this resurgence has focused on religious approaches, it has contributed to the return of religion. At the same time, there is nothing intrinsically religious about morality and citizenship. Writing in the *Chronicle of Higher Education*, Templeton program officer Arthur Schwartz rejected the notion that character education is a "code word for a religious or conservative ideology," adding that "[s]ources of conviction come in many shapes and sizes."[139]

Adding to this diversity, a *new religious pluralism* is reshaping the academy. Founded in 1991, the Pluralism Project at Harvard University has monitored the "changing contours of American religious demography." Documenting new forms of cultural diversity, it recently completed a study on the interfaith infrastructure of twenty American cities. Over the years, it has received funding from the Arthur Vining Davis Foundations, the Ford Foundation, Lilly Endowment, the National Endowment for the Humanities, the Pew Charitable Trusts, the Rockefeller Foundation, and the John Templeton Foundation. Framing the study of religious diversity in the language of pluralism, founding director Diana Eck emphasizes "the active seeking of understanding across lines of differences." Published in 2001, Eck's *A New Religious America* was the first major study to explore the landscape of post-Protestant America.[140]

In a post-Protestant university, more faculty are bringing the insights of Buddhism and other contemplative traditions into the classroom. For almost two decades, the Center for Contemplative Mind in Society has worked to "integrate contemplative practices into academic life." Partnering with the American Council of Learned Societies, the Nathan Cummings Foundation, and the Fetzer Institute, the Center awarded over 150 fellowships between 1997 and 2009. Most recipients taught in public and private research universities, including Columbia, MIT, and Virginia. Only 15 percent were from religiously affiliated institutions. While 82 percent of fellows reported a "deeper sense of personal and professional integration," 65 percent continued to use contemplative approaches in the classroom. From 1998 to 2011, a separate grant program explored the role of contemplative practices in the legal profession. Participants included Ivy League law students, professors, judges, and lawyers from top law firms.[141] Though a self-described secular organization, the Center's programs reflect the influence of Buddhism and other contemplative traditions.[142] Laying out an agenda for the future, the Center has issued a report on meditation and higher education, coauthored by John A. Astin (the son of higher education researchers Alexander and Helen Astin). Established in 2008, the Association for Contemplative Mind in Higher Education promotes "the recovery and development of the contemplative dimensions of teaching, learning, and knowing."[143]

Complementing these efforts, the addition of Buddhist studies, Hindu studies, and Sikh studies positions has contributed to the diversity of American higher education.[144] Centers and institutes are also sprouting up across the country, including the UCLA Center for Buddhist Studies and the Center for the Study of Hindu Traditions at the University of Florida. Though many of these programs and organizations are committed to teaching *about* Asian religions, some are taking a more engaged approach. Robert Buswell, the director of UCLA's Center for Buddhist Studies, is a former monk who speaks autobiographically about his immersion in Buddhist culture. A university publication praised Buswell for bringing "Buddhist principles of modesty, wisdom, and compassion to his work."[145]

In particular, Islamic studies is experiencing steady growth, buoyed by the increasing number of Muslim Americans and the resurgence of global Islam. In 2005, a Saudi Arabian prince donated $40 million to the interdisciplinary Islamic studies programs at Harvard and Georgetown, gifts that were announced in two full-page color advertisements in the *New York Times*. Centers for the study of Islam can be found at institutions as diverse as Oxford, Villanova, Duke, and San Diego State. The growth of Islamic studies has been accompanied by the founding of new scholarly organizations. Formed in 1972, the North American Association of Islamic and Muslim Studies (formerly the Association of Muslim Social Scientists) is an interdisciplinary organization with a diverse membership. Established in 1981, the International Institute of Islamic Thought (IIIT) has taken a more normative approach, publishing the *American Journal of Islamic Social Sciences*. Most recently, the International Qur'anic Studies Association has emerged as the main academic professional organization for the study of Islam's foundational text. Originating in a Henry Luce Foundation grant to the Society of Biblical Literature, the organization began in 2012.[146]

While not a product of the new immigration, Jewish studies is also thriving in the contemporary academy. Before World War II, there were fewer than a dozen full-time scholars of Judaism in the academy. By the 1970s, 250 faculty were teaching Jewish studies courses full time, with an additional 300 to 400 teaching at least one class in this area.[147] In 2001, there were approximately 600 Jewish studies courses, 150 endowed chairs, and 800 to 1,000 faculty positions in American higher education. A 2005 survey found that 45 percent of Jewish college students had taken at least one Jewish studies class. Alumni of such courses are more likely to identify with Jewish values and feel close to Jewish people.[148] The vigor of the field can be seen in the swelling ranks of the Association for Jewish Studies. Formed in 1969, the AJS had a 2017 membership of 1,800. Though the vast majority of Jewish studies programs separate scholarship from religious advocacy, some scholars bring their personal religious commitments into their research and teaching. Since the 1990s, the Posen Foundation has supported a number of initiatives on Jewish secularism, funding courses at thirty colleges and universities and a ten-volume Library of Jewish Culture and Civilization. Advancing a more traditional vision of Judaism, the Tikvah Fund has backed the *Jewish Review of Books*. Commenting on these philanthropic initiatives, one specialist called the present a "golden age for Jewish studies in North America."[149]

While enriching the academic conversation, the new religious diversity has created special challenges. As in the past, real-world conflicts have made their way into academia. At Columbia University, the creation of a Modern Arab Studies position honoring the late Palestinian American scholar Edward Said drew sharp criticism from some Jewish groups. Providing another perspective on Middle Eastern history, Columbia established an endowed professorship and institute for Israel and Jewish studies.[150] In the field of South Asian studies, a very different conflict has embroiled scholars of Hinduism. Unhappy with the way some religious studies faculty are portraying their religious tradition, some Hindu groups are challenging the academic study of Hinduism. Similar tensions led Penguin India to halt the publication of Wendy Doniger's *The Hindus: An Alternative History*.[151]

To address the challenge of diversity on campus, the Ford Foundation initiated its Difficult Dialogues Initiative in 2005. In a letter signed by the presidents of fifteen leading American universities (including Harvard, Berkeley, and Princeton), Foundation president Susan Berresford invited proposals on cultural differences and religious pluralism. Out of the 675 institutions that applied, 136 were invited to submit final proposals. In the end, 27 colleges and universities received $100,000 grants.[152] At the University of Michigan, thirty faculty took part in a seminar on "Student Religion, Faith, and Spirituality in the Classroom and Beyond." At Columbia University, the initiative led to several innovative projects, including a class on "Religion versus the Academy." The Difficult Dialogues programs were profiled in an issue of *Academe*, the official magazine of the American Association of University Professors.[153] Such projects reflect the contentious state of religious discourse in the academy.

Faculty Reponses to the Return of Religion: Indifference, Anxiety, and Engagement

Perhaps the most difficult dialogue of all may be between scholars of religion and their academic colleagues. Confirming the irrelevance of the sacred to many faculty, 62 percent of college students said their professors never encourage discussions of religious or spiritual topics.[154] While systematic data are not available for every field, most scholars do not focus on religion as an object of study. And yet attention to religion varies widely by discipline. While religion is the most popular specialization among historians (7.8 percent of the American Historical Association), psychologists of religion make up just 1.4 percent of the American Psychological Association's division memberships. By contrast, members of the Society of Christian Philosophers (who often specialize in the philosophy of religion) comprise about 11 percent of the American Philosophical Association. While both the American Sociological Association and the American Political Science Association sponsor thriving religion sections, section members are better represented in sociology than political science (4.7 percent versus 2.9 percent). Not surprisingly, the top twenty sociology journals pay twice as much attention to religion as their counterparts in political science.[155]

While many faculty have ignored the academic study of religion, others have criticized the direction of recent scholarship. Analyzing the religious turn, they have interrogated the cultural biases of their colleagues. In a 2010 working paper for the Social Science Research Council, David Smilde and Matthew May criticized the rise of proreligiousness in the sociology of religion. Documenting a thirty-year increase in the positive portrayal of religion, they noted a persistent focus on the religious causes of well-being. In their judgment, an overemphasis on religion's autonomy has masked its relationship with the hierarchies of race, class, and gender.[156]

Still others have challenged the role of normative religious convictions in academic scholarship. Drawing a firm boundary between theology and religious studies, Robert Orsi has questioned the influence of Niebuhrian neo-orthodoxy on American religious historians. Rejecting the distinction between good and bad religion, he argues that such categories obscure our understanding of the sacred. In a similar way, Jon Butler has criticized the recent emphasis on the religious backgrounds of historians, arguing that personal confession provides a "false explanation of why the individual is interpreting something one way or another." Though a regular participant in the Lilly Seminar on Religion and Higher Education, David Hollinger has challenged much of its agenda, questioning whether the university should be more accommodating to Christian perspectives. In "Enough Already: Universities Do Not Need More Christianity," Hollinger noted that higher education remains one of the few American institutions not dominated by religion, warning that "the history of Christianity is too important to be left exclusively in the hands of those who believe in it, however well funded." Making a similar point, sociologist Darren Sherkat writes that the "sociology of religion is once again being dominated by cadres of Christians with non-scientific agendas, funded heavily by quasi-religious foundations seeking to prove the superiority of their religious beliefs."[157]

Some forms of religious scholarship are more controversial than others. In particular, the movement for intelligent design has been widely criticized by the scientific community. Attracting the support of philosopher Alvin Plantinga, intelligent design was actively promoted in *First Things* and by InterVarsity Press. Early on, its leaders had high hopes for reshaping the conversation on religion and science. In a 1999 IVP book, philosopher William Dembski exemplified such confidence, predicting that "in the next several years intelligent design will be sufficiently developed to deserve funding from the National Science Foundation."[158] According to a 2005 survey, it has scant support among elite scientists.[159]

While somewhat less controversial, the John Templeton Foundation's initiatives have elicited similar criticism. As early as 1999, the physicist Lawrence Krauss expressed serious reservations about Templeton's agenda, concluding that "science and religion don't mix."[160] As noted above, Richard Sloan of Columbia University Medical Center has been an especially vocal critic of the Foundation's projects, calling them "garbage research." In direct response to Templeton, some scholars have formed organizations and networks of their own. In 2006, three dozen faculty, journalists, and academic leaders gathered for a conference sponsored by the investor Robert Zeps, the self-described anti-Templeton. Bearing the title "Beyond Belief: Science, Religion, Reason, and Survival," the gathering was a response to the perceived vulnerability of science. Warning of the "twilight for the Enlightenment project," the conference organizers urged scientists to "create a new rational narrative as poetic and powerful as those that have traditionally sustained societies." The presenters included scientists Richard Dawkins and Sam Harris, best-selling authors and leaders in the New Atheist movement, as well as Templeton program officer Charles Harper.[161]

While intended as a critique, such initiatives may have heightened the profile of religion in American higher education. Judging by the spirited reactions, the publications of the New Atheists have energized religious intellectual life, inspiring responses from the novelist Marilynne Robinson and the literary theorist Terry Eagleton.[162] More recently, historian T. Jackson Lears has criticized "the revival of positivism in popular scientific writing."[163] With the publication of *The Language of God: A Scientist Presents Evidence for Belief* (2006), former Human Genome Project director Francis Collins emerged as the New Atheists' chief debating partner.[164] A convert to evangelical Christianity, Collins is the founder of the BioLogos Foundation, an organization that promotes the "integration of science and Christian faith." While widely respected for his genetic research, he remains a controversial figure. In particular, President Obama's decision to make Collins the director of the National Institutes of Health elicited strong criticism. Writing in the *New York Times,* Sam Harris warned against entrusting Collins with the "future of biomedical research in the United States." With an annual budget of $30 billion, the NIH is the largest biomedical agency in the world.[165]

Surveys of the professoriate reveal a mix of secular and religious commitments. While just 20 percent of American faculty identify as born-again Christians, about 23 percent are atheists or agnostics. Yet only 19 percent describe themselves as "not spiritual and not religious," suggesting that most faculty have a spiritual or religious identity. Though a majority of college and university professors claim a religious affiliation, they are much less likely to do so than the general population. To be sure, the number of nonreligious faculty is much higher at leading research institutions. The higher the institutional prestige, the lower the religiosity. Consistent with this pattern, a 2005 survey found that over half of elite scientists had no religious affiliation. While one-third said they did not believe in God, 30 percent identified as agnostic.[166] Such findings suggest that the story of religion and higher education cannot be reduced to a struggle between the secular and the religious. Embracing uncertainty and ambiguity, many top scientists straddle the boundary between belief and unbelief. In the same survey, 69 percent of elite natural scientists and social scientists identified as "spiritual," including half of the atheists in the sample. In a similar way, the 2012 UCLA Faculty Beliefs and Values study found that one-fifth of college and university professors described themselves as spiritual-but-not-religious.[167]

Far from a binary conflict, the current situation has been described as post-secular, a term whose many meanings reflect the ambiguous role of religion in contemporary scholarship. By one count, there have been over forty books, seventeen dissertations, and a half dozen conferences on the topic of the post-secular. Since 2001 there have been over 13,000 references to the "postsecular" on Google Scholar. While some scholars have called for the replacement of secular reason with Christian theology, most have envisioned a space that makes room for both secularism and religion. Rejecting secular and religious triumphalism and binary thinking, they have discussed the coexistence of both in a pluralistic public sphere. This is the stance of philosopher Jürgen Habermas. In a 2001 speech to the German Book Trade, Habermas spoke of "keeping religion at a distance, but without completely closing one's mind to its perspectives." Later he engaged in a public dialogue with the future Pope Benedict XVI. According to Habermas, a post-secular society is one where religious "communities continue to make relevant contributions to public opinion and to political decision-making."[168]

Approaching the post-secular from a different angle, other theorists have trafficked in "odd combinations." Combining Lenin and St. Paul, the philosopher Slavoj Žižek has forged a hybrid discourse. Drawing on St. Augustine and his own autobiography, Jacques Derrida spent his final years reflecting on the possibility of "religion without religion." Commenting on these developments, theologian Mark Lewis Taylor wondered why there were "avowed atheist political thinkers writing on the incarnation or the trinity." Like Derrida, Jean-Francois Lyotard wrote a work on St. Augustine. In the United States, Stanley Fish recently predicted that religion would "succeed high theory and the triumvirate of race, gender, and class as the center of intellectual energy in the academy." Fulfilling Fish's prediction, Richard Rorty published a work on the future of religion, praising his coauthor's emphasis on Christian love.[169]

Though some religion scholars have celebrated the coming of the post-secular, most are engaged in the specialized study of particular groups. Systematic surveys and anecdotal evidence suggest that faculty pursue widely divergent approaches to religious studies. A 1991 study found that public university religion departments were much less sympathetic to theological studies than their counterparts in church-related colleges and seminaries.[170] More recently, a 2006 survey of introductory religious studies courses uncovered a similar divide. While 42 percent of religion faculty at church-related schools thought it was essential or very important for courses to "develop students' own religious beliefs," only 8 percent of faculty at secular institutions felt the same way.[171] The same gap emerged when faculty were asked whether "colleges should be concerned with facilitating students' spiritual development." While over 60 percent of faculty at religious colleges endorsed this goal, less than 20 percent of faculty in public universities concurred (though this still represents thousands of scholars).[172]

From the point of view of students, it may not matter what the syllabus says. Although professors at religious and nonsectarian colleges embrace very different goals, students at both types of institutions view the classroom as a place for spiritual discovery. In the 2006 study mentioned above, over 50 percent of undergraduates at secular colleges agreed that it is essential or important for introductory religion courses to help students develop their own religious beliefs.[173] According to the UCLA study of college student spirituality, 48 percent of American freshmen want colleges and universities to "encourage their personal expression of spirituality."[174] At all four of the institutions profiled in the book *Religion on Campus* (including a large public university), students reported growing spiritually in religion classes.[175] Such findings suggest that undergraduates take what they want from the classroom.

In recent decades, scholars have rediscovered the sacred. In almost every discipline, faculty can point to the existence of religious professional associations, high-profile scholars, influential books, and religion-oriented centers and institutes. Far from homogeneous, the religious resurgence is animated by competing frameworks and agendas. While some emphasize religion as an object of study, others focus on the moral and spiritual development of students. Despite deep differences, such movements have inhabited some of the same institutional spaces.

This chapter has described the heightened attention to religion among American scholars. The next two chapters discuss two further expressions of religion's increased visibility, examining religiously affiliated colleges and student religious life. Not surprisingly, there is substantial overlap between these sectors and the academic study of religion. Nearly half of undergraduate religion programs are located in religiously affiliated colleges and universities. Religiously affiliated institutions are also well represented in graduate education.[176] Because of the multireligious character of campus religious life (the focus of chapter 4), the relationship between student religiosity and the academic study of religion is even more complex. Ethnographic studies suggest that campus ministries and religious studies courses attract many of the same students.[177]

Far from monolithic, the return of religion has influenced multiple institutional spheres. Intersecting at many points, these different contexts cannot be collapsed into each other. The following chapters explore the revitalization of the church-related sector and the campus religious marketplace. Like this chapter, they document the heightened attention to religion in American higher education. Challenging the secularization narrative, they show how church-related colleges and student religious groups have reinvented themselves in a pluralistic era.

3

CRISIS AND RENEWAL IN CHURCH-RELATED HIGHER EDUCATION

There are 768 religiously affiliated colleges and universities in the United States, which together constitute about a third of the nation's postsecondary four-year educational institutions.[1] Reflecting the full spectrum of higher education, the religious sector includes liberal arts institutions and major research universities. Some struggle to meet payroll, while others benefit from hearty endowments. Many are small and largely unrecognized beyond their own locale, while others enjoy national and even international renown. Enrollments range from a few hundred to more than 20,000. The stronger institutions appear in national rankings of the best colleges, with the very strongest scoring near the top of annual surveys, such as those conducted by *U.S. News and World Report*. Meanwhile, other religious colleges are recognized as "best value" or "best regional" institutions.

Church-related higher education also reflects the diversity of American religion. Within mainline Protestantism, the United Methodist Church claims approximately 90 affiliated institutions, the Presbyterian Church (USA) nearly 60, and the two largest Lutheran bodies around 40 colleges.[2] Within evangelical circles, there are nondenominational colleges and others associated with the Baptist, Pentecostal, Holiness, and Church of Christ traditions, among others. The 220 colleges and universities associated with the Roman Catholic Church comprise the largest bloc, with about a dozen institutions sponsored by dioceses, while the remainder is affiliated with various religious orders.[3] The Jesuits claim the largest single portion of the field, with 28 colleges and universities. The rest are sponsored by dozens of religious orders including the Franciscans, Dominicans, Benedictines, as well as the Sisters of Mercy, Sisters of Providence, and Sisters of St. Joseph. Although a non-Christian religious presence is maintained in the United States with the inclusion of a handful of Jewish institutions, four Buddhist universities, and one accredited Muslim institution, the vast majority of the nation's religious colleges and universities are Christian.[4]

The heightened visibility of religion in American higher education is evident in the academic improvement and religious revitalization of church-related colleges and universities. Since 1980 the number of students in the church-related sector has modestly expanded, growing faster than total postsecondary enrollment. Though many church-related colleges and universities remain academically undistinguished, the better institutions have made substantial progress in student quality, faculty prominence, and academic standing. And many church-related institutions have become more serious about their religious identity.[5]

The religious vitality of the church-related sector comes after a period of soul-searching, when key stakeholders worried about the loss of institutional religious identity. A perennial issue in religious colleges and universities, such concerns became more pronounced in the early 1990s. Concerned educators wondered whether church-related colleges and universities were becoming more secular. Religious leaders pointed to the weakening of denominational identity. Though the strength of religious ties varied greatly, colleges across the nation were grappling with similar questions.

But even as much of the church-related sector struggled with the issue of religious identity, it experienced religious renewal. Conversations about the nature, purpose, and relevance of church-related higher education became more frequent. Faculty and administrators published books and articles on the topic, framing the question in different ways. While some warned of impending secularization, others were more optimistic. Religious activity increased, with much of it aimed at strengthening the bonds between the colleges and their sponsoring churches. *Local, regional,* and *denominational* efforts to renew Christian higher education proliferated, coalescing into *national* networks and movements. Aided by religious philanthropy, they worked to revitalize the church-related sector. While their impact was uneven, such initiatives succeeded in strengthening the religious identities of hundreds of colleges and universities.

Renewed interest in religion within church-related institutions marks a turning point, for in most cases the churches' involvement in higher education and colleges' interest in religion waned during the twentieth century. The emergence of the modern research university, a massive commitment to higher education on the part of the state, and the rise of specialized academic disciplines diminished the role of religion throughout higher education, even within the church-related sector. Church-related colleges felt a tension between their founding traditions and a desire to emulate the nation's pace-setting institutions. Responses to these cross-pressures varied greatly. Some colleges gave up their religious affiliations altogether. Others attempted to maintain a balance, selectively adapting to the academic revolution. Among those retaining their ties to their religious sponsors, the bonds weakened as the colleges limited the role of the churches in their affairs, and the churches grew less interested in their colleges.[6] Those with the strongest religious ties often struggled with poor finances and weak academics, remaining on the margins of American higher education.

The revitalization of church-related colleges and universities is part of a broader shift in religion's academic profile. Like the developments described in the previous chapter, efforts to strengthen church-related higher education were far from inevitable. Like the growth of the academic study of religion, the renewal of the church-related sector gained momentum with the emergence of leaders, organizations, and networks. Echoing calls for intellectual and cultural diversity within American higher education, they developed new justifications for the survival of distinctively religious institutions, earning critical support from foundations and donors. Reflecting denominational and institutional particularities, they focused on different parts of the church-related universe.

This chapter documents the renewal of church-related higher education. Focusing especially on mainline Protestant and Catholic institutions (the focus of earlier works lamenting the secularization of religious higher education), it also devotes substantial attention to evangelical colleges.[7] After a brief account of the rise of modern higher education and the weakening of denominational ties, it explores the intertwined stories of reflection and renewal as advocates moved to strengthen the religious identities of church-related colleges. Challenging the secularization thesis, it concludes by assessing both the progress and the limits of revitalization.

Religious Beginnings

The roots of American higher education run deep in ecclesial soil. While ties were often loose, the ten extant institutions of higher learning founded in the colonial period were denominationally sponsored or sanctioned. In the nineteenth century, hundreds of religiously affiliated institutions cropped up as the population grew and pushed westward.[8] The early leaders—Presbyterians, Episcopalians, and Congregationalists—continued building colleges as newcomers entered the field. The Baptists and the Methodists, whose ranks swelled dramatically in the first half of the nineteenth century, made strong showings, while newly arrived Lutherans from northern Europe sprinkled the upper Midwest with ethno-religious schools and colleges. Catholic religious orders established dozens of colleges.

Counting colleges is difficult. Some changed their names and locations, while others quickly folded.[9] Nonetheless, even rough approximations document the popularity of the nineteenth-century denominational college. According to one study, more than 200 colleges operated between 1800 and 1860; by 1890, the total topped 400. In 1890, the U.S. Commissioner of Education enumerated 415 institutions of advanced learning, including colleges, universities, schools of science and technology, normal schools, medical schools, and commercial colleges. All but 99 of this diverse group were religiously affiliated.[10]

Many institutions served local needs, contributing to the civic life of their surrounding communities. At the same time, an expansive vision of a Protestant America sustained and fueled the era of the denominational college. Filled with romantic ideals and evangelical fervor, nineteenth-century Protestants envisioned a Christian Zion carved out of the wilderness. Colleges figured prominently in this vision. Denominational rivalry further fueled the drive to found institutions of higher learning. It was, for example, Methodists' desire to keep up with the Presbyterians in Ohio that helped establish Ohio Wesleyan, Baldwin, and Mount Union.[11] Concurrently, Catholics built colleges to educate their own youth and protect them from what were perceived as the spiritually deleterious effects of Protestantism. Likewise, most of America's Historically Black Colleges and Universities (HBCUs) were founded by Protestant denominations, including 70 started by American Methodists.[12]

For the churches, the colleges were critical. From the earliest days of colonial history, when Harvard sought funds for ministerial education,[13] the churches have looked to the colleges to identify and train future clergy. Some colleges housed seminary divisions, while others simply evolved from seminaries. Calvin College, for example, began as a theological school of the Christian Reformed Church. Founded by Free Methodists in 1891, Seattle Pacific University began as Seattle Seminary.[14] Seeking to raise up a "succession of laborers in this vineyard," the nation's first Catholic bishop, John Carroll, founded Georgetown Academy in 1789. It grew into the nation's first Catholic college, with hundreds of students and graduates becoming priests.[15]

Whether seminary bound or not, students' collegiate experience included large doses of Christian teaching and piety. In the classroom and the chapel, students were exposed to the religious beliefs and practices of the sponsoring religious body. While theology per se had little place in the course of studies, students learned the tenets of the faith through preaching, scriptural study, catechetical instruction, and a capstone course on moral philosophy. Students and faculty attended daily religious services, in many instances worshipping in chapels that dominated the campus, where they listened to biblical texts and sermons and sang hymns dear to their denominations.[16]

The relationship between colleges and churches was mutually supportive. While the colleges fostered vocations to the clergy and piety among youth, the churches, in turn, helped the colleges. Throughout this era, denominations, general assemblies, dioceses, and religious orders authorized establishment of the colleges and then, in many cases, provided human and financial resources. Protestant colleges relied heavily on ministers to advance their cause. Methodists in Indiana, for example, expected their ministers to "solicit funds, procure students, and collect what books the liberality of the public may bestow" for DePauw.[17] In 1843, the Congregationalists and Presbyterians formed the Society for the Promotion of Theological and Collegiate Education at the West to fundraise in the East (the "money frontier").[18] Catholic colleges relied heavily on the contributed labor and the financial sacrifices of religious orders, as well as donations from the Catholic community.[19]

Drifting Apart

Until the end of the nineteenth century, the church and college are well-described as partner institutions. Denominations founded, staffed, and supported the colleges, where specific denominational and religious cultures infused the campuses through leadership, worship, and instruction. In turn, the colleges produced educated young people for the pulpit and the pew.[20] But the close connections between church and college did not endure. The age of the denominational college ended between 1870 and 1900 as an academic revolution remade higher education and eroded the churches' academic warrant. Innovation swept through higher education; traditional ways were set aside in favor of the new. No aspect of academic life went untouched. By the end of the century, a whole new institution, the modern nonsectarian university, had displaced the denominational college at the head of an increasingly regularized and complex academic order.[21] As the age of the college gave way to the age of the university, the trajectory was set for the twentieth century: higher education would increasingly move beyond the purview of the churches.

The leaders of the academic revolution, who created the modern university and forged a new academic order, fundamentally altered Americans' understanding of the relationship between religion and higher education. They convinced important constituencies that denominational sponsorship hindered intellectual life and higher education needed liberation from the stultifying effects of church control. They successfully recast the churches, the primary sponsors of higher education for more than two centuries, as vestiges of higher education's medieval past and inhibitors of free inquiry. For the most part, these reformers were not crusading secularists, for most were committed liberal Protestants. They were not antireligious per se, but averse to institutional religious authority. For example, the first president of the University of Chicago, William Rainey Harper (1891–1906), was a devout Baptist whose religious commitments infused his vision for the new university. Nonetheless, he identified freedom from church control as constitutive of a university.[22]

Denominational sponsorship took a rhetorical beating during the academic revolution. When describing the colleges, educational reformers linked religion to undesirable denominational interests; tenets and creeds "shackled men's minds," while religious homogeneity fostered intolerance. On the other hand, when describing the new nonsectarian universities, reformers took advantage of cultural opportunities and sensibilities by linking religion to the beneficent causes of national progress and "true Christianity."[23] Late nineteenth-century Americans were enamored of the concept of progress, creating sympathy for the modern university. Moreover, American Protestantism overall became more liberal in the postbellum era, making the concept of nonsectarian education not only palatable, but even desirable among those who considered the proliferation of denominations and sects (especially when occasioned by strife) an affront to true Christianity.

Though the leading agents of the academic revolution supported the cause of a Protestant nation, their reforming efforts helped set in motion a process of disestablishment. By disestablishing religion academically, the university builders ensured that no religious tradition would formally enjoy institutional or intellectual privilege, although Protestantism's role in society guaranteed it a first-class berth in American universities for decades to come.[24] Yet the logic of nonsectarian education eventually prevailed. No religion, including American Protestantism, could long maintain cultural privilege in a scholarly milieu where ties between faith and reason were waning. Thus, the nation's pace-setting academic institutions, the leading universities, no longer needed their denominational sponsors. They did not, however, banish Christianity or religion in general. In many institutions, the academic study of religion could be found in theology and religious studies departments, divinity schools, and a handful of other courses. Despite this presence, the exercise of religion became private, voluntary, and much less visible.[25]

The Academic Revolution and the Church-Related College

During the twentieth century, the churches' role in the overall ecology of higher education gradually diminished. With the ascent of the modern university to the head of an expanding academic order, nonsectarian education became what denominational control had been: normative. Gradually, new partners entered the field of higher education and eclipsed the churches. With the triumph of industrial capitalism, colleges and universities catered to the needs of a newly emergent middle class and a social order transformed by expanding markets and new technologies. They tailored the curriculum to the needs of a "learned laity rather than a learned clergy," that is, to those who would teach children, build dams, schedule trains, staff banks, create factories, and engage in commercial pursuits.[26] The great Gilded Age philanthropists poured fortunes into the establishment of nonsectarian universities such as Chicago, Stanford, Johns Hopkins, and Cornell.[27] Most notably, in the mid-nineteenth century the state entered the field and quickly became what the church once was: the primary sponsor of higher education.

Although eventually dwarfed by the nonecclesial sector, church-related higher education persisted and expanded, with hundreds of colleges maintaining ties to religious bodies. But sustaining a religious identity grew increasingly difficult within a complex system dominated by institutions, associations, and ideals that owed little to the church. Increasingly subject to secular organizations, religious educators were no longer able to determine the standards for their own institutions. Noting such shifts in the 1920s, a Jesuit worried about the future of Catholic higher education: "Were Catholics in this country many times more influential than they are, they might succeed in enforcing educational standards different from those actually in vogue."[28] Forty-plus years later, the Danforth Commission's study on church-related colleges and universities painted a sober portrait: "religiously the church colleges are in a difficult position. The academic world today is essentially a secular world. . . . Probably no contemporary institution, however strong its religious foundation, can wholly escape the inroads of secular thought."[29]

New institutions influenced the church-related sector. Accrediting agencies set standards that forced church-related colleges to invest heavily in laboratories, libraries, and faculty members equipped with doctoral degrees instead of religious credentials. The Association of American University Professors promoted the ideal of academic freedom, making uneasy accommodations for faculty employed at religiously affiliated colleges.[30] Money flowed toward nonsectarian institutions, ignoring or undermining denominational subcultures. Philanthropist Andrew Carnegie, for example, established a pension fund for academics in 1906 that excluded denominationally affiliated institutions; by one count, fifteen colleges responded by severing their denominational ties. Though many embraced a broad Christian identity, commitment to church-relatedness waned.[31] Court decisions and federal regulations in the second half of the twentieth century making religious colleges eligible for government funding—if they were not "pervasively sectarian"—made some church-related institutions cautious about expressing their religious character.[32]

New ideas of academic excellence compounded challenges faced by church-related institutions. The leaders of the academic revolution successfully argued that denominational ties were an impediment to robust intellectual life and academic excellence.[33] The famous quip by George Bernard Shaw—that the phrase "Catholic university" was "a contradiction in terms"—was taken as fact in some circles. In 1956, sociologist David Riesman placed denominational colleges at the tail of a "snake-like procession" led by nonsectarian research universities.[34] Of course, many were undistinguished. As Alexander Astin and Calvin Lee wrote in *The Invisible Colleges: A Profile of Small, Private Colleges with Limited Resources* (1972), "The history of invisible colleges in the United States can be traced back to the religious influences that were at work in America." For every Notre Dame or Davidson, there were a dozen schools with meager endowments and low salaries.[35]

Many factors shaped institutional responses to the academic revolution. Within the church-related sector, theological orientation and social context played a decisive role. With a religious faith identified with the dominant culture, mainline Protestant schools were among the first to distance themselves from their denominational sponsors. For colleges that developed into universities, such as Princeton and Vanderbilt, adaptation almost always involved secularization. Accepting the premise that a "true" university needed to be religiously unencumbered, they evolved from denominational colleges into nonsectarian (yet broadly Christian) universities, then, in time, to broadly pluralistic institutions with no religious affiliation.[36] Compared with universities, colleges were more likely to maintain their religious affiliations, although relationships between the churches and colleges often changed significantly. While continuing to claim a religious identity, many colleges sought and gained greater autonomy in the area of governance. Despite weaker ties to denominations, colleges could still point to strong religion departments and an active campus ministry. Only when the mainline Protestant establishment faded in the 1960s did it become apparent that religion faculty and university chaplains were not able to sustain the religious ethos of their institutions.

Not all mainline schools traveled the same path. Always more loosely bound, colleges founded by Congregationalists were among the first to disaffiliate. In the 1960s, one writer likened them to a "chain of fortresses" extending across America. In reality, few had retained strong church ties, though this varied greatly by geography. Nurtured by midwestern Congregationalists, Carleton College maintained its denominational affiliation for well into the post–World

War II era. This was not the case in New England. Methodist and Presbyterian connections fared somewhat better, especially in the South. While northern Presbyterian colleges abandoned formal control by the late 1960s, southern schools held on for a little while longer. In the upper Midwest, ethnic communities served as a buffer for German and Scandinavian Lutherans. At a time when many institutions were shedding their religious affiliations, schools like St. Olaf and Valparaiso remained proudly Lutheran, producing sweeping statements on Christian higher education. Recognizing such institutional commitments, a 1966 study found that among Protestants, "Lutheran bodies have, as a group, the most extensive relationships with their churches."[37]

Other denominational traditions encompassed wide variations in church-relatedness. Among liberal Protestants, Episcopalians had some of the weakest ties, though even here there were significant differences. The Anglican ethos of Sewanee should not be confused with the cosmopolitanism of Bard College. While the former educated southern elites, the latter was home to secular iconoclasts like A. J. Ayer and Dwight Macdonald. Even more diverse, Quaker colleges covered a spectrum, from the loose connections of Whittier (alma mater of Richard Nixon) to the evangelicalism of George Fox (alma mater of Herbert Hoover). Located on Philadelphia's Main Line, the tricollege community of Bryn Mawr, Swarthmore, and Haverford experimented with different ways of being Quaker. While Bryn Mawr wore its religious heritage lightly, Haverford cultivated a liberal Quaker spirituality. Despite this midcentury religious renaissance, all three institutions grew more distant from their Quaker roots. As Daniel Coit Gilman observed at the dedication of Bryn Mawr, "the Society of Friends inclines to the idea of planting rather than to the idea of building institutions." The same was true in many mainline denominations. Where the churches planted, others built.[38]

Wary of modern intellectual currents, Catholics offered more resistance to secularization. In response to the academic revolution, Catholic higher education made institutional (and structural) adjustments. But Catholics also resisted ideologically, until the Second Vatican Council began a period of dramatic change. From 1900 to the early 1960s, American Catholics created their own academic subculture, founding religious scholarly societies in nearly every discipline. In an age of intellectual fragmentation, they looked to the Neo-Scholastic revival for coherence. Revering the Middle Ages, they produced works like *The Thirteenth, Greatest of Centuries*. Despite such romantic rhetoric, Catholic colleges and universities struggled with mundane realities. Weighed down by heavy teaching loads, faculty often had little time for research. A 1952 study found that barely half of Catholic sociologists had published a scholarly article or a book. Embarrassed by such statistics, Monsignor John Tracy

Ellis questioned whether American Catholicism could sustain the life of the mind. In spite of these challenges, American Catholic colleges and universities possessed a strong sense of their own distinctiveness. While parietals enforced an environment of *in loco parentis,* daily Mass and intercollegiate sports gave ritual form to undergraduate life. In the words of a 1957 Notre Dame alumnus, "the campus I knew 50 years ago was an enclosed human habitat."[39]

All of this changed during the 1960s. Influenced by Vatican II and the upheavals of the decade, Catholic colleges and universities were very different places in 1975. Some viewed these developments as liberating, including the drafters of the Land O'Lakes Statement of 1967. Holed up at Notre Dame's lakeside retreat center in the Wisconsin woods, a group of clergy presidents and Catholic intellectuals crafted a new vision for Catholic higher education. Dubbed a Catholic Magna Carta by educational reformers, it declared that the "Catholic University today must be a university in the full modern sense of the word," while making the tradition "perceptively present and effectively operative." For its signatories it was a sign of a church come of age. For its critics it was a prelude to secularization. The ensuing years would see the creation of lay boards of trustees, the hiring of non-Catholic faculty, and an improvement in academic reputation. President of the nation's leading Catholic institution, Father Theodore Hesburgh was one of the key figures behind the document. Looking back on his thirty-five-year tenure, Hesburgh wrote that he left Notre Dame "*more Catholic* today than we were in the past—both big C and little c." Others saw Hesburgh's presidency as a time of religious accommodation.[40]

Even more than Catholic higher education, evangelical colleges resisted the academic revolution. Maintaining a Protestant Christian ethos, they hired evangelical faculty and staff, requiring signed statements of faith and adherence to strict moral codes as conditions of employment. Students, faculty, and staff met regularly for mandatory religious services. With some notable exceptions, few faculty had ambitious research agendas. By remaining insulated from the academic mainstream, evangelical schools emerged with their religious missions intact, though at great cost to their intellectual development.[41]

Yet even here there were changes. Shaped by the "new evangelicalism" of the postwar era, many of these institutions replaced denominational particularities with a generic Protestantism. This was true at Wesleyan and Pentecostal schools, where transdenominational influences eroded theological distinctiveness. From the Mennonite institutions of the Kansas prairies to the Dutch Calvinist enclaves of western Michigan, dozens of conservative Protestant colleges struggled with the tension between denominational traditions and the nondenominational Christianity of American evangelicalism. For many schools, involvement with evangelical scholarly and academic organizations weakened denominational identity.[42]

No matter what their theological orientation, the twentieth century was not easy for church-related colleges and universities. For decades, many institutions lived on the margins of American higher education. Maintaining religious identity was costly. For most of the century, only a minority of religious colleges achieved academic respectability.

And yet Catholic and Protestant higher education witnessed significant changes. Even in the church-related sector, the effects of academic disestablishment were felt as colleges became less confessional. Church-related colleges increasingly turned to laypeople to serve as trustees, administrators, and faculty. Many hired faculty and staff with little if any regard to denominational affiliation, sometimes downplaying the religious identity of the school in order to attract stronger candidates for academic posts. Once mandatory, daily chapel services and mass became voluntary. On not a few campuses, sacred symbols and art went into storage.

Focusing on Mission and Identity

On the margins of higher education, the church-related sector became self-conscious about its place in American society. In the postwar era, many proponents of church-related higher education articulated a new vision. Religion was not an academic liability, they argued; in fact, religiously affiliated colleges had something distinctive and valuable to bring to the table. Spurred by a postwar theological renaissance, advocates argued that church-related colleges could be beacons, serving the academy and nation, morally and religiously, through the integration of faith and learning. Still confident of the central place of Protestantism in American culture, in 1956 one commentator asked, "Shall we Presbyterians of the twentieth century forfeit our heritage of being molders of American culture?" In 1961, well-known leader Merrimon Cuninggim spoke of church-related higher education's potential to serve as the "conscience" of American higher education. The same year, Henry Luce's *Time* called Methodists a "college-building church."[43]

In the mid-1960s, the locus of concern shifted. Leaders still carried the flag on behalf of religious colleges; representatives of the Danforth Foundation, the National Council of Churches Commission on Higher Education, the Council of Protestant Colleges and Universities, and the National Catholic Educational Association, among others, held forth on the value of church-sponsored higher education.[44] Like their predecessors, leaders in the 1960s remained concerned about the viability and vitality of religious colleges vis-à-vis their secular counterparts. But a new, critical concern emerged: the religious identity of religious colleges. The very thing that distinguished them from other institutions and justified their existence came into question. The major study of the period, Manning Pattillo and Donald Mackenzie's *Church-Sponsored Higher Education in the United States: Report of the Danforth Commission* (1966), sounded the first major warning. Finding that religion was "not as strong . . . as one would expect," the authors concluded that the "most basic problem of church-sponsored higher education is, in a very real sense, theological. The shifting sands of religious faith today provide an uncertain foundation for religiously oriented education programs."[45]

Symptomatic of religion's changing place within the church-related sector, definitions and typologies of church-relatedness surfaced in the 1970s. Beginning with Pattillo and Mackenzie's typology of "Defender of the faith colleges," "Free Christian colleges," "Non-affirming colleges," and "Church-related universities," scholars developed criteria to describe and measure religion's place in church-related colleges.[46] A 1972 typology grouped colleges into historically Protestant, nominally Protestant, denominationally connected, and interdenominational evangelical institutions.[47] While Merrimon Cuninggim compared embodying, proclaiming, and consonant institutions, Richard Anderson developed a "religiosity index" based on eight variables, including the religious affiliation of students and board members, compulsory chapel and religion courses, and denominational identification in public documents.[48] Such typologies captured the diversity of the church-related sector.

This diversity could be seen in denominational reports on higher education. Noting the proliferation of these studies in the 1970s, Martin Marty concluded that "'[r]elationships' are clearly on the minds of responsible leaders." One Lutheran body reported an "erosion of church-related colleges." By contrast, the Southern Baptist Convention perceived its institutions to be "in remarkably good shape," failing to anticipate the conflicts ahead. Facing demographic reality, the Society of Jesus admitted "there will be fewer Jesuits in the educational apostolate in our institutions, and they will be older." Marking its diminishing presence in higher education, the United Church of Christ called church-related colleges "an endangered species."[49]

By the late 1980s and early 1990s questions about religious identity of church-related colleges and universities began to surface with greater regularity; by the mid-1990s concern had become widespread. In examining governance, curriculum, discipline, and ethos, even the friendliest of critics wondered whether church-related colleges, individually or corporately, were on a secular trajectory. This soul-searching exercise was repeated over and over, at the local, regional, denominational, and national level.[50]

In the 1990s, supporters of church-related higher education came to a new realization: religious colleges must be more intentional about mission and identity. At a 1995 symposium sponsored by the Association of Catholic Colleges and Universities, journalist Peter Steinfels described an "emerging consensus" on the precariousness of Catholic identity. In a speech to 450 faculty and administrators from 200 schools, he called for "a new moment in Catholic higher education." Many Protestant educators agreed, initiating a new discussion of religious mission.[51]

In the quest for institutional survival and academic prestige, church-related institutions had sometimes downplayed their founding traditions. Many denominational colleges "would be hard-pressed," concluded one clergyman writing in the *Christian Century*, "to demonstrate how their church relationship affects their academic program or campus life."[52] Another observer wondered whether Baptist higher education would end up treating its religious heritage "like an old beau from decades before with whom things did not quite work out."[53] In 1990, sixty-nine Presbyterian college and university presidents issued a statement acknowledging the extent of secularization of their institutions and concluding that the "Presbyterian Church could be close to the point where its involvement in higher education might be lost forever."[54]

Historical studies published in the 1990s emphasized the vulnerability of religious institutions to outside pressures. Chronicling the secularization of America's pace-setting universities, George Marsden's *The Soul of the American University* was quickly accepted as a cautionary tale for contemporary church-related institutions. The following year Philip Gleason published *Contending with Modernity: Catholic Higher Education in the Twentieth Century*. After a sweeping account of Catholic higher education's response to the rise of modern American higher education, Gleason concluded that Catholic educators "are no longer sure what remaining Catholic means." In 1998, James Burtchaell published *The Dying of the Light*, a highly critical work documenting "the disengagement of colleges and universities from their Christian churches."[55] Identifying a problem, these declension narratives raised concerns about the future of church-related colleges, convincing many that Catholic and Protestant schools were traveling a well-worn path cleared by secular institutions that once had a religious identity. As one Mennonite educator put it, "The recent studies of George Marsden and James Burtchaell have put the fear of God into church-related colleges and universities."[56]

Not everyone was so pessimistic. Defending church-related higher education, retired foundation executive Merrimon Cuninggim highlighted the strength of the colleges relative to their denominational sponsors. Improving in academic quality and prestige, they had become the senior partners in the church-college relationship. Criticizing conservative efforts to restore church control, Cuninggim celebrated institutional autonomy. Others called attention to the enormous variety in the church-related sector. Noting the vast middle ground, they questioned the assumption that colleges "are either thoroughly religious or they are not religious at all." Such critics noted that there is more than one way to be church-related.[57]

While scholars debated its veracity, the declension narrative did much to motivate the advocates of church-related higher education. For those concerned about the future of religious colleges, two interrelated challenges were in play: religious diversity and religious identity. Some focused on the impact of religious diversity on institutional culture. This concern surfaced regularly in discussions of mainline Protestant institutions, where members of the sponsoring religious group rarely comprised a majority. Many wondered how a college could be vitally Methodist, Presbyterian, or Disciples of Christ when those who identified with the tradition were outnumbered on campus. A 1998 study of Presbyterian colleges documented demographic realities in many mainline Protestant institutions. At 2.7 percent of the general population, it was not surprising that no Presbyterian college had a Presbyterian majority of students. The Presbyterian share of enrollment ranged from 10 percent at historically denominational institutions to 19 percent at schools with a pervasive connection to the Presbyterian Church (USA).[58] United Methodist institutions faced a similar situation, with Methodist enrollment in their schools, colleges, and universities ranging between 5 and 32 percent and averaging 20 percent.[59] The phenomenon of religious pluralism could also be found among the faculty, where hiring without regard to religious affiliation left many institutions with a paucity of adherents from the sponsoring religious group. According to a 1995 survey of 317 institutions, "61 percent of church-related colleges report that fewer than half their faculty are members of the denomination to which the college is related, and another 31 percent report that fewer than a quarter of their teachers are members."[60]

Many rued a "broken pipeline," focusing on the ecology of religious institutions. Congregations, denominational schools, summer camps, and other denominational associations that once channeled students into denominational colleges no longer functioned well. The colleges could no longer rely on their denominational partners. In considering the future of Methodist higher education, for example, the General Board of Higher Education and Ministry presumed that "many United Methodist congregations will continue the pattern of not recruiting students for United Methodist schools."[61]

Since the 1960s increased access for underrepresented groups has been a first-order priority throughout higher education. As a result, enrollments have increased significantly for various groups, including African Americans, Latinos, international students, the economically disadvantaged, and those with disabilities. In tandem, colleges and universities have tried to make all feel welcome, regardless of race, ethnicity, gender, sexual orientation, or religion. Grounding these efforts is a two-sided premise. On the one hand, every person, regardless of background or identity, is entitled to be treated like everyone else. On the other, every person has a right to a distinctive identity that should be respected, even celebrated. These sometimes contradictory commitments—inclusiveness and particularity—have heightened sensitivity to differences in ways that have, on occasion, complicated efforts to emphasize an institution's religious identity. Concerned that emphasizing one religious tradition will make some people feel excluded, some colleges have muted their religious identities. In other instances, specific denominational identity is tempered in a sea of many religious voices, as representatives of multiple faith traditions are invited to participate in and contribute to public gatherings and forums.[62]

Those concerned about the weakened relationship between churches and colleges also point to the phenomenon of religious identity. As early as 1968, Christopher Jencks and David Riesman recognized that the survival of Protestant colleges depended on the existence of vital, distinctive Protestant communities with members who were "willing and able to pay for a brand of higher education that embodies their vision."[63] The insight was sound: denominational colleges rely on denominations for their religious identity—and denominations are far from static. In the late twentieth century, denominationalism declined as a source of personal identity.[64] Furthermore, those who do identify with a denomination may not be deeply versed in its tenets. The implications for church-related colleges are significant, for even if a critical mass of individuals from the sponsoring religious body exists, their commitment to and understanding of the beliefs and practices of the denomination are not guaranteed. Faculty and staff may not be familiar with the basic concepts and vocabulary of their own religious tradition, undermining their capacity to advance the religious mission or sustain the religious identity of the college. One observer, in examining Augsburg College, noted that in "Lutheran colleges of yore," students and faculty were "our kind of people." Going forward, he claimed, it would be difficult "to find serious Lutherans."[65] Baptist historian Bill Leonard went further, arguing that maintaining the religious identity of Baptist institutions has been "complicated by the essential collapse of Anglo-Baptist culture in the South."[66]

Worries about religious identity have also been acute in Catholic circles. In recent decades, post–Vatican II Catholics have joined the ranks of the faculty and administration. As a cohort they have not been as closely tied to the church as their pre–Vatican II predecessors. The same has been true of young adult Catholics. A 1996 study found that younger Catholics could no longer articulate their religious beliefs.[67] This sense of loss has been fueled by an additional shift: the paucity of younger priests, brothers, and sisters working in Catholic colleges and universities. While religious identity in Protestant colleges is often constructed denominationally, in Catholic colleges religious identity is most often constructed around the sponsoring religious order—the Jesuits, Benedictines, Dominicans, Franciscans, and so on. Between 1965 and 2017 the number of religious order priests dropped from 22,707 to 11,424; the number of brothers from 12,271 to 4,007; the number of sisters from 179,954 to 45,605.[68] The declining number of men and women in religious life has deprived Catholic higher education of the personnel who literally embodied the religious identity of the college. Today, a priest or sister in the president's office is the exception to the rule, as 64 percent of the nation's Catholic colleges and universities employ a lay president. In Catholic colleges and universities, where religious identity is often refracted through the sponsoring religious congregation, the issue of identity is thus doubly acute. It is not solely the question of how an institution might express its Catholic identity, but how it will continue to express its founding charism with few, if any, members of the religious congregation involved in the work of the college.[69]

Religious Renewal: *Apologia Pro Sacra Collegio*

After enduring a period of soul-searching, the church-related sector experienced religious renewal, with the former fueling the latter. Deepening concern over the loss of religious identity spurred a host of initiatives aimed at strengthening the bonds between colleges and their sponsoring churches. Simply put, the soul-searching proved motivational. The "dying of the light?" asked Rev. David O'Connell in his 1998 inaugural address as president of the Catholic University of America, invoking the title of James Burtchaell's book about the "disengagement of colleges and universities from their Christian churches." "Not here. Not now. Not again," he rejoined.[70] Invoking the heritage of Reformed higher education, the editor of a 2003 book on Presbyterian colleges argued that "now is the time to consider whether that light should be revived." In 1995, *Commonweal* magazine editor Margaret O'Brien Steinfels warned that "we have a decade—ten years—in which this question of identity must be honestly addressed and definitively taken on as a commitment and core project of institutions that hope to remain Catholic."[71]

Whether real or imagined, a perceived problem is a necessary ingredient for a social movement.[72] Within Christian higher education, several discrete problems vied for the attention of academic reformers. For some faculty and administrators, religion's weak showing on campus was the issue. This was, however, more than a simple descriptive exercise. Some of the proponents of church-related higher education began redefining conceptual frameworks in their favor. Appropriating the framework of secularization, they identified the *absence* of religion in the academy as problematic. This marked a shift. A century ago, the leaders of the academic revolution that gave birth to the modern university had argued that religion's *presence* in the academy was problematic. Today's argument reverses the relationship, contending that religion's *absence* is the problem. Having spent most of the twentieth century arguing that church-related colleges were respectable *in spite of* their religious ties, proponents now argue that they are valuable *because of* their religious ties. Two faculty members from Presbyterian colleges summarize this view: "We believe that the time is right to challenge the widely held assumption that connection to the Presbyterian Church is a weakness rather than a strength."[73]

Another popular defense of church-related colleges and universities pragmatically asserted that institutional diversity encourages intellectual vitality.[74] Though the contributions of the modern university are substantial, some have warned against the pressures of homogenization. Chronicling the transformation of undergraduate institutions into graduate and professional institutions, they have focused on the "disappearing liberal arts college." Recognizing that "small is different," others have celebrated the variety in American higher education. In *Colleges That Change Lives*, journalist Loren Pope profiled forty schools where "values are central." Half were church-related. In a similar way, college administrator Samuel Schuman argued that small colleges play an important role in America's educational ecology, adding that religious institutions occupy a valuable niche.[75]

From this perspective, higher education runs the risk of "bland conformity" by reproducing the same content in every school.[76] In the judgment of sociologist Alan Wolfe, a lack of diverse viewpoints encourages "scholarship that is seemingly daring yet bloodless, unorthodox yet thoroughly predictable, and politically motivated without any political content." By privileging their religious identities, church-related colleges have resisted this homogenization. While most of the academy busies itself working on methodology and scientific concepts, in Catholic institutions Wolfe finds philosophy departments taking great ideas seriously, humanities departments exploring religious themes in art and literature, and political science departments studying political theory and institutions.[77] In a similar way, Mark Schwehn writes that Lutheran colleges "contribute to the general good of institutional pluralism."[78]

Arguments in defense of religious higher education have often assumed a philosophical and theological cast. While Wolfe and others have stressed the value of religious colleges and universities in simply broadening the intellectual scope, others have argued more epistemologically. As noted in the previous chapter, a number of scholars have invoked the language of postmodernism and multiculturalism to make a case for religious ways of knowing. Extending these arguments, proponents have pointed out that church-related colleges cultivate certain types of questions and thinking not encouraged in secular settings. Religious issues are not avoided; questions about meaning are not ignored. The empirical is not the only road to truth. Insofar as religious questions are considered taboo in many secular settings, former Notre Dame president Reverend Edward "Monk" Malloy has argued that a "Catholic university is more open than its secular counterparts, and not less." Here, too, a small college justifies its existence: as a representative of a Mennonite college put it, "What we 'know' is not the same as what Harvard knows."[79]

Focusing on the moral life, some educators stress the ethical and spiritual benefits of Christian colleges and universities. Here proponents argue that colleges should foster virtue and nurture faith, and that religious schools are better positioned to do so than many other institutions. Proponents invoke the critics of the contemporary university who deem it too beholden to corporate funders to function in an ethical manner, too fragmented to set a meaningful agenda, or too constrained epistemologically to take up moral issues.[80] The alleged moral and spiritual failings of the modern university have afforded advocates of church-related higher education occasion to make another case for church-related higher education. Religion provides moral and spiritual resources that higher education needs, advocates claim. In *Exiles from Eden*, for instance, Schwehn argues that Christianity fosters virtues that are badly needed in academic life, such as charity and humility.[81]

Putting their institutional research dollars to work, a number of church-related colleges and universities have launched "spiritual assessment" projects to document their impact on undergraduates. In recent years, the Lutheran Educational Conference of North America, the Council for Christian Colleges and Universities, the National Catholic College Admission Association, and the Council of Independent Colleges have conducted quantitative studies on the spiritual and moral development of their students.[82] A mixture of evaluation research and marketing, they have documented clear differences between the graduates of church-related colleges and secular institutions. The research firm Hardwick-Day found that Lutherans who graduated from Lutheran schools were more spiritually and religiously engaged during and after college than those who attended other institutions. While 53 percent of Lutheran college graduates said that college helped them integrate faith into everyday life, only 15 percent of public university graduates felt the same way. A brochure distributed by the Lutheran Educational Conference of North America trumpeted these findings for parents.[83] Another Hardwick-Day study yielded similar results, finding that alumni of Catholic institutions were more likely to say that college facilitated their spiritual development.[84]

A final argument for church-related higher education has assumed an ecclesial cast. This argument draws on the frame of denominational identity. Reports by the Presbyterian Church (USA) and the Evangelical Lutheran Church in America have grounded the case for church-related colleges in the educational legacies of their respective traditions. While a Presbyterian task force highlighted the Reformed commitment to education (the word "Reformed" appears many times in their report), an ELCA committee noted that from "the time of the Reformation, the Lutheran church has been a teaching and learning church."[85] Articulating an ecclesial vision for Roman Catholic higher education, former Notre Dame president Theodore Hesburgh famously argued that the "university is where the church does its thinking." As a setting for theological reflection, the church-related college tempers the strains of anti-intellectualism found in some denominations. Acknowledging the relative lack of an academic tradition among Baptists, Baylor University's David Jeffrey spoke of the need for "an intellectual community that is vibrant, that is able to be of service to the church in the wider world, and evangelicals need that more desperately than most folks."[86]

Found in numerous talks, essays, and books, newly articulated arguments on behalf of Christian higher education have provided the rhetorical justification for a more robust religious identity in church-related higher education. Such works have been published by both religious and secular publishers, reaching a significant audience. According to a survey of participants in Lilly Endowment programs, 55 percent of respondents had read at least one of sixteen books on religion in American higher education, including *The Soul of the American University* (read by 20 percent of participants), *From the Heart of the American Church* (13 percent), *Exiles from Eden* (13 percent), and *Models for Christian Higher Education* (10 percent).[87] Each book resolutely affirmed the value of church-related higher education. Many were published by Eerdmans and Oxford University Press. Most had ties to Lilly-funded projects.[88]

Resolve in Religious Identity and Mission

As scholars set pen to paper in defense of Christian higher education, a number of church-related colleges crafted strategic plans that gave more attention to religion. In 1995, Pepperdine University's Seaver College recognized "sources of truth deeper than those of secular culture," including "Christian beliefs regarding the origin, nature, and destiny of humanity."[89] In 2006, the University of Dayton made a commitment to "strengthen and promote the University's distinctive Catholic and Marianist identity."[90] The most visible of these new documents, Baylor University's 2012 vision statement, expressed the ambitious goal of entering the "top tier of American universities while reaffirming and deepening its distinctive Christian mission." By simultaneously hiring more faculty who connect Christianity and learning *and* putting more emphasis on research, Baylor hoped to become a Protestant Notre Dame. According to Lutheran theologian Robert Benne, Baylor 2012 represented nothing less than an attempt to "reverse the trend" of secularization.[91]

The religious revitalization of church-related colleges has also been marked by new mission statements. A 1999 study of twelve Catholic colleges found each had recently revised its mission statement, with religious identity becoming clearer in each instance.[92] So too with the Lutherans. In 1987 St. Olaf College adopted a mission statement with greater emphasis on its faith tradition than in previous versions, declaring that the college "provides an education committed to the liberal arts, rooted in the Christian Gospel, and incorporating a global perspective."[93] Likewise, Roanoke College adopted a new statement of purpose which states that the college "honors its Christian heritage and its partnership with the Lutheran church by nurturing a dialogue between faith and reason."[94] Among the Methodists, Kentucky Wesleyan College endorsed a statement noting its partnership with the denomination.[95] Finally, a number of Presbyterian institutions have produced new statements on church-relatedness, including Waynesburg College. According to a Waynesburg trustee, "It was a preamble for our decision making going forward."[96]

In American Catholic higher education, religious orders play a similar role in shaping institutional culture. For this reason, Catholic colleges founded by congregations of religious women make an interesting case study. While new mission statements can be an exercise in empty rhetoric, renewed attention to religious heritage has helped strengthen the identity of some colleges founded by women's religious orders. A large group, they have experienced monumental challenges since the 1960s. Suffering all the stresses faced by other small liberal arts institutions, Catholic women's colleges have faced two additional challenges: the loss of their traditional constituency to coeducation and a rapid decline in the number of nuns. The colleges that survived made many market-driven changes, developing new constituencies, including women of color, single parents, older students, and men, and augmenting the curriculum with evening and weekend programs, paraprofessional training, and distance education. In some instances, the drastic shift from a traditional single-sex, four-year, residential program provoked friction among trustees, administrators, faculty, alumni, and students. Amid tension, the religious heritage of the college proved a stabilizing factor, as advocates of change invoked the mission of the sponsoring congregation, recalling how sisters founded colleges to serve first-generation college women who often came from disadvantaged backgrounds. As one administrator put it, "We have not changed. Only the needy women whom we serve have changed."[97]

The connection between the religious mission of the founding congregation and institutional vitality is clear in the case of Trinity Washington University. Founded in 1897 by the Sisters of Notre Dame de Namur (SNDdeN) to serve the first generation of female Catholic collegians, the college flourished and was considered by some to be the Catholic version of the "Seven Sisters" colleges. Prominent graduates from this period include House of Representatives Speaker Nancy Pelosi (class of 1962) and Health and Human Services Secretary Kathleen Sebelius (class of 1970).[98] But Trinity faltered in the 1970s as the daughters of alumnae enrolled in other institutions, the popularity of single-sex education waned, the number of sisters dropped, and the neighborhood around the campus declined. No longer viable as a four-year, residential, liberal arts college catering to middle- and upper-class Catholics, the college experimented with alternative programs and new degrees to attract new students, including working-class women of color from the Washington area. The changes provoked outcry among alumnae and some faculty who felt that Trinity was straying from, even betraying, its roots and mission. As one concerned graduate put it, "We don't mind all this diversity. But are they Catholic?"[99]

Trinity experienced renewed vitality by revisiting its mission to "educate women and to serve the poor." According to President Patricia A. McGuire, "The extension of Trinity's mission to new populations of urban women who had previously been left out of higher education became a true social justice ministry."[100] The effects are clear. Trinity's student body is now 75 percent African American and 20 percent Latino. Three-fourths are eligible for Pell Grants. In 2003, Trinity opened a $20 million, state-of-the-art athletic center for women to serve its students and the neighborhood, and finished a $12 million centennial capital campaign.[101]

Trinity is not alone in its multicultural mission. Several Catholic institutions are full members of the Hispanic Association of Colleges and Universities, maintaining a Latino enrollment of at least 25 percent. Most were created by religious women. Located in San Antonio, Texas, Our Lady of the Lake University has the one of the largest Latino student bodies of any Catholic college or university in the United States. Founded by the Sisters of Divine Providence, the university engages San Antonio's Mexican American culture.[102] By embracing ethnic diversity, colleges founded by women religious are reinventing themselves.

Heightening Religion's Profile

In the recent past, some have ridiculed the prose of institutional mission documents. Often vague and bureaucratic, they are an easy target. Absent structural changes, institutional rhetoric cannot guarantee church-relatedness. Yet such rhetoric can serve as a catalyst for deeper reforms. At many institutions, increased seriousness about church-relatedness has led to structural changes. Such shifts have helped create an organizational infrastructure for the promotion of mission and identity. One strategy has involved establishing senior-level administrative positions or committees vested with responsibility for the religious heritage of the school. For example, in 2000 the president of Villanova University created an office that would, among other things, "provide initiatives that address our Augustinian intellectual and moral heritage." About the same time, Roanoke College hired a director of church relations who has forged stronger connections with the local church.[103]

Creating an administrative post devoted to religion near the top of the organizational flowchart marks a departure from the general twentieth-century pattern, wherein the campus minister or chaplain operated near the margins and rarely took center stage except during convocations, commencements, or times of tragedy. Today, the chaplain finds senior-level company as colleges bring religion back toward the center of operations. This strategy is particularly common in Catholic institutions where priests and sisters—the individuals who embodied the religious identity of the college—are becoming scarce. A large-scale study published in 2000 found that 20 percent of Catholic colleges had appointed individuals to oversee the mission of their institutions, with most at the vice-presidential level. Today 159 out of 220 Catholic institutions have established an office of mission and identity. Recognizing this trend, the Association of Catholic Colleges and Universities published *A Mission Officer Handbook* in 2014.[104] Along the same lines, some Protestant colleges have elevated the job of campus chaplain to administrative status, creating a Dean of the Chapel position.[105]

Growing interest in religious identity is evident in efforts to "hire for mission."[106] From this perspective, church-related colleges need a critical mass of people committed to the institution's religious tradition. Yet this is a difficult goal to reach. Campus politics further complicate the issue, as some fear that adding religious criteria might limit the pool of desirable candidates or undermine the institution's academic reputation.[107] The importance and the complexity of hiring for mission is evident in the large numbers of speeches, panels, and essays on the topic.

Despite concerns and even resistance, church-related colleges are increasingly seeking candidates who "fit" religiously. Some institutions give preference to members of the sponsoring religious body, while others are hiring nonmembers who are willing and able to contribute to the school's religious mission. To find such candidates, colleges are taking concrete steps. Job listings are becoming more explicit about the religious affiliation and mission of the school, and candidates are vetted more thoroughly about their views about and commitment to advancing the college's religious identity and mission. St. Olaf College's recruitment statement exemplifies this purposeful approach to hiring; individuals exploring positions at the college are informed that the Lutheran college prefers "persons who have a strong appreciation of the church and the church college. While we do not insist on particular answers to religious questions or to the question of the relation of religion to learning, we do seek persons who will take such questions seriously."[108] At Loyola Marymount University, a 2008 document presented guidelines on "recruiting and hiring faculty for mission," including questions for job candidates. Such institutions are not alone. As early as 1999, a study of twelve Catholic colleges and universities found that candidates were interviewed about their commitment to the religious mission.[109] The University of Notre Dame gives preference to Catholic candidates and creates new positions in order to attract high-profile Catholic academics. In 2005, Notre Dame began compiling a database of Catholic scholars. Within a year, the university had accumulated over 700 names. A decade later, it is expanding this database.[110]

To bolster the presence of mission-centered faculty and heighten the focus on religion, church-related colleges and universities have also created chairs and professorships for scholars whose work enhances the religious identity of the institution. At the College of the Holy Cross, for example, Catholic studies professorships were established in English, sociology, religious studies, and philosophy, with the goal of encouraging sustained engagement with Catholicism across the disciplines. In 2004, Georgetown University established the Ignacio Ellacuria, S.J., Chair in Catholic Social Thought. While Gustavus Adolphus College boasts the first ever endowed chair in Lutheran studies, Davidson College created the Craig Family Distinguished Professorship in Reformed Theology.

Church-related colleges and universities have established a remarkable number of centers devoted to religion. A 2000 study of church-related colleges found over 130 centers and institutes focused on religion, with most established within the past fifteen years.[111] They include the McFarland Center for Religion, Ethics and Culture (College of the Holy Cross), the Institute of Catholic Studies (John Carroll University), the Dovre Center for Faith and Learning (Concordia College–Moorhead), the Institute for Faith and Learning (Baylor University), the Lantz Center for Christian Vocations (University of Indianapolis), the

Center for Faith and Learning (Pepperdine University), the Benne Center for Religion and Society (Roanoke College), and the Ignatian Center for Jesuit Education (Santa Clara University). In a 2000 survey of participants in Lilly Endowment programs, 68 percent of respondents said they had participated in activities at a religion-oriented center at their college or university.[112] In recent years, the number of centers has continued to multiply. In 2015, there were over 1,000 centers and institutes at Catholic colleges and universities. Many explore topics related to mission and identity. Along the same lines, thirty-six church-related institutions have created programs in Catholic studies.[113]

While the goals of these initiatives vary, most are described as vehicles for advancing the religious identity and mission of the home institution. Some make explicit the connection with the sponsoring religious body. Established in 1997, Baylor's Institute for Faith and Learning is designed to help it become a "university of the first rank" while retaining its commitment to its Baptist and Christian heritage. Dating from 1999, Pepperdine's Center for Faith and Learning helps faculty integrate Christianity with scholarship and teaching. In its inaugural year, seventy-five faculty took part in seminars sponsored by the Center.[114] Named after Methodism's founder, Hamline University's Wesley Center for Spirituality, Service, and Social Justice connects "the pursuit of the common good with growth of the whole person."[115] These new centers, along with long-established Offices of Church Relations, have provided an infrastructure for religious revitalization.

New Programs for Fostering Mission and Identity

As initiatives multiply, faculty and staff have had numerous opportunities to talk about what it means to work in church-related higher education. Over the past thirty years denominational colleges, associations, and new organizations have rolled out a host of religiously focused seminars, workshops, lectures, retreats, and mentoring programs. These programs are designed to strengthen faculty and staff engagement with the religious mission and identity of the colleges. In some cases, this entails programming designed to build religious or denominational literacy. In other instances, programs aim to create sympathy for the project of Christian higher education and the integration of faith and learning.

Many programs focus on newly hired faculty and staff. In the 1990s, Seattle Pacific University inaugurated a seminar for new faculty to "reflect on the distinctive feature of Christian higher education, namely the combination (or integration) of faith and learning."[116] At Loyola in Chicago, junior faculty write reflection papers on a 2009 document on Jesuit education. Along the same line, St. Louis University created a three-part video and discussion series examining the history and character of Jesuit education; it is used with new faculty and staff in several Jesuit institutions. Since 1996 over 3,500 individuals have participated in the program. In a similar way, Augustana College in South Dakota has used Ernest Simmons' *Lutheran Higher Education: An Introduction for Faculty* as part of its faculty orientation program.[117] Likewise, Pepperdine's Center for Faith and Learning sponsors summer faculty seminars on the relationship between Christianity and scholarship.[118] Reflecting the popularity of mentoring programs at religious institutions, Caroline Simon and a team of seven other authors published *Mentoring for Mission: Nurturing New Faculty at Church-Related Colleges* (2003). The book itself was the fruit of the Lilly Fellows Program in the Humanities and Arts at Valparaiso University, which has supported faculty mentoring programs at fifty colleges and universities.[119]

Other programs are open to all faculty and staff. At St. John's University and the College of St. Benedict (coordinate institutions for men and women), Benedictine monks and sisters invite faculty into conversation about religious values and education. In recent years, the Benedictine Institute of St. John's has sponsored Benedictine Heritage Study Tours to sites in Italy and Germany.[120] At the Jesuit-run College of the Holy Cross, faculty participated in Catholic studies seminars for a half-dozen years, discussing faculty research-in-progress over dinner. More recently, Holy Cross has taken groups of faculty and staff on an Ignatian Pilgrimage to Spain and Italy, a program which revisits places important in the life of St. Ignatius of Loyola, the founder of the Jesuits. The perquisite of European travel has proved an effective incentive for heightening interest in the college's Jesuit tradition. Between 2004 and 2017, over a hundred individuals took part in the pilgrimage.[121]

Beginning in the early 1990s, *national* programs aimed at strengthening the religious character of church-related institutions developed. Conferences, workshops, and seminars proliferated, attracting thousands of individuals from hundreds of institutions. These initiatives have heightened consciousness of the issues and challenges attendant on institutional religious identity, even as they increased enthusiasm for Christian higher education. More than any other organizations, they have established national networks of like-minded people in church-related colleges.

Established in 1991, the Lilly Fellows Program at Valparaiso University seeks "to strengthen the quality and shape the character of church-related institutions of higher learning in the twenty-first century." With hopes of creating a hiring "pipeline" for church-related institutions, its founders established a two-year residential postdoctoral fellowship program to foster "intellectual and spiritual virtues in young scholars." Though only some fellows have taken jobs at religious schools, the Lilly Fellows Program quickly evolved into a flagship service organization for a network of Protestant and Catholic colleges and universities. Each year, hundreds of representatives from dozens of church-related institutions participate in national and regional conferences, workshops, and mentoring initiatives. About one hundred institutions belong to the program's Lilly Network of Church-Related Colleges and Universities.[122]

Catholic colleges have developed a handful of their own initiatives. Motivated in large measure by the declining number of priests and sisters, programs have provided faculty, staff, and trustees, both religious and lay, with opportunities for in-depth conversation about leading and working in Catholic colleges and universities. Founded in 1992, Collegium is a week-long program combining study, discussion, and worship for faculty and graduate students. It has nearly 2,000 alumni at 64 member institutions. Begun in 1995, the Institute for Student Affairs in Catholic Colleges (ISACC) led to the creation of the Association for Student Affairs at Catholic Colleges and Universities in 1999. In 2017 ASACCU had over 160 member institutions.[123] In 2001, Boston College launched the Institute for Administrators in Catholic Higher Education, an annual week-long program that gives senior-level administrators opportunities for substantive conversation about the nature and mission of a Catholic higher education. During its first ten years, over 200 administrators took part in the institute.[124] In 2003, the Association of Jesuit Colleges and Universities, in conjunction with the Association of Catholic Colleges and Universities, created a similar program for trustees.[125]

These national networks have disseminated new strategies for strengthening church-related higher education. For example, the Lilly Fellows Program and Collegium have sponsored discussions on hiring for mission, with that phrase entering the lexicon of church-related colleges and universities. Sociologists note the tendency of organizations in a particular sector to adopt similar procedures and goals, engaging in organizational mimicry. Such *institutional isomorphism* has led church-related colleges to employ the same methods, including faculty mentoring programs, centers and institutes, endowed chairs, Catholic studies programs, and cabinet-level positions in mission and identity.[126] Networks like Collegium have accelerated institutional isomorphism through books on best practices in Catholic higher education.[127] According to Lilly Fellows Program founder Mark Schwehn, network schools "are constantly learning from the central theological insights of the others," with "the Evangelical schools learning from the depth of Catholic tradition" and the Catholic and mainline institutions "taking cues from the Evangelical schools."[128]

Extending the network of church-related institutions, Lilly Endowment launched a major new initiative in 1999. Called the Programs for the Theological Exploration of Vocation (PTEV), it was the largest undertaking in the history of the Endowment's Religion Division, awarding over $225 million in the space of a decade. Hoping to raise up strong candidates for the ministry, as well as thoughtful lay leaders, it made initial grants of up to $2 million to institutions that developed programs to encourage students to view their work and aspirations "in terms of a calling or vocation, which endows their lives and work with lasting meaning." The vocation initiative spurred many church-related colleges to examine the religious character of their schools. During three funding cycles, over 400 institutions submitted proposals; 88 were funded and 83 received follow-up grants. The grants spawned an array of new courses, internships, campus ministry programs, faculty seminars, retreats, centers, and collaborative efforts with theological schools, congregations, and denominations. The new funds allowed many colleges and universities to hire an additional chaplain or campus minister, positions that many schools have retained after the grant period ended.[129]

Many Lilly vocation programs have drawn on the theological and cultural resources of their sponsoring traditions. While Messiah College has emphasized Anabaptist, Pietist, and Wesleyan themes, Gustavus Adolphus College connects the Lutheran concept of vocation with approaches from other faiths.[130] In many institutions, the PTEV initiative has also had an impact on curriculum. Through courses such as "Discernment and Christian Decision Making" (College of St. Benedict / St. John's University), "Finding Your Calling" (Santa Clara University), "Lives of Commitment" (Simpson College), and "Finding the Good Life" (Austin College), students have explored the moral and religious dimensions of work.[131] The initiative has also led to the publication of several books, including *Claiming Our Callings: Toward a New Understanding of Vocation in the Liberal Arts*.[132]

At many of the 88 schools, the PTEV award from Lilly was the largest grant in the history of the institution. Because $2 million is hard to miss at a small or medium-sized college, the grants have increased the visibility of religion (and vocation) on campus. The goal of PTEV was to influence the institutional culture of grantees. As Lilly Endowment vice president Craig Dykstra told the final gathering of PTEV grantees in 2007, "You have drawn on, renewed and reshaped the deep cultures of your institutions." In some denominational traditions, the impact of this and other Lilly programs has been quite noticeable. "Among Lutherans," noted a Valparaiso professor, "there are many new collaborative efforts and initiatives that are creatively changing the 'ecology' of the church to invite more reflection on vocation and to deepen our shared discourse about it." A similar story could be told for church-related higher education as a whole, as the word "vocation" has reentered the campus lexicon. While the *Presbyterian Outlook* reported a "quiet trend among Presbyterian-related colleges and universities," the United Methodist *Interpreter* noted that Methodist colleges are helping students think about their future careers.[133]

Two studies have examined the impact of Lilly Endowment's initiatives on church-related colleges and universities. Focusing on faculty and staff in five Lilly-funded programs, a 2000 survey found that 71 percent of participants were more aware of the "relationship between religion and work."[134] A more recent survey of participants in PTEV revealed a similar pattern. While 80 percent of faculty said the programs would influence their campuses "long after the grant money is gone," 62 percent reported a positive impact on their departments. As these findings indicate, the Lilly vocation initiatives made an impression on faculty. They also reached many students, who were, after all, the main focus of the programs.[135] Current efforts have focused on expanding the conversation to more institutions. Toward that end, Lilly sponsored the Network for Vocation in Undergraduate Education (NetVUE). Formed in 2009, it has 224 institutional members. Through its partnership with the Council for Independent Colleges, it has access to over 700 private colleges, universities, and organizations.[136]

Denominations and denominational college associations have also mounted efforts to foster interest in the religious mission of church-related institutions. Publishing a brochure series on strengthening Catholic identity (topics include boards of trustees and chief academic officers), the Association of Catholic Colleges and Universities has cohosted many gatherings on Catholic higher education. In 1999, St. Joseph's University welcomed 300 educators to a meeting on "The Future of Jesuit Higher Education." In the year 2000, 30 faculty, administrators, and church leaders gathered at Centre College for a consultation on the Reformed tradition, resulting in *Called to Teach: The Vocation of the Presbyterian Educator.*[137] Other Protestant denominations have organized gatherings on denominational higher education. Beginning in 1999, the Evangelical Lutheran Church in America sponsored the Lutheran Academy of Scholars in Higher Education. For over a decade, some 80 faculty from 23 ELCA colleges participated in this program.[138] Similar efforts have been underway in the world of Baptist higher education. In 2005, a conference on the future of Baptist church-related colleges and universities drew over 300 faculty, administrators, and denominational officials to the campus of Baylor University, producing the volume *The Future of Baptist Higher Education.* Likewise, the Young Scholars in the Baptist Academy program has met annually since 2004, bringing over 70 faculty together for focused conversations about faith and intellectual life held at Oxford University's Regent's Park College and at North American Baptist institutions.[139]

While not affiliated with a particular denomination, the largely evangelical Council for Christian Colleges and Universities has also become a major force in the revitalization of church-related higher education, sponsoring faculty development workshops, conferences for administrators, study-away programs, and other networking opportunities. Founded in 1976 with only 38 institutions, it has gradually increased its reach. Today over 150 North American colleges and universities belong to the CCCU, including Southern Baptist, Nazarene, Presbyterian Church (USA), Wesleyan, American Baptist, Assemblies of God, and Christian Reformed Church institutions.[140]

Distinct from Catholic and mainline institutions, evangelical colleges have faced their own challenges. Imposing religious tests on faculty and staff, most have adopted a "homogeneous model" of campus religious life. Discussing the pros and cons of such a model, a recent study noted that "[h]omogeneous institutions may be prone to navel-gazing." At the same time, theological homogeneity may lead to a more vigorous discussion of shared commitments. Less vulnerable to secularization, evangelical colleges are preoccupied with the more pressing issue of academic respectability. No book has done more to frame the conversation than Mark Noll's *The Scandal of the Evangelical Mind* (1994). Arguing that the "scandal of the evangelical mind is that there is not much of an evangelical mind," Noll offered a blunt diagnosis of the shortcomings of evangelical intellectual life.[141] Though much has changed since 1994, evangelicalism still struggles with the legacy of anti-intellectualism. While recognizing a "renaissance of Christian scholarship," a recent survey found that faculty at evangelical colleges publish significantly less than their counterparts at other institutions. Asked to identify the most difficult aspects of being a Christian college professor, a significant minority cited the problem of weak academics, complaining of "parochialism, close-mindedness, and lack of curiosity displayed by many students."[142]

Despite these difficulties, evangelical colleges are among the most visible advocates of Christian higher education in America. Of the fourteen institutions profiled in Richard Hughes and William Adrian's *Models for Christian Higher Education*, nine belonged to the CCCU. Likewise, some of the most prominent evangelical scholars in America have spent part of their careers at CCCU institutions, including Edith Blumhofer, Joel Carpenter, James Davison Hunter, Mark Noll, Alvin Plantinga, and Nicholas Wolterstorff. Together with their colleagues, these scholars have created a cottage industry of books on the integration of faith and learning. In cooperation with HarperCollins, the CCCU published eight books in its Through the Eyes of Faith series, including *History through the Eyes of Faith*, *Biology through the Eyes of Faith*, and *Psychology through the Eyes of Faith*. Faculty at CCCU institutions have also produced such general faith and learning titles as *Christianity in the Academy* and *Scholarship and Christian Faith*.[143]

Besides these generically evangelical publications, a host of books have addressed the question of denominational identity. Lutheran colleges now have *Lutheran Higher Education: An Introduction for Faculty*, while *Teaching to Transform: Perspectives on Mennonite Higher Education* has informed the discussion of religious identity at Anabaptist institutions.[144] Catholic institutions have used, among others, *Enhancing Religious Identity: Best Practices from Catholic Campuses* and *Revisioning Mission: The Future of Catholic Higher Education*. Bearing witness to a diverse tradition, *Founded by Friends: The Quaker Heritage of Fifteen American Colleges and Universities* shows that religious identity assumes many forms.[145]

These programs and books have helped faculty and staff understand the distinctive theological traditions that Protestant denominations and Catholic religious orders bring to the table of American higher education. For many Lutherans a doxological sensibility, historically articulated by Johann Sebastian Bach and expressed today by Lutheran college choirs, serves as a visible reminder of the Lutheran tradition. Likewise, Martin Luther's emphasis on paradox and tension has helped Valparaiso and St. Olaf reflect on what it means to be a Lutheran college. In a similar way, the Mennonite contributors to the volume *Teaching to Transform* highlight the pacifist orientation of the Anabaptist tradition. Perhaps the most visible effort to articulate the meaning of denominational identity can be found in Richard Hughes and William Adrian's *Models for Christian Higher Education*. Exploring seven traditions (Catholic, Lutheran, Reformed, Mennonite, evangelical/interdenominational, Wesleyan/Holiness, and Baptist/Restorationist), the contributors highlighted the ways in which denominational traditions contribute to campus culture. In *The Vocation of the Christian Scholar*, Hughes explores similar terrain, discussing the ways that the Anabaptist, Catholic, Lutheran, and Reformed traditions shape scholarly inquiry. As in the previous volume, the message is clear: denominations matter.[146]

Denominational Response

Discussions about the religious identity of church-related colleges assume the existence of church communities with beliefs and traditions to shape, as well as commitment and resources to support, institutions of higher learning. Quite simply, church-related higher education needs college-related churches. As early as 1968, Christopher Jencks and David Riesman noted the connection: recognizably Protestant colleges depended "on the survival within the larger society of Protestant enclaves whose members believe passionately in a way of life radically different from that of the majority, and who are both willing and able to pay for a brand of higher education that embodies their vision."[147] This theme has been picked up more recently by other commentators, including Robert Benne, who notes that a church-related college "needs a living religious tradition to supply students, faculty, administrators, board members, and donors for the college."[148]

Recent historical literature on religion and higher education traces religion's decline during the nineteenth and twentieth centuries, focusing on the rise of the modern, nonsectarian university and the expansion of secular knowledge. Far less attention has been paid to the churches.[149] The literature is imbalanced, for the churches have also contributed to the erosion of religious identity. Overall, church interest in colleges waned. Local communities stopped sending their young people to their denominational colleges as a matter of routine. And when denominational budgets got tight, support for the colleges dried up.

In recent decades, a number of denominations have started paying more attention to their colleges. They are increasingly viewed as denominational assets. More immediately they are viewed as vehicles for maintaining and developing denominational leadership. Increasing the number of Mennonite youth at Mennonite colleges "represents an important investment in the future of the denomination," noted a 1997 report for the Mennonite Board of Education.[150] In a more recent strategic plan, the Methodist General Board of Higher Education and Ministry (GBHEM) committed to increasing the number of Methodist students at Methodist colleges by 10 percent.[151]

In a series of denominational statements, church leaders have affirmed their support for church-related colleges. Recognizing its commitment to the formation of children and young people, the Evangelical Lutheran Church in America approved a statement on education at its 2007 Churchwide Assembly. The process leading up to the statement included a series of more than forty hearings across the United States at Lutheran churches, synod offices, campus ministries, and colleges. Prepared by a task force cochaired by former Concordia College President Paul Dovre, the statement urged the ELCA's colleges to "maintain a living connection with the Christian faith," sponsor distinctively Lutheran worship, and nurture ties with the denomination.[152] After a similar process of institutional self-examination, the 2003 Presbyterian General Assembly approved the report *Reclaiming the Vision: A Mission Strategy to Strengthen the Partnership between the Presbyterian Church (USA) and Its Related Schools, Colleges, and Universities*. The PCUSA report urged Presbyterian schools and colleges to "place more emphasis on biblical literacy, theological foundations, spiritual development, and the Reformed tradition."

In 2014, the Presbyterian Mission Agency drafted new guidelines on what constitutes a Presbyterian-related institution.[153]

Marketing church-related colleges, denominations are doing more to promote their distinctive brands. In the late nineties, the Lutheran Educational Conference of North America launched an initiative to reclaim Lutheran students. The marketing campaign included a website touting the benefits of Lutheran higher education and a *Here I Study* brochure. In 2010, the ELCA released a video on Lutheran colleges. At sites such as www.whygolutheran.org and lutherancolleges.org, students can investigate the benefits of a Lutheran higher education.[154] In 2012, the National Association of Schools and Colleges of the United Methodist Church sponsored a video contest. In a similar vein, the *Presbyterian Outlook* asked college seniors to reflect on the topic "How my education at a PC(USA)-related college has shaped my faith and prepared me for significant service and leadership."[155]

Several Protestant church-related institutions have signed covenants of understanding with their local synods. Waynesburg College's covenant with the Presbyterian Church (USA)'s Synod of the Trinity affirms both a "historic relationship as well as our contemporary commitments." While Waynesburg pledges to hire faculty who reflect the Christian tradition, nurture the religious lives of students, and advertise its Presbyterian identity, the Synod promises to promote the school to potential students, offer financial support, and send representatives to visit the campus at least once a year.[156] Hoping to institutionalize a covenantal relationship between denomination and colleges, the United Methodist Church approved "An Education Covenant of Partnership" at its 2000 General Conference. The agreement was signed by the president of the Council of Bishops, the head of the General Board of Higher Education and Ministry, and the president of the association of Methodist schools, colleges and universities.[157] Today its words can be found on the websites of several Methodist institutions. Citing the agreement, Birmingham-Southern College notes the presence of "a Christian chapel in the heart of campus, a United Methodist chaplain, a United Methodist campus ministry, and strong ties to the Church—whose North Alabama Conference headquarters is located on the campus." Such connections give tangible form to church-relatedness.[158]

Limits of Religious Revitalization

Over the past three decades, many initiatives have worked to strengthen Christian higher education. Together, national networks of religious colleges, interested foundations, conferences and seminars, centers and institutes, revised mission statements, denominational discussions, and new literature have encouraged colleges to reconsider the importance of religious identity. Since the early 1990s, attention to church-relatedness has significantly increased. Thirty years ago there was less discussion of the religious aspects of denominational higher education. Today, discussions of religious sponsorship are routine.

Despite heightened attention to mission and identity, the outlook for some colleges remains uncertain. In particular, three issues challenge the project of church-related higher education: uneven participation in revitalization efforts, denominational tensions, and faculty ambivalence about religion's role on campus.

Not surprisingly, efforts to revitalize religious colleges have not resonated in every quarter. Not all church-related schools have taken steps to strengthen their religious identities. Although such initiatives have reached hundreds of schools, some have participated more fully than others. Institutional participation rates are suggestive. During the 1990s, for example, only a quarter of religiously affiliated colleges and universities participated in Lilly Endowment's $15.6 million religion and higher education initiative.[159] Likewise, just 88 schools were funded through Lilly's $225 million Programs for the Theological Exploration of Vocation (PTEV). Though 224 schools currently belong to the Network for Vocation in Undergraduate Education (NetVUE is an outgrowth of PTEV), several hundred church-related institutions do not.[160] Participation in denominationally oriented programs and organizations has also been uneven. Only 64 of America's 220 Catholic colleges are members of Collegium, the summer colloquy for faculty, while just 160 schools belong to the Association for Student Affairs at Catholic Colleges and Universities.[161]

Recent challenges facing several American denominations have also hampered efforts to strengthen the religious identity of church-related schools. In denominations experiencing significant declines in membership, the pipelines connecting church and college have felt the strain. In recent years, mainline Protestant denominations have faced tighter budgets, reflecting decades of shrinking membership rosters. Budget constraints have prompted cuts in the number of staff devoted to higher education, undermining the ability of church bodies to maintain strong connections with and support for their colleges. In some cases, entire divisions have fallen under the budget axe. Reflecting these constraints, the Presbyterian Church (USA) did away with its Higher Education Program Area, an office that oversaw Presbyterian colleges, replacing it with a new Office of Collegiate Ministries. In 2009, that unit merged with the Office of Youth Ministries, only to be revived as a stand-alone collegiate ministries office in 2010. In 2012, the denomination approved a new campus strategy, resulting in the creation of UKirk ("kirk" is Scottish for "church"), a clearinghouse for collegiate and higher education ministry.[162] Facing severe budget pressures in 2005, the Evangelical Lutheran Church in America folded its Division for Higher Education and Schools into a new program unit on Vocation and Education. Following the recession, the ELCA suffered further budget cuts, eliminating Vocation and Education as part of another denominational restructuring. While the denomination employs an executive director for its Network of ELCA Colleges and Universities, finances remain tight.[163]

By far the most serious erosion in denominational relations has occurred in the Southern Baptist Convention, America's largest Protestant denomination. Like the Presbyterians and the Lutherans, the SBC cut its national staff responsible for colleges and schools, eliminating the Southern Baptist Education Commission in 1996.[164] Far more damaging to the church-college relationship, internal conflicts have plagued Southern Baptist life in recent years. During the past three decades, polarization between conservative and moderate Baptists has shaken the foundations of Southern Baptist higher education. Since the conservative takeover of the Convention in 1979, the denomination has lost over a dozen institutions. In most cases, colleges and universities have declared their independence in order to protect themselves from conservative state Baptist conventions. At Georgetown College, President William H. Crouch Jr. resisted calls by the Kentucky Baptist Convention to hire a biblical studies professor who took a literal approach to the Scriptures. Officials at other institutions have also expressed concerns that state conventions will name conservatives to their boards of trustees. Such was the case at Shorter University in Georgia, where the board demanded that faculty declare their opposition to homosexuality and alcohol consumption. While many professors complied, one-third of the faculty resigned. Elsewhere, conflicts over Calvinism and evolution have plagued Baptist colleges. According to former Mercer University president Kirby Godsey, "Baptist politics are wreaking havoc on Baptist higher education," adding that "Baptist higher education has never been more fragile."[165]

For several years, the turmoil was pronounced at the world's largest Baptist university. At a secret board meeting in 1990, Baylor University president Herbert Reynolds presided over a charter change that freed the university from the control of the Baptist General Convention of Texas. Dubbed the "thief of the Brazos" by conservatives, Reynolds was concerned about the threat they posed to Baylor's academic reputation. The new charter reduced the proportion of regents appointed by the Baptist General Convention to one-fourth of the board. Unlike other Baptist institutions that have diminished denominational control, Baylor maintained an official tie to the state Baptist convention through an agreement ratified in 1991. Despite its newfound autonomy, Baylor's problems were not over. Under Reynolds' successor, Robert Sloan, the university embarked on an ambitious plan to become a tier-one institution (a "Baptist Notre Dame"), while simultaneously heightening its focus on the integration of faith and learning. Called Baylor 2012, the plan proved controversial with older professors who resented the heightened emphasis on faculty religious beliefs and on research productivity. The tensions came to a head in the summer of 2003 at a Baylor "family dialogue" that "often resembled a family feud." Faculty and alumni squared off at public dialogues, football games, and in the pages of the *Houston Chronicle* and the *Dallas Morning News*. In the end, Sloan was unable to heal the rift in Baylor's culture that he had helped to create, resigning from the university's presidency in 2005. Since then Baylor has attempted to preserve the core goals of 2012. Under the leadership of Kenneth Starr, the institution adopted *Pro Futuris*, affirming "its identity as a research university with a strong Christian commitment." Using its endowment to attract scholars like Rodney Stark, Alan Jacobs, Philip Jenkins, and Thomas Kidd, Baylor has gradually raised its academic profile. A national opinion poll, an institute on faith and learning, and a flurry of conferences have further enhanced the university's scholarly reputation. After several years of relative calm, the university was shaken by a sexual assault scandal in Baylor's athletic program, resulting in Starr's resignation. While this scandal has caused great anguish for the Baylor community, the conflicts over the university's academic vision have lessened in recent years. The 2017 appointment of Linda Livingstone as Baylor's first female president has raised hopes for a new beginning at evangelicalism's leading research institution.[166]

Far from unique, Baylor is not the only church-related institution where faculty and alumni have argued about mission and identity. A 2000 survey of participants involved in projects funded through Lilly Endowment's religion and higher education found that 34 percent of faculty at conservative Protestant schools, 73 percent of those at mainline Protestant schools, and 53 percent of those at Catholic schools agreed with the statement "Faculty at my college/university are divided over the religious identity of the institution." Such divisions have persisted on many campuses. Some have worried that greater emphasis on religion signals a return to confessional statements, oaths, and a loss of academic freedom. Still others are concerned that the reassertion of religious identity will undercut efforts in the areas of gender equality and cultural diversity. For example, nearly half of the female participants in national programs funded under Lilly's religion and higher education initiative felt that "discussions of religious identity at my college/university fail to address the concerns of women faculty and staff." Similar reservations were expressed in a 2007 report from the University of Notre Dame's women's faculty collective. According to the report's authors, the university's policy of "affirmative action for Catholics" has provided the department in question with "an even greater excuse to hire more white Catholic males."[167]

Tensions flared within the Catholic higher education community for the better part of the 1990s and beyond as the U.S. bishops developed norms for Catholic colleges and universities based on the vision for Catholic higher education found in Pope John Paul II's apostolic letter *Ex Corde Ecclesiae*. A committee of bishops and Catholic college presidents spent innumerable hours working out implementation norms to submit to Rome for approval. As they met, administration and faculty spoke out, often heatedly, expressing concerns about the potential consequences of greater church oversight. Episcopal involvement in academic affairs, they claimed, could seriously undermine Catholic higher education by raising questions within and without about academic freedom. Colleges might not be able to attract high-quality scholars who might be concerned about potential infringement on their scholarly agendas and research. Current faculty expressed concerns that they would be subject to new religiously informed expectations for their teaching and research.

The guidelines approved by Rome in 2001 call for Catholic theologians at Catholic institutions to obtain, from their local bishop, a *mandatum*, a recognition that their teaching and research are orthodox. The directive for Catholic theologians to seek a *mandatum* has produced soul-searching among individual theologians and within theology departments. Though many faculty in religion and theology departments have supported efforts to strengthen the religious identity of their respective institutions, some have resisted the *mandatum*. One predicted the "impending death of Catholic higher education," while another well-known theologian decried oversight by nonacademics. An impasse was avoided, with bishops making a *mandatum* a private matter between theologians and their local bishops. Concerns died down, although some conservatives were displeased with the privatization of the *mandatum*.[168] With this as backdrop, Pope Benedict XVI delivered a well-received address to Catholic educators during his 2008 visit to the United States, in which he held up the value of academic freedom as well as the obligation of scholars to respect Catholic teachings. Catholic colleges and universities are even more hopeful about Pope Francis, a reformer whom some compare to Pope John XXIII.[169]

The tensions surrounding the development of norms for *Ex Corde Ecclesiae* defined something of a limit to the revitalization of religion on campus. The religious revitalization of church-related higher education depends on faculty convinced of its value and willing to contribute to it. In their book on Catholic higher education, Melanie Morey and John Pidiret argue that efforts to introduce faculty to Catholic intellectual traditions face a "political challenge," adding that "faculty will claim (perhaps quite rightly) that they were not hired to teach Catholic material in their courses."[170] That said, thousands of faculty and staff have participated in programs designed to strengthen church-relatedness. The challenge has been making such programs voluntary and persuasive.

Faculty hiring remains the most contentious issue in church-related colleges. In the modern academy, the power to hire and tenure has been located primarily at the departmental level. In many institutions, senior-level administrative involvement in the hiring process has been considered intrusive and even a threat to academic freedom. Top-down directives to "hire for mission" have not always been welcomed. One study, published in 2002, found that the majority of faculty members at Boston College and Notre Dame, though not Baylor and Brigham Young, were against giving preferential treatment to candidates from the sponsoring tradition.[171] Only a minority of church-related institutions mandate the hiring of faculty from the sponsoring denomination or religious tradition. A few utilize institutional carrots, such as new faculty lines, to encourage departments to hire mission-friendly candidates. Most religious colleges and universities rely on the power of persuasion. Talk about landing the best candidate continues to dominate the hiring process, but "best" only occasionally takes into consideration candidates' willingness and ability to advance the religious mission of the college.

The State of Church-Related Higher Education

The issues facing church-related higher education are real. Uncertainty about institutional mission, expanding religious pluralism, budget cuts in the denominations, and ambivalence among the faculty—all pose challenges to the religious identities of denominational colleges and universities. Nonetheless, religious colleges and universities manifest more interest in church-relatedness than just three decades ago.

For much of the twentieth century, the religious identity of church-related institutions was taken for granted. During this era of relative complacency, the leadership of most institutions focused on raising academic standards and enhancing the reputation of their particular institutions. Today, a broadened agenda includes the foundational question of what it means to be a church-related institution. Though many religious colleges and universities still vie for coveted spots on various "top 100" lists, many have also made religious identity a priority. The sheer volume of discourse about church-related higher education has made it difficult to ignore the topic. Hundreds of conferences, seminars, programs, books, and articles are both the drivers and the product of recent concerns.

Of course, not all religiously affiliated institutions have demonstrated interest in strengthening their religious character. Robert Andringa, the former president of the Council for Christian Colleges and Universities, estimates that only around 250 Protestant liberal arts colleges are "intentional about integrating their faith with their mission." Together with 220 Roman Catholic schools, these colleges and universities make up a majority of America's religiously affiliated institutions of higher learning. By contrast, about 150 colleges and universities "have pretty much neglected their faith tradition."[172] If this number is correct, fewer than 500 schools have experienced religious revitalization.

Yet not all movements to revitalize church-related higher education are cut from the same cloth. While some emphasize a homogeneous faculty, others retain a critical mass from the sponsoring tradition. Still others work to transmit the college's mission to and through a diverse faculty. As other advocates of religious higher education have noted, "many colleges and universities that seem secular on the surface still possess convictional traits that, properly understood, are supportive of rather than antithetical to religious faith." Macalester College is one of those schools. In 2001, the college received a $1.8 million Lilly vocation grant. According to the *Minneapolis Star Tribune*, 120 out of 500 freshmen applied to two Lilly-funded programs (there were 30 spaces). With support from the grant, Jeanne Halgren Kilde completed *Nature and Revelation: A History of Macalester College*. Rejecting claims that "everything has changed or nothing has changed," it chronicles the college's complicated relationship with American Protestantism.[173]

Such stories could be multiplied many times over, illustrating different models of church-relatedness. In the late 1980s, Haverford College established a committee to ensure that "Quakerism remains strong and vibrant at Haverford." Home to a thriving peace studies concentration, it has recently created a new Friend in Residence program. At Grinnell College, a $1.4 million Lilly grant increased the visibility of the college's chaplaincy. Housed at Vassar College, a Teagle Foundation project on secularity and the liberal arts inspired new questions: "How open are these secular institutions to religious expression and experience in the classroom that falls outside the consensus? Should we teach in ways that encourage breaks with that consensus? What if any religious expression should be encouraged or discouraged?" Such questions suggest a bigger tent.[174]

The tent is also expanding at many denominational schools, reflecting a new commitment to religious diversity. Unlike Vassar, St. Olaf College remains a "college of the church," identifying with the Evangelical Lutheran Church in America. At the same time, it welcomes faculty from diverse religious backgrounds. While affirming her college's Lutheran identity, St. Olaf religion professor L. DeAne Lagerquist wonders whether secularization is always harmful. Noting Luther's distinction between the church and the temporal realm (one definition of the secular), Lagerquist advocates hospitality to those outside the household of faith. In the recent past, an observant Hindu served as chair of Lagerquist's department. Cultivating close ties with the World Council of Churches, Professor Anantanand Rambachan has participated in many interreligious gatherings. Though St. Olaf is committed to interfaith dialogue, it retains a critical mass of Lutheran faculty and students. While 8 percent of entering students identify with non-Christian traditions, Lutherans make up one-fourth of the freshman class. In 2015, the college's religion department employed eleven graduates of Lutheran colleges, including seven St. Olaf alumni. In the words of St. Olaf's president, "We come at religious dialog from a distinct perspective, the Lutheran one. As a result we are going to have ongoing tension between our commitment to the particular faith tradition in which the College was founded and to which we belong and our desire, and need, to welcome and invite dialog with the differing faith traditions of our students and staff and faculty."[175] Along the same lines, Georgetown University's Office of Mission and Ministry endorses the concept of "centered pluralism." While emphasizing Georgetown's Jesuit and Catholic identity, it recognizes the "the wide variety of religious and humanist perspectives of our colleagues."[176]

Surveys indicate that faculty at church-related colleges support the religious aims of their institutions. A UCLA study of the American professoriate found that over 60 percent of professors at religiously affiliated institutions agree that colleges and universities should facilitate students' spiritual development, compared to just 18 percent of public university professors.[177] Along the same lines, a survey administered to faculty at Baylor, Notre Dame, Boston College, and Brigham Young found that most "appear broadly supportive of their university's religious commitment."[178] Such sentiments set church-related schools apart. This should not be surprising given the higher levels of religiosity enjoyed by professors at church-related colleges and universities. While over 65 percent of faculty at religious institutions see integrating spirituality into their own lives as essential or very important, only 41 percent of public university faculty feel the same way.[179]

In the final analysis, efforts to strengthen the religious identity of denominational colleges and universities have enjoyed modest success. On the whole, church-related colleges are academically and religiously stronger than they were a few decades ago. Until recently, they have also enjoyed steady growth. Between 1990 and 2004, enrollment in four-year independent religious colleges and universities rose by 27.5 percent, compared to just 12.8 percent for public four-year institutions. Enrollment in the member institutions of the evangelical Council of Christian Colleges and Universities rose from 135,000 to 230,000, a 71 percent increase that far outstripped the growth rates of nonevangelical institutions. During the 1990s, enrollment increased by 19 percent at Catholic colleges and universities. Since then they have enjoyed further growth, rising from 636,000 students in 2000 to 730,000 in 2015.[180]

Granted, all is not well at America's religious colleges. Though many are thriving, others are in poor health. With lagging SAT scores, small endowments, and shaky finances, some evangelical colleges face steep challenges. The same could be said for plenty of smaller Catholic and mainline Protestant colleges. As discussed in chapter 6, some institutions have struggled since the recent recession.[181]

Despite these challenges, many religious institutions have made headway in renewing their identities. While institutional mission has been strengthened, there has not been a return to a golden age of religion on campus. Articulating old traditions in fresh ways, religious colleges have embraced new forms of diversity. Though church-related colleges have experienced revitalization, this is not true on all campuses. And on those campuses which have seen revitalization, it has not reached all quarters. That being said, the turnaround has been notable. The institutional drift evident throughout the church-related sector has lost momentum; the distance that developed between colleges and their sponsoring religious traditions has lessened. Over the past three decades, church-related colleges have actively strengthened their religious identities. In many institutions, secularization no longer seems a likely trajectory.[182]

This chapter has documented the renewed attention to religious identity at church-related colleges and universities. Like religious schools, undergraduate religious life has also experienced revitalization. The following chapter shifts the discussion to campus religious organizations at nonsectarian institutions, including public universities. Focusing on the voluntary sector of student religion as well as student affairs, it chronicles the rise of a pluralistic campus religious marketplace at all levels of American higher education.

4

THE REVITALIZATION OF STUDENT RELIGIOUS LIFE

Higher education has long been perceived as a threat to youthful piety.[1] Writing in the *Atlantic,* a 1928 Harvard graduate described the "wholesale apostasy of the younger generation," recounting "what college did to my religion." Recent works have sounded a similar theme. In popular books such as *How to Stay Christian in College* (2004), evangelicals have portrayed higher education as corrosive to religious faith. In a more academic vein, historians have chronicled the marginalization of campus religious groups, telling a tale of declension.[2]

There is a good deal of truth in this secularization narrative. After the abolition of compulsory chapel, the Gothic edifices on many campuses sat empty except for Sunday morning services that did not begin to fill up the pews. After disbanding in the late 1960s, the once-massive ecumenical student movement was a shadow of its former self. Reflecting a wider disenchantment with American institutions, many undergraduates distanced themselves from campus religious groups. So did student affairs professionals, abandoning an earlier focus on the spiritual development of the whole person. Student religiosity ebbed. Once overflowing with young Methodists and Presbyterians, Wesley and Westminster Foundations faced tighter budgets and lower participation. Campus Hillels encountered similar challenges. As recently as the 1980s, researchers found a correlation between college attendance and religious disaffiliation.[3]

This is no longer the case. Although the ecumenical student movement no longer dominates undergraduate religious life, newer movements have emerged, sharing the college union with their mainline counterparts. Nearly invisible at the end of World War II, evangelical parachurch groups are among the largest religious organizations on campus. Reflecting a renaissance in campus Judaism, Hillel and Chabad have enjoyed a period of impressive growth, constructing new Jewish centers on dozens of campuses. Likewise, the number of Muslim Students' Associations in North America has risen from 10 in 1963 to 500 today, while the presence of Buddhist, Hindu, and Sikh groups continues to expand. Responding to the new diversity, a burgeoning interfaith movement is engaging the campus. Last but not least, student affairs professionals have rediscovered spirituality. Instead of secularizing, the campus has become a "spiritual marketplace." Reflecting this religious vitality, surveys of college graduates now show a positive correlation between higher education and religious affiliation.[4]

Contrary to the secularization thesis, the history of campus religion is not a declension narrative. A mixture of cyclical and linear motifs, it resembles the larger fluctuations in American religion. As older denominations lose their followers, they are replaced by religious newcomers. In a similar way, flagging campus ministries are replaced by newer religious groups. Sometimes they recycle elements from the past. Sometimes they introduce new forms of cultural diversity. As in the wider story of American religion, innovation leads to religious revitalization.[5]

Over the past two hundred years, colleges and universities have experienced periodic waves of religious mobilization and decline, reflecting wider shifts in American culture and the dynamics of campus life.[6] The founding of student religious clubs in the aftermath of the Great Awakenings, the birth of the YMCA and the Student Volunteer Movement, the rise of denominational campus ministries, the growth of evangelical parachurch groups, and the arrival of non-Western religions have punctuated these cycles.[7] As one set of organizations has declined in popularity, another has emerged to take its place. Such innovation exemplifies the protean quality of American religion, a flexibility that extends to campus religion.[8]

This chapter provides an overview of the student religious landscape in America. Highlighting the recurring motifs in campus religion, it notes the parallels between today's period of religious revitalization and earlier episodes in American higher education. After recounting the history of campus religious organizations, it identifies six signs of religious vitality: (1) the expansion of campus evangelicalism; (2) the retooling of Catholic campus organizations; (3) the reinvention of campus Judaism; (4) the rise of religious pluralism, new immigrants, and alternative religions; (5) the beginnings of a renewal in mainline Protestant campus ministries; and (6) the embrace of spirituality by student affairs professionals. This chapter concludes by discussing the impact of college on student religiosity and the place of campus ministry organizations in the wider university.

This chapter relies on the official statistics of campus ministries. No systematic study of their accuracy has ever been conducted. Like the self-reported statistics of some congregations, they may be inflated. A more comprehensive study would include ethnographic observations from campus religious groups. Absent such qualitative research, organizational statistics are the best available data.

The Roots of Voluntary Student Religious Life

Conceived in the medieval church, the university was once inseparable from its ecclesiastical parent. On the post-Reformation colonial American campus, Protestant Christianity maintained a similarly high profile. With most colleges founded by religious bodies for the purpose of training clergy, religion and campus life were deeply intertwined. Required chapel, grace at meals, Bible study, and worship services were part and parcel of the educational experience for undergraduates.[9]

The piety of college students waxed and waned throughout the eighteenth and early nineteenth centuries. As early as the 1740s, leaders of the First Great Awakening complained about the secularization of the colleges. In the post-revolutionary period, the influence of the French Enlightenment seemed to dampen student religious life. Law supplanted ministry as the most popular profession for college graduates. Critics complained that infidelity ran rampant on campus. There was some "occasion to rejoice," noted one critic of Harvard, that "the Lord Jesus has, even there, a remnant who worship him in spirit and in truth." At Williams College, few students professed to be religious; those who did were subject to scorn.[10]

Whether real or imagined, campus apostasy helped fuel religious renewal. Buoyed by the enthusiasm of the revivals, New Light proponents founded several new institutions, including Princeton, where student piety was assumed. The religious regimen included morning and evening prayer each day, Sunday worship and catechetical instruction on Sunday afternoon. New student organizations proliferated. Between 1810 and 1858 over ninety new religious societies formed on seventy campuses.[11]

Even at the early public universities, religion flourished. As late as 1840 clergy comprised two-thirds of state college presidents (and 80 percent of denominational college presidents). On some state campuses, participation in chapel services was mandatory; other campuses held voluntary services.

According to a survey of twenty-four institutions, 71 percent of state university faculty belonged to Christian churches. In many college towns, faculty taught Sunday school and led Bible classes.[12]

In the second half of the nineteenth century, the driving force behind religion at most state and private universities was the collegiate Y.[13] The first university YMCA chapter was established at the University of Virginia in 1858, part of a national revival. A chapter soon followed at the University of Michigan. At Virginia 85 percent of the student body belonged to the Y, making it by far the largest student club on campus. The Y spread rapidly to other campuses, becoming a staging ground for religious organizing. Between 1868 and 1877 the number of student associations quadrupled, a trend some attribute to the voluntaristic character of the religious marketplace. This rapid growth occurred among both men and women. At coeducational institutions, female students participated in male missionary societies, as well as single-gender organizations. Founded in 1873, the first collegiate YWCA was created at Illinois State Normal University. Sixteen years later, there were 142 chapters.[14]

During the first decades of its existence, the YMCA promoted a revivalistic brand of Protestantism emphasizing individual conversion and evangelistic zeal. Anticipating the evangelical parachurch groups of the late twentieth century, it pioneered the use of student-run small groups, keeping statistics on the number of conversions. While in later years YMCA secretaries were appointed to some campus chapters, many groups were student led.[15] By the 1910s the YMCA had developed a more systematic approach. At one university the Y used a map to keep track of the participants in student Bible studies.[16]

Such focused organizational strategies produced tremendous growth, with the Y becoming the leading student organization in American higher education. Between 1880 and 1887 the number of students participating in the collegiate YMCA rose from 5,000 to 12,000, while the number of associations grew from 96 to 258.[17] On most campuses, the Y possessed a virtual religious monopoly.[18] In 1905, it claimed one-fifth of college men and half of college women. In 1921, one out of seven college students in America participated in the collegiate Y, a ratio never exceeded by a campus ministry. In that year Christian Associations were present on over 700 campuses with some 90,000 members, performing many functions now the purview of university student development offices. Student handbooks, new student orientation, dormitories, and extracurricular social activities could all be found at the Y. Housed in newly constructed buildings, it became an integral part of the campus landscape.[19]

Fueled by the expansion of the Y, the student missionary movement gathered momentum in the late nineteenth century. Following an 1886 summer Bible conference at Dwight L. Moody's Mount Hermon School, Princeton graduates Robert Wilder and John Forman embarked on a missionary recruitment journey, traveling to 162 campuses and signing up 2,106 students for the cause of student missionary service. This cross-country, intercollegiate organizing effort resulted in the formation of the Student Volunteer Movement for Foreign Missions in 1888. Like the domestic YMCA/YWCA, this movement engaged both men and women. In the SVM's first two decades, 30 percent of missionary volunteers were women. Its central message was summed up by the text on its famous pledge cards: "We are willing and desirous, God permitting, to become foreign missionaries."[20] During the next thirty years, 175,000 signed the pledge. Over 20,000 became foreign missionaries.[21]

Like the collegiate Y, the Student Volunteer Movement's efficient organizing style was partially responsible for its success. Part of a new professional-managerial class, the SVM's leaders combined muscular Christianity with business acumen. Forging transnational connections, they hoped to bring their message to the wider world.[22] Reflecting these global aspirations, the YMCA, YWCA, and SVM were also key players in the formation of the World's Student Christian Federation. Encouraged by the American Y, indigenous movements arose in Europe and Asia. In an 1895 gathering held at a Swedish castle, these movements united to form the World's Student Christian Federation. Ten years later, over 100,000 faculty and students belonged to eleven national Christian movements.[23]

Well into the twentieth century, the student Christian movement remained connected to the Protestant establishment. An elder statesman in both the YMCA and the SVM, John R. Mott advised President Woodrow Wilson and philanthropist John D. Rockefeller Jr. In 1946, Mott won the Nobel Peace Prize, reflecting the global reach of his activities. Beyond American shores, many of the founders of the World Council of Churches had SVM connections. At its height, the student Christian movement shaped a generation of ecumenical leaders, including Union Theological Seminary president Henry Van Dusen, theologian Georgia Harkness, archbishop of Canterbury William Temple, and Swedish bishop Nathan Söderblom.[24]

During the late nineteenth century, voluntary student groups became the dominant form of undergraduate religious life in America and in many quarters of the globe. In the campus religious marketplace, student-run groups spread from school to school. A lay-oriented expression of popular evangelicalism, such groups did not rely on formally trained clergy. Instead, they functioned as parachurch groups, literally *beside* or *alongside of* the church.[25]

For several decades, the collegiate Y preserved a place for religion in higher education. Its strength was a capacity to mobilize on multiple campuses. Its weakness was its separation from the educational mission of American colleges and universities.[26] Without a functional connection to the university's core activities, student religious groups risked becoming irrelevant. Reflecting this vulnerability, the growth of student affairs hurt the YMCA. As the universities assumed more and more of the Y's functions, it experienced a sharp decline in membership.[27] Between 1920 and 1940 the number of YMCA college chapters fell from 731 to 480, while student participation decreased from 94,000 to 51,350.[28] The situation in the Student Volunteer Movement was even worse. While 2,783 students became Volunteers in 1920, this number dropped to 25 in 1938.[29]

In an era of fraternities, football, and bathtub gin, students no longer gravitated to the YMCA. In *This Side of Paradise* (1920), F. Scott Fitzgerald painted a boozy portrait of Princeton University. At Fitzgerald's alma mater, revelers vandalized a statue of the "Christian Student," pulling it to the ground. The removal of the statue, formerly located outside Princeton's intercollegiate Y, signaled a national shift in campus culture. This shift was compounded by internal changes in the YMCA's theology and mission. During the 1920s, it adopted a more radical approach, embracing the goals of social justice and world peace. Soon the Y's national meetings welcomed socialists Norman Thomas and Harry Ward. While remaining largely segregated, the organization promoted interracial dialogue. So did the YWCA, taking a more progressive stance than its male counterpart.[30] Such activism was not always popular with white Protestant undergraduates. While some students gravitated to other campus ministries, many disengaged from organized religion. Though the YMCA remained highly involved with progressive causes, most notably the nascent civil rights movement, it was no longer a major force in campus ministry.[31]

The Era of Denominational Campus Ministry

The history of campus ministry has alternated between periods dominated by voluntary student organizations and those dominated by denominations. The YMCA's nondenominational approach prevailed between 1880 and 1925. Overlapping the Y's era, denominational efforts came to the fore in the early twentieth century and became dominant after World War II. Providing a template for a wide variety of campus religious groups, the denominational model found expression in Protestant, Catholic, and Jewish settings. While differing in beliefs and practices, campus ministries came to look a lot alike, reflecting the influence of a common organizational environment.[32]

The ascendancy of the newly created, nonsectarian university—which displaced the denominational college at the head of the academic order—created the impetus for the denominational campus ministry. As long as their youth attended church colleges, denominational leaders could be confident that the faith was being passed down to the younger generation. As more and more collegians opted for state universities, church officials began to worry about their religious lives. And while the Y was active on most state university campuses, it did little to connect students to the denominations.[33]

The first Protestant denominational centers were established at the University of Michigan in 1887. Replication and experimentation followed. The Presbyterians, Congregationalists, Baptists, Methodists, Lutherans, and Episcopalians established student pastorates. The Disciples of Christ were most active and started the Bible Chair movement. With the first Chair established at the University of Michigan in 1893, Bible Chairs soon spread to universities across the Midwest and South. Offering formal instruction in biblical studies, they provided a religious supplement to the course offerings at state universities.[34]

A major expansion in denominational campus ministries occurred between 1910 and 1920. By 1923, there were 128 Protestant university pastors employed by mainline denominations, a number that rose to 209 by 1933. Together with 174 Bible Chairs and 1,145 local Protestant churches, they represented a growing mainline presence on or near university campuses.[35]

During this era, Catholics and Jews also entered the campus ministry arena, establishing Newman Clubs and Hillels on public and private university campuses. Catholics created their own clubs in part, to maintain a distinctive religious identity, in part as a response to anti-Catholicism. The first Catholic Club, the "Melvin Club," was formed at the University of Wisconsin in 1883. Over the next fifteen years this model spread to Cornell, Minnesota, Brown, Berkeley, and other campuses.[36]

The papal encyclical *Acerbo Nimis* (1905) provided ecclesiastical sanction for the nascent Catholic student movement. Urging the establishment of "schools of religion" at secular institutions, it encouraged the founding of a dozen new Catholic student clubs.[37] Created in 1915, the Federation of College Catholic Clubs united groups across the country under one organization. By 1926 there were 134 Catholic clubs in the United States, most identifying with the Newman Movement, named after the British Catholic apologist John Henry Newman.[38] While opposition from Catholic colleges and several bishops threatened this emerging movement, the number of Newman Clubs continued to grow, reaching 262 colleges and universities by 1938.[39]

American Jews faced significant prejudice and bigotry on Protestant-dominated campuses, especially in the early twentieth century. At many Ivy League institutions, quotas were used to restrict the enrollment of Jews. Many of Harvard's Gentile students favored numerical limits on Jewish admissions. Along the same lines, the *Yale Daily News* asked the university administration to "institute immigration laws more prohibitive than those of the United States government." Such policies remained on the books until the postwar era.[40]

In this hostile environment, Jewish students sought out the company of fellow Jews. The first Jewish campus group in North America was established in 1898 as the ZBT fraternity (*Zion Bemishpat Tipadeh*).[41] By the end of the 1920s, around twenty multicampus Jewish fraternities had been established in the United States.[42] Providing a home for Jewish religious life, the Harvard Menorah Society was founded in 1906 and could be found on fifty campuses by 1930. The first B'nai B'rith Hillel Foundation was established on in 1923 at the University of Illinois. By 1938 over 10,000 students had become involved in Hillel, making it the leading campus Jewish organization. Like their Protestant and Catholic counterparts, Hillel Foundations provided opportunities for religious study and socializing with coreligionists. "Except for this distinctive Jewish cultural note," observed Protestant Clarence Shedd, the activities of a Hillel looked "very much like that of a Wesley, Westminster, Roger Williams or Pilgrim Foundation." While open to all branches of Judaism, it embraced the model of the denominational foundation.[43] At a time when Protestants dominated campus religious life, Hillel was a place that Jewish students could call their own.

During an era that some described as a "religious depression," denominational foundations became the primary locus of campus ministry in America.[44] After World War II, the economic and religious depression was over. College-age men participated in the postwar religious revival. As millions of GI's crowded the campuses, participation in student ministries swelled to new heights. Surveys of collegians showed an increase in religiosity. Responding to these trends, Protestant denominations increased funding for campus ministers. Methodist appropriations for campus ministry rose from $97,574 in 1944 to $151,590 in 1947, while the number of campuses reached by Presbyterian university pastors increased from 53 in 1939 to 101 in 1948. In 1960, there were 144 Westminster and 181 Wesley Foundations in the United States.[45]

Like their mainline Protestant counterparts, Catholic ministries expanded considerably following World War II. In the 1950s, the number of Newman Clubs grew from 385 to 496, reaching an estimated 45,000 students by 1960. Reflecting a building boom in campus ministry, the number of free-standing Newman Centers increased from 79 in 1962 to 300 in 1967.[46] In the words of a Catholic chaplain, they were more than a "place and provision for Catholic ping-pong."[47]

In the triple melting pot of postwar America, Jewish student organizations were part of the wider expansion of denominational campus ministries. Gone was much of the stigma of the 1920s and 1930s. Hillel leader Maurice Pekarsky celebrated these advances in 1961, noting that "[h]undreds of thousands of Jewish students are at our universities. They are third-generation Americans and at home in America. There is no sense of underprivileged position. There is no quota system."[48] As Jewish enrollment surged, Hillel Foundations mobilized to meet the need. With seventy-seven foundations in 1963, Hillel was a growing presence on the American campus.[49] Jewish learning was also flourishing. In 1963 Hillel offered a total of 600 courses, while instruction in Judaic studies was available on thirty-eight campuses.[50]

Denominational foundations were not the only campus ministries booming in postwar America. Beginning in the 1920s and 1930s, American colleges and universities established university-sponsored chapels and religious life offices overseen by newly appointed deans, chaplains, and directors of religious life. In a 1941 survey of 263 colleges and universities, 68 percent reported holding regular chapel services, including 19 state universities.[51] In *The American College Chaplaincy* (1954), Seymour Smith reported that new chaplaincy positions were being created "at a startling rate," noting that "[p]robably no other religious development in higher education has had a longer incubation in its infancy or a more rapid growth in its adolescence." In 1902 just 14 institutions had hired college chaplains. By the 1940s, chaplains could be found at half of America's independent colleges and universities.[52] Surveying the situation in 1947, Methodist educator Merrimon Cuninggim wrote that American colleges had "recaptured much of their lost concern for the religious development of their students."[53] Believing that "our campuses are ready right now for a spiritual awakening," Ralston-Purina chairman William Danforth funded the construction of two dozen Danforth chapels. Though bankrolled by a private philanthropist, many were built on public university campuses. Each chapel included a print of Heinrich Hofmann's *Christ in the Garden*.[54]

Leading a postwar theological renaissance, Reinhold Niebuhr and Paul Tillich became heroes to many campus ministers. Likewise, scholars associated with the student Christian movement produced seminal works, including Peter Berger's *The Noise of Solemn Assemblies* (1961) and Harvey Cox's *The Secular City* (1965).[55] Along with a new religious intellectualism came a heightened focus on social action. Building on the legacy of the YMCA, campus ministers redefined evangelism to mean the structural reform of American society. While the 1955 quadrennial meeting of the Student Volunteer Movement focused on the theme of "Revolution and Reconciliation," subsequent gatherings featured civil rights leaders Martin Luther King Jr. and Fannie Lou Hamer. Recalling her own years as a Methodist student, women's historian Sara Evans writes that "the SCM [student Christian movement] trained a remarkable generation of leaders who moved directly into the civil rights movement, the student antiwar movement, and women's liberation."[56]

Reflecting this renewed activism, the ecumenical student movement reorganized after World War II. In 1945, Yale professor Clarence Shedd called for a "more inclusive Student Christian Movement in the United States," one that united denominational efforts with the smaller YMCA and SVM.[57] Shedd's dream became a reality in 1959, when the Interseminary Committee of the YMCA/YWCA, the SVM, and the United Student Christian Council combined to form the National Student Christian Federation (NSCF). The NSCF was joined in 1960 by the United Campus Christian Fellowship (a newly formed association of student movements from four mainline denominations). The NSCF signaled a new ecumenism among both denominational campus ministries and student religious movements. In 1963, the NSCF published Russian Orthodox theologian Alexander Schmemann's *For the Life of the World*. A classic of American Orthodoxy, it was the study guide for the Federation's 19th Ecumenical Student Conference.[58]

This ecumenism received further expression with the formation of the United Ministries in Higher Education and the National Campus Ministry Association in 1964, and the University Christian Movement in 1966. The embodiment of liberal Protestantism's ecumenical vision, the UCM also included Catholic and Eastern Orthodox students. Under the auspices of the UMHE, campus ministers from a dozen mainline Protestant denominations joined forces to staff ecumenical campus ministries, dismantling their own denominational foundations.[59]

In the mid-1960s Protestant campus ministries had over 1,300 campus clergy on the ground, most in the mainline denominations. In 1963, about 3,000 full-time campus ministry staff workers (including mainline and conservative Protestant campus ministers) operated on American campuses. Launched the same year, the Danforth Study of Campus Ministries illuminated the importance of the campus ministry profession. In another sign of vitality, up to 40,000 individuals subscribed to the Methodist journal *motive*, the unofficial journal of the student Christian movement. Known for radical commentary and artistic experimentation, it catered to the spiritual avant-garde. Its readers included a young Hillary Rodham. Too radical for its denominational sponsors, *motive* lost its funding after a provocative issue on women's liberation. The magazine's last two issues explored the topics of lesbian feminism and gay men's liberation.[60]

With little warning, the great age of the ecumenical student movement and Protestant denominational ministries came to an end in the late 1960s. With the universities in turmoil, students and campus ministers distanced themselves from formal religious organizations, aligning themselves with the campus social movements. Some became leaders in the civil rights movement and second-wave feminism.[61] This anti-institutional spirit culminated in the disappearance of the University Christian Movement in 1969. At a national meeting sponsored by the Danforth Foundation, a UCM task force called for the radical reconstruction of American society. Frustrated with its inability to effect social change, as well as the demands of its own black caucus, the UCM's general committee voted to disband before sharing a meal of bread and wine.[62]

Though mainline Protestant campus ministries survived the death of the UCM, they were greatly weakened by the growing distance between students and organized religion. In the wake of the counterculture, the percentage of students attending religious services dropped precipitously in the late 1960s. During the same period, many young people left the mainline denominations.[63] Compounding the decrease in student religiosity, mainline Protestant denominations drastically cut funding to campus ministries. Between 1970 and 1981, the national staff of the ecumenical United Ministries in Higher Education shrank from 31 to 14.5.[64]

In an era when conservative churches were growing, mainline Protestants faced shrinking membership rolls and tighter finances. With fewer people in the pews, denominational coffers had less money for campus ministry. They also had fewer students, reflecting a breakdown in the pipelines connecting congregations with campus ministries. In the 1970s, mainline campus ministries weathered new challenges.[65] Underfunded and unrecognized, denominational campus ministers were increasingly marginal.[66] Since then, mainline Protestant support for campus ministry has been less than generous. While some denominations increased their funding in the 1980s, this development was short lived. In 1995, the *Christian Century* reported budget cuts in mainline Protestant and Catholic campus ministries, adding that 10 percent of the programs said they could disappear.[67] Consistent with this prediction, over a dozen Episcopal campus ministries went out of business in the 1990s, leading one chaplain to lament the "abandonment of campus ministry."[68] In 2002, the *United Methodist Reporter* noted a "steep decline in church funding of campus ministry." Such trends have continued into the new millennium.[69] Once the dominant player in Christian campus ministry, mainline Protestant denominations have struggled to maintain their presence in student religious life.

Religious Vitality on a Pluralistic Campus

The marginalization of mainline Protestantism left a hole in the religious ecology of American higher education. Yet rather than secularizing the campus, the collapse of the ecumenical Protestant student movement ushered in a new era of religious innovation. Like the decline of the Protestant establishment in American society, the decline of mainline Protestant campus ministries made room for a host of religious newcomers.[70] Some were more conservative than the groups they replaced, recycling older forms of student religion. Others reflected growing religious diversity.

Present since the 1940s, evangelical parachurch groups enjoyed new growth. After a period of stagnation, Catholics and Jews developed creative ministries and new funding sources. Newcomers to the American campus, Muslims and Hindus established hundreds of student groups. While continuing to struggle, mainline Protestant campus ministries showed signs of renewal. Finally, student affairs professionals rediscovered spirituality, returning to the roots of their field. The rest of this chapter explores the vitality of student religious life, beginning with campus evangelicalism.

The Expansion of Campus Evangelicalism

More than any other major religious tradition, evangelicals have thrived on the American campus. Approximately 140,000 students are active in parachurch groups like InterVarsity Christian Fellowship, Campus Crusade for Christ (now known as Cru), the Fellowship of Christian Athletes, the Navigators, and Young Life. An additional 130,000 college students are involved in ministries sponsored by conservative Protestant denominations. These figures probably underestimate the presence of evangelicalism on American campuses because they ignore local groups unaffiliated with national organizations or denominations. At many institutions, the largest evangelical campus ministries have no national affiliation.[71] Some have attributed the vitality of conservative Protestantism to the decline of the mainline. Noting that "nature abhors spiritual vacuums," a veteran of the ecumenical student movement wrote that its dissolution was "partly responsible for the active presence of more evangelical and conservative Christian groups."[72]

It did not start out that way. In 1960, only 60 campus ministers worked for InterVarsity. Campus Crusade had just 109 staff members. Both were dwarfed by the 1,300 clergy employed in denominational and ecumenical campus ministries. Not surprisingly, the landmark studies of campus ministry published in the 1960s barely mentioned either group. Only Harvey Cox was prescient enough to note the rise of campus evangelicalism. In a forgotten passage of *The Secular City* (1965), Cox called InterVarsity "a remarkable organization," notable for its "lay-led, highly visible, and extremely mobile" approach to ministry. Criticizing mainline Protestants for erecting denominational foundations "*next to* the world of the university," he praised InterVarsity's decision to "live in the same world with everyone else."[73]

Rather than reinventing campus religion, evangelical parachurch groups took their cues from the voluntary student religious movements of the nineteenth and early twentieth centuries. Conservative in theology yet entrepreneurial in strategy, they carried on the tradition of the early YMCA/YWCA and the Student Volunteer Movement.

The model of the evangelical parachurch group arrived on college and university campuses through what might be called a campus ministry British invasion. In the 1930s, InterVarsity Christian Fellowship moved from England to Canada to the United States. Formally incorporated as a separate organization in Canada in 1929 and in the United States in 1941, the American branch of InterVarsity Christian Fellowship reintroduced forms of student religious organization common in the era of the YMCA and the Student Volunteer Movement.[74] First and foremost was the principle of student responsibility. Like the Y and the SVM, InterVarsity was a lay-led and student-run group. Though it employed a paid staff, InterVarsity looked for staffers who could coach and develop student leaders. Undergraduates took campus religion into their own hands, leading small-group Bible studies and daily prayer meetings, and engaging in one-on-one ministry with peers. Local chapters were also responsible for raising their own support, providing an entrepreneurial motivation for students and staff.[75]

Such entrepreneurial initiative helped InterVarsity to spread from campus to campus. Starting with 22 chapters in 1939–1940, it had established a presence on 277 campuses by the 1946–1947 academic year. In 1969, the year the mainline student movement voted to disband, InterVarsity served 7,822 students in 400 campus groups. By 1981 InterVarsity reached 32,126 students in 859 chapters. Like Campus Crusade, InterVarsity went through a slump in the 1980s, dipping to 23,273 students by 1989. Along with Crusade, it experienced renewed growth in the 1990s and early 2000s. In 2016–2017, InterVarsity ministered to 38,404 students and faculty in approximately 1,000 chapters.[76]

Besides its campus fellowships, InterVarsity has gained visibility by sponsoring large gatherings on foreign missions. Beginning with a 1946 conference in Toronto, InterVarsity revived the missionary conventions once central to the Student Volunteer Movement. Between 1948 and 2003 these events took place on the campus of the University of Illinois at Urbana-Champaign. In 1976, attendance at the Urbana Student Missions Conference reached 17,000, triple the attendance at the SVM's national gatherings. Recycling an old tactic, attendees were presented with a version of the SVM pledge card, renamed the World Evangelism Decision Card by InterVarsity. At the 1976 gathering, 8,500 students (50 percent of attendees) pledged to serve God as foreign missionaries or support overseas missions if they did not go themselves. In 2006, attendance reached 23,000 when Urbana moved to the Edward Jones Dome in St. Louis, Missouri. Since 1946 over 300,000 people have attended InterVarsity's student mission conference.[77]

In reviving the evangelical movement on campus, InterVarsity drew on a tradition of indigenous student organizing going back to John Wesley's Holy Club, the early collegiate missionary societies, and the YMCA. Though part of a long tradition, the leaders of American InterVarsity in the 1940s were unaware of their own lineage. "For various reasons," wrote IVCF pioneer Charles Troutman, "we thought we were pioneering a new thing. . . . It came as a complete surprise when we discovered the Holy Club of Oxford, the early history of the intercollegiate YMCA, and especially our own background in the CICCU [Cambridge Inter-Collegiate Christian Union]." Troutman and his colleagues "began ransacking every second-hand bookstore we could find" for works on the earlier student evangelical movements. They soon discovered remarkable similarities between IVCF and its predecessors.[78] The parallels were not accidental. As Troutman learned, the origins of InterVarsity can be traced back to the Cambridge Inter-Collegiate Christian Union of the 1920s, an evangelical group that grew out of the same international student movement that produced the YMCA and the Student Volunteer Movement.[79] When InterVarsity came to the United States, it was importing a style of student religious organizing with deep roots in Anglo-American evangelicalism.[80]

One crucial difference between InterVarsity and the YMCA has been the willingness of the former to draw theological boundaries between insiders and outsiders. Unlike the noncreedal Y, the American branch of InterVarsity composed a doctrinal statement of five nonnegotiable beliefs in the 1940s: the authority of the Bible, the deity of Jesus, the death and resurrection of Christ, the presence of the Spirit, and the second coming of Jesus.[81] This statement of faith was designed to prevent InterVarsity from following the path of the YMCA. Convinced the Y had sunk into a "liberal morass," InterVarsity's North American founders attempted to restore the faith. Along with entrepreneurial organizing, a return to core teachings paved the way for religious mobilization. Compared to the more ambiguous theology of the ecumenical student movement, InterVarsity advanced a well-defined belief system that differentiated the group from other campus movements. It was a recipe for growth.[82]

InterVarsity is not the only evangelical parachurch group to thrive on the American campus. Founded in the 1930s as a ministry to military personnel, the Navigators soon spread to American high schools and colleges. Active on 160 campuses, the Navigators reached an estimated 5,000 students by 2001. Besides the Navigators and InterVarsity, several other evangelical ministries are active on American college campuses, including Reliant Mission (formerly Great

Commission Ministries), Every Nation campus ministry, Student Mobilization, the Coalition for Christian Outreach (better known as CCO), Campus Ambassadors, and Young Life. In 2017 Young Life's college ministries attracted over 9,500 students per week.[83] Conservative denominations also maintain significant ministries to college and university students. Present on 312 campuses, the Assemblies of God ministers to 28,000 college students through its Chi Alpha program, up from 13,000 in 2003. Active on 140 campuses, Reformed University Fellowship represents the evangelical Presbyterian Church in America. Served by 170 campus ministries, 8,000 students worship in the centers run by the Lutheran Church–Missouri Synod. In the early 2000s (the last time such data were publicly reported), 87,000 students were actively involved in Baptist Collegiate Ministries, while 248,000 had some connection to BCM. As a Baptist official noted at the time, "Campus ministries outside the Bible Belt—such as in New England, California and the Northwest—are multiplying rapidly." Currently, Baptist Collegiate Ministries has over 800 campus ministers in its online database.[84]

The biggest evangelical ministry in America was founded in 1951 by California businessman Bill Bright. Like InterVarsity, Campus Crusade for Christ was a response to a perceived problem, in this case the "present pagan condition of our campuses." Lamenting the spiritual plight of American undergraduates, Bright called for a Christian response. Beginning with one chapter at UCLA, Campus Crusade expanded to forty chapters by 1960.[85]

Influenced by the *pragmatist* and *pietist* streams of American evangelicalism, Campus Crusade combined business methods with Christianity. Dubbed the Henry Ford of campus ministry by theologian J. I. Packer, Bright packaged the faith in a new way.[86] Adopting a businesslike orientation, Crusade emulated the collegiate YMCA. Echoing the Y, it kept careful track of the statistical bottom line, tallying the number of "decisions," "exposures," and "total students involved" each year.[87] It also adapted the famous watchword of the Student Volunteer Movement, "the evangelization of the world in this generation," changing it to the "fulfillment of the Great Commission." This goal led Campus Crusade to systematically evangelize the campus at home and abroad. The organization's four-stage process of *penetration, concentration, saturation,* and *continuation* is reminiscent of the Y's own methodical approach.[88]

In the past two decades, Campus Crusade's collegiate ministry has enjoyed steady growth, increasing from 20,755 students in 1995–1996 to 82,000 in 2015–2016. Meanwhile, the number of chapters rose from 200 in 1990 to 2,400 today.[89] This growth followed a period when the campus ministry lost staff and students. From the mid-1970s to the late 1980s, Campus Crusade turned its attention to noncampus projects, including Washington's Christian

Embassy and the internationally known Jesus film. This slump lasted until the early 1990s, when Campus Crusade began its recovery.[90]

Reflecting the impact of immigration on American religion, campus evangelicalism has become more diverse. Since the 1960s, the racial and ethnic composition of evangelical parachurch groups has shifted dramatically. The number of Asian Americans in InterVarsity surged from 992 in the late 1980s to 3,640 in the early 2000s, an increase of 267 percent. In 2000, Asian Americans comprised 80 percent of the participants in evangelical Christian groups at Berkeley and UCLA. Single-ethnicity ministries have provided a home for hundreds of first- and second-generation Americans. Among Asian Americans these include Korea Campus Crusade (now known as SOON Movement). Though such groups feature kimchi and Korean-style intercessory prayer, the main draw is the presence of coethnics.[91] Along the same lines, InterVarsity and Campus Crusade have stepped up their efforts to connect with African Americans and Latinos. While Campus Crusade's Impact Movement has attracted over 15,000 African Americans to its national conferences, InterVarsity's Black Campus Ministry reaches over 5,000 students. In 2016–2017, 41 percent of the students participating in InterVarsity were racial or ethnic minorities. The percentage of InterVarsity employees who are ethnic minorities has also increased. In 2015–2016, the organization employed 247 Asian American, 92 African American, and 70 Latino staff members.[92]

This focus on diversity has led evangelical parachurch groups to engage issues of social justice. This shift is especially evident in InterVarsity, which has emphasized global poverty, racial reconciliation, and environmental awareness at its triennial student missions conferences. Like its overall approach, InterVarsity's embrace of social justice is rooted in the history of its British predecessors.[93] It can also be traced to the YMCA of the 1910s. Just as the Y expanded its definition of evangelism to include "Christian sociology" and "social evangelism," IVCF has increasingly redefined evangelism in holistic terms. Since the 1990s, InterVarsity has created a number of social action–oriented programs, including the Pilgrimage for Reconciliation and Urban Programs. Along the same lines, Campus Crusade currently sponsors Cru Inner City, an initiative that seeks to "break down walls of social injustice, like racism, sexism, and classism" through holistic ministry.[94]

Despite such efforts, historically African American denominations have rarely felt a part of the evangelical subculture. Though some African American students participate in IVCF and Cru, others frequent groups that are rooted in the black church. While the African Methodist Episcopal Church maintains a campus ministry at Virginia Tech, Princeton sponsors a worship service focused on African American students. Similar opportunities are available at

Cornell, Tufts, Yale, and many other institutions. Present on over 200 campuses, student gospel choirs straddle the line between religion and the performing arts. Such groups foster ethnic and religious community. Aside from InterVarsity and Campus Crusade, most African American campus groups are organized at the local level. A search of the national websites of the African Methodist Episcopal Church, Church of God in Christ, National Baptist Convention, Inc., and the Progressive National Baptist Convention revealed little or no discussion of campus religious groups. To the extent that such denominations support campus ministries, they are usually sponsored by individual congregations. According to the National Study of Youth and Religion, 28 percent of college-educated black Protestants have participated in a campus religious group.[95]

Despite these limitations, evangelicals have pioneered the niche marketing of campus religion, establishing thriving ministries to fraternities and sororities. In 2016–2017, Greek InterVarsity reached 3,253 students. Holding its very first meeting at UCLA's Kappa Alpha Theta sorority back in 1951, Campus Crusade now sponsors a website for Greek students. Such initiatives parallel six decades of evangelical outreach in intercollegiate sports. Founded in 1954 by a mixture of mainline and evangelical Protestants, the Fellowship of Christian Athletes repackaged the muscular Christianity of the YMCA for the postwar generation. In 2013, FCA reached 450,000 high school and college students on over 9,323 campuses. Adopting a similar tactic, Campus Crusade started Athletes in Action in 1966, building a network on over 200 campuses. In both groups, the idea was to capitalize on the popularity of sports. At many universities, evangelicalism is now the de facto religion of intercollegiate athletics.[96]

While aimed at a very different audience, evangelical ministries to Ivy League students have a similar goal: "to influence the influencers." Since the 1980s, parachurch ministries have surged in the Ivy League. One-tenth of the student body participates in evangelical groups at Princeton University, where campus ministries converge on the former building of the intercollegiate YMCA. At Harvard the membership of Campus Crusade doubled between 2000 and 2006, paralleling similar increases at Brown and Yale. Founded in 2002, newcomer Christian Union has also targeted the Ivy League. Maintaining ministry centers at Brown, Cornell, and Princeton, it has a multimillion-dollar budget. Since 2005 the organization has hosted a gathering with students from all eight Ivy League institutions. In appeals to donors, Christian Union has combined references to Ivy League influence with dire warnings of secularization, noting that "these institutions are among the most secular, anti-God places in the U.S. and the world."[97]

Similar concerns motivated a recent project to preserve the faith of evangelical college students. Beginning in 2007, the Youth Transition Network worked to bridge the domains of high school and college. Its partners included InterVarsity, Campus Crusade, Reformed University Fellowship, Chi Alpha, and the Navigators. Its objective was to "address the dramatic loss of youth occurring from the church." Noting that 70 percent of youth ministry alumni lose the faith, Youth Transition appealed for funds. This goal motivated its donors and partners to create a database of campus ministries, as well as a series of videos and ministry curricula. Like other parachurch organizations, Youth Transition Network focused on a perceived problem: the threat of the secular campus.[98]

In actuality, the study touted by Youth Transition Network found no statistically significant difference between the religious dropout rates of college and non-college attenders. Other studies suggest that college campuses may be a better place for religious faith than the workplace. Like other emerging adults, many evangelical college students drop out of church. Yet they are less likely to do so than evangelicals who do not go to college. In a recent survey, the National Study of Youth and Religion found that 40 percent of conservative Protestants with some college have been involved in a college-based religious group. Far from destructive to evangelical faith, colleges and universities may actually strengthen it. According to a 2011 study, evangelicals who attend college have higher rates of church attendance and prayer than those who do not.[99]

Such studies have not found their way into the fundraising appeals of evangelical parachurch groups. In promotional materials, many ministries have portrayed higher education as a threat. Commenting on this tendency to accentuate the negative, sociologist Christian Smith charges that evangelicals have been "behaving badly with statistics," adding that "they are usually trying desperately to attract attention and raise people's concern in order to mobilize resources and action for some cause." As in the past, a perceived problem has proved motivational for campus religious movements.[100]

The Revitalization of Catholic Campus Ministries

Like evangelicals, Catholics have maintained a large presence in American higher education, with approximately 2,200 campus ministers on 4,000 campuses. They serve a potential audience of 5.5 million Catholic students. A national survey found that 22 percent of Catholic seniors at nonsectarian institutions frequently attended religious services, while 50 percent did so occasionally. Beyond Mass attendance, the National Study of Youth and Religion found that 15 percent of Catholics with some college have participated in a campus-based religious group.[101]

Now a widely accepted ministry, Catholic campus organizations were not always embraced by the church. Well into the twentieth century, the Catholic hierarchy regarded them with suspicion. Yet unlike mainline Protestants, Catholics emerged from the 1960s with their campus ministries more or less intact. In sharp contrast to the pessimistic outlook of ecumenical Protestant ministers, observers of Catholic campus ministry, commonly called Newman Centers, after John Henry Newman, were guardedly optimistic. Boasting 1,450 chaplains on 1,200 campuses in the early seventies, the Newman Movement was thriving.[102] No longer resented by Catholic colleges and an insular hierarchy, Catholic campus ministries were becoming a key component of the church's outreach to young people. In 1985, the U.S. Catholic Bishops issued a landmark pastoral letter, "Empowered by the Spirit: Campus Ministry Faces the Future."[103] According to one campus minister, the pastoral letter marked the end of the older philosophy of "protecting the fragile faith of the young from a supposedly hostile atmosphere."[104]

As Catholic campus ministries entered the 1990s, they faced new challenges. On the one hand, many Newman Centers reported healthy attendance and a surge in student interest.[105] On the other hand, budget cuts made it difficult for campus ministries to take advantage of this hunger for spirituality and meaning. In 1996, the *National Catholic Reporter* described "dramatic cutbacks . . . in a number of dioceses."[106] Many campuses saw their campus ministry positions eliminated. On other campuses, programs made do with part-time staff. Such staffing problems have been accentuated by a growing priest shortage. Within a generation, the number of ordinations dropped from nearly 1,000 in 1965 to less than 500 in 2002. Priests must be replaced with lay chaplains, who cost more money. Paying for them is increasingly difficult since church finances have grown precarious, especially in dioceses with large legal settlements related to clerical sex abuse. Reflecting these constraints, the number of full-time Catholic campus ministers declined from 2,000 to 1,700 between 1988 and 1998 (though this is still more than the 1,450 campus ministers at work in the late 1970s).[107]

If there is a silver lining to the budget cuts, it is that Catholic campus ministries have been forced to become more entrepreneurial. Some Catholic campus centers have engaged in serious development work, with 15 percent employing a development officer. Since the mid-1990s, the well-funded St. Lawrence Catholic Campus Center at Kansas University has received most of its budget from private donations. More recently, Yale University's Catholic campus ministry raised $75 million for a new Catholic student center. Such approaches have spread to other colleges and universities. Across the nation, the Petrus Development firm and the Catholic Campus Ministry Association are helping campus ministries professionalize their fundraising operations.[108]

The recent upsurge in development activities has allowed Catholic campus ministries to launch several large new initiatives. At Yale, the Thomas E. Golden

Jr. Catholic Center includes space for offices, as well as a lecture hall, music room, volunteer center, dining room, meditation chapel, and library. Comprising 29 percent of the student body, Catholics are now the largest religious group at Yale.[109] At the University of Kansas, the St. Lawrence Catholic Campus Center sponsors a great books symposium, courses on Catholic doctrine, an Institute for Faith and Culture, as well as a full schedule of Masses and service activities. Successful fundraising projects have also been completed at Duke and Ohio State. While Duke's Newman Center has tripled its staff, Ohio State's Catholics completed a $1.2 million capital campaign.[110]

At most schools, the mainstays of Catholic campus ministry programs are Sunday and weekday Masses, retreats, and volunteer projects serving the poor. Sixty-four percent of programs at private non-Catholic institutions and 73 percent of those at public universities offer lectures on church teachings, while about half of programs at both types of institutions offer the Rite of Christian Initiation for Adults, a program leading to baptism.[111] Social engagement also remains a priority. According to the National Study of Campus Ministries, 39 percent of Roman Catholic campus ministers see fostering a commitment to social justice as a top three goal.[112]

Studies of Catholic emerging adults show a drop-off in religiosity in the early twenties, yet college has no negative influence on piety. If anything, college-educated Catholics are more religious.[113] Campus ministries play a role in this outcome. Compared to other Catholics, campus ministry alumni are more likely to attend Mass regularly, donate money to the church, consider a religious vocation, and participate in other church activities. Of alumni who took part in campus ministries on non-Catholic campuses, 81 percent attended Mass at least a few times a month. Almost half of male campus ministry participants on non-Catholic campuses considered a religious vocation.[114]

Reflecting wider conflicts in the church, Catholic campus ministries have not been without conflict or controversy. Articulating a progressive vision of post–Vatican II Catholicism, they have attracted the criticism of conservative Catholics. Welcoming the gay Catholic group Dignity, the University of Minnesota's Newman Center soon ran afoul of the local archdiocese. After repeated clashes between archdiocese-appointed Paulist priests and a progressive staff of laypeople, the archdiocese closed the center in 1998. The campus ministry was subsequently relocated to a nearby parish. Similar conflicts have erupted on other campuses, including the University of Toronto, where conservative protesters complained about the appearance of theologian Gregory Baum.[115]

Emphasizing renewal, some groups have taken a page from the playbook of evangelical parachurch organizations. Established in 1998, the Fellowship of Catholic University Students (FOCUS) has embraced Pope John Paul II's call for a "new evangelization." Like the evangelical ministries it emulates, FOCUS has experienced a dramatic increase in campus participants, growing from 24 students in 1998 to 25,000 in 2016, when it maintained a presence at 125 institutions. Almost 13,000 students attended the ministry's SEEK2017 gathering. Practicing traditional devotions such as eucharistic adoration, FOCUS also emphasizes "a personal relationship with Christ." Funded by local dioceses, Newman Centers, and individual donations, it is a new player in Catholic campus ministry. Signaling its traditionalist leanings, its board of directors has included Archbishop Charles Chaput, a leading conservative.[116] Focusing on a more elite population, the conservative lay organization Opus Dei has been active at several Ivy League universities, purchasing a residence near the Princeton campus. Together with Princeton's Catholic chaplaincy, the organization has tried to foster a "Catholic renaissance."[117] Though they reach only a fraction of Catholic students, such groups show the potential for new organizations to reshape campus religious life.[118]

The Revival of Jewish Campus Ministry

Like their Catholic counterparts, Jewish campus organizations have experienced revitalization. Between 1963 and 2001, the number of full-fledged Hillel Foundations increased from 77 to 110. Through its foundations and other groups, Hillel is currently active on 550 North American campuses.[119] Joining Hillel on campus is a global network of 256 Chabad Houses. Founded by the Chabad-Lubavitch movement, most have been established since 2000. In 2011 alone, over 8,000 attended weekly Shabbat dinners sponsored by Chabad.[120]

Though Jewish groups are thriving, their growth has been uneven. Hillel lost ground in the late 1960s. While local groups attracted a core constituency, they represented a minority of Jewish students. Like mainline Protestant campus ministry, Hillel struggled in the 1970s and 1980s. Even though Jewish enrollment was at an all-time high, it could not support a presence on many campuses. The problem lay in large measure with B'nai B'rith, Hillel's parent organization, which experienced significant financial difficulties. With funding cut in half in the 1980s and facing additional cutbacks, Hillel disaffiliated with B'nai B'rith in the early 1990s.[121]

Facing these financial troubles, Hillel reinvented itself. President Richard Joel engineered the "remaking of Hillel." One of his key allies in this effort was philanthropist Edgar Bronfman, CEO of Seagram's and a leader in the World Jewish Congress. Enlisting Bronfman's help, Hillel attracted new funding from Jewish family foundations and Jewish federations. As in the world of Catholic campus ministry, one of the cornerstones of this transformation was better development. In 1998 Hillel's Campaign for a Jewish Renaissance raised over

$37 million. Highlighting the impact of assimilation on Jewish identity, it used the 1990 National Jewish Population Survey (which found that Jewish college students were an at-risk population) to secure greater support from the Council of Jewish Federations.[122]

More importantly, the campus organization reinvented its vision of Jewish life. During this period, Hillel described its mission as maximizing "the number of Jews doing Jewish with other Jews." It replaced the synagogue model with a religio-cultural community model and expanded the organization's staff to include laypersons.[123] This strategy resembled the student-centered approach of other campus religious organizations. Using undergraduate interns to mentor uninvolved Jewish peers, Hillel engaged over 12,000 students in 2010. Welcoming students from every branch of American Judaism, it has taken a big-tent approach to the tradition.[124]

Hillel has also enjoyed a construction boom. According to the *Chronicle of Higher Education*, many chapters have upgraded their facilities, replacing "rickety old houses" with "ultra-modern student unions complete with pool tables, rooms for meetings and studying, coffeehouses, and computer workstations." Between 1994 and 2005, Hillel built or renovated buildings on thirty-seven campuses. Since then, Jewish centers have risen at Alabama, Tulane, Virginia, and Emory. Among the newer facilities, Princeton's Center for Jewish Life offers kosher meals and discussions of topics ranging from social justice to Jewish art. A similar center was established at Yale in 1995. As the Yale alumni magazine noted at the time, "there's something of a Jewish revival on campus," with several hundred students attending Friday night Shabbat dinners.[125]

A decade later, *Reform Judaism* magazine heralded a "Jewish-style Greek revival," noting the popularity of Shabbat dinners cooked in kosher kitchens and college dances featuring Hava Nagila. Currently, there are over one hundred chartered chapters of the sorority Alpha Epsilon Phi. Its 80,000 living alumnae include Supreme Court justice Ruth Bader Ginsburg. Enjoying similar vitality, the Jewish-oriented fraternity Alpha Epsilon Pi boasts over 190 chapters. Though it declined during the 1960s, the fraternity reversed course in the 1970s and 1980s, strengthening its Jewish identity.[126]

More traditional Jewish groups are also expanding their reach. Rooted in the eighteenth-century traditions of Hasidic Judaism, Chabad-Lubavitch has been called the "fastest growing Jewish presence on campus."[127] Blending Jewish mysticism with savvy marketing, Chabad has developed a distinctive brand. Under the charismatic leadership of Rabbi Menachem Mendel Schneerson (1902–1994), the movement sponsored urban advertising campaigns aimed at secular Jews. The same approach has informed its campus outreach. Proclaiming

"Shabbat: Just Do It" (complete with the Nike swoosh), Chabad has repackaged Jewish tradition in the language of popular culture.[128]

The very first Chabad House was established in 1967 on the campus of UCLA. Led by a rabbi who "could talk to the hippies," it migrated quickly to UC Berkeley and UC San Diego. By the end of the 1980s Chabad had spread to 25 campuses.[129] Twenty years later there were 119 Chabad centers in North America. As in the case of Hillel, successful development has played an important role in Chabad's growth. Thanks to the support of philanthropist George Rohr, new houses have received modest start-up grants.[130]

Offering Shabbat meals, religious instruction, and special programs during the Jewish holidays, Chabad is known for its *haimish* feel, serving as a home away from home. Central to this domestic experience is the presence of a rabbi and rebbetzin (rabbi's spouse). Traditional Jewish foods are also used to attract students. In 2008 alone, Chabad served 261,240 slices of gefilte fish during campus dinners. By evoking an experience of family and tradition, such events sometimes facilitate a return to religious practice.[131]

Jewish life has changed a great deal over the past three decades. Writing in the 1999 *American Jewish Yearbook*, historian Jack Wertheimer described a "remarkable revival of Jewish campus programs" that was already underway.[132] By expanding their funding, facilities, and programs, organizations like Hillel and Chabad have gained access to their target constituencies. Two-thirds of America's Jewish college students attend schools with a Chabad chapter. Over 400,000 have access to Hillel.[133] A 2006 study found that 33 percent of Jewish students were involved in Hillel or Chabad, with an additional 12 percent holding leadership positions. Within some Jewish populations, the percentage is even higher. A survey of young adults raised in conservative synagogues found that 68 percent have participated in a Hillel / Jewish Student Union and 8 percent have participated in Chabad.[134] Although campus Jewish organizations face an increasingly nonobservant American Jewish population, they are enjoying a period of relative vitality.[135]

Religious Pluralism: New Immigrants and Alternative Religions

The vitality of Jewish and Catholic campus organizations highlights the pluralistic character of student religious life. No longer dominated by a Protestant establishment of denominational campus ministries, campus religion now includes the full breadth of American religious groups. The Protestant chapel at the center of campus has been joined by multimillion-dollar Catholic centers, evangelical parachurch groups, and newly constructed Chabad Houses. The American university has become a house of prayer for all peoples.

Joining the chorus of religious voices has been a new surge of non-Western religious groups, the result of post-1965 shifts in American immigration. In 2002, an estimated 75,000 Muslims were enrolled in American colleges and universities.[136] The number of Hindus, Buddhists, and Sikhs has also grown by leaps and bounds. As Pluralism Project founder Diana Eck noted in the mid-nineties, colleges "have become microcosms and laboratories of a new multicultural and multireligious America," adding that "it is not uncommon to have a Hindu and Jew, Muslim and Christian in a single rooming group."[137]

The Education as Transformation project, based at Wellesley College, represents one response to the new pluralism. For over a decade, it explored the "impact of religious diversity on education" by hosting conferences, offering consulting services, and sponsoring publications.[138] It is not surprising that Wellesley College hosted the project. Its liberal Protestant heritage and more recent demographics have created an environment conducive for religious diversity. At the outset of Education as Transformation, over twenty religions were represented in the student body. In 2004, the project published a "campus religious diversity kit" complete with instructions for constructing multifaith worship spaces. This guidebook also included suggestions for accommodating religious dietary requirements, holidays, and codes of behavior. Cosponsored by the National Association of Student Personnel Administrators (NASPA, the nation's primary professional association for student affairs personnel, it was disseminated to a large national audience. In the spring of 2008, Wellesley renovated its chapel to make room for new religious groups, creating a new Multifaith Center.[139]

In addition to Wellesley, Mount Holyoke, MIT, and Duke have taken steps to provide what the *Chronicle of Higher Education* calls "pluralism and prayer under one roof."[140] On the West Coast, the University of Southern California calls itself a "religious laboratory" in the heart of a cosmopolitan city. Though USC cut its ties to the Methodist church in 1928, it has reflected its ecumenical roots. Under the leadership of Rabbi Susan Laemmle, USC's Office of Religious Life established a student Interfaith Council. Hosting eighty campus religious organizations, it serves a region home to both Buddhist temples and evangelical megachurches. During her years as Dean of Religious Life, the university started groups for Buddhists, Hindus, and Muslims. "We're hoping to get a Zoroastrian group going soon," she explained to the alumni magazine back in 2004. After Laemmle's retirement, the university hired a Hindu chaplain to replace her, a first for an oldline Protestant institution.[141]

On many American campuses, the job of managing religious diversity falls on the shoulders of university chaplains and deans of religious life. Like Rabbi Laemmle and her replacement, Varun Soni, many have worked hard to foster interreligious harmony. Some belong to the Association for College and University Religious Affairs, established in 1959. Its principles include fostering "an understanding and respect for the multifaith reality of higher education." In 2017, its officers hailed from Duke, Northwestern, Stanford, Yale, and other elite private schools. Attracting an even larger constituency, the National Association of College and University Chaplains (NACUC) equips its members for "multifaith religious, spiritual, and ethical life at public and private institutions." Founded in 1948, NACUC serves chaplains at over 160 institutions. Originating among mainline Protestants, both organizations have gradually embraced multifaith ministry. In a 1996 survey of 650 chaplains and campus ministers, 74 percent observed an increase in religious diversity among students.[142]

These efforts to diversify campus religious life are part of a wider movement. In 2005, Princeton University hosted the first annual conference of multifaith university councils. Offering sessions on "The Challenges of Creating Sacred Spaces in the University Setting" and "Multi-Faith Councils 101," it attracted over ninety students from thirty schools. Six years later, the keynote speech was given by Eboo Patel, a Muslim American and the founder of Interfaith Youth Core.[143] Established in 2002, IFYC is the most visible advocate of interreligious dialogue on campus. In 2010, Interfaith Youth Core helped the Obama White House lead a series of meetings on religious dialogue and higher education, issuing a set of recommendations for students, staff, faculty, and administration. These discussions laid the groundwork for a White House initiative on interfaith service projects. Initiated by the Office of Faith-Based and Neighborhood Partnerships, it sponsored programs on over 250 campuses, engaging 100,000 students in 2011–2012 and 2012–2013 alone. Involving 450 local groups, these projects included representatives of Campus Crusade, InterVarsity, Hillel, the Hindu Students Council, the Muslim Students' Association, the United Methodist Church, the Evangelical Lutheran Church in America, and the Secular Student Alliance. According to President Obama, the goal was to "unite people of all faiths or even no faith around a common purpose of helping those in need." By disseminating its Spiritual Climate Survey, Interfaith Youth Core helps colleges and universities be more sensitive to religious diversity.[144]

Of all the new immigrant religions on campus, none has a higher profile than Islam. In 2016, Muslims made up 1.6 percent of American freshmen, up from 0.1 percent in 1974.[145] During the post–World War II era, a growing number of Muslims chose to study in the United States, forming an informal network of student organizations. These groups came together to found the Muslim Students' Association. Founded in 1963, it now has over 500 chapters in the United States and Canada.[146] Paralleling their Christian and Jewish counterparts, Muslim Students' Associations offer courses in Islamic studies, prayer services, and special events geared to the Muslim calendar. The fasting month of Ramadan is an especially important time for MSAs, as is the celebration of Eid al-Fitr. Recently, MSA has established a management training program, offering courses on "How to Run a Fortune 500 MSA" and "Media Relations." In 2000, Hartford Seminary created an Islamic Chaplaincy Program, enrolling a dozen future chaplains.[147] In 1999, Georgetown hired the first Muslim chaplain at a major American university. As early as 2001, seventy-five campuses had designated areas for Muslim prayer. Princeton's Muslim prayer room can be found on the third floor of Murray-Dodge Hall, a building once used by the intercollegiate YMCA.[148]

Given political realities, campus Islam faces challenges after the September 11 terrorist attacks. Some Muslim students have been the victim of hate crimes. A small number of groups have come under the suspicion of law enforcement officials. Tighter controls on foreign student visas have reduced the number of Muslim students on campus. Yet on balance, campus Islam has weathered the storms of the post-9/11 era. Electing a female president in 2004, the MSA has appealed to a wide range of Muslims. According to the organization's guiding principles, "Moderation is the compass for our journey." On many campuses, Muslim students have been asked to explain their religious beliefs in interfaith dialogues. This is especially difficult for Muslim women, who must often explain their distinctive dress. Though Muslims have become more integrated into campus life, they have also suffered from marginality and exclusion.[149]

Less numerous than Muslims, Hindus are becoming more visible on the American campus. In 2016, just under 1 percent of freshmen identified as Hindu.[150] Founded by three collegians in 1990, the Hindu Students Council (HSC) has established over fifty chapters on college and university campuses, serving over 130,000 Hindu and non-Hindu students during the past quarter century. Part of a "Hindu revival on campus," they have provided a home for both immigrants and American-born Hindus (the latter make up about 60 percent of Hindu undergraduates).[151] In 2015, the HSC celebrated its twenty-fifth anniversary by hosting a Global Dharma Conference in Edison, New Jersey.[152] Comprised mostly of second- and third-generation Hindu-Americans, the group has fostered a dialogue between Hinduism and American culture. Several HSC chapters have quoted Mark Twain's observation that in "religion and culture, India is the only millionaire," using the quintessential American writer to affirm Hindu traditions.[153] In recent years, schools such as Princeton and Duke have hired full-time Hindu chaplains, reflecting the growth of the community on campus.[154]

Alongside Hindu Students Councils and Muslim Students' Associations, Sikh Student Associations can be found on at least fifty campuses, including the University of California, Riverside and the University of Illinois at Urbana-Champaign. While Trinity University's association held a "Tie a Turban Day," other groups have called attention to anti-Sikh persecution on the Indian subcontinent. With the help of Sikh American philanthropists, Sikh studies chairs have been established at the University of California, Santa Barbara; Hofstra University; the University of California, Riverside; and the University of Michigan–Ann Arbor.[155]

Both inside and outside the classroom, interest in "Eastern spirituality" has surged in recent decades. While such curiosity characterized the Harvard transcendentalists and the postwar Beats, the growth in Asian American students has facilitated a new encounter with non-Western religions.[156] Currently, 1.2 percent of American freshmen identify as Buddhists. Accommodating a multireligious constituency, Yale University maintains a Buddhist shrine and a nonsectarian meditation space. While Buddhist groups at Yale and other elite universities are predominantly white, many Asian Americans flock to evangelical student groups.[157] A practicing Buddhist with deep roots in the Protestant establishment, Middlebury College professor Steven Rockefeller describes the ways that "college can provide students with opportunities for understanding, appreciating, and practicing the meditative and contemplative disciplines."[158] The oldest Rockefeller to bear the family name, his advocacy of meditation in the classroom represents a major sea-change for his influential family. While his Baptist great-grandfather John D. Rockefeller funded the construction of the Protestant chapel at the University of Chicago, Steven Rockefeller has called for greater attention to non-Western spirituality in higher education.[159]

Since then such approaches have become more mainstream. Growing in popularity, several varieties of meditation have become part of the wellness programs at North American colleges and universities. A 2008 survey of students at a midwestern university found that many undergraduates have participated in mind-body therapies, including relaxation techniques (43.8 percent) and yoga (34.6 percent). While often detached from their historic contexts, such practices are sometimes perceived as religious or spiritual. According to the Pew Research Center, 23 percent of the general population identifies yoga as a spiritual practice. Though scholars debate yoga's religious status, few doubt it is becoming more prevalent on campus.[160]

While not a function of new immigration, a host of neo-pagan groups are also part of the new religious pluralism on campus. Many of these groups date back to the religious experimentation of the 1960s. At the time, sociologist Andrew Greeley described what he called a "new-time religion on campus," arguing that "there has been a very notable increase . . . in interest in the sacred and particularly the bizarrely sacred among students on the college and university campuses in the last few years."[161] Five decades later, neo-paganism is now a recognizable part of the campus religious landscape. A comprehensive website for "Pagans on Campus" lists groups on about one hundred campuses, including the University of Arkansas, Iowa State, St. Olaf College, and Montana State University.[162]

Other religious groups are flourishing on campus. In the United States, over 150,000 eighteen- to thirty-year-olds participate in the Mormon Institutes of Religion, which are often located near colleges and universities. The first Institute was established in 1926 at the University of Idaho. Its goal was to "take care of the L.D.S. students registered at the university." By the late 1960s, there were 200 Institutes serving a population of 35,000 Mormons, more than the enrollment of Brigham Young University. Today they can be found in over 2,700 locations worldwide. Not restricted to undergraduates, they provide instruction to other single adults, offering courses in Church History, Old Testament, the Book of Mormon, and the Pearl of Great Price.[163]

Providing another form of religious diversity, the Orthodox Christian Fellowship has established a presence at over 200 North American colleges and universities. Rooted in centuries of Christian tradition, this outreach began in the postwar era with groups at Columbia, McGill, and Penn State. In the mid-1960s, the Standing Conference of Canonical Orthodox Bishops in the Americas established a national Campus Commission. After reaching nearly 100 campuses with student groups, the Bishops eliminated the commission in 1973. During the 1970s, Orthodox campus ministry entered a period of decline, reaching fewer than 50 institutions by the end of the decade. In the late 1990s, a trio of priests helped to revitalize this neglected area, paving the way for the Orthodox Christian Fellowship. Supported by a Lilly Endowment grant, the OCF expanded its staff. According to the organization's website, "the number of OCF chapters on universities across the continent has exploded," increasing from 50 to over 200 groups in ten years. This new campus outreach may also reflect the influence of evangelical converts to Eastern Orthodoxy. At least one OCF board member spent time with Campus Crusade for Christ.[164]

Unlike Orthodox believers, Unitarians and Universalists are not new to the American campus, having established a nineteenth-century presence at Harvard, Tufts University, and St. Lawrence University. The first Unitarian campus group was established at the University of Wisconsin in 1886 under the banner of the Channing Club. Presently, there is a "concerted campaign" to revitalize Unitarian Universalist (UU) campus ministries. Billing themselves as the "liberal evangelists on campus," they are reaching out to a new generation of students.[165] Between 1997 and 2002, the number of UU young adult groups grew from 100 to 250. Such groups focus on eighteen- to thirty-five-year-old individuals. Through its Office of Youth and Young Adult Ministries, the Unitarian Universalist Association offers grants to campus groups. Published in 2008, a *Campus Organizer's Handbook* is now available, along with UU posters and videos.[166]

If Unitarian Universalists are the liberal evangelists in American higher education, the students within the network affiliated with the Center for Inquiry on Campus are the ambassadors of organized atheism and agnosticism. Formed in 1996 by students from 15 institutions, the network has expanded to include groups at 240 colleges and universities in the United States which sponsor lectures on scientific critiques of religion, atheism, and skepticism. The Center also makes available campus posters with statements such as "Privatize Religion," "Skeptics Do It with Their Eyes Open," and "Extraordinary Claims Demand Extraordinary Evidence."[167] The network's original Declaration of Necessity urged atheists, agnostics, and secularists to organize. Mentioning Campus Crusade, Catholic Newman Centers, Hillel, and Muslim student organizations, it called for a freethinking alternative. The rapid growth of campus free thought is just one more sign of the vitality of the student religious marketplace.[168] So is the appointment of humanist chaplains at Harvard, Rutgers, and Adelphi universities.[169] Other groups have also emerged to serve atheists and freethinkers. Emphasizing the "values of naturalism, reason and compassion," the nontheistic Secular Student Alliance now has nearly 200 campus chapters. In an environment where religious and secular groups often coexist, organizational models are freely borrowed.[170]

Revitalizing Mainline Protestant Campus Ministry

Amidst the flurry of evangelical, Catholic, Jewish, Muslim, Mormon, and Unitarian groups, mainline Protestantism is still a significant presence in student ministry. According to the National Study of Youth and Religion, 26 percent of mainline Protestant young adults participated in a campus religious group during their time in college. According to data available in 2017, there were 1,300 Presbyterian, 580 Evangelical Lutheran Church in America, 510 United Methodist, 266 Episcopal Church USA, 140 Disciples of Christ, 61 American Baptist, and 19 United Church of Christ campus ministries or campus ministry locations in the United States. Twenty years ago there were more campuses served by Presbyterian Church (USA) ministries and congregations than by InterVarsity or Campus Crusade. While Cru reaches more institutions today, there are still more PCUSA campuses than InterVarsity chapters.[171]

Though these numbers are impressive, they mask some important realities. First, many mainline Protestant collegiate ministries are based in nearby congregations where staff only devote part of their time to campus work. Second, there is a significant amount of double counting, reflecting the large number of ecumenical campus ministries. The same campus ministry may show up on the list of more than one denomination. Third, this one-time snapshot of denominational campus ministries obscures a very important long-term trend: the number of mainline Protestant campus ministries has declined in some groups. As recently as 2005, the United Methodist Church reported over 700 campus ministries. By 2017 that number had fallen to 510. According to the denomination's news service, "the number of United Methodist campus ministries is gradually shrinking." Though precise numbers are hard to come by, campus clergy in other denominations have identified a similar pattern. Lamenting the state of campus ministry in the Episcopal Church, one chaplain wrote that the "campus mission field was effectively shut down." While maintaining a larger presence than the Episcopalians, Presbyterians have seen older ministries disappear. In the words of a 2009 report, "The ways of ministering on campus that have nourished the faith of generations of Presbyterians are breaking down."[172]

At the dawn of the twenty-first century, mainline campus ministries are best described as down but not out. Despite severe challenges, they have shown signs of renewal. This renewal can be seen in the rebirth of the mainline student movement, the emergence of new fundraising strategies, the rise of new forms of campus ministry, and the crafting of new denominational statements.

The first chapter of the mainline Protestant student movement ended abruptly when the University Christian Movement voted itself out of existence in 1969. Its resurrection indicates that mainline campus ministries are recovering from the losses suffered in the late 1960s. For the first time in two decades, 2,100 campus ministers and students from eleven mainline Protestant denominations attended an ecumenical gathering held from December 28, 1990, to January 1, 1991. Christened the "Celebrate" conference, it reconvened four more times between 1994 and 2006. All told, Celebrate managed to attract some 7,000 students.[173]

Building on these developments, a group of college students revived the U.S. branch of the Student Christian Movement at a 2010 conference. Part of the international World Student Christian Federation (WSCF), it is the American affiliate of a worldwide ecumenical network. Established in 1895, the WSCF is a direct descendant of the YMCA and the Student Volunteer Movement. By resurrecting this organization, mainline students are returning to the roots of student religious activism in America. Still in its infancy, it is a much smaller version of its 1960s predecessor. Like its precursor, the Student Christian Movement–USA has articulated a progressive agenda of "standing up for the poor, downtrodden, sick, and oppressed as Jesus taught." Currently, its partners include the Lutheran Student Movement USA, the United Methodist Student Movement, the National Council of Churches, and the National Campus Ministry Association. As of 2013, chapters had formed at Boston University, Elmhurst College, New York University, Princeton University, and four other institutions. Chapter development is a major priority. The WSCF's North American donors include the Episcopal Church USA, the Minnesota Council of Churches, the Presbyterian Church (USA), the Riverside Church in New York City, the United Methodist Church, and the United Church of Christ.[174]

It remains to be seen whether mainline denominations can make the necessary investments in student religious life. At both the national and the regional level, denominations have cut funding for campus ministry. Yet, as in the Catholic Church, tight budgets have prompted innovative development strategies. Episcopalians have been particularly successful in advancement efforts, especially in establishing endowments to support specific campus-based ministries. Faced with the possibility of extinction, Cornell launched the first major endowment campaign in 1979. After two decades of diligent fundraising that produced a $2 million endowment, Cornell's Episcopal Chaplaincy is now "fully endowed and financially self-sustaining." Seeking to stem Episcopal campus ministry closures, the Episcopal Church Foundation drew on the Cornell example, providing ministries with small grants to jump start their development efforts as well as training in the basics of fundraising. Over thirty campus ministries benefited, including those at Boston University, Oklahoma State University, Stanford, and the University of Florida. Looking back on this episode in Episcopal campus ministry, Cornell chaplain Gurdon Brewster called it "a crisis overcome." Fifteen years later, the denomination sponsors grant programs to fund new and innovative campus ministries.[175]

Mainline Protestants are also experimenting with congregational approaches to campus ministry. One of the leaders of this movement is University Presbyterian Church in Seattle, which attracts between 1,000 and 1,200 students to weekly services in its fellowship hall. Through spirited worship, retreats, service projects, and small groups, the Seattle church has pioneered congregational approaches to campus ministry. In recent years, University Presbyterian Church has promoted its model through a handbook on congregation-based campus ministry and the Ascent Network, an interdenominational association of campus ministries. In the Presbyterian Church (USA) about 700 churches are engaged in collegiate ministry.[176] Other denominations are also utilizing congregation-based approaches. According to the Evangelical Lutheran Church in America, 400 congregations have committed themselves to some form of campus ministry.[177]

In another form of innovation, campus ministers in several denominations have revived the model of the religious dormitory. Hearkening back to the days of the YMCA, Berkeley's Westminster House opened in 2003, providing a home to 126 students from the University of California. Though it closed in 2011, other residential ministries have flourished at the University of Wisconsin, Kansas State University, and the University of Illinois. While Presby Hall offers suite-style residences to undergraduate Illini, Kansas State's Wesley Foundation provides a Christian residential community. In 2013, the *Wall Street Journal* described a new wave of "religious dorms" at Troy University, the Florida Institute of Technology, Texas A&M University, and the University of Nebraska–Lincoln. Several of these dormitories were built by the Newman Student Housing Fund, a private business that builds campus housing for Roman Catholics.[178]

Though most innovations bubble up from the grassroots, national denominations are also talking about campus ministry. Over the decades, the Methodists, Lutherans, and Presbyterians have produced dozens of reports and resolutions on campus ministry. The most recent wave of these self-studies and statements has called for a greater presence in campus life. Released in 2001, *Renewing the Commitment* urged the church to "affirm, pray for, and financially support the restoration and renewal of our denomination's commitment to the oldest continuing mission of the Presbyterian Church (USA) beyond the congregation."[179] Framed as an effort to "begin reversing the decline," this plan encountered significant obstacles in 2009. Facing budgetary pressures, the PCUSA's General Assembly eliminated its Office of Collegiate Ministries, combining it with youth ministries.[180] Responding to a groundswell of criticism, the denomination reestablished the office in 2010, creating a task force on Presbyterian collegiate ministries. In 2012, this committee presented a new campus ministry strategy to the General Assembly, proposing a capital campaign to "fund the important and ongoing work of the Office of Collegiate Ministries in perpetuity." Formed the same year, UKirk represents campus ministers, chaplains, and associate pastors ministering to college students. By 2014, UKirk had developed 66 campus ministry sites around the country. At that time, the organization hoped to establish 101 new worshiping communities.[181]

In a similar way, United Methodists have worked to revitalize campus ministry, albeit from different ends of the church. On the evangelical side of the denomination, the Foundation for Evangelism created College Union, an online community focused on rebuilding the Methodist campus network. In 2005,

College Union hosted a campus ministry summit. Since then it has sponsored several Refresh conferences, featuring evangelicals like Andy Crouch, a former staff member with InterVarsity Christian Fellowship.[182] Emphasizing a more progressive vision, the denomination's General Board of Higher Education and Ministry (GBHEM) has stressed social justice and interfaith dialogue. Fostering close ties with the United Methodist Campus Ministry Association, it has promoted virtual communities through social networking and blogs. In 2009, the GBHEM held a conference on "The Promise of United Methodist Campus Ministry." Describing these competing networks, Methodist historian Russell Richey notes that campus ministers "seem to welcome all the help they can get and from wherever."[183]

Like the Presbyterian Church (USA) and the United Methodist Church, the Evangelical Lutheran Church in America has tried to sustain its presence on campus. Along these lines, recent ELCA documents have affirmed the denomination's commitment to campus ministry, most recently in a churchwide social statement on education. In *Our Calling in Education* (2007), the denomination acknowledged the financial pressures on campus clergy, calling for "new models of ministry, of partnership, and of staffing and support."[184]

Sometimes mainline campus ministries take two steps forward and one step back. Four years after *Our Calling in Education*, the ELCA announced a 38 percent cut in campus ministry.[185] As recently as 1997, the denomination claimed to possess "the strongest campus ministry of any mainline denomination." Since then the ELCA's organizational chart has gone through several changes. In 2005, the denomination folded its Division for Higher Education and Schools into a new unit on Vocation and Education. Following the Great Recession, the ELCA went through yet another restructuring, eliminating the Vocation and Education area altogether. Despite these shifts, it continues to employ a program director for campus ministry, albeit at half time.[186]

Taken together, grassroots innovations, better fundraising, and denominational statements may strengthen campus ministry in the mainline. Then again, such efforts may not be enough to counteract the effects of steep budget cuts. Whether mainline Protestantism continues to maintain its considerable presence in higher education remains to be seen. That it is still a major player in the campus religious marketplace is undeniable.

Student Affairs Rediscovers Spirituality

What is now referred to as "student affairs" emerged as a distinguishable part of higher education in the first half of the twentieth century as colleges and universities grew into more rationalized, specialized, and bureaucratic institutions. While professors tended to the intellectual lives of students, those who worked in the new field of student affairs focused on other areas, seeing that undergraduates became "well-rounded" men and women. What was once the responsibility of presidents and professors, namely the spiritual and religious development of students, migrated to student affairs personnel, including those affiliated with the YMCA and the early denominational campus ministries.[187]

Early works in the field of student affairs and student development proclaimed the importance of holistic student development and, by extension, spiritual growth. According to a 1949 publication of the American Council on Education, student affairs must "include attention to the student's well-rounded development—physically, socially, emotionally and spiritually, as well as intellectually."[188] Despite this initial focus on spirituality, the religious lives of undergraduates soon became increasingly peripheral to student development work.[189] Though postwar public universities sometimes employed personnel to coordinate the array of collegiate religious organizations, religious and spiritual development was not seen as a central aim of student affairs staff.[190]

Serious interest in religion and spirituality reemerged in the late 1980s. A landmark article in the *Journal of College Student Personnel* called attention to the "blind spot" of spirituality in student affairs work, advocating new "principles and strategies." According to the authors, students should be given the "same opportunity to attain spiritual development as they are given in all other areas."[191] In 1989, Jossey-Bass published *Religion on Campus* as part of its New Directions for Student Services series. In the concluding chapter, the volume's editor argued that establishing a "relationship with religion on campus is possible, practical, and needed."[192]

In the 1990s, religion and spirituality became a regular topic at the national meetings of the two major student development professional associations, the American College Personnel Association (ACPA) and NASPA. Paper titles from this period include "Spirituality in the Counseling Process" (ACPA 1990), "Spiritual Development Theory and Practice" (NASPA 1991), "Have You Spoken to a Buddhist Lately?" (ACPA 1992), "Taking Responsibility for Student Spiritual Development" (NASPA 1993), "A Spiritual Awakening: Giving Students Permission to Explore their Spiritual Wellness" (ACPA 1994), and "The Spiritual Development of Lesbian Gay Students" (NASPA 1999).[193] An article in NASPA's flagship journal called spiritual development "an integral part of students' overall development."[194] In a similar way, New York University administrator Patrick Love noted "a surge of interest" in the topic.[195]

Over the past two decades, several conferences have reintroduced spirituality into the discourse of student affairs professionals. In 2000, the ACPA sponsored a one-day institute on "Spiritual Maturation" for campus ministers, student affairs staff, faculty, and administrators. In 2002, NASPA convened a pair of workshops on spirituality and student affairs. Reflecting on these events, NASPA's executive director wrote that "[c]onsideration of the spiritual in education has become a part of the context in which we do our work." For the past several years, NASPA and the ACPA have sponsored subgroups on religion and spirituality. In 2017, NASPA hosted a major national conference at UCLA on the convergence of religious, spiritual, and secular identities, cosponsored by Hillel, Interfaith Youth Core, major chaplaincy organizations, and the Secular Student Alliance.[196]

Complementing the work of NASPA and the ACPA, the Jon C. Dalton Institute on College Student Values at Florida State University has become a clearinghouse for discussions on spirituality and student affairs. Featured speakers have included Eboo Patel, Robert Nash, Thomas Ehrlich, and Anne Colby.[197] At the 2004 Institute, UCLA researchers Alexander and Helen Astin joined Jennifer Lindholm in presenting preliminary findings from *Spirituality in Higher Education: A National Study of College Students' Search for Meaning and Purpose*. As noted in chapter 2, the Astins and Lindholm have published *Cultivating the Spirit: How College Can Enhance Students' Inner Lives* (2011). A companion volume presents case studies from American colleges and universities, offering a "guidebook of promising practices" for promoting spiritual development.[198]

Now an official NASPA publication, the *Journal of College and Character* (founded in 2000) has also fostered such discussions. In a 2004 article, founding editor Jon Dalton recommended several steps colleges and universities could take to enhance "students' spiritual growth in college." According to Dalton, schools should offer space for prayer and meditation, integrate spirituality into wellness programs, and forge ties with clergy and campus ministers.[199] More recently, the journal has turned its attention to interfaith dialogue, campus atheists, and college chapels.[200]

By talking about spirituality and student affairs programming, student development professionals have come full circle. One hundred years ago, the overtly Christian YMCA took responsibility for functions now performed by student affairs offices, including new student orientation, student handbooks, and extracurricular activities. Like the turn-of-the-century Y, today's student life administrators are paying careful attention to spirituality and religion. As in other areas of campus religious life, student affairs professionals are recycling older models. At Penn State University, the Division of Student Affairs manages the Pasquerilla Spiritual Center. Dedicated in 2003, it resembles the Danforth chapels of the postwar era, with some very important differences. It houses the Center for Spiritual and Ethical Development, home to nearly sixty religious groups, including Catholic Campus Ministries, the Vedic Society, the Muslim Students' Association, and Chabad. It also hosts numerous wedding ceremonies. Like many of the Danforth chapels, it serves a public university campus. In a 2011 report, Jennifer Lindholm and her colleagues described the proliferation of sacred spaces in American colleges and universities. From chapels to meditation rooms, such spaces are the meeting places for a new religious pluralism.[201]

Unlike the Danforth chapels, contemporary student development educators make a distinction between religion and spirituality. By focusing on the meaning and purpose of life, they have distinguished spirituality in student development from formal religious institutions.[202] Such definitions resonate with a growing segment of American college students. According to a 2013 survey, 32 percent identify as spiritual but not religious. An earlier survey found that 80 percent of undergraduates have an interest in spirituality, while 47 percent think it is important to seek out opportunities for spiritual growth. Like the baby boom generation, they have been influenced by the "quest culture" of the 1960s.[203]

Still in its infancy, the movement for spirituality in student development has a long way to go. A survey of student affairs professionals found that most did not integrate religion and spirituality into their work. Despite an emphasis on holistic student development, they have ignored this dimension of campus life. Along the same lines, a study of graduate programs in student affairs found that most ignore religion and spirituality. Like the comeback of religion in the academic disciplines, the heightened focus on spirituality is confined to a subset of student affairs practitioners.[204]

Religious Vitality on Campus: Competition, Conflict, and Cooperation

This brief overview has explored the size and scope of student religious organizations in the United States. While membership statistics cannot tell us anything about the spiritual and religious experiences of campus groups, they can debunk some common myths about religion on campus.

First, the decline of one kind of student religious organization should not be interpreted as the secularization of campus life. Over the course of American history, the fortunes of specific groups have waxed and waned. The dominant student religious organizations in America, the YMCA and the YWCA, almost disappeared in the decades following World War II. Inevitably, new religious groups arose to take their place. Often these newcomers recycle cultural forms from the distant past, combining them with novel approaches. A similar dynamic is going on today as mainline Protestant denominational ministries yield some of their territory to other forms of campus ministry. With a few exceptions, the Y and the Student Volunteer Movement are gone from the American campus. Yet their student-centered organizational strategy lives on in Hillel's peer mentoring program, evangelical parachurch groups, Muslim Students' Associations, and the Student Christian Movement–USA.

Second, student religious participation remains strong. The proliferation of Catholic Newman Centers, Chabad Houses, Mormon Institutes of Religion, and neo-pagan clubs suggests that campus religion endures. So does the presence of congregation-based campus ministries. Surveys of college students bear this out. According to the National Study of Youth and Religion, one-fourth of eighteen- to twenty-three-year-olds with some college have been involved in a campus-based religious group. Likewise, the 2009 College Senior Survey found that 26.4 percent of seniors frequently attended religious services (36.4 percent did so occasionally).[205] This rate of campus religious involvement compares quite favorably to figures from the 1920s, when one out of seven students took part in the collegiate Y and a smaller number of students were involved in denominational campus ministries.[206]

Given the wealth of religious options available on campus, it is not surprising that undergraduates are less likely than other young adults to lose their religion. Though religious participation tends to decrease in the young adult years, a University of Texas study found that going to college decreases the risk of religious decline.[207] Another study confirmed this relationship, noting a positive correlation between higher education and attendance at religious services. For each year of college and graduate school, attendance increases by 15 percent. So do Bible reading and prayer.[208] Though the percentage of American freshmen with no religion rose from 15.4 percent in 1971 to 31 percent in 2016, this was not a result of college. Taken in the fall of the freshman year, this survey looked at students at the very beginning of their college careers.[209] Other research indicates that college may intensify religious and spiritual seeking, a trait already associated with today's emerging adults. The UCLA study of spirituality and higher education found growing interest in "integrating spirituality in my life" between the freshman and the junior year. In another survey, 38 percent of college seniors reported stronger religious faith. Just 14 percent said their faith had weakened.[210] Researchers have also uncovered a positive correlation between higher education and religious liberalism. College-educated Americans tend to switch to mainline denominations and hold more liberal views of the Bible.[211] Yet liberalization is not the same as secularization. Far from secular, the vast majority of college students identify with a religious tradition. While 69 percent of undergraduates pray, 79 percent believe in God.[212]

While fostering a lively religious marketplace, campus ministries have been unable to challenge another aspect of secularization: the separation of piety and knowledge. In the late nineteenth century, student religious life migrated from the classroom to the student union. From this location, it has been almost impossible to shape the core academic work of the university.

To be sure, campus religious organizations have had a modest impact on the world of scholarship and teaching. In an earlier era, Jewish students paved the way for Jewish studies.[213] More recently, Catholic student centers have played a role in the creation of Catholic studies positions. Found at a dozen non-Catholic institutions, most have received funding from campus ministries or their supporters.[214] In a similar way, evangelical groups have tried to influence the professoriate. In 2016–2017, InterVarsity's graduate and faculty ministries served 4,560 students and 1,959 professors. In the judgment of historian Mark Noll, "the grad-faculty IVCF may be doing as much in its low-key way to improve evangelical intellectual life as any other ongoing national program." Along the same lines, Campus Crusade has built a network of 9,000 professors at 1,100 universities. Both ministries regularly sponsor academic conferences. A spin-off of InterVarsity's graduate ministry at Harvard, the Veritas Forum has hosted 2,000 forums on faith and knowledge at 200 universities. Featuring speakers such as Francis Collins and Alvin Plantinga, they have reached over 100,000 students. Pursuing similar goals, 23 Christian study centers help faculty and students integrate faith and learning on nonsectarian campuses. Active at Arizona State University, Cornell University, Duke University, and the University of Virginia, they formed the Consortium of Christian Study Centers in 2008.[215] Taking a different approach, the advocates of campus spirituality have pursued a holistic curricular and a cocurricular agenda. As noted in chapter 2, the UCLA study on spirituality in higher education urges faculty to address questions of meaning and value. In *A Guidebook of Promising Practices: Facilitating Students' Spiritual Development* (2011), the UCLA team lists exemplary academic degree programs, courses, and pedagogies.[216]

While student religion and spirituality take a back seat in the classroom, they are quite consequential for campus life. Their influence can be seen in the tensions that surround student religious organizations. Sometimes conflicts arise *within* particular religious traditions. On many campuses, Chabad and Hillel compete for the same students. The same is true of InterVarsity and Campus Crusade. In other places, Hindu Students Councils and Indian cultural organizations vie for the allegiance of Indian Americans.[217] Despite the prevalence of *intra*-religious tensions, the most serious conflicts are between different religious traditions. At some universities, disagreements over the Israeli-Palestinian conflict have led to friction between Muslim Students'

Associations and Jewish student groups.[218] Proselytizing is also a perennial concern. Part of the cultural DNA of evangelicalism, it evokes uneasiness in other groups. While INDOlink discusses "how Christian evangelists target Hindu American students," similar experiences are common among Jewish students. Along the same lines, a mainline Protestant chaplain compares evangelical campus ministries to religious fast food, arguing that "students who are involved in parachurch campus organizations are suffering from poor nutrition."[219] Still others warn of conservative campus organizing, pointing to ties between Campus Crusade and the new Christian Right.[220] Evangelical groups have also run afoul of university nondiscrimination policies. By excluding gays and lesbians, as well as non-Christians, from leadership positions, they have invited dozens of legal challenges. These conflicts pit appeals to religious freedom against the values of inclusiveness and tolerance. As social mores change, evangelical groups may encounter growing pressure to abandon such restrictive membership criteria. In 2014, the California State University system derecognized InterVarsity Christian Fellowship on all twenty-three of its campuses, citing the organization's requirement that officers sign a statement of faith. Although this decision was reversed in 2015, InterVarsity faces similar policies on other campuses.[221]

Though such conflicts persist, student religious organizations have learned to get along, endorsing both *inter-* and *intra-*faith cooperation. At Swarthmore College, campus freethinkers called for a dialogue with evangelicals. At Harvard University, Chabad and Hillel have learned to coexist. Across the country, the two often learn from each other. Reaffirming a 1971 statement, a dozen evangelical ministries, including InterVarsity and Campus Crusade, have pledged not to compete for students.[222] Across the nation, Muslim and Jewish students have cosponsored Shabbat and iftar dinners. At Rutgers University, the presidents of Hillel and the Muslim Students' Association coauthored a letter to the campus newspaper.[223]

Responding to aggressive proselytizing, some universities have adopted a religious code of ethics. While allowing students to share their faith, the University of Southern California's ethical framework requires that they do so "in a manner that avoids harassing, demeaning, or disregarding the integrity and freedom of other persons." Developed by the university's Office of Religious Life, it governs the activities of over eighty religious groups.[224] At other institutions, student affairs personnel, university religious councils and interfaith groups have tried to ensure an inclusive environment. At the University of Delaware, the University Religious Leaders Organization (URLO) appoints a liaison to the Division of Student Life. At the University of Kentucky, an Interfaith Dialogue Organization worked to overcome the "polarization of religious groups." At Penn State, the university-sponsored Center for Spiritual and Ethical Development serves as a spiritual referee. Groups that sign off on the Center's code of ethics pledge "not to coerce or diminish, so as to take advantage of anyone's vulnerability."[225] After the passing of the mainline Protestant chapel, such organizations are the closest thing to a religious establishment in American higher education.

Not all religious traditions have embraced interfaith dialogue. Historically, evangelicals have been more resistant, while the mainline has taken the lead. Although this remains the case on many campuses, evangelicalism is beginning to change. Responding to the new pluralism, InterVarsity published *Can Evangelicals Learn from World Religions?* (2000). On the evangelical left, *Sojourners* magazine has featured the writings of Muslim Eboo Patel, the founder of Interfaith Youth Core. In campus ministry, InterVarsity has embraced the issues of poverty and environmentalism, combining evangelism and social action. In a 2006 survey, 87 percent of InterVarsity staff agreed that social justice was at the heart of the gospel. While remaining more conservative, Campus Crusade has distanced itself from the political activities of its late founder. By changing its name to Cru in 2012, it has acknowledged the "negative associations" of the word "crusade," adapting to global developments and a multireligious America.[226]

Once dominated by a Protestant establishment, American society has always been religiously diverse. While some groups have identified with a common "religious center," others have existed on the margins. Much of the dynamism of American religious history has come from the tensions between the center and the periphery. As our multireligious society has become even more diverse, this dialectic between conflict and consensus has intensified. Like American religion, student religious organizations have displayed both centripetal and centrifugal tendencies. Emphasizing theological differences, they have carved out their distinctive niches. Searching for common ground, they have tried to understand each other. At the beginning of the twenty-first century, the American campus remains a place of both competition and cooperation. Both impulses have contributed to the vitality of student religious life.[227]

5

THE WIDER SIGNIFICANCE OF RELIGION ON CAMPUS

Over the past three decades, higher education has become more open to the teaching and the practice of religion.[1] Across the university, the advocates of religious scholarship have carved out new organizational niches. Paying more attention to institutional mission, church-related colleges have revitalized their religious identities. At both public and private institutions, diverse expressions of student religiosity have become more visible, turning the campus union into a lively religious marketplace. In some cases, these developments have challenged the institutional differentiation of religion from American higher education. They have also resisted the privatization of faith, taking religion and spirituality into public life.

To be clear, such changes have been limited. In most disciplines, a minority of scholars have turned their attention to religion. Even fewer have attempted to integrate religious perspectives into the content of their research. Eschewing confessional approaches, most focus on the detached study of religion. Though church-related colleges have emphasized mission and identity, many have been unable to halt the attenuation of denominational ties. Despite the vitality of undergraduate religious groups, many students never participate in a campus ministry. Although the return of religion has been modest, clearly something has changed. Once portrayed as an island of secularity, higher education is more open to religious discourse and practice. It is also more open to critical scholarship about the sacred.

The preceding chapters have documented the return of religion in American higher education. This chapter considers the meaning of these developments for the wider society. In the 1990s, the *Chronicle of Higher Education* called the university "a bellwether for society's religious revival."[2] As a bellwether, the university is continually buffeted by the winds of public opinion. Yet the academy can also serve as a rudder, steering the conversation in new directions. Because of their training, scholars of religion have played a special role in bridging the divides in American society (and occasionally widening them). From domestic policy debates to international relations, religious studies has shaped public discourse. In different ways, church-related colleges have also influenced the public square. So have student religious organizations. Promoting distinctive religious traditions, they have contributed to the institutional pluralism of American society.

This chapter explores the wider significance of religion and higher education in three arenas of American culture: civic education, the arts, and public intellectual life.[3] Examining the relationship between religion and civic education, it highlights the role of colleges in fostering religious literacy and engaging cultural diversity. Acknowledging the limits of campus dialogue, it recognizes the persistence of political and religious divisions, as well as the challenges of American pluralism. Moving beyond politics, it examines the connections between religious higher education and the creative arts. Last, but not least, it discusses the ways that colleges and universities have sustained the ecology of religious intellectual life. Documenting the public relevance of American higher education, it shows how the teaching and the practice of religion have shaped politics, art, and the world of ideas.

Religion and Civic Education: Fostering Religious Literacy and Engaging Diversity

In a country of red and blue zip codes, fewer and fewer Americans have regular contact with those who think differently from themselves. As Bill Bishop argued in *The Big Sort*, the geographical clustering of Americans into ideologically homogeneous neighborhoods is dividing the country. Already visible in 2008, this polarization is even more apparent after the 2016 presidential election. While such differences should not be exaggerated, our political discourse suggests that Americans are divided by race, class, and generation. Now the "world's most religiously diverse nation," we are also divided by religious faith. Even before the events of September 11, 2001, Americans were coming to grips with the new diversity. In a post-9/11 world, it is both easier and more difficult to talk about religious differences.[4]

Frustrated by the divisions in American culture, Senator John Danforth wrote *Faith and Politics: How the "Moral Values" Debate Divides America and How to Move Forward Together* (2006). In an effort to elevate the national conversation, his family's foundation established the John C. Danforth Center on Religion and Politics in 2009, pledging a $30 million gift to Washington University in St. Louis. Focusing on the academic study of religion, the Danforth Center aspires to be "an ideologically neutral venue." Cultivating a climate of civility, it has hosted high-profile figures from the left, right, and center, including columnist George Will and women's rights activist Sandra Fluke. Its advisory board has been equally diverse, bringing together academics (John McGreevy and the late Jean Bethke Elshtain), journalists (Michael Gerson and Krista Tippett), and religious leaders (Eboo Patel and Joel Hunter) from across the political and religious spectrum. During the 2016 election, the Center sponsored a series of Danforth Dialogues featuring David Brooks, Patel, poet Natasha Trethewey, and *Washington Post* columnist E. J. Dionne Jr. Commenting on the contemporary political climate, founding director R. Marie Griffith said that the "bridging work we attempt to do at the Center has seemed more crucial than ever this year."[5]

Besides fostering civility, the academic study of religion has helped Americans become religiously literate. Conducted in 2010, the Pew Religious Knowledge survey examined the effect of taking a college religion course. According to the study, "People with higher levels of education tend to be more knowledgeable about religion." Alumni of religion courses did the best on a religious knowledge quiz, answering an average of twenty-two out of thirty-two questions correctly. Falling somewhere in between, collegians with zero religion courses got an average of eighteen items right, suggesting that other classes may contribute to religious literacy. By contrast, those with no college experience had an average score of thirteen.[6]

Religious literacy is especially relevant to the world of the professions. In contemporary America, colleges and universities play a key role in professional education. If the professional project is about training future workers, the academy is at the center of law, medicine, and social work. In all of these occupations, practitioners must deal with the challenge of religious pluralism and the boundary between church and state. To the extent that professional schools can give practitioners a basic knowledge of religion, they will be better prepared.[7]

Religious literacy is also essential for American diplomats. In 1994, Douglas Johnston and Cynthia Sampson called religion the "missing dimension of statecraft." Following the events of September 11, 2001, religion took center stage. From the Council on Foreign Relations to the Carnegie Endowment for International Peace, the foreign policy establishment turned its attention to the sacred. While George W. Bush emphasized the issue of religious freedom, Barack Obama called for a new dialogue with the Muslim world. During the Obama administration, the Department of State created an Office of Religion and Global Affairs (originally known as the Office of Faith-Based Community Initiatives). Directed by Wesley Theological Seminary Professor Shaun Casey, it focused on international development, religious freedom, and conflict resolution. Speaking at the office's dedication, Secretary of State John Kerry emphasized the importance of religious literacy, adding, "If I went back to college today, I think I would probably major in comparative religion." Recalling an era when theologians helped shape American foreign policy, Casey noted that Reinhold Niebuhr once "walked these halls."[8]

Though the Trump administration has ended many of these initiatives, the wider foreign policy community remains engaged with religious issues. Located in the nation's capital, Georgetown University has become a center for such conversations. Long a training ground for the diplomatic corps, Georgetown established the Berkley Center for Religion, Peace, and World Affairs in 2006, now directed by Casey. Under the auspices of the Center, scholars have explored such topics as religious liberty, globalization, and interreligious dialogue.[9] In a similar way, Yale University's "Faith and Globalization" course examined the role of religion in international affairs, poverty alleviation, and gender relations. Cotaught by theologian Miroslav Volf and former British prime minister Tony Blair, it was sponsored by Blair's Faith and Globalisation Initiative (now part of the Tony Blair Institute for Global Change). In a 2013 speech to the Counter-Terrorism Committee of the United Nations, Blair declared that "Education in the 21st century is a security issue." In Blair's judgment, "The battles of this century are less likely to be the product of extreme political ideology . . . but they could easily be fought around the questions of cultural or religious difference."[10]

Such rhetoric makes some religion scholars nervous. Commenting on the post-9/11 climate, Islam scholar Edward E. Curtis IV cautions against "deploying one-dimensional explanations of religion to justify our own usefulness to the academy and to the nation." Still others challenge the ways that policymakers have engaged the sacred. Criticizing a report on international relations, religion and law specialist Winnifred Sullivan warns of the "extra-territorial establishment of religion." Highlighting the unintended consequences of efforts to promote religious freedom, political scientist Elizabeth Shakman Hurd notes that "official religious engagement with 'religion' can harden lines of division between communities by defining identities and interests in religious terms." Others disagree, arguing that religious freedom advocacy need not exacerbate global conflicts. By debating the role of religion in international affairs, scholars have modeled yet another form of academic citizenship. Though they disagree about the direction of American foreign policy, few doubt the importance of religious literacy.[11]

Beyond mere literacy, the academic study of religion can reveal new social worlds. In the late nineteenth century, Max Weber pioneered the tradition of *Verstehen* sociology, cultivating an empathetic approach to human social life. Following Weber, interpretative social scientists have struggled to understand the meanings ordinary people impute to religious practices. In the 1970s, Clifford Geertz encouraged researchers to see things from "the native's point of view." Since then, anthropologists have continued to blur the boundaries between researchers and informants. Anthropologist T. M. Luhrmann models such an approach in *When God Talks Back*, experimenting with the prayer practices of her respondents. So does Danforth director Griffith, emphasizing the virtue of "critical empathy." Pioneering the study of lived religion, historian Robert Orsi urges scholars to "enter into the otherness of religious practices in search of an understanding of their human ground." Presiding over a "polytheistic classroom," Orsi welcomes the "presence of many different histories, memories, experiences—and moral idioms."[12]

Such encounters have real-world implications for students. By learning about the religious practices of others, they prepare themselves for a culturally diverse world. In a recent survey of American undergraduates, Interfaith Youth Core found that 81 percent of undergraduates have talked with a diverse group of students about shared values. Though only 3 percent were highly engaged in interfaith activities, 45 percent had taken a course exploring another religious tradition. Related research has found that classroom discussions of religion foster a pluralistic orientation and an ecumenical worldview. These findings are consistent with the rhetoric of religious studies programs. In the words of a 2009 report from the American Academy of Religion, "Americans increasingly accept the idea that we need better to understand the diverse range of religious phenomena." Focusing on similar themes, former Harvard Divinity School dean William A. Graham argues that the study of religion leads to "[i]ncreased acceptance, or at least tolerance, of the 'other,'" adding that religious literacy makes citizens "more open to a diversity of views, heritages, allegiances, faiths, and religious as well as social and political systems." Toward that end, Harvard's Religious Literacy Project has sponsored initiatives on teacher education and interfaith mediation.[13]

Despite their ubiquity in departmental mission statements, some faculty question such lofty goals. For these critics, the language of ecumenism and pluralism is too closely tied to the liberal Protestant history of religious studies. Criticizing the crypto-theological outlook of the field, they favor a sharp break with the past. Many in the humanities agree. Literary theorist Stanley Fish writes that "[t]eachers of literature and philosophy are competent in a subject, not in a ministry," adding that the "humanities are their own good." In *Save the World on Your Own Time* (2012), he advances a circumscribed understanding of the academic vocation, emphasizing specialized expertise over civic engagement. Like Fish, many religion scholars reject a normative agenda for the field, emphasizing the critical interpretation of human cultural phenomenon.[14]

While nervous about religious moralizing, many American faculty recognize a civic component to higher education. Emphasizing cultural pluralism, they view the campus as a microcosm of the larger society. Adopting a more capacious vision of multiculturalism, some have added religion to their definitions of diversity. Voicing these concerns, Interfaith Youth Core founder Eboo Patel wants campuses to include religious identity in discussions of cultural differences. Seeing "campuses as models," IFYC urges colleges and universities to model interfaith understanding. Embracing a more philosophical approach, University of Vermont education professor Robert Nash promotes the value of "moral conversation." Moving beyond the detached study of religion to religious encounter, Nash urges students to debate the merits of different worldviews, "without watering down those intractable intellectual, political, and philosophical differences."[15]

Some of the most intense religious conversations take place outside of the classroom. Focusing on the cocurricular dimensions of undergraduate life, groups like Interfaith Youth Core have emphasized interfaith relationships. Research on cultural diversity reveals a strong link between social segregation and religious intolerance. By contrast, cocurricular encounters with other religions make students more open to religious pluralism.[16] Other studies have documented the correlation between diverse social networks and support for religious dialogue. While people with homogeneous networks tend to resist cross-cultural conversations, those with diverse friendships often thrive in interreligious settings. Law professor Cass Sunstein makes a similar point about American politics. Analyzing the conditions for resisting ideological polarization, he advocates a vigorous exchange of ideas. Rather than segregating themselves in homogeneous enclaves, Americans should embrace the "architecture of serendipity," exposing themselves to a variety of magazines, newspapers, radio stations, and books. At its best, the campus can promote such a social architecture. More than many American institutions, the university welcomes all religions and those with no religion at all. In the campus religious marketplace, students hear from many different traditions.[17]

And yet there are homogeneous contexts within higher education. From Greek letter organizations to women's colleges, the American campus remains a community of communities. No less diverse, the campus religious marketplace includes numerous subcultures. While Muslim Students' Associations work largely with Muslims, evangelical colleges educate an overwhelmingly Protestant student population. Based on what researchers know about cultural homogeneity, we would expect them to heighten political and cultural differences.

Such polarization was on display during presidential candidate Donald Trump's visits to Liberty University, leading one scholar to claim "there is something in the air at evangelical colleges that contributes somehow to evangelical support for Trump." Promoting a nostalgic vision of Christian America, schools like Liberty and Patrick Henry College have prepared their students for Trump's message. Reflecting this orientation, a preelection poll found that 78 percent of Liberty's students planned to vote for the New York businessman. Yet not all evangelical undergraduates think alike. When the candidate visited Liberty's chapel, some students criticized him on social media. Mike Pence's visit to Patrick Henry was even more contentious, provoking visible student protests. At several evangelical schools, support for the Republican presidential candidate declined in 2016. Given the history of evangelical higher education, this is not so surprising. Politically divided, Christian college professors have played a key role in the emergence of an evangelical Left, founding organizations such as Evangelicals for Social Action. In a country split between red and blue, they have cultivated a "purple state of mind." Positioned between a conservative religious subculture and an academy that leans to the left, they have frequent interchange with both sides of the political spectrum.[18]

Looking beyond American shores, Jewish and Muslim groups often hold contrasting views on the Middle East. While often divisive, such commitments do not always put an end to dialogue. In recent years, Jews and Muslims have participated in campus discussions about Israel and Palestine (Palestinian Christians are also part of these discussions). At Tufts University, the Chaplains Office sponsored a series on "Restoring Dignity in the Israeli-Palestinian Conversation." According to a Jewish participant, the series represented "a wide spectrum," adding that there were "lots of people in the group that actually don't usually engage in these kind of conversations." Similar dialogues have taken place on other campuses. While some have resulted in greater understanding, others have led to increased polarization. At Boston College, students destroyed literature by a pro-Israeli speaker. At the University of California, Berkeley, a pro-Palestinian protest was interrupted by pepper spray. In the words of the *Daily Michigan*, it is often a polarized discussion.[19]

Human sexuality is another contentious issue. While many mainline Protestant and some Catholic institutions have welcomed gay and lesbian student groups, most evangelical colleges and campus ministries remain opposed to homosexual relationships. Bridging this divide, some evangelical and LGBT students have worked together on HIV/AIDS initiatives. Others have talked about religion and homosexuality. At Eastern Mennonite University, faculty and staff organized a semester-long conversation on LGBT issues, including books from a wide range of viewpoints. Describing his institution's commitment to dialogue, EMU's president noted, "As a church college, we will debate every issue the church is, or should be, debating." To be sure, such face-to-face conversations often result in greater polarization. Despite the formation of LGBT support groups at seventy-five evangelical colleges (many go unrecognized by their home institutions), the debate remains unresolved. In the years ahead, it may be the most significant issue separating evangelical higher education from other institutions. While some observers worry that evangelical colleges could lose their tax-exempt status, others believe such claims are overblown. Still others argue that religious colleges should voluntarily change their policies. In 2015, Eastern Mennonite University and Goshen College dropped bans on hiring faculty in gay marriages, later resigning from the Council for Christian Colleges and Universities. Like conflicts over nondiscrimination policies (see chapter 4), these controversies pit demands for tolerance and inclusiveness against appeals to religious liberty.[20]

Because real differences exist among America's religious traditions, it is important to differentiate among the various expressions of campus religion. As noted earlier, not all church-related institutions follow the same pattern. Mapping the spectrum of religiously affiliated schools, Douglas and Rhonda Hustedt Jacobsen distinguish between *homogeneous* and *one-party-rule* institutions. Though one-party-rule schools privilege a single religious tradition, they welcome others to the table. Adopting this approach, some Catholic and mainline Protestant institutions have become leaders in the interfaith movement. In 2010, Interfaith Youth Core was active on over thirty Catholic campuses. Welcoming a multifaith student body, DePaul University's Office of Religious Diversity strives to "create a genuine Spirit of Hospitality in all our services and encounters." Articulating a similar vision, Augustana College theologian Jason A. Mahn explained "why interfaith understanding is integral to the Lutheran tradition." At their best, notes Interfaith Youth Core's Eboo Patel, Lutheran colleges "bridge identity and diversity." As discussed in chapter 3, this tension is reflected in the hiring practices of mainline Protestant institutions. By contrast, many evangelical colleges restrict employment to fellow believers, emphasizing the benefits of shared religious commitments. Though several evangelical institutions have participated in interfaith programs, they must look beyond their own campuses for conversation partners.[21]

The same variations that occur among colleges can be found among campus religious organizations. Historically, most campus ministries have been led by students from their sponsoring religious bodies. Emphasizing religious homogeneity, groups like InterVarsity Christian Fellowship and Cru require leaders to adhere to an evangelical statement of faith, a practice they have followed for decades. While most universities allow student religious groups to choose their own leaders, policies vary. During the 2014–2015 academic year, the California State University network adopted an "all comers" policy. Evangelical groups that refused to abandon religious tests for leadership positions were no longer recognized by the Cal State system. Though this decision was later reversed, similar policies exist on some private college campuses.[22]

New immigrant religions have faced similar challenges. While some Hindu Students Councils have emphasized Hindu nationalism, this is beginning to change. According to the HSC's national website, the group is "open to anyone regardless of their religion, race, gender, sexual orientation or national origin," adding that chapter officers have included students from diverse ethnic backgrounds and at least one Buddhist. Along the same lines, a Cal State University Muslim Students' Association welcomes non-Muslim members. On some campuses, religious tests for leaders have created unlikely alliances between Muslims and evangelicals. At the Ohio State University, the Muslim Students' Association and several evangelical parachurch groups criticized a new non-discrimination policy that barred them from using religious criteria to select leaders and members. Challenged by a Christian-Muslim coalition, the university later reversed its decision. An unresolved issue in higher education, such policies continue to spark debate.[23]

So has Duke University's refusal to broadcast the Islamic call to prayer from its chapel bell tower. Responding to external criticism from conservative Protestants, including the evangelist Franklin Graham, Duke reversed an earlier decision to open the tower to Muslim students. By contrast, Syracuse University's decision to install *wudu* stations in Hendricks Chapel has "caused no stir," despite the fact they are intended for Muslim ritual washing. Articulating a "Wesleyan Praxis of Interreligious Engagement in Higher Education," Syracuse's chaplain has called for "rigorous engagement with religious pluralism." By both welcoming and excluding religious minorities, colleges and universities illustrate the strengths and weakness of the multifaith campus. In the words of the anthropologist Shabana Mir, "liberal pluralism in U.S. higher education both falters and succeeds."[24]

By representing distinctive religious traditions on particular campuses, student religious organizations have contributed to intellectual and cultural diversity. By increasing variety *among* American colleges, religious institutions have increased the institutional pluralism of American higher education. Noting the "role of private colleges and universities in sustaining religious traditions and communities," Wake Forest University president Nathan Hatch highlights their contribution to American society. According to Hatch, such institutions "can avoid two extremes—religious homogeneity or the relativism of the modern university."[25]

Reflecting deep divisions in American culture, such bridge building is not always possible. In today's polarized political environment, institutions frequently take sides. Such divisions could be seen in the opposing reactions to the Affordable Care Act of 2010. While many welcomed the new health care law, others raised concerns about its implications for religious institutions. Such conflicts came to a head when Secretary of Health and Human Services Kathleen Sebelius announced that the law would require many religious nonprofits to provide contraception coverage. Hailed by progressives as a victory for women's health, the contraception mandate provoked a backlash from administrators at some church-related institutions. Describing the requirement as a threat to religious freedom, several Catholic and evangelical schools, including the Catholic University of America and Wheaton College, sued the Obama administration. Responding to this litigation, the Obama administration developed new rules which permitted religious nonprofits to opt out of contraceptive coverage, while requiring insurance companies to provide free contraception. Though such compromises placated many critics of the law, some institutions remained dissatisfied. In 2017, the Trump administration announced plans to eliminate the contraception mandate.[26]

While Georgetown University did not fight the Affordable Care Act, it came under fire for inviting Secretary Sebelius to speak at its 2012 commencement. A practicing Catholic, Sebelius is an alumna of Trinity Washington University, a distinction she shares with House Minority Leader Nancy Pelosi. Praised by the Trinity alumni magazine, both women were criticized by conservative Catholics for their positions on abortion and contraception. In her speech, Sebelius observed that "[p]eople have deeply-held beliefs on all sides of these discussions," noting that "these debates can be contentious." Such divisions are not confined to social issues. The same year, a group of Georgetown faculty criticized Republican Paul Ryan for his "misuse of Catholic teaching." In a related controversy, a coalition of Catholic college professors blasted Catholic University for accepting a $1.75 million grant from the Charles Koch Foundation, noting the philanthropy's views "are in direct conflict with traditional Catholic values." Far from unified, religious colleges and universities have reflected wider tensions in American society.[27]

Religion and the Imagination: Engaging Art and Culture

Frustrated by these conflicts, some have turned from partisan politics to literature and the arts. Once a staff writer at William F. Buckley's *National Review*,

Gregory Wolfe burned his "draft card to the culture wars." A Roman Catholic who teaches at an evangelical university, Wolfe founded *Image* magazine in 1989. Dedicated to "spanning the gap" between faith and the imagination, the journal reflects Wolfe's belief that the "secular forms and innovations of a particular time can be assimilated into the larger vision of faith." In an era when artists often draw the ire of religious conservatives, *Image* gives them the benefit of the doubt. This was the case in the magazine's discussion of Chris Ofili, the creator of a Virgin Mary painting made out of elephant dung. Though many critics accused Ofili of blasphemy, an *Image* contributor praised his "serious, embodied spirituality." While acknowledging the painter's "apparent sacrilege," the magazine discussed "why an artist like Ofili is worth appreciating." Such small "c" catholicity reflects the journal's diverse constituency. Currently, the *Image* editorial board boasts such luminaries as Robert Coles, Mary Gordon, Kathleen Norris, and Richard Rodriguez. Housed at an evangelical institution, it bridges the worlds of religion and the arts.[28]

Far from unusual, such initiatives are becoming the public face of American religion. Sponsoring organ concerts, choral music, and liturgical dance, congregations foster artistic activity. The same is true in higher education.[29] Historically, the arts have mattered at church-related schools. Thanks to St. Olaf, Concordia, Augsburg, and Gustavus Adolphus colleges, Minnesota became known as "the land of ten thousand choirs." Across the United States, college and university chapels helped introduce the European liturgical movement to American Christians. While Valparaiso University experimented with modern architecture, Marcel Breuer's Abbey Church at St. John's University anticipated the reforms of the Second Vatican Council. St. John's was also the birthplace of Minnesota Public Radio. Created to "bring historic Benedictine culture to surrounding communities," KSJR broadcast Mozart to "Stearns County farmers as they went about milking the cows on dark winter mornings."[30]

Inspired by Paul Tillich's theology of culture, mainline Protestants vigorously engaged the postwar era's art worlds. Founded in 1961, the Society for the Arts, Religion and Contemporary Culture (ARC) attracted figures such as Robert Motherwell and W. H. Auden, as well as Museum of Modern Art director Alfred Barr Jr. Present in the seminaries and divinity schools, such currents also influenced mainline Protestant student groups. At the 1959 Convocation for Methodist youth, 6,000 young people took in performances by Dave Brubeck, Odetta, and New York's Mary Anthony Dancers. Mainline student publications also celebrated the imagination. Published by the Methodist Student Movement between 1941 and 1972, *motive* magazine reproduced images by Pablo Picasso, Edvard Munch, and Jacob Lawrence. Featuring fiction and poetry, social criticism, and the visual arts, it had a circulation of about

40,000. Reaching an even larger public, Flannery O'Connor, Thomas Merton, and Walker Percy led a renaissance in American Catholic literature. Educated in nonsectarian institutions, they often lectured on Catholic campuses.[31]

Looking back on that era, some dream of a new engagement between faith and culture. In an interview with *Commonweal* magazine, the poet Dana Gioia calls for "a recognizable Catholic element in the arts." A recipient of the University of Notre Dame's Laetare medal for service to church and society, he served as chairman of the National Endowment for the Arts from 2003 to 2009. Along the same lines, the organizers of an *Image* seminar on the arts envision a "healthier ecosystem for the creation of works that advance the true, the good, and the beautiful."[32]

If these efforts flourish, it will be because of organizations like Christians in the Visual Arts. Comprised of 1,000 members in twenty-eight countries, it has served as a clearinghouse for discussions of theology and art. Embracing a similar mission, Calvin College's Festival of Faith and Writing has provided a public venue for religious writers, drawing the attention of the *Christian Science Monitor* and the *Wall Street Journal*. In 2008, it attracted a crowd of 1,900 festivalgoers. Founded in 1990, it has hosted prominent speakers from outside the world of evangelical Protestantism, including George Saunders, Salman Rushdie, Michael Chabon, John Updike, Joyce Carol Oates, and Elie Wiesel.[33] Along the same lines, Baylor University sponsored a series of Art and Soul conferences featuring music, literature, theater, and the visual arts. Plenary speakers included *Publishers Weekly* religion editor Phyllis Tickle, Cambridge theologian Jeremy Begbie, and best-selling novelist John Grisham.[34]

Similar developments are taking place among Catholics and mainline Protestants. As the editor of *Image*, Gregory Wolfe has observed a "re-coalescing of Catholic writers and of Catholic artistic and literary cultures," citing figures such as Alice McDermott, Oscar Hijuelos, and Ron Hansen. Such writers are often found on college campuses, whether as visiting speakers or as faculty. While Vanderbilt Divinity School and Wesley Theological Seminary have established programs on religion and art, Yale's Institute of Sacred Music fosters "engagement with the sacred through music, worship, and the arts." Celebrating its fortieth anniversary in 2013, the Institute hired poet Christian Wiman as a senior lecturer in religion and literature. The former editor of *Poetry* magazine, he is one of America's leading poets. Eight years after being diagnosed with cancer, Wiman published *My Bright Abyss: Meditation of a Modern Believer* (2013). After immersing himself in the midcentury theology of Karl Barth, Paul Tillich, and Karl Rahner, he says "poets can learn from theologians and vice versa." Like Wiman, novelist Marilynne Robinson has wrestled with dead theologians. A self-described narrative Calvinist, she won the Pulitzer Prize for her 2004 novel *Gilead*. In 2015, she received the Religion and Arts Award from the American Academy of Religion. As a faculty member at the prestigious University of Iowa Writers' Workshop, Robinson often visits colleges she has never heard of before. Praising their contributions to the national culture, she notes, "You can go almost anywhere in America and find an interesting cultural life. Big or small, all these campuses are in effect Chautauquas. They bring in poets and lecturers, they offer musical performances and stage plays."[35]

Part of the "creative ecosystem" of American culture, colleges and universities have revitalized religion and the arts. At several church-related institutions, museums and galleries have provided a space for religious visual culture. Recently profiled by *Architectural Digest*, Saint Louis University's Museum of Art boasts a large collection of Jesuit pieces. Housed on the same campus, the Museum of Contemporary Religious Art has featured the *Papercut Haggadah* and Andy Warhol's *Silver Clouds*. In a similar way, Regis University's Faith and Art Program affirms the Jesuit conviction that "God is to be found in all things." While less developed than their Catholic counterparts, art and design programs are also proliferating in the member institutions of the Council for Christian Colleges and Universities. A 2010 report from the Christian in the Visual Arts identified eighty-eight art departments at CCCU institutions. Citing the "burgeoning number of artists, books, groups, galleries, and even church galleries," the report noted that this environment "simply did not exist sixty years ago." Across the country, the visual arts are expanding at Christian colleges, with eighty-five schools adding new degree programs within the past decade.[36]

Such initiatives would not exist without religious colleges. Campus art museums and literary festivals depend on the generosity of their home institutions. So do centers and institutes. While King College's Buechner Institute focuses on "the intersections—and collisions—between faith, art, and culture," Loyola University's Walker Percy Center honors a renowned Catholic novelist and former faculty member. Since 1974, Wheaton College's Marion E. Wade Center has introduced American evangelicals to the writings of C. S. Lewis and his fellow Inklings. Demonstrating a similar commitment to religion and literature, Georgetown's Faith and Culture lecture series has welcomed Alice McDermott, James Wood, Richard Rodriguez, and Martin Scorsese to the Jesuit campus. The series is coordinated by the writer Paul Elie, a former editor at Farrar, Straus and Giroux. Author of an acclaimed book on Dorothy Day, Thomas Merton, Flannery O'Connor, and Walker Percy, Elie also directs Georgetown's partnership with StoryCorps.[37]

Like their counterparts in church-related higher education, nonsectarian institutions are exploring the nexus between spirituality and the arts. Since 1996 Indiana University–Purdue University Indianapolis (IUPUI) has cosponsored the annual Spirit and Place Festival. Through concerts, exhibits, and public conversations, it has fostered "creative collaborations among the arts, humanities, and religion." Beginning with a panel discussion featuring John Updike, Kurt Vonnegut, and Dan Wakefield, the festival has become Indiana's largest civic gathering. Supported in part by Lilly Endowment, it was an offshoot of IUPUI's Project on Religion and Urban Culture. On a much smaller scale, USC's Office of Religious Life has used concerts, films, plays, and exhibits to examine the big questions. Bringing together scholars and practitioners, the Architecture, Culture, and Spirituality Forum draws its 450 members from all over the world. Since 2009 the Forum has met at a Benedictine retreat house, Harvard Divinity School, St. John's University, and the ancient Mayan site of Chichen Itza. Its sponsors include Harvard University, North Carolina State University, Texas A&M University, and the University of Minnesota.[38]

Across the United States, faculty have pioneered the study of religion and visual culture. Much of this research has been supported by the Henry Luce Foundation. Beginning in the nineties, Luce funded a number of initiatives on religion and the arts, exploring "what binds the arts and religion to each other, and what drives them apart." In a Lilly Endowment–funded project, sociologist Robert Wuthnow documented the diverse spiritual practices of Tony Kushner, Madeleine L'Engle, and Andres Serrano. Other scholars have recovered the religious dimensions of art history. Chronicling a "'return' of religion in the scholarship of American art," historian Sally Promey has been a key player in these discussions. Director of the Center for the Study of Material and Visual Cultures of Religion, she is a faculty member in Yale University's Institute of Sacred Music. Together with historians David Morgan and Colleen McDannell, Promey has brought the insights of cultural and social theory into the study of religious material culture. Focusing on critical scholarship rather than religious advocacy, such efforts have found a home in the American Academy of Religion. Currently, five AAR program units focus on art, literature, media, and visual culture. Founded in 2002, the Society for the Arts in Religious and Theological Studies combines confessional approaches with critical inquiry.[39]

Campus initiatives on religion and the arts have a modest impact on students. According to a recent survey, college-educated Americans favor more artistic activities in their churches. Compared to the graduates of flagship public universities, Lutheran college alumni recalled much higher rates of participation in music and theater during their undergraduate years. Graduates of Lutheran schools are also more likely to say that their colleges helped them develop an appreciation for the fine arts. The same is true at other religious institutions. In a 2006 survey, 58 percent of Catholic college alumni said their institutions were effective in helping them develop an appreciation for the arts. This compares with 45 percent of graduates from flagship public institutions.[40]

From Eero Saarinen's modernist MIT Chapel (dedicated in 1955) to Philip Johnson's postmodern Chapel of St. Basil (a 1997 structure at the University of St. Thomas), sacred architecture has long had a home in American higher education. Offering places "where an individual can contemplate things larger than himself" (Saarinen's description of his creation), such buildings are often the most visible meeting point for religion and the arts. While Brandeis University's three postwar chapels symbolized "tri-faith America," today's multifaith facilities at Penn State University and Wellesley College give shape and form to the new religious diversity. The commissioning of artistically compelling meditation spaces at dozens of institutions has also influenced campus spirituality. Yet this is not true everywhere. In an era when much of student religious life takes place away from formal chapels, they have sometimes been described as "white elephants on campus."[41]

Instead of sacred choral music, many of the largest student religious organizations promote the more commercial genre of praise and worship music. Rooted in the youth culture of evangelicalism, such music has transformed the sound of congregational worship in America. Some of the same campus religious groups maintain active arts ministries. Currently, InterVarsity's National Arts Ministry has a presence at several institutions, including the Manhattan School of Music and the School of the Art Institute of Chicago. In 2017, over 1,600 students took part in InterVarsity's arts chapters. In a similar way, Catholic campus ministries serve up "gourmet liturgy" that cannot be found in ordinary parishes. Whatever their impact, such ministries do not reach most students. Because only one-fourth of undergraduates participate in a student religious group, any exposure to religion and the arts is likely to come from outside the walls of the campus chapel.[42]

Sustaining the Ecology of Religious Intellectual Life

Rather than tracing a direct influence on aesthetic preferences, it is more helpful to consider the role of colleges and universities in sustaining the cultural ecology of public religious discourse. From publishing houses and periodicals to libraries and exhibitions, it is impossible to separate religious intellectual life from American higher education. Disseminating the work of academic theologians and philosophers, publishers like Harper and Brothers relied on an educated audience of religious laypersons. Paving the way for today's spiritual supermarket, Christian theology gradually gave way to alternative spirituality, as the religious book trade reached beyond its Protestant readership. Religious magazines were no less dependent on the college-educated middle class.

Central to the rise of mainline Protestantism, the *Christian Century* cultivated an educated readership. Emerging out of the same milieu as Drake University (a Disciples of Christ institution), the *Century* has maintained close ties to the University of Chicago Divinity School, most notably through the career of Martin Marty. Appealing to moderate-to-liberal Protestants, the magazine's circulation has long hovered around 35,000. Equally important to the subculture of liberal Catholicism, *Commonweal* magazine has recruited its best writers from Catholic colleges and universities. Recalling his student days at Chicago's Loyola University, journalist Peter Steinfels noted that "there was a whole series of conveyor belts for someone like me," adding that "I fell in with Catholic intellectuals and was conveyed to that network to work at *Commonweal*." In recent years, *Commonweal* has sponsored a college subscription program, enrolling over 1,500 undergraduate and graduate students. According to the magazine's website, 40 percent of subscribers began reading it in college, "by far the most significant source of future readers we have ever discovered."[43]

The Dutch Calvinist network around Calvin and Hope colleges has played a similar role in evangelical intellectual life. Through periodicals like *Perspectives* and the *Reformed Journal*, it has served as a training ground for conservative Protestant scholars, including Alvin Plantinga and Nicholas Wolterstorff. Emerging from the same ethno-religious subculture, book publishers Eerdmans, Zondervan, Kregel, and Baker have served an expanding market of Christian colleges and seminaries. Other publications have addressed the same audiences. Published between 1995 and 2016, the magazine *Books and Culture* nurtured faculty in both religious and nonsectarian institutions. Reflecting a high level of educational attainment, its 12,000 subscribers purchased an average of twenty-five books a year and read nearly fifteen hours per week. Founded in 1947, InterVarsity Press has published works by N. T. Wright, John Stott, and Mark Noll. Along with its British counterpart, it has revitalized the intellectual life of Anglo-American evangelicalism. Uniting book culture and campus religion, InterVarsity's publishing activities recall the heyday of the British Student Christian Movement Press. As early as 1952, IVP was selling 178,000 books and booklets per year. Today it is 2.3 million.[44]

In a similar way, religious minorities and new immigrants have nurtured the cultural and intellectual life of their communities. Founded in 1974 by an exiled Tibetan monk, Naropa University has attracted a diverse faculty and student body. Drawing on the Buddhist strains in the American Beat movement, the university has established the Jack Kerouac School of Disembodied Poetics and the Allen Ginsberg Visiting Fellowship in poetry. Recognizing a "poet that changed America," Naropa's library is named after Ginsberg, who taught at the institution from 1974 to 1996. Along with Ginsberg, the school has welcomed composer John Cage and writer bell hooks. In the words of its president, Naropa sits "at the confluence of two rivers: one river flowing out of classical India and the Buddha's contemplative experience" and another reflecting the "liberal arts tradition that originated, almost at the same time, in the Mediterranean."[45]

Slowly but surely, American Muslims are also creating their own cultural institutions. In particular, the Muslim Students' Association has served as an organizational incubator. Founded in 1963, it has given birth to the Islamic Book Service (1966), the Islamic Medical Association of North America (1967), the Association of Muslim Scientists and Engineers (1969), and the Association of Muslim Social Scientists of North America (established in 1972, it is now known as the North American Association of Islamic and Muslim Studies). In 1982, the MSA helped start the Islamic Society of North America, an umbrella association for most of the major Muslim associations in America. At the time, the MSA was the largest American Muslim organization. Since then Muslims have built a thriving organizational infrastructure, leading Georgetown University Islam specialist Osman Bakar to predict "the possible emergence of the United States in the next few decades as the most creative and productive center of Islamic intellectual life in the world." Seeking to become a Muslim Georgetown or Notre Dame, Zaytuna College is the first accredited Muslim liberal arts institution in America. Embracing a great books approach, its has adapted Islam to American culture. Like most religious colleges, it serves as a bridge between a particular community and the wider academic world. According to interfaith activist Eboo Patel, Zaytuna is "led by some of the preeminent Muslim intellectuals in America." In 2017, the college founded the journal *Renovatio*, a publication "drawing from the enduring texts of revelatory faith traditions and current thinking."[46]

Such close connections between religious intellectual life and higher education are not limited to religiously affiliated institutions. As sociologist Charles Kadushin wrote in *The American Intellectual Elite* (1974), the university is "the first gatekeeper to the intellectual community." Surveying a sample of leading intellectuals, Kadushin found that about 40 percent worked in the academic professoriate. Though the intellectual elite included plenty of academics, publications such as *Commentary* and *Dissent* drew from a wider community of writers and social critics. These circles were especially significant in the development of American Jewish intellectual life. Like the sociologist Daniel Bell, many Jewish scholars began their careers outside academia. Once a journalist for Henry Luce's *Fortune*, Bell went on to teach at Columbia and Harvard. With the growth of Jewish studies programs, today's informal Jewish intellectual life is even more connected to American higher education. Mapping the ecology of Jewish organizations in the San Francisco Bay Area, a recent study explored the role of museums, libraries, synagogues, and community centers in "the production of Jewish art and culture." Along with Hillel and Chabad, the report cited the presence of Jewish studies programs and Holocaust centers at California's universities. Drawing on a national network of Jewish academics, the editorial board of the *Jewish Review of Books* includes the scholars Robert Alter, Jon Levenson, Michael Walzer, and Ruth Wisse. Edited by Oberlin College professor Abraham Socher, it is a leading platform for Jewish intellectual life. To be sure, there are hundreds of Jewish cultural organizations outside of the academy. In New York City, for example, the 92nd Street Y remains a high-profile venue, welcoming over 300,000 people to its public events. Yet without the presence of college and university professors, its programming would be very different.[47]

Besides fostering thoughtful reflection on religious topics, colleges and universities have improved media coverage of religion. Through programs sponsored by the Pew Charitable Trusts and Lilly Endowment, journalists have gathered for seminars with leading scholars of religion. Housed in the University of Missouri's School of Journalism, the Religion News Association creates tools for reporters, including a religion stylebook and an online guide to topics and sources. Such projects have put journalists in touch with experts in religious studies.[48]

Reflecting changes in technology, much of the discourse about religion and current affairs has moved into cyberspace. A 2010 study commissioned by the Social Science Research Council identified nearly one hundred websites focused on religion and the public sphere, concluding that "blogs have created a new kind of public intellectual." In 2011, the SSRC received a $300,000 grant from the Henry Luce Foundation to support its Project on Religion, Media, and Digitization. Another SSRC report found that digital initiatives are bridging the gap between scholars and the general public. Like the little magazines of the past, they could not survive without faculty. Adapting their scholarship for the Internet age, they have taken religious intellectual life to new audiences.[49]

Conclusion

From civic engagement and foreign policy to literary fiction and the visual arts, the return of religion in higher education has had significant implications for American public life. Responding to the resurgence of politicized religion, the academy has influenced the national conversation. Exposing American citizens to the world's religions, it has increased the religious literacy of college graduates. Fostering the creative imagination, it has provided an institutional home for novelists, poets, and artists. Energized by big debates in little magazines, it has strengthened the ecology of religious intellectual life.

To be sure, it is difficult to quantify the influence of religious higher education on the public sphere. While the Pew study on religious literacy has documented the impact of university religion courses, more research needs to be done in this area. The same goes for research on tolerance for diversity and the outcomes of church-related higher education. Though Lutheran college graduates are more engaged with the arts, it is impossible to prove a causal link between religious higher education and artistic involvement. Despite these challenges, we can say some things about campus religion and public life. First, some of the most significant ventures on religion and art can be found in the academy. Second, most religious magazines of ideas rely on the contributions of college professors. Third, the university is one of the few American institutions where secular and religious voices can engage in civil conversation about religion and public life. Representing the full range of American religious groups, the campus is a haven for religious diversity.[50]

In each of these domains—politics, art, and ideas—organizations in higher education have formed partnerships with institutions outside the university's gates. Far from monolithic, these partnerships have varied enormously. While some have promoted interfaith dialogue and religious tolerance, others have provoked cultural conflict and political polarization. Still others have emphasized the importance of music and visual culture, blending religion and the creative arts. Like the teaching and the practice of religion on campus, they cannot be reduced to a single pattern. Reaching beyond the ivory tower, such partnerships have connected campus religion with the American public square.

6

THE FUTURE OF RELIGION IN HIGHER EDUCATION

The past thirty years have witnessed a comeback of religion in higher education. From public universities to elite liberal arts colleges, scholars have rediscovered the sacred. While church-related institutions have strengthened their religious identities, campus ministries have flourished in a pluralistic spiritual marketplace.

Once relegated to the margins of scholarship, the academic study of religion is taken seriously in many disciplines. While the philosophy of religion has experienced a modest revival, religious history is now the most popular specialization in the American Historical Association. In several social science disciplines, new sections on religion have institutionalized growing subfields. Similar developments can be seen in social work and medicine. Promoting interdisciplinary reflection, centers and institutes have initiated university-wide conversations about the sacred. In a more normative vein, religious scholarly societies have fostered the integration of faith and learning, while leading higher education researchers have emphasized the importance of spirituality. From social scientific inquiry to overtly confessional approaches, the return of religion has taken many forms.[1]

Safeguarding the future of religious higher education, church-related colleges have experienced renewal. In the 1990s, works on religious colleges warned of weakening denominational ties and impending secularization. Countering these trends, foundation-sponsored initiatives have focused renewed attention on institutional religious affiliation. Through faculty mentoring programs and networks of colleges, a host of new organizations have sustained a national conversation about the future of church-related higher education. While colleges and universities have strengthened their denominational ties, denominations have reaffirmed the importance of religious higher education. Fostering theological reflection and vocational discernment, unprecedented philanthropic initiatives have focused on faith and work, pouring hundreds of millions of dollars into the church-related sector. Reaching a wide swath of religiously affiliated institutions, such programs have raised the profile of religion on campus.[2]

The same is true of student religious life. From the growth of evangelical parachurch groups to the rise of Muslim Students' Associations, universities have offered a wealth of religious options. Campus Jewish organizations, Hindu student groups, and Eastern Orthodox Christian fellowships are all experiencing renewal. Once a predictor of disaffiliation, college attendance is now associated with higher rates of religiosity. A laboratory for religious pluralism, the student union has reflected the diversity of American religions. Managing this diversity, student affairs professionals have adopted a more holistic understanding of student development. Constructing multifaith worship spaces and meditation rooms, they have welcomed a wide range of student groups. Far from secular, higher education has become a place of religious discovery for many.[3]

In all three areas—academic scholarship, church-related higher education, and student life—religion has enjoyed a comeback. In each case, it was facilitated by private philanthropy, campus organizations and networks, and the return of religion in public life.

Despite the success of religion's comeback, its future—like the future of the wider academy—remains uncertain. Benefiting from a red-hot stock market, the teaching and the practice of religion grew during a period of relative prosperity. From the late 1980s to the early 2000s, the American economy expanded at a steady pace, feeding philanthropic coffers and university endowments. Briefly interrupted by the recession of 2001–2002, the bull market underwrote a host of new initiatives. From religion-oriented centers and institutes to faculty mentoring programs, many were dependent on foundation support. Underwriting an overlapping set of organizations and networks, religious philanthropy peaked between 1999 and 2003.[4] Everything changed in 2008, when the United States entered the worst economic downturn since the Great Depression. Several years into a sluggish recovery, the economy remains uneven. Undermining foundation support for religious colleges and universities, the volatility of the stock market has not been good for American philanthropy. The economy has also threatened college and university budgets, weakening both enrollment and fundraising. Relying on the contributions of cash-strapped individuals and denominations, student religious groups have found it harder to raise money. Taken together, these developments raise serious questions about the sustainability of religious initiatives in higher education.

Even before the recession, religious philanthropy was in flux. Between 2000 and 2005, the Pew Charitable Trusts cut its support for religion programs by 90 percent. Like the abandonment of campus religion by the Danforth and Rockefeller foundations, Pew's change of direction has removed a key source of funding.[5] Though Lilly Endowment has continued to fund in this area, it has reduced its support. In 2016, Lilly's Religion Division awarded $114 million in grants, less than half the amount in 2002, a banner year for religious philanthropy. In a similar way, Jewish nonprofits have suffered financial constraints, creating uncertainty for campus religious groups and Jewish studies programs. Likewise, the recession hurt the finances of American denominations, compounding the damage caused by shrinking membership rolls. At the state and local level, such deficits have translated into less money for campus ministries and church-related colleges.[6]

Like American denominations, religious colleges and universities have faced significant financial pressures. While larger schools have remained intact, they have adjusted their expectations. At Baylor University, a Texas-sized strategic plan was scaled back.[7] The bad economy exacted a heavier toll on smaller institutions. Once dubbed the "invisible colleges," schools with limited endowments are often rural and church-related. Some did not survive the recession. Recently, the Evangelical Lutheran Church in America lost two of its twenty-nine colleges. In 2009, the century-old Waldorf College went for-profit, cutting its ties with the ELCA. Founded in 1884 by Danish immigrants, Dana College closed its doors in 2010. Most recently, Roman Catholic Marian Court College in Massachusetts ended its fifty-year run as a liberal arts college, citing "insurmountable financial challenges." From historically black institutions to evangelical colleges, others have encountered similar challenges.[8]

Slashed during the economic downturn, state higher education funding has not returned to prerecession levels. In many public universities, budget cuts pose a serious threat to the academic study of religion. In 2009, the *Religious Studies News* profiled two public university programs that narrowly escaped the scalpel. At Florida International University, a $100,000 donation from the Dalai Lama helped save the religious studies department. Not all schools were so fortunate. At Miami University of Ohio, the MA program in Comparative Religion lost its teaching assistants. At Arizona State University, religious studies merged with two other departments, while the University of California eliminated its major. Such reductions have influenced the job market. According to the American Academy of Religion and the Society of Biblical Literature, the number of open religion positions declined by 46 percent in 2009, following a period of steady hiring. While the hiring situation improved in 2010, the number of religion listings was lower than in 2001. Religion scholars in other disciplines face similar challenges. Out of 536 openings in sociology, only 4 called for a specialist in religion.[9]

Transcending budgets and the bottom line, the Great Recession revealed a set of deeper challenges. Whether bowling alone or socializing online, Americans are reevaluating their commitment to many cultural and social institutions. Long part of the social fabric, newspapers and bookstores are weathering tough times. While symphony orchestras are experiencing an economic crisis, the weekly newsmagazine is disappearing from supermarket shelves. In the age of the Internet, many Americans are withdrawing from face-to-face groups. In each of these cases, critics have called attention to new economic realities, urging cultural institutions to change or die.[10] As in the 1930s, America may be facing a "religious depression." Church attendance has "softened" as the percentage of Americans with no religion (the so-called "nones") has grown. While religious giving has plateaued, church construction is at a fifty-year low. In sharp contrast to a few years ago, most Americans believe that religion is losing ground.[11]

Many have questioned the future of both religion *and* higher education. At a time when the secularization of higher education storyline has been seriously challenged, two new declension narratives have taken its place. Each has implications for religion on campus. While one announces the *end of the university*, the second describes the *decline of American religion*. A third narrative points to the *globalization of religious higher education*, arguing that the future of campus religion may be in the non-Western world. Seeing immigration as the answer to both softening church attendance and declining enrollments, this storyline argues that globalization could revitalize both American religion and higher education. This chapter considers each of these potential futures, beginning with the first declension narrative on the end of the university.[12]

The End of the University

Despite past difficulties, the university has rarely contemplated its own demise. While the history of higher education is filled with defunct colleges, few have predicted the disruption of hundreds of institutions. As gloomy as that sounds, that is exactly what some are forecasting. In 2015, a trio of books proclaimed the "end of college," the "crisis" of American universities, and the "great unbundling of higher education." Heralding the power of creative destruction, Harvard Business School professor Clayton Christensen predicted that half of all universities will go bankrupt within fifteen years. In Christensen's account of "disruptive innovation," technological and organizational change will radically reshape higher education. Others have advanced a similar vision of the future. Three months after *Time* magazine declared, "College is dead. Long live college!" the *New Criterion* published "Higher Ed: An Obituary." Equally pessimistic, Columbia University's *Hechinger Report* warned that "some U.S. universities and colleges may be going the way of the music and journalism industries."[13]

Diagnoses vary, but most observers agree that higher education faces a host of fiscal challenges. Since the late 1970s, the cost of a college education has increased by 1,120 percent. Decades of state budget cuts and spiraling costs have led public universities to rely more on tuition. While state funding decreased 21 percent between 2000–2001 and 2010–2011, tuition increased by 45 percent. Rising expenses have posed even more of a challenge for private colleges and universities. Exacerbating these pressures, many analysts expect the number of undergraduates to decline over the next decade. In 2013 almost 50 percent of schools anticipated a drop in full-time enrollment. Five years later, the outlook remains negative.[14]

Some observers have singled out the humanities for special scrutiny, adopting the rhetoric of declension. While *New York Times* columnist Verlyn Klinkenborg chronicled the "decline and fall of the English major," the *Wall Street Journal* asked, "Are humanities degrees doomed?" In recent years, the "crisis in the humanities" has elicited a great deal of commentary, spawning blue-ribbon reports from Harvard University and the American Academy of Arts and Sciences. Commenting on the AAAS report, *New York Times* columnist David Brooks argued that the humanities are "committing suicide" by thinking "less about the old notions of truth, beauty and goodness." Others have identified different culprits. Pointing to the defunding of the liberal arts, Columbia University historian Alan Brinkley cited a "dangerous decline in both absolute and relative support for research across most areas of humanistic scholarship."[15]

Appropriating the rhetoric of neoliberalism, many critics of higher education have emphasized economic efficiency, market-driven reforms, and new technologies. Comparing universities to newspapers, bookstores, and the music industry, they argue that disruptive innovation will radically reshape higher education. Such views are promoted by think tanks and political interest groups. Arguing that colleges and universities are ripe for restructuring, they question traditional models of higher education. By reaching more students at a lower cost, so the argument goes, American higher education can improve college access and reduce government spending. Dispensing with student affairs programs and intercollegiate athletics, they argue that schools should unbundle academics from campus life. While some push online courses, a growing number tout smaller-scale experiments with technology. Still others stress practical job skills and the STEM disciplines over the liberal arts.[16]

These claims are especially popular on the right. According to conservative publisher Steve Forbes, "The Internet is about to do to America's universities and colleges what it's done to media and entertainment—profoundly upend them."[17] Questioning the value of a liberal arts education, former secretary of education William Bennett denigrates the humanities, calling them dead-end majors (including his own discipline of philosophy).[18] Privileging "degrees where people can get jobs," Florida governor Rick Scott proposes cutting the social sciences, questioning whether it is a "vital interest of the state to have more anthropologists."[19] In light of such critiques, some have concluded that "conservatives killed the liberal arts." In reality, the situation is far more complex. While later apologizing for his remarks, President Barack Obama has made similar claims, noting that "folks can make a lot more, potentially, with skilled manufacturing or the trades than they might with an art history degree." He has also called for "more online learning," arguing that technology can "reduce the overall cost of higher education." While some Republicans have defended the liberal arts, prominent Democrats have jumped on the disruptive innovation bandwagon. Emphasizing technological solutions and market-driven approaches, these proposals are best thought of as neoliberal rather than conservative or progressive.[20]

If implemented, such approaches could have serious consequences for religion in American higher education. With some notable exceptions, major online vendors have ignored religious studies and the academic study of religion, focusing on business, education, and the health professions. They have also ignored extracurricular life. By decoupling academic coursework from undergraduate culture, online education could leave student religion without an institutional home. Outside of brick-and-mortar institutions, it is difficult to envision a place for campus ministries and student religious organizations. It is also hard to imagine a cohesive campus community.[21]

By denigrating the humanities and social sciences, the critics of higher education have targeted the very disciplines where religion matters. Following the Great Recession, religious studies has regularly appeared on lists of the ten worst college majors, while articles on college-educated baristas have painted a negative picture of the liberal arts. If the past few years are any guide, such critiques are having an effect. Between 2011 and 2014, the number of religious studies graduates declined by 6.8 percent, the largest drop in twenty-eight years. During the same period, the share of bachelor's degrees awarded to humanities majors dropped to 6.1 percent, the lowest since 1948. At a time when parents warn their children not to major in English, postrecession economic pressures are influencing student choices. Such pressures also shape the funding decisions of universities, making it harder for humanities and social sciences departments to defend their budgets.[22]

Small, religiously affiliated institutions are especially vulnerable to market forces. A 2015 survey found that 38 percent of baccalaureate private college business officers believe their institutions may eventually have to close. According to Moody's, "Smaller, tuition dependent universities with lower credit ratings are most vulnerable to revenue and pricing pressures." Analyzing the recent closure of fourteen church-related institutions, a Vanderbilt University study notes that religious affiliation is now a risk factor for American colleges. Many church-related schools have encountered serious financial challenges. In 2013, one-third of the Council for Christian College and University's schools fell into Bain and Company's "financially unsustainable" category, while another third were "at risk." Though no one has compiled a similar breakdown of mainline Protestant and Catholic institutions, several earned a "D" from a *Forbes* magazine analysis of college finances. Some anticipate a shakeout. Noting that "our model of student development requires significant expenditures on residence halls, and athletic fields, and food services, and a chapel, and staff for all of them," St. Olaf College president David Anderson acknowledged that "[t]here will be fewer institutions like ours."[23]

Taken together, such assessments paint a bleak picture of American higher education. From the crisis in the humanities to the finances of liberal arts colleges, the future looks increasingly grim. According to some observers, "a 'perfect storm' is enveloping higher education," one that could radically transform the university. Widely reported in the press, such pronouncements are quickly becoming the new conventional wisdom.[24]

While some accept these tales of doom and gloom, others are not so sure. Launching a broader Campaign for the Liberal Arts, the Council of Independent Colleges has defended the value of small classes, cocurricular experiences, and face-to-face communities. Founded in 1956, the organization represents over 700 midsized private liberal arts colleges and universities, including many church-related institutions. Marshalling data and personal stories, the Council hopes to "dispel persistent and false stereotypes about independent colleges." Using the fictional characters Libby and Art, the Council has posted thousands of tweets on topics ranging from student debt ("Myths and Facts") to the future earnings of liberal arts graduates. According to Libby and Art, "#LiberalArts learning is more practical than training in a specific skill that may well be obsolete almost upon graduation." Such claims are backed up by a survey commissioned by the Association of American Colleges and Universities. Conducted by

Hart Research Associates, it found that 55 percent of employers value learning "about global cultures, histories, values, religions, and social systems."[25]

Taking a closer look at the facts, many argue the liberal arts disciplines are holding their own. Listening to the declension narratives, one would never guess that the percentage of humanities majors rose in the eighties and nineties. As historian David Silbey notes in the *Chronicle of Higher Education*, the data "don't support the stories we want to tell about marginalization or declension." This is also true in philosophy and religious studies, fields that grew at a faster pace than the rest of the university. As noted in chapter 2, the number of philosophy and religious studies graduates increased by 75 percent between 1991 and 2011, growing faster than the number of graduates in computer science, engineering, mathematics, and other STEM disciplines. Despite recent challenges, there were still more religion degrees awarded in 2014 than in 1987. Far from unemployable, humanities and social sciences graduates command respectable midcareer salaries (an average of $66,185 at age 56–60), outearning many professional and preprofessional majors. Humanities majors also report a greater sense of personal satisfaction. According to PayScale, 59 percent of religious studies graduates said their current job "makes the world a better place." While it is fashionable to lament the decline of the liberal arts, such rhetoric does not always fit the facts. This is especially true in the humanities, where talk of crisis often descends into hyperbole.[26]

Hyperbole also distorts discussions of new technologies. While 30 percent of college students study online, only 14 percent restrict themselves to Internet courses. At a time when boosters present online education as all but inevitable, a small number of schools dominate the field. In the Fall of 2015, 5 percent of institutions enrolled about half of all online students. At most universities, skepticism continues to prevail. While only 13 percent of college presidents believe that Massive Open Online Courses (MOOCs) will "improve the learning of all students," just 11 percent see them as a solution to higher education's financial difficulties. Many educators are more critical, denouncing the "MOOCs delusion" and the "unsustainable gimmick" of free online classes. Still others question the rhetoric of disruption, calling it "the most pernicious cliché of our time." Defending the value of face-to-face mentoring, Trinity Washington University president Patricia McGuire challenges the claims of online boosters, noting there is "an awful lot of hype about disruption and the need for reinvention that is being fomented by people who are going to make out like bandits on it."[27]

Taking this argument a step further, others emphasize the benefits of physical copresence. Such arguments resonate with faculty at religious colleges and universities. Criticizing "overconfident prophecies that 'the residential college will become largely obsolete'," Wheaton College art professor Matthew Milliner notes that "college students, most reports seem to indicate, are as yet embodied creatures—and where they study matters at least as much as what." Valparaiso University architectural historian Gretchen Buggeln concurs, emphasizing the importance of "campus places and placemaking."[28]

In spite of these critiques, online education continues to gain ground. Documenting this growth, a 2017 *Chronicle of Higher Education* survey found that 98 percent of public and 89 percent of private institutions offer Internet courses, suggesting that online learning has "reached a tipping point in higher education." Embracing this trend, many religion programs have experimented with online modalities. Offered in the Spring 2014 semester, edX's course on early Christianity and the letters of Paul became a runaway success. Taught by Harvard professor Laura Nasrallah, it had an online enrollment of 22,000 during the first week. Attracting students from 180 countries, it was dubbed the "world's largest Bible class." Building on this success, edX and Harvard have established a six-course series exploring "world religions through their scriptures."[29] A leader in Internet education, Arizona State University offers an online religious studies major. Designed to expand the university's student body (which includes hundreds of Starbucks employees), it has many of the same courses that are taught on campus. Along the same lines, the *Religious Studies News* published a special section on Internet courses, noting that "online education's moment has arrived."[30]

Some of the biggest online programs can be found at conservative Protestant schools. In 2015, for-profit Grand Canyon University had an enrollment of 69,000 (54,000 online), thanks in part to a president recruited from the University of Phoenix. According to GCU investor Michael Clifford, "The only thing that is going to save Christian colleges is a robust online operation." While many evangelical educators would disagree, others have followed a similar playbook. Founded in 1971 by the Reverend Jerry Falwell, Liberty University enrolled 80,000 students in 2015 (72,000 online), making it the largest private nonprofit university in North America. According to Religion News Service, such classes are largely responsible for Liberty's $1 billion endowment, providing over 60 percent of the university's income. Between 2001 and 2011, total enrollment at Liberty grew by 940 percent. Reflecting this online presence, Liberty was the only church-related school to appear on Google's list of the top twenty most searched universities, joining the University of Phoenix, Stanford, Cambridge, and the University of Mumbai. Describing an "online kingdom come," the *Chronicle of Higher Education* called Liberty "an unexpected model for the future of higher education." The university is also a national leader in graduate student loan debt. In 2013–2014, the government awarded $800 million in federal aid to Liberty's students, much of it student loans.[31]

Elsewhere in evangelical higher education, Indiana Wesleyan University has generated large enrollments, attracting 10,000 students to its nonresidential courses. With a 2017 student body of 13,850, it is the largest member of the Council for Christian Colleges and Universities. Such numbers have attracted the attention of America's leading consulting firm, which highlighted the "strategies of highly productive higher-education institutions" in 2010. Commissioned by the Bill and Melinda Gates Foundation, the report also discussed the growth of Brigham Young University–Idaho. With a 2015 enrollment of 43,000 (33,000 online), BYU-Idaho has reinvented Mormon higher education, adopting a host of cost-saving reforms, including the elimination of intercollegiate athletics. Led by former Harvard Business School dean Kim Clark, the university combines a strong commitment to religious identity with a focus on undergraduate education.[32]

Like their evangelical counterparts, some mainline Protestant schools are embracing the rhetoric of disruption. Praising "traditioned innovation," Duke Divinity School theologian L. Gregory Jones urges religious institutions to "explore risk-taking mission and service." Along the same lines, a group of Lutheran colleges has participated in Project DAVID. Focusing on Distinction, Analytics, Value, Innovation, and Digital Opportunities, this initiative is a "call for reinvention at Lutheran (and similar) colleges and universities." Emphasizing Lutheran identity *and* pedagogical innovation, the project encourages institutions to "leverage cloud technologies and social media." Several United Methodist institutions are also experimenting with new technologies. In recent years, Baker University, Hendrix College, and Texas Wesleyan University have developed an Internet presence. By 2012 a majority of Baker's 2,100 undergraduates were enrolled online.[33]

While conventional online classes are relatively common at small liberal arts colleges, only a handful of church-related institutions offer bona fide MOOCs, including Georgetown University, the University of Notre Dame, and Davidson College. As three of the best-endowed religiously affiliated schools in the country, they have the resources to experiment with online education. While Georgetown's bioethics course explores morality in health care, Davidson's "Introduction to Philosophy: God, Knowledge, and Consciousness" was one of the first religion-oriented courses in the MOOC universe.[34]

Combining social justice with distance education, the world's Jesuit universities have developed an online resource of their own. Dubbed Jesuit Worldwide Learning, it has provided online course content to refugee camps in Malawi Kenya, and Jordan. Focusing on the poor and powerless, it reaches one of the world's most vulnerable populations. Funded entirely by Jesuit institutions and their partners, it educates people who cannot afford a college degree. Founded in 2010, the project draws on a global network of colleges and universities.[35]

In the end, debates about online courses raise larger questions about the purposes of higher education. Many advocates of new technologies are skeptical of the liberal arts. Others want to remake colleges and universities in the image of American corporations. Chronicling the rise of the "corporate university," sociologist Gaye Tuchman writes that "higher education is turning from the fields that ask who we are as a society and from the disciplines that nourish the soul." Embracing a neoliberal emphasis on pragmatic job skills and workplace readiness, today's reformers have privileged STEM disciplines over the humanities and social sciences. Instead of serving as a "hedge against utilitarian values" (Andrew Delbanco's phrase), many universities have adopted the rhetoric of big business. Criticizing these developments, Harvard University historian Jill Lepore argues that "[f]aith in disruption is the best illustration, and the worst case, of a larger historical transformation having to do with secularization, and what happens when the invisible hand replaces the hand of God as explanation and justification." From health care to higher education, the rhetoric of disruption is being applied to "arenas whose values and goals are remote from the values and goals of business." Living in the tension between corporatization and liberal learning, colleges and universities must negotiate between competing visions of the future.[36]

The Decline of American Religion

Like higher education, American religion is facing new challenges. It was not always so. Throughout the 1980s and 1990s, attendance at religious services remained remarkably stable, as did belief in the importance of religion. While evangelicals enjoyed steady growth, new immigrants were transforming the religious landscape. When asked about the influence of religion on American life, a majority of respondents replied that it was increasing, a percentage that soared in the months following September 11, 2001. In light of such statistics, it was easy to believe that religion mattered.[37]

Much has changed in the past decade. Despite relatively high levels of religiosity, attendance at religious services has softened. While the Christian share of the U.S. population has declined, the percentage of Americans identifying with no religion has risen to 23 percent. In the most recent Pew religious landscape survey, 36 percent of younger millennials identified with no religion.[38]

The growth of the "nones" has led some to proclaim the "end of religion as we know it," urging scholars to "[f]orget churches; forget priests and pastors; forget the Bible; forget organized religion generally." A reversal of the "churching of America," it suggests that the United States may follow the path of Western Europe. Several other indicators point in the same direction. Once a sign of vitality, conservative churches have stopped growing. Though most evangelical denominations are holding their own, some have begun a slow decline. At the same time that confidence in religious institutions has plummeted, 77 percent of Americans believe that religion is losing its influence, a conviction shared by many scholars. Summarizing these trends, sociologist Mark Chaves notes that "every indicator of traditional religiosity is either stable or declining."[39]

Far from inconsequential, such developments have broad implications for religion on campus. If the growth of religious studies was a function of student interest, it is possible that the decline of American religion could lead to smaller classes and shrinking departments. In a country where religion is losing its influence, the sacred may lose its academic luster. Coupled with growing doubts about the humanities, the secularization of American culture could pose real problems for the academic study of religion. The same is true for student religious groups. At a time when more and more students identify as "nones," campus ministries must work harder to attract new members. Church-related colleges and universities may be particularly vulnerable to the decline of institutional religion. In a society where denominational brand names are no longer meaningful, it will be difficult to sustain distinctively Lutheran and Presbyterian colleges. Even more so than in the past, the incentive will be to play down signs of overt religious affiliation in order to appeal to a wider applicant pool. The result may be further secularization and the demise of the church-related college.

So far such things have not come to pass. Though the recent recession proved difficult for many departments, religious studies enrollment is higher than it was before the rise of the "nones." Far from depressing student interest, there are strong indications that a religiously diverse student body may actively seek out such courses. Shaped by a hermeneutic of suspicion, campus freethinkers and skeptics have embraced the critical study of religion. In a similar way, spiritual seekers have gravitated to courses in world religions and new religious movements. Fueling this interest, the growth of religious studies has contributed to the emergence of new spiritualties. At a time when Barnes and Noble and Amazon have served as spiritual supermarkets, colleges and universities have helped students negotiate the shifting religious landscape. Experimenting with new curricular offerings, religious studies departments have helped students explore the religious meanings of popular culture and alternative spiritualities. The same experimental attitude has fostered the growth of a pluralistic student religious marketplace.[40]

The language of spirituality can also be found among the "nones." Though only 18 percent think of themselves as religious persons, 37 percent identify as spiritual. Embracing a wide range of alternative beliefs and practices, 30 percent believe that "spiritual energy is located in physical things such as mountains, trees, and crystals"; one-fourth believe in reincarnation; and 28 percent view yoga as a spiritual practice. While 40 percent pray at least monthly, 68 percent believe in God or a universal spirit.[41]

Far from a "zero-sum proposition," the relationship between religion and spirituality is complex and multidimensional. Surveys find that most Americans identify as both religious *and* spiritual.[42] Though often portrayed as anti-institutional, these emerging forms of spirituality are embedded in a dense network of organizations and groups, including religious congregations. Many of these institutional sites intersect with American higher education. In Cambridge, Massachusetts, there are multiple connections between Harvard University and the purveyors of alternative spirituality. From the nineteenth century to the new millennium, America's most prestigious university has played a key role in producing the spiritual. In the same institution where William James and the nineteenth-century Metaphysical Club explored the "varieties of religious experience," Harvey Cox and the Harvard Psychedelic Club fed off the spiritual energy of the 1960s, experimenting with LSD. More recently, Cambridge has played host to mind-body medicine and spiritual arts groups.[43]

The same mix of identities and practices can be found on other American campuses. Increasingly diverse, undergraduates embrace a wide range of spiritual and religious identities. According to a 2013 survey of 38 institutions, college students identify with three distinct categories: religious (32 percent), spiritual (32 percent), and secular (28 percent). Students with spiritual identities are especially prevalent in the humanities and social sciences. Far from secular, many spiritual-but-not-religious students affirm the reality of miracles (55 percent), life after death (45 percent), ghosts and spirits (44 percent), and karma (38 percent). While 43 percent believe in the efficacy of prayer, 20 percent affirm the reality of faith healing. Such findings are consistent with other studies of undergraduate spirituality, including those documenting the growth of the "nones." In the 2016 edition of UCLA's annual American Freshman Survey, 31 percent of students identified with no religious preference (up from 15.4 percent in 1971). According to UCLA, "self-rated spirituality" has also declined since the 1990s. It is important to note that the American Freshman Survey is administered in the first semester of college. Any drop in religious and spiritual identification is likely due to the changing backgrounds of freshmen, not the undergraduate experience. As noted in chapter 4, a more comprehensive UCLA survey found that most students reported an increased interest in spirituality *during* their college years. The same study found that 80 percent of college students had an "interest in spirituality."[44]

Instead of depressing student interest, the growth of the "nones" may actually heighten undergraduate demand for campus religion. While nonreligious students embrace the critical investigation of religion, spiritual seekers make religious studies part of their personal quests. This is especially true at church-related colleges and universities. Increasingly diverse, Catholic higher education is attracting more non-Catholic students. In a time of spiritual experimentation, schools that address the big questions will continue to remain relevant. Whether spiritual, religious, or secular, college students live in a world where differences matter. Such diversity is often the *raison d'être* of religious studies. By helping America deal with cultural differences, the academic study of religion has demonstrated its relevance. Whether or not Americans go to church, they often retain an interest in religion and spirituality.[45]

The Globalization of Religious Higher Education

Of course, America is not the world. Neither is Western Europe. Not surprisingly, the future of religion looks quite different outside of North America. As Peter Berger notes in *The Desecularization of the World*, the world today is "as furiously religious as it ever was, and in some places more so than ever." According to the *Yearbook of International Religious Demography*, the percentage of the world's population identifying with a religious group rose from 80 percent in 1970 to 88 percent in 2013. Extrapolating from current trends, the Pew Research Center predicts the unaffiliated will make up a smaller percentage of the world's population in 2050, while Christianity and Islam will continue to grow. Summarizing these projections, the *Washington Post* notes that the "world is expected to become more religious—not less." Accompanying this growth, the world's religions have experienced dramatic changes in geographical distribution. Over the past century, Christianity's "center of gravity" has shifted to the global South.[46] Reflecting centuries of movement and migration, Islam has expanded beyond its cultural hearth in the Middle East and North Africa. Like Islam and Christianity, Buddhism and Hinduism have spread across the globe.[47]

These developments have had important consequences for religion and higher education around the world. Paralleling the religious turn in American higher education, the globalization of religion has fostered the academic study of religion, the proliferation of religiously affiliated universities, and the growth of student religious organizations.

Facilitated by rising educational levels, cheaper travel, and global media (including the Internet), religious studies is undergoing a period of internationalization. Analyzing long-term trends in faculty employment at British Commonwealth universities, sociologists David Frank and Jay Gabler found that the academic study of religion grew between 1975 and 1995.[48] Since World War II, new religion programs have formed in China, Japan, Nigeria, South Korea, and many other countries. Beyond individual departments, groups like the Korean Association for the History of Religions, the Japanese Association for Religious Studies, the African Association for the Study of Religions, and the Chinese Association of Religious Studies have provided the organizational infrastructure for a global discipline. Founded in 1950, the International Association for the History of Religions has served as a clearinghouse for religious studies, linking together over forty national and regional associations, including the American Academy of Religion.[49]

Along with the globalization of religious studies, the developing world has witnessed the creation of hundreds of religiously affiliated universities, including many established during the past few decades. While the *Chronicle of Higher Education* heralds a global "renaissance in Christian higher education," historian Joel Carpenter notes the founding of dozens of institutions since 1980. In 2011, there were 579 Christian colleges and universities outside of North America, including 311 Asian, 135 Latin American, and 68 African institutions. One-fifth were founded after 1989. Reflecting on these developments, historian Rick Ostrander wonders whether America is "destined to become a backwater of a global Christian college movement centered in Africa, Asia, and Latin America." While most third-world institutions are small and underfunded, they may eventually outnumber their North American counterparts.[50] In a similar way, Muslim higher education has expanded across Asia and sub-Saharan Africa. Bolstered by Saudi philanthropy, these institutions complement older Muslim universities in the Middle East and North Africa, such as the Al-Azhar University in Egypt (founded in 971 C.E.). While 120 schools belong to the Islamic University League, the Federation of the Universities of the Islamic World has 193 member institutions.[51] Beyond Christianity and Islam, religious universities in other traditions are thriving. Formed in 2007, the International Association of Buddhist Universities and the International Association of Theravada Buddhist Universities have attracted dozens of member institutions. In a similar way, Banares Hindu University (founded in 1916) celebrates "all that was good and great in the ancient civilization of India."[52]

Accompanying the growth of religious universities, student religious groups have flourished around the world. Appropriating the voluntaristic methods of Protestant evangelicalism, global student movements in multiple religious traditions have proliferated since the 1890s. Emerging out of the Anglo-American YMCA, the Student Christian Movement (SCM) later spread to India, China, and other developing nations, building on existing campus groups. By 1905 it had attracted over 100,000 students. Part of the World's Student Christian Federation and the international YMCA, the SCM could be found in Africa, Asia, Latin America, as well as Europe and North America.[53] Emulating the YMCA, Buddhists and Muslims formed student movements of their own. In a similar way, the Young Men's Hindu Association and the Young Men's Sikh Association resisted Christian proselytizing. More overtly political, the Young Men's Muslim Association influenced the early Muslim Brotherhood. Several of these movements are active today.[54]

Over 120 years old, the World Student Christian Federation maintains a presence in Africa, Asia, Latin America, Europe, and North America, serving two million members in more than ninety countries. Despite this global reach, the WSCF has a much smaller footprint than it did in the decades following World War II.[55] Paralleling the WSCF, evangelical campus ministries have expanded around the globe. Over 500,000 students participate in the International Fellowship of Evangelical Students, an outgrowth of InterVarsity Christian Fellowship. Present in 160 countries in Latin America, Asia, Europe, and North America, it is especially popular in sub-Saharan Africa. Like IFES, Campus Crusade (now known as Cru) has participated in the globalization of evangelicalism, maintaining a presence on 366 international campuses.[56] In addition to these Anglo-American ministries, many indigenous evangelical student movements are active across the non-Western world. In South Korea, groups such as University Bible Fellowship and Korea Campus Crusade for Christ (SOON Movement) attract thousands of students. Once confined to Europe and North America, evangelical student groups are more numerous in the global South.[57]

Around the globe, higher education has engaged the sacred. From the internationalization of religious studies to the growth of student religious groups, the world's universities have fostered the teaching and the practice of religion. These developments also have implications for American higher education. As in the past, globalization promises to heighten the visibility of religion on American campuses, reinforcing the trends discussed in this book.

Far from isolated, religious studies has been shaped by the global movement of people and ideas. In the 1940s and 1950s, a generation of European émigré scholars exerted a powerful influence on American intellectual life. From Jacques Maritain and Abraham Joshua Heschel to Paul Tillich and Peter Berger, they changed the ways Americans thought about religion and culture. Today the United States remains the most popular destination for international scholars. Many have emigrated from non-Western countries, including China (22 percent), India (9.4 percent), and South Korea (9.3 percent).[58] In recent years, three immigrant scholars have served as president of the American Academy of Religion. While Kwok Pui Lan (Hong Kong) and Otto Maduro (Venezuela) have shaped the development of liberation and feminist theology, Vasudha Narayanan (India) has written about Hinduism in Cambodia and India. Similar insights can be found in the research agendas of AAR presidents Diana Eck and Mark Juergensmeyer. While Eck has celebrated new religious immigrants, Juergensmeyer has urged religion scholars to "understand the religiosity of the emerging global society." In 1989, the British scholar Ninian Smart called for a new Global Academy of Religion, reiterating this proposal in his 2000 presidential address to the AAR. Founded in 1991, the International Connections Committee of the AAR has worked to foster global understanding. In a similar way, the Society of Biblical Literature is paying more attention to international developments. During the early 2000s, foreign membership in the SBL more than doubled, reaching 2,600 in 2011.[59]

American students are part of the global flow of people and ideas. According to the Institute of International Education, 15 percent of bachelor's degree recipients studied abroad during their degree programs. In 2014–2015 alone, over 300,000 students earned academic credit in another country, a figure that has quadrupled since 1990. Consistent with these trends, many religious studies programs emphasize the benefits of foreign study. While one department "strongly encourages its students to study abroad," another notes that study abroad participants "report an elevated understanding of cultural and religious influence in a region."[60] As Americans flock to other countries, more international students are studying in America. Over the past sixty years, international enrollment has surged, rising from 25,000 in 1948–1949 to one million in 2015–2016. The leading countries of origin are China, India, South Korea, and Saudi Arabia, nations with diverse and distinctive religious profiles. Currently, internationals make up 5.2 percent of the American student population, while immigrant and second-generation students constitute 23 percent of all undergraduates. Though applications from internationals dropped following the election of Donald Trump, they still comprise a significant proportion of American college students.[61]

As noted in chapter 4, both internationals and immigrants have contributed to the diversification of student religious life. Founded in 1911, the Berkeley Young Men's Buddhist Association "provided a true home away from home," catering to California's growing Japanese American community. In the 1940s, foreign students organized some of the first Muslim groups on campus, while Indian immigrants and their children played a key role in the formation of Hindu Students Councils and Sikh Student Associations. In a case of reverse missionizing, Korea Campus Crusade for Christ (SOON

Movement) is currently active on over forty American campuses, including Berkeley, UCLA, and USC.[62]

Internationals are also a growing presence at many religiously affiliated institutions. Several of the top forty baccalaureate colleges hosting international students are church-related, including Brigham Young University (Hawaii), Calvin College, Earlham College, and St. Olaf College.[63] Many other students are recent immigrants. Welcoming this influx, several Catholic colleges and universities have developed extensive support systems for both documented and undocumented immigrants. A 2013 study explored the treatment of the undocumented at six Jesuit institutions. Sponsored by the Ford Foundation, it suggested several ways the schools could assist immigrants on campus. Following the 2016 election, the presidents of twenty-eight Jesuit institutions reaffirmed their support for undocumented students. Reflecting the Latino surge in American Catholicism, several Catholic colleges and universities can be classified as Hispanic-serving institutions, including Our Lady of the Lake University (63 percent Latino) and St. Mary's University (71 percent Latino).[64]

By educating immigrants and their children, church-related colleges are following in the footsteps of their Irish, Swedish, and German founders. In the nineteenth and twentieth centuries, multiple waves of European immigration fueled the growth of religious higher education. From the Scandinavian enclaves of the upper Midwest to the Dutch-Calvinist heartland of western Michigan, immigrant educators built a network of church-related colleges. Without immigration there would be no "Fighting Irish" or "Flying Dutch."[65]

Central to the American experience, such ethno-religious pluralism helps account for the vitality of American religion *and* American higher education. Noting the influence of mass migration, sociologist R. Stephen Warner argues that American religion provided "social space for cultural pluralism."[66] The same could be said for America's colleges and universities. Though access to higher education remains stratified by class and race, it is more diverse than many other American institutions. Seldom do so many groups come together within a single organization. As in the past, today's newcomers could revitalize both religion and higher education. At a time when many religious denominations are declining or holding steady, immigration is one of the few sources of new members. The same holds true in American higher education, where colleges depend on immigrants and internationals to maintain enrollments. If current projections are correct, the number of white high school graduates will decrease by 2020, while the population of Asian and Latino applicants will grow. Like their early twentieth-century predecessors, many are the children and the grandchildren of immigrants. These demographic shifts have broad implications for campus religion. While immigrants and internationals could swell the ranks of student religious groups, an increase in cultural diversity would underscore the need for more religion courses. Along with the globalization of religious higher education, the recent surge in immigration may end up strengthening the place of religion on campus.[67]

The Future of Religion on Campus

In an era of online courses and declining enrollments, shrinking budgets and softening church attendance, globalization and religious migration, it is difficult to predict the future of religion in American higher education. Though the teaching and the practice of religion are enjoying a comeback, it is unclear whether that will continue. In the 1950s, many spoke of a campus revival paralleling "the surge of piety in American society." A decade later, it was over. Today's "religious studies revival" may follow a similar trajectory. At a time when some speak of the decline of religion and the disruption of higher education, the future of religion on campus remains uncertain.[68]

In one admittedly farfetched scenario, disruptive innovation ends higher education as we know it. While half of American colleges declare bankruptcy, the Internet becomes the university of choice. Though the Ivy League remains a formidable presence, large segments of higher education disappear from the map. Gone are the second-tier public institutions, along with many church-related schools. While STEM disciplines thrive, the humanities and social sciences begin a long, slow decline. As online education takes over more of the academic market, the infrastructure of campus religion gradually shrinks. With academic instruction unbundled from campus life, there is no place for student religious groups or the college chapel.

Though this scenario contains an element of truth, it is unlikely to come to pass. For starters, American higher education has been here before. In the early 1970s, education researchers forecast a similar outcome. Noting that two-thirds of colleges and universities were in financial peril, the Carnegie Commission on Higher Education predicted a "new depression." Despite these warnings, the vast majority survived, including several on the Commission's watch list. Once in financial danger, Boston College went from a struggling commuter school to a major research university. Between 1973 and 2017, the Jesuit university's endowment rose from $5 million to $2.4 billion.[69] Though the future will be challenging, most institutions will make it. Though online modalities will spread, few see them taking over the market. According to historian John Thelin, the Internet and MOOCs are "no more and no less consequential than the introduction of affordable Xerox and photocopying machines in the 1960s, televised courses in the 1950s, carbon paper in the 1920s, typewriters in 1900, or a sophisticated, excellent postal system that allowed for correspondence courses in the 1890s." Education researcher Arthur Levine concurs, arguing that "higher education will be a blend of brick, click, and brick-and-click-institutions."[70]

The future of American religion is far less certain. Noting the growth of the "nones" and the softening of religiosity, some foresee a future of empty churches. In the judgment of Philip Jenkins, "The U.S. may be heading toward European-style secularization." Political scientist Tobin Grant agrees, arguing that "[w]e are in the midst of the 'Great Decline of Religion' in America." Were America to continue along this path, campus religious life could meet a similar fate. So would church-related colleges, theological seminaries, and divinity schools. Describing the religious climate of contemporary Scandinavia, sociologist Phil Zuckerman notes that "few people spend much time thinking about theological matters." In a more secular America, we would expect a similar decline in religious scholarship and theological reflection.[71]

To be sure, this scenario is not a given. While U.S. religiosity has dipped, it is much higher than in most of the developed world. Despite the rise of the "nones," most Americans identify with a religious tradition. Though church membership peaked in the 1980s, it is still higher than it was during most of U.S. history. Even if America follows a European trajectory, the academic study of religion might continue to thrive. This is certainly the case in Europe, where religious studies has enjoyed steady growth. Despite the secularization of European society, student religious life is also far from dead. This is especially true in England, where 66 percent of undergraduates identify with a religious tradition. While 27 percent of Christian students participate in a campus ministry, 30 percent attend church on a weekly basis. Summarizing these findings, *Times Higher Education* declared that "[r]eligious belief is alive and well on campus." Given the growth of alternative spiritualties on both sides of the Atlantic, the campus will continue to be a place for religious seeking.[72]

Beyond Europe and North America, new expressions of campus religion are proliferating across the globe. From university religion departments to student religious movements, non-Western institutions are engaging the sacred. While Muslim and Christian universities are growing in sub-Saharan Africa, Buddhist schools are thriving in East Asia. In one version of globalization, religious higher education shifts to the global South, as non-Western campuses overshadow their American counterparts. In another, new immigrants help revitalize American religion, reversing the process of secularization.[73]

Both scenarios assume a higher level of religiosity in non-Western countries. Given the dynamic character of religion around the world, this may be a faulty assumption. While many scholars highlight the religiosity of the global South, it is not immune to secularization. Today the religiously unaffiliated make up an estimated 16 percent of the world's people. Raising the possibility of a secular Latin America, historian Philip Jenkins points to falling birthrates and liberalizing social attitudes. Currently, the proportion of religious "nones" ranges from 9 percent in Brazil to 40 percent in Uruguay. In the United States, 12 percent of Latinos are religiously unaffiliated, up from 6 percent in 1990. The percentage of "nones" is even higher among Asian Americans. Similar patterns can be seen in other groups, including people who grew up Muslim.[74]

Secularization is also occurring at the institutional level. While many Latin American Protestant universities are Christian in name only, several South Korean schools have lost their religious distinctiveness. In a similar way, some Buddhist institutions have downplayed their religious identities. In the words of a Japanese educator, "We feel sad as Buddhists, but [changing school and faculty names] is perhaps inevitable for private universities to survive." Even the nonconfessional study of religion faces new challenges. At both private and public institutions, the humanities and social sciences are under fire. In many parts of the world, universities have embraced a narrow focus on vocational education, endangering the academic study of religion. Describing the situation in East Asia, Philip Altbach writes that the "humanities and to a lesser extent the social sciences are in crisis."[75]

Far from linear, the story of religion and higher education has many twists and turns. During the peak of the postwar campus revival, few anticipated the collapse of the mainline Protestant student movement. Even fewer noticed the growth of evangelical parachurch groups and new immigrant religions. Blinded by theories of modernization and secularization, most social scientists missed the resurgence of global Islam. In light of this history, it is hazardous to predict the future of religion in higher education. Though it is impossible to say, several recent studies suggest that the teaching and the practice of religion will remain relevant to the American campus.

At the dawn of the twenty-first century, the Pew Research Center reported a surge in social hostilities involving religion. While one-third of countries had a religious conflict in 2012, 18 percent experienced sectarian or communal violence. According to the *Economist*, we are witnessing "the new wars of religion."[76] Of course, there are other ways to interpret these developments. Highlighting the secular influences on ISIS, some point to the legacy of Revolutionary France. Others argue that violent extremism is rooted in politics, not religion. Besides exploring the sources of sacred violence, scholars can examine why some phenomena get labeled as religious and others as secular. The contested nature of these categories suggests that religious studies has a role to play in analyzing global conflicts.[77]

Another recent study challenges the conventional wisdom about religion and higher education. Released in 2014, it notes that the relationship between religiosity and education has undergone a dramatic shift. From the greatest generation to the baby boomers, exposure to college increased the likelihood of leaving the faith. For those born in the 1970s, the pattern is reversed. For members of generation X, going to college increases the chances of affiliating with a religious group. Such findings suggest that higher education is no longer a secularizing influence on emerging adults. Questioning the secularization thesis, others have commented on this reversal. Noting the positive correlation between religiosity and college attendance, sociologist Christian Smith perceives "a major shift in the role of higher education in American religion." In Smith's judgment, the growth of campus religious groups, the influence of religious colleges, and the presence of sympathetic faculty have made higher education more open to religious concerns. These are precisely the developments chronicled in this book.[78]

Far from pessimistic, many are hopeful about the future of religion in higher education. Taking the floor at a 2013 conference, Yale University professor Kathryn Lofton offered an impassioned defense of religious studies. Blending the academic and the sermonic, she urged her colleagues to ignore the declension stories scholars tell about both religion and higher education. According to Lofton, "to predict the future of the study of American religion requires predicting the future of American religion itself." Rejecting "the hysteria of some colleagues about the end of the university" and the "claims that religion will end," she argued that both institutions are changing their shapes. Asked about the future of American religion, she urged scholars to pay attention: "Wherever we find individuals gathering in collectivities for the purpose of moral debate and social self-making, *there* it is. Wherever we see propositions for transformation, for regulation, and for survival, *there* it is. Wherever we find people both paying attention to common subjects and offering ritual, commentarial, and critical reply to them, *there* it is." According to Lofton, "If we pay attention to these locations, we will not only perpetuate the study of religion, but also propound the life blood of our classrooms, and our institutions, as we see and really listen—really listen—to where and who we are."[79]

Nobody knows how long the university will listen to the sacred. In the final analysis, the place of religion on campus depends on the key stakeholders in American higher education, as well as the wider contexts they inhabit. As in the past, their choices have consequences for life beyond the campus. If international relations specialists ignore the academic study of religion, they will misunderstand the world. If politicians cut funding for religious studies departments, they will foster religious illiteracy. If religious groups fail to invest in colleges and campus ministries, they will undermine their own traditions. If interfaith movements do not flourish on campus, they will languish in the wider culture. Whatever its trajectory, the relationship between religion and higher education matters for American society. An expression of American culture in all its diversity, the campus has become a place for religious pluralism and critical reflection about the sacred. If the key stakeholders remain committed to such conversation, it will remain so in the future.

NOTES

Chapter 1

1 Peter Berger, *The Sacred Canopy* (Garden City, NY: Doubleday, 1967); Harvey Cox, *The Secular City* (New York: Macmillan, 1965); Bryan Wilson, *Religion in a Secular Society* (London: Penguin, 1969).

2 Richard Hofstadter, *Academic Freedom in the Age of the College* (New Brunswick, NJ: Transaction, 1995); Laurence R. Veysey, *The Emergence of the American University* (Chicago: University of Chicago Press, 1965); George M. Marsden, *The Soul of the American University: From Protestant Establishment to Established Nonbelief* (New York: Oxford University Press, 1994); Douglas Sloan, *Faith and Knowledge: Mainline Protestantism and American Higher Education* (Louisville, KY: Westminster John Knox Press, 1994); Julie A. Reuben, *The Making of the Modern University: Intellectual Transformation and the Marginalization of Morality* (Chicago: University of Chicago Press, 1994); James T. Burtchaell, *The Dying of the Light: The Disengagement of Colleges and Universities from Their Christian Churches* (Grand Rapids, MI: Eerdmans, 1998); Philip Gleason, *Contending with Modernity: Catholic Higher Education in the Twentieth Century* (New York: Oxford University Press, 1995).

3 On the postwar academic revival and theological renaissance, see Sloan, *Faith and Knowledge*.

4 Our use of the term "post-secular" was inspired by Peter Steinfels, "Swapping 'Religion' for 'Postsecularism,'" *New York Times*, 3 August 2002. More recently, Douglas Jacobsen and Rhonda Hustedt Jacobsen have edited *The American University in a Postsecular Age* (New York: Oxford University Press, 2008). See also Gregor McLennan, "The Postsecular Turn," *Theory, Culture, and Society* 28 (4): 3–20 (2010).

5 The American Academy of Religion has 9,000 members, up from 5,500 in 1990. For current AAR membership, see the AAR website, https://www.aarweb.org/. Figures on past membership from the 2000 annual report, http://web.archive.org/web/20070226105611/

http://www.aarweb.org/about/annualreport/AR2000.pdf. The membership of the Society of Biblical Literature is 8,697, 30 percent more than in 2001. The 2010 SBL annual report can be found at the SBL website, http://www.sbl-site.org/. On the popularity of religious history, see Robert B. Townsend, "AHA Membership Grows Modestly, as History of Religion Surpasses Culture," *AHA Today*, 30 June 2009. Data on the growing attention to religion in sociology's top three journals reported in David Smilde and Matthew May, "The Emerging Strong Program in the Sociology of Religion," Social Science Research Council Working Paper, 8 February 2010, http://blogs.ssrc.org/. On the "desecularization" of philosophy, see Quentin Smith, "The Metaphilosophy of Naturalism," *Philo* 4 (2) (2001). For a list of the thirty-three centers and institutes focused on the study of religion in North America, see the website of the Centers and Institutes Project, https://web.archive.org/web/20111104142248/http://iupui.edu/~raac/CIP.html.

6 A 2011 ACCU study identified 128 centers and institutes at Catholic colleges and universities. "Advancing Knowledge and Mission," *Update: The Newsletter of the Association of Catholic Colleges and Universities*, Winter 2011. The ACCU database now lists over 1,000 centers and institutes. See http://www.accunet.org/. On the growing attention to mission and identity in the 1990s, see Kathleen A. Mahoney, John Schmalzbauer, and James Youniss, "Revitalizing Religion in the Academy: An Evaluation of Lilly Endowment's Initiative on Religion and Higher Education," unpublished report to Lilly Endowment, 7 August 2000. A summary is available online: *Revitalizing Religion in the Academy: Summary of the Evaluation of Lilly Endowment's Initiative on Religion and Higher Education* (Chestnut Hill, MA: Boston College, 2000), 10, http://www.resourcingchristianity.org/sites/default/files/transcripts/research_article/Mahoney_Schmalzbauer_Youniss_Revitalizing_Religion_Essay.pdf. See also Tim Clydesdale, *The Purposeful Graduate: Why Colleges Must Talk to Students about Vocation* (Chicago: University of Chicago Press, 2015).

7 Campus Crusade (now known as Cru) grew from 20,000 students in 1995 to 82,000 in 2015–2016. Ministry statistics for Campus Crusade from https://web.archive.org/web/19990203144419/http://www.uscm.org/aboutus/stats.html and http://demoss.com/newsrooms/cru/background/cru-overview. The number of Orthodox Christian Fellowships has quadrupled since the 1970s. On the OCF, see http://www.ocf.net/about/. On the rise of Muslim and Hindu groups, see Altaf Husain, "Envisioning a Continent Wide Student Organization," *MSA Link*, Fall/Winter 2008, 8–9; Aditya Kashyap, "Hindu Students Council Celebrates 20th Anniversary at Annual Camp," press release, *Hinduism Today*, 20 June 2010, https://www.hinduismtoday.com/. New models of ministry are discussed in "A New Theme for Dorms: God," *New York Times*, 30 July 2006; Arian Campo-Flores, "Religious Dorms Sprout Up," *Wall Street Journal*, 3 September 2013; "A Model for Church-Based Campus Ministry: Real Life in Jesus Christ," University Presbyterian Church, Seattle, Washington, https://ukirk.pcusa.org/. For more on development, see the website of the Petrus Development firm, http://www.petrusdevelopment.com/; Gurdon Brewster, "Ministry on the Frontier: The Contribution of Episcopal Campus Ministry to the Present and Future Church," July 2000, http://web.archive.org/web/20030305031227/http://www.esmhe.org/ministryonthefrontier.htm.

8 Alexander W. Astin, Helen S. Astin, and Jennifer A. Lindholm, *Cultivating the Spirit: How College Can Enhance Students' Inner Lives* (San Francisco: Jossey-Bass, 2011).

9 Alan Wolfe, "A Welcome Revival of Religion in the Academy," *Chronicle of Higher Education*, 19 September 1997; Diane Winston, "Campuses Are a Bellwether for Society's Religious Revival," *Chronicle of Higher Education*, 16 January 1998, A60. Marsden is quoted in Beth McMurtrie, "Future of Religious Colleges Is Bright, Say Scholars and

Officials," *Chronicle of Higher Education*, 20 October 2000, A41. The ethnographic study is Conrad Cherry, Betty DeBerg, and Amanda Porterfield, *Religion on Campus* (Chapel Hill: University of North Carolina Press, 2001), 4. See also Douglas Jacobsen and Rhonda Hustedt Jacobsen, *No Longer Invisible: Religion in University Education* (New York: Oxford University Press, 2012). The terms "comeback," "revitalization," and "resurgence" appear in Kathleen A. Mahoney, John Schmalzbauer, and James Youniss, "Religion: A Comeback on Campus," *Liberal Education*, Fall 2001. In the *Merriam-Webster Dictionary*, "revitalization," "revival," "resurgence," and "renewal" are listed as synonyms. For the sake of the reader, this study uses multiple terms to describe the return of religion, acknowledging that no term captures the complexity of religion on the ground. Like other historians and sociologists, we employ these words in a descriptive sense, avoiding their normative or theological connotations.

10 Roger Finke and Rodney Stark, *The Churching of America, 1776–2005: Winners and Losers in Our Religious Economy* (New Brunswick, NJ: Rutgers University Press, 2005), 46. Religiosity is substantially higher in the United States than in most Western European countries. According to the 2010–2014 wave of the World Values Survey, in America 43 percent of respondents attend religious services at least once a month, compared to 19 percent in Germany and 9.1 percent in Sweden. Figures generated from the online data analysis page of the World Values Survey, http://www.worldvaluessurvey.org/WVSOnline.jsp.

11 Catherine L. Albanese, "Religious Diversity in Early America," 19 August 2008, *eJournalUSA*, August 2008, https://web.archive.org/web/20170107051810/http://iipdigital.usembassy.gov/st/english/publication/2008/08/20080819130107cmretrop0.2322962.html; Jon Butler, *Awash in a Sea of Faith: Christianizing the American People* (Cambridge, MA: Harvard University Press, 1992).

12 Martin E. Marty, *Righteous Empire: The Protestant Experience in America* (New York: Dial Press, 1970); Robert T. Handy, *A Christian America: Protestant Hopes and Historical Realities*, 2nd ed. (New York: Oxford University Press, 1984).

13 On the second disestablishment, see Handy, *A Christian America*, 159–84.

14 Dorothy C. Bass, "Ministry on the Margins: Protestants and Education," in *Between the Times: The Travail of the Protestant Establishment in America, 1900–1960*, ed. William R. Hutchison (New York: Cambridge University Press, 1989), 48–71. On de-Christianization, see David Hollinger, *Science, Jews, and Secular Culture* (Princeton, NJ: Princeton University Press, 1996).

15 Roger L. Geiger, ed., *The American College in the Nineteenth Century* (Nashville, TN: Vanderbilt University Press, 2000); Frederick Rudolph, *The American College and University: A History*, 2nd ed. (Athens: University of Georgia Press, 1990); Colin B. Burke, *American Collegiate Populations: A Test of the Traditional View* (New York: New York University Press, 1982); James Findlay, "The SPCTEW and Western Colleges: Religion and Higher Education in Mid-Nineteenth Century America," *History of Education Quarterly* 17: 31–62 (1977).

16 Veysey, *The Emergence of the American University*; Edward Shils, "The Order of Learning in the United States from 1865 to 1920: The Ascendancy of the Universities," in *The Order of Learning: Essays on the Contemporary University*, ed. and with with an introduction by Philip G. Altbach (New Brunswick, NJ: Transaction, 1977), 1–38.

17 On the fragmentation of the "unity of truth," see Reuben, *The Making of the Modern University*; Conrad Cherry, *Hurrying toward Zion: Universities, Divinity Schools, and American Protestantism* (Bloomington: Indiana University Press, 1995), 267; Roger L. Geiger, *The*

History of American Higher Education: Learning and Culture from the Founding to World War II (Princeton, NJ: Princeton University Press, 2015), 337; Sloan, *Faith and Knowledge*. On the specialization of knowledge, see Jon H. Roberts and James Turner, *The Sacred and the Secular University* (Princeton, NJ: Princeton University Press, 2000).

18 Marsden, *The Soul of the American University*; Gleason, *Contending with Modernity*.

19 For two contrasting perspectives on these developments, see Merrimon Cuninggim, *Uneasy Partners: The College and the Church* (Nashville, TN: Abingdon Press, 1994); Burtchaell, *The Dying of the Light*. James Axtell describes "the gradual secularization of institutional leadership" in *Wisdom's Workshop: The Rise of the Modern University* (Princeton, NJ: Princeton University Press, 2015), 289.

20 David P. Setran, *The College "Y": Student Religion in the Era of Secularization* (New York: Palgrave Macmillan, 2007); Clarence P. Shedd, *Two Centuries of Student Christian Movements: Their Origin and Intercollegiate Life* (New York: Association Press, 1934); Marsden, *The Soul of the American University*; Dorothy C. Bass, "Ministry on the Margins"; Dorothy C. Bass, "The Independent Sector and the Educational Strategies of Mainstream Protestantism, 1900–1980," in *Religion, The Independent Sector, and American Culture*, ed. Conrad Cherry and Rowland A. Sherrill (Atlanta: Scholars Press, 1992), 51–72.

21 Louis Menand, *The Metaphysical Club: A Story of Ideas in America* (New York: Farrar, Straus and Giroux, 2001); S. E. Henking, "Sociological Christianity and Christian Sociology: The Paradox of Early American Sociology," *Religion and American Culture* 3 (1): 49–67 (1993); the quotation appears in an excerpt from Friedrich Wilhelm Nietzsche's *The Antichrist* (1895), from *The Portable Nietzsche*, ed. Walter Kaufmann (New York: Penguin, 1954), 576. Hollinger, *Science, Jews, and Secular Culture*; John McGreevy, "Thinking on One's Own: Catholicism in the American Intellectual Imagination, 1928–1960," *Journal of American History* 84 (1): 97–131 (1997). On the shifts in postwar religion, see Kevin Schultz, *Tri-Faith America: How Catholics and Jews Held Postwar America to Its Protestant Promise* (New York: Oxford University Press, 2011). On the demise of the Protestant establishment, see E. Digby Baltzell, *The Protestant Establishment: Aristocracy and Caste in America* (New Haven, CT: Yale University Press, 1964).

22 On the state of religion in higher education in the 1970s, see Sloan, *Faith and Knowledge*; Nancy T. Ammerman, "Sociology and the Study of Religion," in *Religion, Scholarship, and Higher Education: Perspectives, Models, and Future Prospects*, ed. Andrea Sterk (Notre Dame, IN: University of Notre Dame Press, 2002), 77, 78; Bass, "The Independent Sector." Jacobsen and Jacobsen call the 1970s the "privatized era" in *No Longer Invisible*, 16.

23 Richard Hofstadter, *Anti-intellectualism in American Life* (New York: Knopf, 1963); Richard Hofstadter and C. DeWitt Hardy, *The Development and Scope of Higher Education in the United States* (New York: Columbia University Press for the Commission on Financing Higher Education, 1952); Richard Hofstadter and Walter P. Metzger, *The Development of Academic Freedom in the United States* (New York: Columbia University Press, 1955).

24 For a discussion of the conceptual vocabulary of secularization theory (including privatization and differentiation), see Olivier Tschannen, "Secularization Theory: A Systematization," *Journal for the Scientific Study of Religion* 30 (4): 395–415 (1991). On the privatization of religion in American higher education, see Jacobsen and Jacobsen, *No Longer Invisible*, 16–30.

25 Peter Berger, "Protestantism and the Quest for Certainty," *Christian Century*, 26 August 1998, 782; Harvey Cox, *Fire from Heaven: The Rise of Pentecostal Spirituality and the Reshaping of Religion in the Twenty-First Century* (Reading, MA: Addison-Wesley, 1995), xv.

26 José Casanova, *Public Religions in the Modern World* (Chicago: University of Chicago Press, 1994), 5. On de-differentiation, see Charles L. Harper and Bryan F. LeBeau, "Social Change and Religion in America: Thinking beyond Secularization," in *The American Religious Experience*, http://are.as.wvu.edu/sochange.htm.

27 Martin E. Marty, "Our Religio-Secular World," *Daedalus* 132 (3): 42 (2003).

28 On the connections between campus religion and the religious resurgence in American public life, see Diane Winston, "Campuses Are a Bellwether for Society's Religious Revival," *Chronicle of Higher Education*, 16 January 1998, A60.

29 Jonathan Judaken and Jennifer L. Geddes, "Black Intellectuals in America: A Conversation with Cornel West," *Hedgehog Review*, Spring 2007, 81–91; Robert Boynton, "The New Intellectuals," *Atlantic*, March 1995, 53–70.

30 This paragraph draws on John Schmalzbauer, "Big Shots, Born Again" (Review of *Faith in the Halls of Power*), *Wall Street Journal*, 18 October 2007. On the emergence of an evangelical professional class, see John Schmalzbauer, "Evangelicals in the New Class: Class versus Subculture Explanations for Political Ideology," *Journal for the Scientific Study of Religion* 32 (4): 330–42 (1993). On the emergence of social justice evangelicals, see Brian Steensland and Philip Goff, eds., *The New Evangelical Social Engagement* (New York: Oxford University Press, 2014).

31 Andrew Greeley, "Is There an American Catholic Elite?" *America*, 6 May 1989, 428. For a list of the members of the Association of Catholic Colleges and Universities, see http://www.accunet.org.

32 David Hollinger, "After Cloven Tongues of Fire: Ecumenical Protestantism and the Modern American Encounter with Diversity," *Journal of American History* 98 (1): 21–48 (2011).

33 Schultz, *Tri-Faith America*; Will Herberg, *Protestant—Catholic—Jew: An Essay in American Religious Sociology* (New York: Doubleday, 1955).

34 Diana Eck, *A New Religious America: How a "Christian" Country Has Become the World's Most Religiously Diverse Nation* (San Francisco: HarperSanFrancisco, 2001). Numbers on Buddhist centers from the Pluralism Project website, http://www.pluralism.org/.

35 On seeker spirituality, see Wade Clark Roof, *Spiritual Marketplace: Baby Boomers and the Remaking of American Religion* (Princeton, NJ: Princeton University Press, 2001); Leigh Schmidt, *Restless Souls: The Making of American Spirituality* (New York: HarperCollins, 2005); Catherine L. Albanese, *A Republic of Mind and Spirit: A Cultural History of American Metaphysical Religion* (New Haven, CT: Yale University Press, 2007); Wade Clark Roof, *A Generation of Seekers: The Spiritual Journeys of the Baby Boom Generation* (San Francisco: HarperSanFrancisco, 1993). The UCLA study of spirituality and higher education found that one-third of college juniors scored high on a Spiritual Quest scale. See Astin, Astin, and Lindholm, *Cultivating the Spirit*, 31.

36 On cultural innovation and unsettled times, see Ann Swidler, "Culture in Action: Symbols and Strategies," *American Sociological Review* 51 (2): 273–86 (1986). On the diffusion of religion into other spheres, see Winston, "Campuses Are a Bellwether," A60; Michelle Conlin, "Religion in the Workplace: The Growing Presence of Spirituality in Corporate America," *Business Week*, 1 November 1999, 3–10; David W. Miller, *God at Work* (New York: Oxford University Press, 2006).

37 Tom Shone, "A Movie Miracle: How Hollywood Found Religion," *Guardian*, 31 July 2014; Mara Einstein, *Brands of Faith: Marketing Religion in a Commercial Age* (New York: Routledge, 2007); Martin E. Marty, "Church Affiliation Colonial and Now," *Sightings*, 5

November 2012, https://web.archive.org/web/20121108031718/http://divinity.uchicago.edu/martycenter/publications/sightings/archive_2012/1105.shtml.

38 Cullen Murphy, "Religion and the Cultural Elite," a lecture given at Saint Ambrose University in Davenport, Iowa, 7 April 1994, http://www.theatlantic.com/past/docs/unbound/cullen/cmrel.htm. See Michael Kazin, "A Difficult Marriage: American Protestants and American Politics," *Dissent*, Winter 2006; Mark Noll, "Jesus and Jefferson," *New Republic*, 18 May 2011; Chris Lehmann, "Little Churches Everywhere: California's Evangelical Conservatism," *Nation*, 27 June 2011. On the gatekeeping role of magazines, see Charles Kadushin, *The American Intellectual Elite* (New Brunswick, NJ: Transaction, 2006), 14.

39 For more on religious intellectual periodicals, see William Placher, "Helping Theology to Matter: A Challenge for the Mainline," *Christian Century*, 28 October 1998, 994–98; Rodger Van Allen, *Being Catholic: Commonweal from the Seventies to the Nineties* (Chicago: Loyola Press, 1993); Mark Oppenheimer, "Adding More Jewish Voices to the Discussion," *New York Times*, 23 April 2010.

40 William Grimes, "Another Top 100: This Time, It's Intellectuals," *New York Times*, 19 January 2002, A19; Richard Posner, *Public Intellectuals: A Study of Decline* (Cambridge, MA: Harvard University Press, 2001). The list of leading thinkers from *Foreign Policy* and *Prospect* was retrieved from the websites of each magazine.

41 Timothy Samuel Shah, Alfred Stepan, and Monica Duffy Toft, ed., *Rethinking Religoin and World Affairs* (New York: Oxford University Press, 2012); Mark Juergensmeyer, *The New Cold War? Religious Nationalism Confronts the Secular State* (Berkeley: University of California Press, 1993). On the "golden age of secular nationalism," see Mark Juergensmeyer, "Rethinking the Secular and Religious Aspects of Violence," in *Rethinking Secularism*, ed. Craig Calhoun, Mark Juergensmeyer, and Jonathan VanAntwerpen (New York: Oxford University Press, 2011), 189. See also Rajeev Bhargava, "States, Religious Diversity, and the Crisis of Secularism," *Hedgehog Review* 12 (3): 8–22 (2010); Madeleine Albright, *The Mighty and the Almighty: Reflections on America, God, and World Affairs* (New York: HarperCollins, 2006).

42 On the exhaustion of modernity, see Vaclav Havel, "The Need for Transcendence in the Postmodern World," *Futurist*, July 1995; Larry Ray, "Post-Communism: Postmodernity or Modernity Revisited?" *British Journal of Sociology* 48 (4): 543–60 (1997); Daniel Bell, "The Cultural Wars: American Intellectual Life, 1965–1992," *Wilson Quarterly*, Summer 1992, 74–107; Madeleine Bunting, "Market Dogma Is Exposed as Myth: Where Is the New Vision to Unite Us?" *Guardian*, 28 June 2009; Bruno Latour, *On the Modern Cult of the Factish Gods* (Durham, NC: Duke University Press, 2010).

43 On multiculturalism and knowledge, see Todd Gitlin, *The Twilight of Common Dreams: Why America Is Wracked by Culture Wars* (New York: Henry Holt, 1995), 200–201. On the critique of objectivity, see Peter Novick, *That Noble Dream: The "Objectivity Question" and the American Historical Profession* (Cambridge: Cambridge University Press, 1988); Mary Field Belenky, ed., *Women's Ways of Knowing* (New York: HarperCollins, 1997). The last quotation is from Cornel West, *Keeping Faith: Philosophy and Race in America* (New York: Routledge, 1993), 36.

44 Daniel Bell, *The End of Ideology: On the Exhaustion of Political Ideas in the Fifties* (Cambridge, MA: Harvard University Press, 1962). On the affinity between postwar liberalism and the ideology of objectivity, see Novick, *That Noble Dream*, 300; Bell, "The Cultural Wars," 74. On the fragmentation of American culture during this period, see Daniel T. Rodgers, *Age of Fracture* (Cambridge, MA: Harvard University Press, 2011). See also Daniel Bell, "The

Return of the Sacred? The Argument on the Future of Religion," in *The Winding Passage: Essays and Sociological Journeys*, ed. Daniel Bell (New York: Basic Books, 1980), 324–54.

45 In a recent cultural history of the United States, sociologist Claude Fischer rejects the myth that "Americans turned away from religion," arguing that the story of our religious development can be summed up with one word—more. See Fischer, *Made in America: A Social History of American Culture and Character* (Chicago: University of Chicago Press, 2010), 4. The 77 percent figure is from the Pew Research Center, *America's Changing Religious Landscape* (Washington, DC: Pew Research Center, 2015). The figure of 53 percent attendance is from Frank Newport, "Three-Quarters of Americans Identify as Christian," Gallup, 24 December 2014, http://www.gallup.com/. On the softening of religious attendance, see Mark Chaves, *American Religion: Contemporary Trends* (Princeton, NJ: Princeton University Press, 2011).

46 Chaves, *American Religion*.

47 Christian Smith, preface to *The Secular Revolution: Power, Interests, and Conflict in the Secularization of American Life*, ed. Christian Smith (Berkeley: University of California Press, 2003), vii.

48 See Smith, "Secularizing American Higher Education: The Case of Early American Sociology," in Smith, *The Secular Revolution*, 97–159. Though scholars disagree about the extent of this shift, Smith offers a useful model for thinking about the role of movements in the transformation of colleges and universities.

49 Smith, "Introduction: Rethinking the Secularization of American Popular Life," in Smith, *The Secular Revolution*, 30, 48–53.

50 On prognostic and diagnostic frames, see Scott A. Hunt, Robert D. Benford, and David A. Snow, "Identity Fields: Framing Processes and the Social Construction of Movement Identities," in *New Social Movements: From Ideology to Identity*, ed. Enrique Larna, Hank Johnston, and Joseph R. Gusfield (Philadelphia: Temple University Press, 1994), 191. On narrative and social movements, see Gary Alan Fine, "Public Narration and Group Culture," in *Social Movements and Culture*, ed. Hank Johnston and Bert Klandermans (Minneapolis: University of Minnesota Press, 1995), 127–43.

51 David Snow and Robert Benford, "Master Frames and Cycles of Protest," in *Frontiers of Social Movement Theory*, ed. Aldon D. Morris and Carol McClurg Mueller (New Haven, CT: Yale University Press, 1992), 133–55. The concept of frame disputes is taken from Robert Benford, "'You Could Be the Hundredth Monkey': Collective Action Frames and Vocabularies of Motive within the Nuclear Disarmament Movement," *Sociological Quarterly* 34 (2): 195–216 (1993). For a defense of scholarly detachment, see Donald Wiebe, *The Politics of Religious Studies: The Continuing Conflict with Theology in the Academy* (New York: Palgrave Macmillan, 1999). For a critique of the secular university, see Marsden, *The Soul of the American University*; C. John Sommerville, *The Decline of the Secular University* (New York: Oxford University Press, 2006). For a discussion of spirituality, see Astin, Astin, and Lindholm, *Cultivating the Spirit*. Anthony Kronman has articulated the case for a nondogmatic spirituality in Kronman, "Why Are We Here? College's Ignore Life's Biggest Questions," *Boston Globe*, 16 September 2007. In *Education's End: Why Our Colleges and Universities Have Given Up on the Meaning of Life* (New Haven, CT: Yale University Press, 2007), Kronman uses the word "spiritual" forty-two times. On civic and moral engagement with some attention to religion, see Anne Colby, Thomas Ehrlich, Elizabeth Beaumont, and Jason Stephens, *Educating Citizens: Preparing America's Undergraduates for Lives of Moral and Civic Responsibility* (San Francisco: Jossey-Bass, 2003).

52 Peter Steinfels, "Catholic Identity: Emerging Consensus," *Occasional Papers on Catholic Higher Education* 1 (1): 11–19 (1995); Eric Childers, *College Identity Sagas: Investigating Organizational Identity Preservation and Diminishment at Lutheran Colleges* (Eugene, OR: Wipf and Stock, 2012). Robert Benne, *Quality with Soul: How Six Premier Colleges and Universities Keep Faith with Their Religious Traditions* (Grand Rapids, MI: Eerdmans, 2001).

53 Concerns about the attenuation of student faith are common in the history of campus religious movements. See Clarence P. Shedd, *The Church Follows Its Students* (New Haven, CT: Yale University Press, 1938); Daniel Smokler, "Why Hillel Matters More than Ever," *Mosaic*, 10 November 2014; John G. Turner, *Bill Bright and Campus Crusade for Christ: The Renewal of Evangelicalism in Postwar America* (Chapel Hill: University of North Carolina Press, 2008). On the importance of spirituality, see Astin, Astin, and Lindholm, *Cultivating the Spirit*; Sharon Daloz Parks, *Big Questions, Worthy Dreams: Mentoring Young Adults in Their Search for Meaning* (San Francisco: Jossey-Bass, 1999); Alyssa Bryant Rockenbach and Matthew J. Mayhew, eds., *Spirituality in College Students' Lives: Translating Research into Practice* (New York: Routledge, 2013). On religious diversity, see Eboo Patel and Cassie Meyer, "Introduction to 'Interfaith Cooperation on Campus': Interfaith Cooperation as an Institution-Wide Priority," *Journal of College and Character* 12 (2) (2011).

54 Mayer N. Zald and John D. McCarthy, *Social Movements in an Organizational Society* (New Brunswick, NJ: Transaction Books 1987), 1.

55 On master-pupil chains, see Randall Collins, *The Sociology of Philosophies: A Global Theory of Intellectual Change* (Cambridge, MA: Harvard University Press, 1998). These multigenerational networks of teachers and students are the primary means of transmitting and transforming academic traditions.

56 On the organizational technologies of the student YMCA and the YWCA, see Lawrence A. Cremin, *American Education: The Metropolitan Experience, 1876–1980* (New York: Harper and Row, 1988), 115. These organizational forms are still being used today.

57 On preexisting networks and organizations, see Jo Freeman, "On the Origins of Social Movements," in *Waves of Protest: Social Movements since the Sixties*, ed. Jo Freeman and Victoria Johnson (Lanham, MD: Rowman and Littlefield, 1999), 7–24.

58 Marsden, *The Soul of the American University*; Smith, "Introduction," 75. On Rockefeller, see James Gilbert, *Redeeming Culture: American Religion in an Age of Science* (Chicago: University of Chicago Press, 1997). On Danforth, see Robert Wood Lynn, "'The Survival of Recognizably Protestant Colleges': Reflections on Old-Line Protestantism, 1950–1990," in *The Secularization of the Academy*, ed. George M. Marsden and Bradley J. Longfield (New York: Oxford University Press, 1992), 182.

59 On the record giving between 1999 and 2003, see Robert Wuthnow and D. Michael Lindsay, "Financing Faith: Religion and Strategic Philanthropy," *Journal for the Scientific Study of Religion* 49 (1): 87–111 (2010); Robert Wuthnow and D. Michael Lindsay, "The Role of Foundations in American Religion," in *American Foundations: Roles and Contributions*, ed. Helmut K. Anheier and David C. Hammack (Washington, DC: Brookings Institution Press, 2010), 305–27. Templeton's 2010 capabilities report is available from the Templeton website, http://www.templeton.org/. Its 2014 assets were $3.2 billion. On Lilly and Templeton, see the Foundation Center's "Top 100 Foundations by Asset Size," available from the Foundation Center website, http://foundationcenter.org/findfunders/topfunders/top100assets.html.

60 On the Pew Evangelical Scholars Program (later called the Pew Christian Scholars Program), see the program website, https://web.archive.org/web/*/www.nd.edu/~csp/

index.html. Rhys Williams and Eugene Lowe's evaluation of the program is described in Janet L. Kroll and Rebecca A. Cornejo, "Onward Christian Scholars," *Trust*, May 2003.

61 For a description of the "Centers of Excellence" program, see http://web.archive.org/web/20060220231717/http://www.pewtrusts.org/ideas/index.cfm?issue=17&misc_idea=2. On Pew's impact on the fields of American religion and philosophy, see Michael S. Hamilton and Johanna G. Yngvason, "Patrons of the Evangelical Mind," *Christianity Today*, 8 July 2002.

62 James H. Madison, *Eli Lilly: A Life, 1885–1977* (Indianapolis: Indiana Historical Society, 1989); Kenneth L. Woodward, "The High Priest of Scholarship," *Newsweek*, 7 August 1989.

63 Mahoney, Schmalzbauer, and Youniss, *Revitalizing Religion in the Academy*. For more on the Programs for the Theological Exploration of Vocation, see https://web.archive.org/web/20090619080547/http://www.ptev.org:80/. The $225 million figure comes from Clydesdale, *The Purposeful Graduate*, 46; "Lilly Endowment Makes Grants to Strengthen Campus Ministries Serving Public Universities," Religion News Service, 4 November 2015.

64 On Templeton, see Nathan Schneider, "God, Science, and Philanthropy," *Nation*, 21 June 2010.

65 See David L. Wheeler, "Foundation Seeks to Create Field Melding Science and Theology," *Chronicle of Higher Education*, 11 April 1997; Tony Carnes, "The $1 Billion Handoff," *Christianity Today*, 19 August 2005. On Templeton's spending in 2009, see its 2010 capabilities report, https://web.archive.org/web/20150327154703/http://www.templeton.org/sites/default/files/capabilities_report_2010.pdf. On Templeton, philosophy, and science, see Nathan Schneider, "The Templeton Effect," *Chronicle Review*, 3 September 2012; Schneider, "God, Science, and Philanthropy."

66 For information on the Notre Dame endowment, see http://investment.nd.edu/history/.

67 See Larry Eskridge and Mark Noll, *More Money, More Ministry: Money and Evanglicals in Recent North American History* (Grand Rapids, MI: Eerdmans, 2000); Michael S. Hamilton, "We're in the Money!" *Christianity Today*, 12 June 2000. See the website of the Gathering, http://www.thegathering.com. The $200,000 figure is from D. Michael Lindsay, *Faith in the Halls of Power: How Evangelicals Joined the American Elite* (New York: Oxford University Press, 2007), 292. On the modest interest of evangelical philanthropists in academic causes, see Michael S. Hamilton, "Philanthropic Funding, the ISAE, and Evangelical Scholarship," *Evangelical Studies Bulletin*, Fall 2014, 6–8.

68 The figure of $70 million comes from Gerald Renner, "Hillel Connects Jewish College Students," *Courant*, 31 March 1999. Chabad's 2010 report can be found at http://chabad.edu/media/pdf/492/SBVf4921608.pdf.

69 Robert Eisen, "Jewish Studies and the Academic Teaching of Religion," *Liberal Education*, Fall 2001, 14. For more on the Posen Society of Fellows, see the Posen Foundation website, http://www.posenfoundation.co.il/. See also "Philanthropist Aiming to Reach Out to Cultural Jews," *Forward*, 5 December 2003.

70 On the Nathan Cummings Foundation's support for the Center for Contemplative Mind in Society, see the Center's website, http://www.contemplativemind.org/about/history. For more on the Muslim Students' Association's fundraising efforts, see http://msanational.org/donate/. See also Gitika Ahuja, "Saudi Prince Donates $40 Million to Harvard, Georgetown Universities," ABC News, 13 December 2005; Lonnie Shekhtman, "Why Did a Saudi Billionaire Donate $10 Million to Yale?" *Christian Science Monitor*, 13 September 2015.

71 John D. McCarthy and Mayer N. Zald, "Resource Mobilization and Social Movements," *American Journal of Sociology* 82 (6): 12–24 (1977).

72 Christian Smith asks what "changes in the sociopolitical environment altered the structure of power relations in ways that increased the opportunities for insurgents to act successfully upon their existing interests and grievances?" See Smith, "Introduction," 31.

73 According to Robert Wuthnow, this "epistemological uncertainty" has created "opportunities for rethinking the place of faith in the academy." See Wuthnow, "Can Faith Be More than a Side Show in the Contemporary Academy?" in Jacobsen and Jacobsen, *The American University in a Postsecular Age*, 35. For a discussion of the religious use of postmodern rhetoric, see Joel A. Carpenter and Kenneth Shipps, "Preface," in *Making Higher Education Christian: The History and Mission of Evangelical Colleges in America* (Grand Rapids, MI: Eerdmans, 1987), xiii; John Schmalzbauer, *People of Faith: Religious Conviction in American Journalism and Higher Education* (Ithaca, NY: Cornell University Press, 2003). For a discussion of religious ethnography, see James V. Spickard, J. Shawn Landres, and Meredith McGuire, *Personal Knowledge and Beyond: Reshaping the Ethnography of Religion* (New York: New York University Press, 2002); T. M. Luhrmann, *When God Talks Back:Understanding the American Evangelical Relationship with God* (New York: Knopf, 2012).

74 Clifford Geertz, "Blurred Genres: The Reconfiguration of Social Thought," in Geertz, *Local Knowledge: Further Essays in Interpretive Anthropology* (New York: Basic Books, 1983).

75 Louis Menand, "Undisciplined," *Wilson Quarterly* 25 (4): 51–59 (2001); Elaine Howard Ecklund, "Abandoning Disciplines," *Chronicle of Higher Education*, 29 August 2010.

76 Roger L. Geiger, "Organized Research Units: Their Role in the Development of University Research," *Journal of Higher Education* 61 (1): 17 (1990); W. Robert Connor, "Why We Need Independent Centers for Advanced Study," *Chronicle of Higher Education*, 17 January 2003, B10; Rebecca Chopp, "Beyond the Founding Fratricidal Conflict: A Tale of Three Cities," *Journal of the American Academy of Religion* 70 (3): 461–71 (2002).

77 *Spirituality and the Professoriate: A National Study of Faculty Beliefs, Attitudes, and Values* (Los Angeles: Higher Education Research Institute, UCLA, 2006), 4; Sean J. Gehrke, "Race and Pro-social Involvement: Toward a More Complex Understanding of Spiritual Development in College," in *Spirituality in College Students' Lives: Translating Research into Practice*, ed. Alyssa Bryant Rockenbach and Matthew J. Mayhew (New York: Routledge, 2013), 41.

78 Benjamin Ginsberg, *The Fall of the Faculty: The Rise of the All-Administrative University* (New York: Oxford University Press, 2011). See also Leo Reisberg, "Proliferation of Campus Clubs: Too Much of a Good Thing," *Chronicle of Higher Education*, 29 September 2009. See also Scott Jaschik, "High Court Rules in Favor of Religious Students," *Chronicle of Higher Education*, 7 July 1995; Eric Kelderman, "U. of Wisconsin Group Cannot Exclude Religious Group from Student Fees, Court Says," *Chronicle of Higher Education*, 1 September 2010.

79 In tracking the religious resurgence in American higher education, we will focus on diverse approaches to the categories of "religion" and "spirituality." Because this study explores the entire range of scholarship on religion in higher education, we do not settle on a single definition. Rather, we pay attention to when scholars, students, and colleges *say* they are engaging with religion or spirituality. In this way, we follow the approach of other recent studies. On the protean forms of the "practice and teaching of religion," see Cherry, DeBerg, and Porterfield, *Religion on Campus*, 5. For a discussion of the pluriform shape of religion in higher education, see Jacobsen and Jacobsen, *No Longer Invisible*, 16. On spirituality

and religion, see Penny Long Marler, "'Being Religious' or 'Being Spiritual' in America: A Zero-Sum Proposition?" *Journal for the Scientific Study of Religion* 41 (2): 289–300 (2002); Nancy T. Ammerman, "Spiritual but Not Religious? Beyond Binary Choices in the Study of Religion," *Journal for the Scientific Study of Religion* 52 (2): 267 (2013).

80 For an account of Princeton's growing religious diversity, see Frederick Houk Borsch, *Keeping Faith at Princeton: A Brief History of Religious Pluralism at Princeton and Other Universities* (Princeton, NJ: Princeton University Press, 2012). See the website of Princeton's Department of African American Studies, http://www.princeton.edu/africanamericanstudies/people/faculty/. The James Madison Program mission statement is available at http://web.princeton.edu/sites/jmadison/mission.html. On the teaching and the practice of religion at Princeton, see Justin Harmon, "Under-Studied Phenomenon: New Center for the Study of Religion to Promote Scholarship on Social, Cultural Practice," *Princeton Weekly Bulletin*, 22 March 1999; Robert Wuthnow, "Is There a Place for 'Scientific' Studies of Religion?" *Chronicle of Higher Education*, 24 January 2003. On African American studies, see Robert S. Boynton, "Princeton's Public Intellectual," *New York Times Magazine*, 15 September 1991; Eddie Glaude, "The Black Church Is Dead," *Huffington Post*, 24 February 2010, http://www.huffingtonpost.com/. On Robert George and the James Madison Program, see Maurice Timothy Reidy, "Catholicism on Campus: How Faith Is Presented at Secular Universities," *Commonweal*, 7 April 2006, 10–15; J. I. Merritt, "Heretic in the Temple," *Princeton Alumni Weekly*, 8 October 2003; George Weigel, "A Catholic Renaissance at Princeton," *Catholic Difference*, 9 November 2005, http://www.catholiceducation.org/. On Paul Raushenbush, see "A Moment with Paul Raushenbush," *Princeton Alumni Weekly*, 9 February 2005. For a list of student religious groups, see http://religiouslife.princeton.edu/chaplaincies-groups. For a discussion of religious diversity at Princeton, see Merrell Noden, "Keeping the Faith," *Princeton Alumni Weekly*, 17 December 2008; Sarah Pease-Kerr, "U to Hire First Full-Time Hindu, Muslim Chaplains," *Daily Princetonian*, 1 April 2008; Belda Chan, "'Coming Together' Sparks Interfaith Dialogue on Campus," *Daily Princetonian*, 18 February 2005.

81 Mahoney, Schmalzbauer, and Youniss, *Revitalizing Religion in the Academy*, 9.

Chapter 2

1 Much of this chapter originally appeared in John Schmalzbauer and Kathleen A. Mahoney, "Religion and Knowledge in the Post-Secular Academy," in *The Post-Secular in Question*, ed. Philip Gorski, David Kyuman Kim, and Jonathan VanAntwerpen (New York: New York University Press, 2012), 215–48, as well as John Schmalzbauer and Kathleen A. Mahoney, "American Scholars Return to Studying Religion," *Contexts*, 16–21 (Winter 2008). Another version was published as a working paper on the website of the Social Science Research Council: http://blogs.ssrc.org/.

For a discussion of the secularization of higher education, see Lawrence Veysey, *The Emergence of the American University* (Chicago: University of Chicago Press, 1965); Richard Hofstadter and Walter P. Metzger, *The Development of Academic Freedom in the United States* (New York: Columbia University Press, 1955); George M. Marsden, *The Soul of the American University: From Protestant Establishment to Established Nonbelief* (New York: Oxford University Press, 1994); Douglas Sloan, *Faith and Knowledge: Mainline Protestantism and American Higher Education* (Louisville, KY: Westminster John Knox Press, 1994); James T. Burtchaell, *The Dying of the Light: The Disengagement of Colleges and Universities from Their Christian Churches* (Grand Rapids, MI: Eerdmans, 1998).

2 For a critique of the secularization storyline as applied to higher education, see Douglas Jacobsen and Rhonda Hustedt Jacobsen, eds., *Scholarship and Christian Faith: Enlarging the Conversation* (New York: Oxford University Press, 2004). See also Mark Noll, "The Future of Religious Colleges: Looking Ahead by Looking Back," in *The Future of Religious Colleges*, ed. Paul Dovre (Grand Rapids, MI: Eerdmans, 2002), 73–94. On pages 88–89, Noll notes that while secularization changed the university, it "would not be responsible to think that the only live possibilities are crabbed sectarian isolation or the steady creep of enervating secularism." For a similar view, see Martin Marty's foreword to *Scholarship and Christian Faith*, vii. Challenging the secularization thesis, Marty rejects "complaints and whimpers" about "what went wrong with Christian scholarship," including such storylines as "In a golden age theology was queen of the sciences and now it is not."

3 Marsden, *The Soul of the American University*; Sloan, *Faith and Knowledge*; Julie A. Reuben, *The Making of the Modern University: Intellectual Transformation and the Marginalization of Morality* (Chicago: University of Chicago Press, 1996); Jon Roberts and James Turner, *The Sacred and the Secular University* (Princeton, NJ: Princeton University Press, 2000), 36; Roger L. Geiger, *The History of American Higher Education: Learning and Culture from the Founding to World War II* (Princeton, NJ: Princeton University Press, 2015), 337.

4 Christian Smith, "Introduction: Rethinking the Secularization of American Public Life," in *The Secular Revolution: Power, Interests, and Conflict in the Secularization of American Public Life*, ed. Christian Smith (Berkeley: University of California Press, 2003); Smith, "Secularizing American Higher Education: The Case of Early American Sociology," in Smith, *The Secular Revolution*, 97–159.

5 On the incomplete status of secularization, see Smith, "Introduction"; Smith, "Secularizing American Higher Education."

6 See Peter Steinfels, "Swapping 'Religion' for 'Postsecularism,'" *New York Times*, 3 August 2002; Douglas Jacobsen and Rhonda Hustedt Jacobsen, eds., *The American University in a Postsecular Age* (New York: Oxford University Press, 2008); Mark Clayton, "Scholars Get Religion," *Christian Science Monitor*, 26 February 2002, http://www.csmonitor.com/2002/0226/p12s01-lehl.html; Alan Wolfe, "A Welcome Revival of Religion in the Academy," *Chronicle of Higher Education*, 19 September 1997, B4; John A. McClure, "Post-Secular Culture: The Return of Religion in Contemporary Theory and Literature," *CrossCurrents* 47 (3): 332–47 (1997). See also John D. Boy, "What We Talk about When We Talk about the Postsecular," Immanent Frame, 15 March 2011, http://blogs.ssrc.org/; Gregor McLennan, "The Postsecular Turn," *Theory, Culture, and Society* 28 (4): 3–20 (2010). For a more critical view, see James Beckford, "Public Religions and the Postsecular: Critical Reflections," *Journal for the Scientific Study of Religion* 51 (1): 1–19 (2012).

7 Sally Promey, "The 'Return' of Religion in the Scholarship on American Art," *Art Bulletin* 85 (3): 581–603 (2003); Bruce Holsinger, "Literary History and the Religious Turn," *English Language Notes* 44 (1): 1–4 (2006); Quentin Smith, "The Metaphilosophy of Naturalism," *Philo* 4 (2) (2001). See also Andreas Andreopoulos, "The Return of Religion in Contemporary Music," *Literature and Theology* 14 (1): 81–95 (2000); Richard Schaefer, "Intellectual History and the Return of Religion," *Historically Speaking* 12 (2): 30–31 (2011); Vendulka Kubalkova, "The 'Turn to Religion' in International Relations Theory," *E-International Relations*, 3 December 2013, http://www.e-ir.info/; Kenneth D. Wald, Adam L. Silverman, and Kevin S. Fridy, "Making Sense of Religion in Political Life," *Annual Review of Political Science* 8: 121–43 (2005); D. W. Miller, "Programs in Social Work Embrace the Teaching of Spirituality," *Chronicle of Higher Education*, 18 May 2001, A12; Katherine S. Mangan, "Medical Schools Begin Teaching Spiritual Side of Health

Care," *Chronicle of Higher Education*, 7 March 1997; Michelle Boorstein, "Study of Health and Religiosity Growing Despite Criticism," *Washington Post*, 6 December 2008; Helen Rose Ebaugh, "Return of the Sacred: Reintegrating Religion in the Social Sciences," *Journal for the Scientific Study of Religion* 41 (3): 385–95 (2002). William Ringenberg estimates that there are about fifty Christian scholarly associations in the United States in *The Christian College: A History of Protestant Higher Education in America* (Grand Rapids, MI: Baker Academic, 2006), 215. This does not include organizations such as the North American Association of Islamic and Muslim Studies and the Association for the Philosophy of Judaism.

8 On organizations and networks in movements, see Smith, preface to *The Secular Revolution*, vii.

9 This formulation of the return of religion draws on language from Schmalzbauer and Mahoney, "Religion and Knowledge," 216.

10 For a fuller discussion of this literature, see John Schmalzbauer, "Marsden and Secularization," in *American Evangelicalism: George Marsden and the State of American Religious History* (Notre Dame, IN: University of Notre Dame Press, 2014), 283–311. For standard statements of the secularization argument, see Marsden, *The Soul of the American University*, 34–44. On Harvard's early history, see Samuel Eliot Morrison, *The Founding of Harvard College* (Cambridge, MA: Harvard University Press, 1935). On the professional aspirations of early collegians, see James Axtell, *Wisdom's Workshop: The Rise of the Modern University* (Princeton, NJ: Princeton University Press, 2016), 18; Bruce A. Kimball, *The "True Professional Ideal" in America: A History* (Cambridge, MA: Blackwell, 1992), appendix 2; John Thelin, *A History of American Higher Education* (Baltimore: Johns Hopkins University Press, 2011), 13.

11 Hofstadter and Metzger, *The Development of Academic Freedom*; Mark Noll, *Princeton and the Republic, 1762–1822: The Search for a Christian Enlightenment in the Era of Samuel Stanhope Smith* (Princeton, NJ: Princeton University Press, 1989); Henry May, *The Enlightenment in America* (New York: Oxford University Press, 1978); Reuben, *The Making of the Modern University*, 19–23. For a discussion of the antebellum colleges, see Roger L. Geiger, ed., *The American College in the Nineteenth Century* (Nashville, TN: Vanderbilt University Press, 2000); David Potts, *Baptist Colleges in the Development of American Society* (New York: Garland, 1988). The idea of an American *paideia* is developed in Lawrence A. Cremin, *American Education: The National Experience, 1783–1876* (New York: Harper and Row, 1980).

12 Reuben, *The Making of the Modern University*, 17–35, 73–76; Julie A. Reuben, "Writing when Everything Has Been Said: The History of American Higher Education following Lawrence Veysey's Classic," *History of Education Quarterly* 45 (3): 412–19 (2007); Marsden, *The Soul of the American University*; Charles W. Eliot, "Address at the Inauguration of Daniel Coit Gilman," in *Educational Reform: Essays and Addresses*, ed. Charles W. Eliot (New York: Century, 1898), 42–43.

13 The first approach can be found in Richard Hofstadter, *Academic Freedom in the Age of the College* (New Brunswick, NJ: Transaction, 1995). The second is described in George Marsden's *The Soul of the American University*, 156–59, 408.

14 Jon H. Roberts and James Turner, *The Sacred and the Secular University* (Princeton, NJ: Princeton University Press, 2000), 36.

15 See Dorothy Ross, *The Origins of American Social Science* (Cambridge: Cambridge University Press, 1991); S. E. Henking, "Sociological Christianity and Christian Sociology: The Paradox of Early American Sociology," *Religion and American Culture* 3 (1): 49–67

(1993); William Swatos, "The Faith of the Fathers: On the Christianity of Early American Sociology," *Sociological Analysis* 44 (1): 33–53 (1983); Smith, "Secularizing American Higher Education," 126; Reuben, *The Making of the Modern University*, 133–229; Bruce Kuklick, *A History of Philosophy in America, 1720–2000* (New York: Clarendon Press, 2003), xii, 282; Bruce Kuklick, *Churchmen and Philosophers: From Jonathan Edwards to John Dewey* (New Haven, CT: Yale University Press, 1985). On Dewey's combination of religious and secular impulses, see Martin E. Marty, *Modern American Religion*, vol. 1, *The Irony of It All, 1893–1919* (Chicago: University of Chicago Press, 1986), 90.

16 David A. Hollinger, *Science, Jews, and Secular Culture: Studies in Mid-Twentieth-Century American Intellectual History* (Princeton, NJ: Princeton University Press, 1998), 29; David A. Hollinger, "The 'Secularization' Question and the United States in the Twentieth Century," *Church History* 70 (1): 132–43 (2001); Edward S. Shapiro, "The Friendly University: Jews in Academia since World War II," *Judaism* 46 (3): 365–74 (1997); Paul Ritterband and Harold S. Wechsler, *Jewish Learning in American Universities: The First Century* (Bloomington: Indiana University Press, 1994); Lila Corwin Berman, *Speaking of Jews: Rabbis, Intellectuals, and the Creation of an American Public Identity* (Berkeley: University of California Press, 2009).

17 Smith, "Secularizing American Higher Education"; Roger Finke and Rodney Stark, *Acts of Faith: Explaining the Human Side of Religion* (Berkeley: University of California Press, 2000), see especially pages 1–41. As Julie Reuben notes, "The scientific study of religion declined rapidly in the 1920's." Reuben, *The Making of the Modern University*, 118.

18 Myer S. Reed, "After the Alliance: The Sociology of Religion in the United States from 1925 to 1949," *Sociological Analysis* 43 (3): 191 (1982).

19 Ted G. Jelen, "Research in Religion and Mass Political Behavior in the United States: Looking Both Ways after Two Decades of Scholarship," *American Politics Quarterly* 26 (1): 110–35 (1998). Historian Charles Beard is quoted in Robert P. Swierenga, "Religion and American Voting Behavior, 1830s to 1930s," in *The Oxford Handbook of Religion and American Politics*, ed. Corwin Smidt, James L. Guth, Lyman A. Kellstedt (New York: Oxford University Press, 2009), 69.

20 On seminaries and church-related colleges, see Dorothy C. Bass, "Ministry on the Margins: Protestants and Education," in *Between the Times: The Travail of the Protestant Establishment in America, 1900–1960*, ed. William R. Hutchison (Cambridge: Cambridge University Press, 1989), 48–71; Conrad Cherry, *Hurrying toward Zion: Universities, Divinity Schools, and American Protestantism* (Bloomington: Indiana University Press, 1995); Sloan, *Faith and Knowledge*; William Halsey, *The Survival of American Innocence: Catholicism in an Era of Disillusionment, 1920–1940* (Notre Dame, IN: University of Notre Dame Press, 1980).

21 Merrimon Cuninggim, *The College Seeks Religion* (New Haven, CT: Yale University Press, 1947), 30, as quoted in Sloan, *Faith and Knowledge*, 35; Will Herberg, *Protestant—Catholic—Jew: An Essay in American Religious Sociology* (New York: Doubleday, 1983), 53.

22 The account of the revival in this paragraph and the ones that follow is drawn from Sloan, *Faith and Knowledge*; Cherry, *Hurrying toward Zion*; D. G. Hart, *The University Gets Religion: Religious Studies in American Higher Education* (Baltimore: Johns Hopkins University Press, 1999).

23 On the popularity of religion classes, see Hart, *The University Gets Religion*, 111. Hart cites data taken from Claude Welch, *Graduate Education in Religion: A Critical Appraisal* (Missoula: University of Montana Press, 1971), 230–35.

24 On the organizational foundings in this era, see Sloan, *Faith and Knowledge*; James Gilbert, *Redeeming Culture: American Religion in an Age of Science* (Chicago: University of Chicago Press, 1997), 252–95.

25 The figures come from Sloan, *Faith and Knowledge*, 85. See also Hart, *The University Gets Religion*; Cherry, *Hurrying toward Zion*; Dorothy C. Bass, "The Independent Sector and the Educational Strategies of Mainstream Protestantism, 1900–1980," in *Religion, the Independent Sector, and American Culture*, ed. Conrad Cherry and Rowland A. Sherrill (Atlanta: Scholars Press, 1992), 51–72.

26 On the blurred boundaries between liberal Protestantism and the academic study of religion in the area of curriculum, see Hart, *The University Gets Religion*; Amanda Porterfield, *The Transformation of American Religion: The Story of a Late Twentieth-Century Awakening* (New York: Oxford University Press, 2001); Cherry, *Hurrying toward Zion*.

27 Arthur Schlesinger Jr., "The Thirteen Books You Must Read to Understand America: Schlesinger's Syllabus," *American Heritage*, February–March 1998, 30–36.

28 Sidney Hook, "The New Medievalism," *New Republic*, 28 October 1940, 604–6. See Hart, *The University Gets Religion*, for a discussion on the role of religion in the curriculum.

29 Dorothy C. Bass in "Church-Related Colleges: Transmitters of Denominational Cultures?" in *Beyond Establishment: Protestant Identity in a Post-Protestant Age*, ed. Jackson Carroll and Wade Clark Roof (Louisville, KY: Westminster John Knox Press, 1993), 157–72; Sloan, *Faith and Knowledge*; Hutchison, *Between the Times*.

30 Sallie TeSelle, "Editorial," *Soundings* 51 (1): 2–3 (1968).

31 On mainline Protestants in higher education, see Sloan, *Faith and Knowledge*, 185. Bass tells the story of the Danforth Foundation's decision to end grants to religion and higher education in "The Independent Sector."

32 On American religious history in the 1970s, see Harry S. Stout and Robert M. Taylor Jr., "Studies of Religion in American Society: The State of the Art," in *New Directions in American Religious History*, ed. Harry S. Stout and D. G. Hart (New York: Oxford University Press, 1997), 15–47; Nancy T. Ammerman, "Sociology and the Study of Religion," in *Religion, Scholarship, and Higher Education: Perspectives, Models, and Future Prospects*, ed. Andrea Sterk (Notre Dame, IN: University of Notre Dame Press, 2002), 77, 78. For a critical assessment of the behavioral revolution in political science, see James F. Farr, "Remembering the Revolution: Behavioralism in American Political Science," in *Political Science in History: Research Programs and Political Traditions*, ed. James F. Farr, John S. Dryzek, and Stephen T. Leonard (Cambridge: Cambridge University Press, 1995), 203, 204; Kenneth Wald and Clyde Wilcox, "Getting Religion: Has Political Science Rediscovered the Faith Factor?" *American Political Science Review* 100 (4): 523–29 (2006).

33 See Sarah Imhoff, "The Creation Story, or How We Learned to Stop Worrying and Love *Schempp*," *Journal of the American Academy of Religion* 84 (2): 466–97 (2016). This paragraph draws on Schmalzbauer, "Fifty Years of Non-sectarian Study of Religion," in *Proceedings: Third Biennial Conference on Religion and American Culture*, Center for the Study of Religion and American Culture, Indiana University–Purdue University Indianapolis, June 2013, 10–12. Data on new programs from Welch, *Graduate Education in Religion*, 174. See Cherry, *Hurrying toward Zion*, 112–23. Porterfield discusses the "Post-Protestant" phase of religious studies in *The Transformation of American Religion*, 209–26. See also Hart, *The University Gets Religion*; Bass, "The Independent Sector."

34 This argument is articulated in N. J. Demerath III, "Cultural Victory and Organizational Defeat in the Paradoxical Decline of Liberal Protestantism," *Journal for the Scientific Study of Religion* 34 (4): 458–70 (1995).

35 See Hart, *The University Gets Religion*; Porterfield, *The Transformation of American Religion*; Cherry, *Hurrying toward Zion*; Sloan, *Faith and Knowledge*.

36 Figures from http://studyofreligion.fas.harvard.edu/profile-type/staff and http://hds.harvard.edu/faculty-research/faculty/faculty-of-divinity.

37 On the growth of public university religious studies departments between 1999–2000 and 2004–2005, see "AAR Undergraduate Departments Survey Shows Increases in Religious Studies," *Religious Studies News*, May 2008, 11–12. On the increased number of Hinduism and Islam sections, see "The Religion Major and Liberal Education: A White Paper," https://www.aarweb.org/about/teagleaar-white-paper. On new funding sources and positions in Islamic studies, see Edward E. Curtis IV, "Explaining Islam to the Public," Immanent Frame, 9 May 2011, http://blogs.ssrc.org/.

38 "AAR Undergraduate Departments Survey," 11–12. On the high proportion of AAR papers on theology, see Hans Hillerbrand, "A Message from the President," *Religious Studies News*, May 2005, 10.

39 See Rebecca Chopp's presidential address in "Beyond the Founding Fratricidal Conflict: A Tale of Three Cities," *Journal of the American Academy of Religion* 70 (3): 461–74 (2002). On the Theological Programs Initiative, see "AAR Announces Major New Program Initiative," *Religious Studies News*, May 2005, 9.

40 On these tensions, see Charlotte Allen, "Is Nothing Sacred? Casting Out the Gods from Religious Studies," *Lingua Franca*, November 1996, 30–40. The reference to a "hegemonic liberal Protestant framework" comes from Luther H. Martin and Donald Wiebe, "Establishing a Beachhead: NAASR, Twenty Years Later," unpublished paper, 2004, 1–2, https://web.archive.org/web/*/http://www.naasr.com/Establishingabeachhead.pdf. Russell McCutcheon, *Critics Not Caretakers: Redescribing the Public Study of Religion* (Albany: SUNY Press, 2001). On the SBL, see John Dart, "Scholars and Believers," *Christian Century*, 5 April 2011, 34–38; Ronald S. Hendel, "Farewell to SBL: Faith and Reason in Biblical Studies," *Biblical Archaeology Review*, July/August 2010; Jacques Berlinerblau, "What's Wrong with the Society of Biblical Literature?" *Chronicle of Higher Education*, 10 November 2006. While Hendel later returned to the SBL's journal, Berlinerblau praised the Society's "new management" under executive director John Kutsko. See Ronald Hendel, "Mind the Gap: Modern and Postmodern in Biblical Studies," *Journal of Biblical Literature* 133 (2): 422–43 (2014); Jacques Berlinerblau, "An Afternoon with the Society for Pentecostal Studies," *Chronicle of Higher Education*, 22 November 2011. Conrad Cherry recognizes both "empathetic participation as well as critical distance" in *Hurrying toward Zion*, 117.

41 Chopp, "Beyond the Founding Fratricidal Conflict."

42 *American Academy of Religion Annual Report*, 2000 and 2008. For the 2000 annual report, see http://web.archive.org/web/20070226105611/http://www.aarweb.org/about/annualreport/AR2000.pdf. The 2008 report and the 2017 membership of the AAR are from the AAR website, https://web.archive.org/web/20120112180731/http://www.aarweb.org/Publications/Annual_Report/2008.pdf. The 2010 SBL report and the 2017 membership of the SBL are from the SBL website, http://www.sbl-site.org/.

43 Data on enrollment and majors from David V. Brewington, "AAR Undergraduate Departments Survey Comparative Analysis of Wave I and Wave II," *Religious Studies News*, May 2008, 14–15. Data on the percentage increase in enrollment between 1996 and 2005 derived from "Table 303.10: Total fall enrollment in degree-granting postsecondary institutions, by attendance status, sex of student, and control of institution: Selected years, 1947 through 2023," *Digest of Education Statistics* (Washington, DC: Department of

Education, 2013). Data on the growth in philosophy and religion graduates from "Change in Number of Bachelor's Degrees Awarded, by Field of Study, 1991–2011," in *Almanac of Higher Education 2013* (Washington, DC: Chronicle of Higher Education, 2013). Between 1991 and 2011, the number of bachelor's degrees increased by 57 percent. During the same period, the number of philosophy and religion graduates increased by 75 percent. See also Lisa Miller, "Religious Studies Revival," *Newsweek Education*, 12 September 2010.

44 In 2014, the University of Melbourne sponsored a conference on the "return of religion in contemporary continental philosophy." See https://blogs.deakin.edu.au/philosophy/the-return-of-religion-in-contemporary-continental-philosophy/. See also Hent de Vries, ed., *Philosophy and the Turn to Religion* (Baltimore: Johns Hopkins University Press, 1999); Linda Alcoff and John Caputo, eds., *Feminism, Sexuality, and the Return of Religion* (Bloomington: Indiana University Press, 2011); Smith, "The Metaphilosophy of Naturalism," https://web.archive.org/web/20051017034837/http://www.philoonline.org/library/smith_4_2.htm.

45 Smith dates the return of theism to Plantinga's book in "The Metaphilosophy of Naturalism." Membership of the Society and the *Time* quote reported in Kelly James Clark, "Introduction: The Literature of Confession," in *Philosophers Who Believe: The Spiritual Journeys of 11 Leading Thinkers*, ed. Kelly James Clark (Downers Grove, IL: InterVarsity Press, 1993), 7–8. The quotation is from Alvin Plantinga, "Advice to Christian Philosophers," *Faith and Philosophy: Journal of the Society of Christian Philosophers* 1 (1984), http://www.leaderu.com/truth/1truth10.html. See also "Religion: Modernizing the case for God," *Time*, 7 April 1980.

46 On the return of theism, see Jennifer Schuessler, "Philosopher Sticks Up for God," *New York Times*, 13 December 2011. See also Nathan Schneider, "Saving Faith: The Renewed Stature of Christian Philosophy," *Commonweal* (Web exclusive), 13 March 2013, http://www.commonwealmagazine.org/saving-faith. On philanthropic support for evangelical scholarship in philosophy and other disciplines, see Michael S. Hamilton and Johanna G. Yngvason, "Patrons of the Evangelical Mind," *Christianity Today*, 8 July 2002, . Plantinga noted the high number of conservative Protestant philosophy graduate students at Notre Dame in the "Spiritual Autobiography" he wrote for the 125th anniversary of Calvin College. See https://web.archive.org/web/20170704180859/http://www.calvin.edu/125th/wolterst/p_bio.pdf. A list of Plantinga's graduate students can be found at http://philosophy.nd.edu/graduate-program/recent-placements/past-ph-d-recipients/. On master-pupil chains, see Randall Collins, *The Sociology of Philosophies: A Global Theory of Intellectual Change* (Cambridge, MA: Harvard University Press, 1998), 76. On Plantinga's influence on Jewish and Muslim scholars, see Kelly James Clark, "Alvin Plantinga and the Revival of Religious Philosophy," *Huffington Post*, 8 May 2017, http://www.huffingtonpost.com/. See also Thomas Morris, ed., *God and the Philosophers: The Reconciliation of Faith and Reason* (New York: Oxford University Press, 1994); and Clark, *Philosophers Who Believe*. For a list of current and past fellows, see the website of the Center for Philosophy of Religion, http://philreligion.nd.edu/.

47 Nathan Schneider discusses Plantinga's student Michael J. Murray in "The Templeton Effect," *Chronicle Review*, 3 September 2012. See also Libby A. Nelson, "Where Philosophy Meets Theology," *Inside Higher Ed*, 21 May 2003.

48 The 2009 PhilPapers Survey had 3,226 respondents, including 1803 faculty and 829 graduate students. Just over 900 respondents were from the United States. For more information, see http://philpapers.org/surveys/.

49 As MIT professor Alex Byrne noted in the *Boston Review*, "Christian philosophers often content themselves with pulling up the drawbridge and manning the barricades, rather than crusading against the infidel." The result is less than convincing to those outside the household of faith. See Byrne, "God: Philosophers Weigh In," *Boston Review*, January/February 2009.

50 McClure, "Post-Secular Culture," 332–47; John A. McClure, "Postmodern/Post-Secular: Contemporary Fiction and Spirituality," *Modern Fiction Studies* 41 (1): 141–63 (1995). See also Michael Kaufmann, "Locating the Postsecular," *Religion and Literature* 41 (3): 68–73 (2009); Magdalena Maczynska, "Toward a Postsecular Literary Criticism: Examining Ritual Gestures in Zadie Smith's 'Autograph Man,'" *Religion and Literature* 41 (3): 73–82 (2009).

51 Edward Said, *The World, the Text, and the Critic* (Cambridge, MA: Harvard University Press, 1983), 291. For a discussion of Said's views on religion, see McClure, "Post-Secular Culture," 334–35.

52 George Steiner, *Real Presences* (Chicago: University of Chicago Press, 1989), 3.

53 Alfred Kazin, *God and the American Writer* (New York: Random House, 1997); McClure, "Post-Secular Culture," 334.

54 See a description of the *English Language Notes* issue in "Literary History and the Religious Turn," special issue, *ELN* 44 (1) (2006), http://www.colorado.edu/english-language-notes/issues/44-1. See also Stanley Fish, "One University under God?" *Chronicle of Higher Education*, 7 January 2005; Terry Eagleton, *Culture and the Death of God* (New Haven, CT: Yale University Press, 2014); Paul Griffiths, "Christ and Critical Theory," *First Things*, August/September 2004, 46–55.

55 On the AAR and the MLA, see Boston College's report on religion and the arts, http://www.bc.edu/content/dam/files/publications/relarts/pdf/institute_proposal.pdf. The CCL membership figure of 1,300 is from http://www.hope.edu/academic/english/huttar/conference.html. See also Harold K. Bush, "The Outrageous Idea of a Christian Literary Studies: Prospects for the Future and a Meditation on Hope," *Christianity and Literature* 51 (1): 79–103 (2001). See also Dennis Taylor, "The Need for a Religious Literary Criticism," *Religion and Arts* 1 (1): 124–50 (1996).

56 Robert B. Townsend, "A New Found Religion? The Field Surges among AHA Members," *Perspectives on History*, December 2009; Robert B. Townsend, "AHA Membership on the Rise Again in 2011," *AHA Today*, 20 July 2011. Ray Haberski discusses the religious turn in "Why Academia Found God," U.S. Intellectual History Blog, 15 March 2013, http://s-usih.org/. See also David Hollinger, "After Cloven Tongues of Fire: Ecumenical Protestantism and the Modern American Encounter with Diversity," *Journal of American History* 98 (1): 21–48 (2011).

57 On the growing interest of secular historians in American religion, see David Hollinger, "Off the Cuff: Religion and the Historical Profession," Immanent Frame, 30 December 2009, http://blogs.ssrc.org/. Urging readers to thank Sarah Palin, Hollinger argues that religion is "harder to ignore if it keeps coming back and hitting you again and again." According to sociologist Peter Berger, scholarship on religious fundamentalism is "a matter of knowing one's enemies." See Berger, "The Desecularization of the World: A Global Overview," in *The Desecularization of the World: Resurgent Religion and World Politics*, ed. Peter Berger (Grand Rapids, MI: Eerdmans, 1999), 2. By contrast, Michael Kazin writes that "more liberal historians and social scientists, whether or not they are Christians, have been writing about the religious underpinnings of American politics and American culture

and arguing that people of faith have been active as often on the left as on the right." See Marvin Olasky, "Unlikely Praise: Liberal Author Michael Kazin on Fundamentalist William Jennings Bryan as a Hero for the Left," *World*, 11 March 2006.

58 Henry May, "The Recovery of American Religious History," *American Historical Review* 70 (1): 79–92 (1964). The account of this period (including the survey) is drawn from Stout and Taylor, "Studies of Religion in American Society," 23, 15, 21. Stout and Taylor discuss the move away from mainline Protestant divinity schools to new departments of religious studies. For a list of Marty's 115 doctoral students, see http://www.illuminos.com/mem/advisees.html. Ahlstrom student Peter Williams estimates his mentor had three dozen doctoral students in Williams, review of *A Religious History of the American People*, 2nd ed., *Anglican and Episcopal History* 76 (1): 119 (2007). For a list of centers and institutes focused on North American religion, see *Centers and Institutes Project 2006* (Indianapolis: Center for the Study of Religion and American Culture, 2006). This list is available at https://web.archive.org/web/20130403143222/http://www.iupui.edu/~raac/CIP.html. On philanthropy and American religious history, see Hamilton and Yngvason, "Patrons of the Evangelical Mind." For the data from the 1993 survey, see Stout and Taylor, "Studies of Religion in American Society," 15, 22. Information on the Young Scholars in American Religion program can be found at raac.iupui.edu. The 4,771 number is from Thomas A. Tweed, "Expanding the Study of U.S. Religion: Reflections on the State of a Subfield," *Religion* 40 (4): 253 (2010).

59 On this shift, see David Lotz, "A Changing Historiography: From Church History to Religious History," in *Altered Landscapes: Christianity in America, 1935–1985*, ed. David W. Lotz with Donald W. Shriver (Grand Rapids, MI: Eerdmans, 1989), 332–36. The phrase "new evangelical historiography" was coined by Leonard Sweet in "Wise as Serpents, Innocent as Doves: The New Evangelical Historiography," *Journal of the American Academy of Religion* 56 (3): 397–416 (1988).

60 Michael Paulson, "Evangelicals Find Place at Mainstream Colleges," *Boston Globe*, 20 February 2000, A1. On philanthropy and American religious history, see Hamilton and Yngvason, "Patrons of the Evangelical Mind." See also Stout and Taylor, "Studies of Religion in American Society," 15, 22.

61 Butler quoted in Stout and Taylor, "Studies of Religion in American Society," 19.

62 On the emergence of new narratives, see Thomas A. Tweed, ed., *Retelling U.S. Religious History* (Berkeley: University of California Press, 1997). On American Catholic Studies, see R. Scott Appleby, "Historicizing the People of God: The Cushwa Center and the Vision of Its Founder," *U.S. Catholic Historian* 19 (1): 93–98 (2001); Deborah Dash Moore, "North American Jewish Studies," paper presented at the Thirtieth Anniversary Conference: At the Cutting Edge of Jewish Studies: The Most Recent Developments in the Field, May 9–10, 1999, http://jewish30yrs.mcgill.ca/moore/index.html.

63 Clarence Taylor, "Review: A Glorious Age for African-American Religion," *Journal of American Ethnic History* 15 (2): 79 (1996); Ann Braude, "Women's History *Is* American Religious History," in Tweed, *Retelling U.S. Religious History*, 87–107. For more on the philanthropic support for Harvard Women's Studies in Religion Program and for information on the research associates, see the Program website, http://wsrp.hds.harvard.edu/.

64 Daniel Bell, "The Return of the Sacred? The Argument on the Future of Religion," in *The Winding Passage: Essays and Sociological Journeys*, ed. Daniel Bell (New York: Basic Books, 1980), 324–54. See also Fran Schumer, "A Return to Religion," *New York Times Magazine*, 15 April 1984, SM90.

65 Berger, *The Desecularization of the World*; Ebaugh, "Return of the Sacred," 385–95; Ammerman, "Sociology and the Study of Religion." The Spring/Summer 2006 issue of the *Hedgehog Review* was entitled "After Secularism."

66 The Wald quotation comes from Wald, Silverman, and Fridy, "Making Sense of Religion," 121. See also David Leege and Lyman Kellstedt, eds., *Rediscovering the Religious Factor in American Politics* (Armonk, NY: M. E. Sharpe, 1993). The August 2014 membership counts for the APSA's sections are from the APSA website, http://www.apsanet.org/. Much of this account of the field of political science is taken from Wald and Wilcox, "Getting Religion."

67 For more on the task force on "Religion and Democracy in the United States," see the committee's website, https://web.archive.org/web/20070713042105/http://www.apsanet.org/section_684.cfm. The committee's conclusions can be found in Alan Wolfe and Ira Katznelson, eds., *Religion and Democracy in the United States: Danger or Opportunity?* (Princeton, NJ: Princeton University Press, 2010).

68 Monica Duffy Toft, Daniel Philpott, and Timothy Shah, *God's Century: Resurgent Religion and Global Politics* (New York: W. W. Norton, 2011); Timothy Shah and Daniel Philpott, "The Fall and Rise of Religion in International Relations: History and Theory," in *Religion and International Relations Theory*, ed. Jack Snyder (New York: Columbia University Press, 2011), 24–59. On the Luce Foundation's initiative, see the Foundation's website, http://www.hluce.org/.

69 David Smilde and Matthew May, "The Emerging Strong Program in the Sociology of Religion," Social Science Research Council Working Paper, 8 February 2010, 3, http://blogs.ssrc.org/tif/wp-content/uploads/2010/02/Emerging-Strong-Program-TIF.pdf.

70 The membership of the American Sociological Association's sections (including Sociology of Religion) can be found at the Association's website, http://www.asanet.org/. On graduate student interests, see Michael Kisielewski with John Curtis, "Faculty Position Opportunities in Sociology Appear to Hold Steady: Position Postings from the 2013 ASA Job Bank," *Data Brief*, August 2014, 6–7, also on the Association's website.

71 A list of SSRC Religion and the Public Sphere publications can be found on the Immanent Frame website, http://tif.ssrc.org.

72 Jonathan Sheehan, "Teaching Calvin in California," *New York Times*, 12 September 2016.

73 On the early SSSR, see Gilbert, *Redeeming Culture*, 253–71. The goals statement from SSSR organizer J. Paul Williams appears on page 256. On the Harvard seminar, see Stark and Finke, *Acts of Faith*, 16. Peter Berger, *A Rumor of Angels: Modern Sociology and the Rediscovery of the Supernatural* (New York: Doubleday, 1969), 59; Linda Woodhead, ed., *Peter Berger and the Study of Religion* (New York: Routledge, 2001). See Bellah, "Christianity and Symbolism Realism," in *The Social Meanings of Religion*, ed. William M. Newman (Chicago: Rand McNally College, 1974), 117, 115.

74 Herbert Gans, "Best-Sellers by Sociologists: An Exploratory Study," *Contemporary Sociology* 26 (2): 131–35 (1997). On the Berkeley Circle and its intellectual offspring, see Stark and Finke, *Acts of Faith*, 17–18; Michael Linsday, "How Bellah's Ideas Spread: The Diffusion of a Scholar's Influence," *ASA Footnotes* (May/June 2007); "Jeffrey Alexander's Comments on the Passing of Robert Bellah," https://web-beta.archive.org/web/20151217222604/http://ccs.research.yale.edu/alexander_bellah/.

75 Robert Wuthnow, "Living the Question—Evangelical Christianity and Critical Thought," *CrossCurrents* 40 (2): 160–76 (1990); Christian Smith, *What Is a Person? Rethinking Humanity, Social Life, and Moral Good from the Person Up* (Chicago: University of Chicago Press, 2010), 99; Christian Smith et al., "Roundtable on the Sociology of Religion:

Twenty-Three Theses on the Status of Religion in American Sociology—A Mellon Working-Group Reflection," *Journal of the American Academy of Religion* 81 (4): 927 (2013).

76 On the Society for the Anthropology of Religion, see Simon Coleman, "Recent Developments in the Anthropology of Religion," in *The New Blackwell Companion to the Sociology of Religion*, ed. Bryan Turner (Chichester, UK: Blackwell, 2010), 103. See also Joel Robbins, "Anthropology and Theology: An Awkward Relationship," *Anthropological Quarterly* 79 (2): 285–94 (2006); Joel Robbins and Matthew Engelke, "Introduction," *South Atlantic Quarterly* 109 (4): 625 (2010); Philip Fountain and Sin Wen Lau, "Anthropological Theologies: Engagements and Encounters," *Australian Journal of Anthropology* 24 (3): 227–34 (2013).

77 Robert A. Emmons and Raymond E. Paloutzian, "The Psychology of Religion," *Annual Review of Psychology* 54: 379 (2003).

78 The 2010 membership of Division 36 is from the APA website, http://www.apa.org/. See also Mary E. Reuder, "A History of Division 36 (Psychology of Religion)," on the APA divisions website, http://www.apadivisions.org/.

79 On the Harvard seminar, see Stark and Finke, *Acts of Faith*, 16. On the debate between Ellis and Bergin, see Michael E. Nielsen, "Psychology of Religion in the USA," http://www.psywww.com/psyrelig/USA.html; P. Scott Richards and Allen Bergin, *A Spiritual Strategy for Counseling and Psychotherapy* (Washington, DC: American Psychological Association, 1997). APA Division 36 index on the psychology of religion from http://www.apadivisions.org/division-36/about/sommervogel.aspx.

80 For more on the North American Association of Christians in Social Work, see http://www.nacsw.org/. On the number of programs with religion courses, see Miller, "Programs in Social Work," A12. On the Society for Spirituality and Social Work, see http://societyforspiritualityandsocialwork.com/. See also Edward Canda, Mitsuko Nakashima, Virginia Burgess, Robin Russel, and Sharon Barfield, *Spirituality and Religion in Social Work Practice* (Alexandria, VA: Council on Social Work Education, 2009); Holly K. Oxhandler and Kenneth I. Pargament, "Social Work Practitioners' Integration of Clients' Religion and Spirituality in Practice: A Literature Review," *Social Work* 59 (3): 271–79 (2014). On the CSWE's Religion and Spirituality Work Group, see the CSWE website, http://www.cswe.org/.

81 On the increase in the number of medical schools with religion-oriented courses see David G. Myers, "Stress and Health," in *Psychology* (New York: Worth, 2006). The quotation on the growth of the literature is from Harold Koenig, "Religion, Spirituality, and Health: The Research and Clinical Implications," *ISRN Psychiatry*, 2012. MEDLINE figures reported in Harold Koenig, *Spirituality in Patient Care* (West Conshohocken, PA: Templeton Press, 2013), 4. See the website of the Center for Spirituality, Theology, and Health, http://www.dukespiritualityandhealth.org/. Information on federal support for alternative health research can be found on the website of the National Center for Complementary and Integrative Health, https://nccih.nih.gov. The David Myers quote is from "On Assessing Prayer, Faith, and Health," *Reformed Review* 53 (2): 119–26 (2000).

82 Richard Sloan, *Blind Faith: The Unholy Alliance of Religion and Medicine* (New York: St. Martin's Press, 2006).

83 Laurel Thomas Gregory, "UM to Lead Major Effort to Solidify Research on Religion and Health," *University Record*, 14 October 2013, http://ur.umich.edu/1314/Oct14_13/4953-um-to-lead.

84 First quotation from Huston Smith, *Why Religion Matters: The Fate of the Human Spirit in an Age of Disbelief* (San Francisco: HarperSanFrancisco, 2001), 72–73. On the Science and Religion Course Program, see the website of the Center for Theology and the Natural

Sciences, http://www.ctns.org/news_090102.html. See the website of the Dialogue on Science, Ethics, and Religion, http://www.aaas.org/DoSER.

85 Dennis Cheek, "Interdisciplinary Dialogue and Issues in Religion," Metanexus Online, 22 June 2004, http://www.metanexus.net/.

86 Varadaraja V. Raman, ed., *Indic Religions in an Age of Science* (Philadelphia: Metanexus Institute, 2011); Marc Kaufman, "For the Dalai Lama, a Meeting of Brain and Mind," *Washington Post*, 9 November 2005, C1. For more on the Local Societies Initiative, see William Grassie's account at http://grassie.net/elements/local-societies-initiative/.

87 Turner and Roberts connect specialization with a focus on secular concerns in *The Sacred and the Secular University*.

88 Chopp, "Beyond the Founding Fratricidal Conflict." On the fuzzy boundaries between disciplines in the contemporary academy, see Eviatar Zerubavel, "The Rigid, the Fuzzy, and the Flexible: Notes on the Mental Sculpting of Academic Identity," *Social Research* 62 (4): 1093–107 (1995). See also Louis Menand, "Undisciplined," *Wilson Quarterly* 25 (4): 51–59 (2001); Mark C. Taylor, *Crisis on Campus: A Bold Plan for Reforming Our Colleges and Universities* (New York: Random House, 2010), 139, 145.

89 Alexander Astin and Helen Astin, *Meaning and Spirituality in the Lives of College Faculty: A Study of Values, Authenticity, and Stress* (Los Angeles: Higher Education Research Institute, 1999), 1. Our 2000 evaluation of Lilly Endowment's work in this area reached a similar conclusion, describing the "emergence of a movement to revitalize religion in higher education." See Mahoney, Schmalzbauer, and Youniss, *Revitalizing Religion in the Academy*, 10.

90 For an earlier version of this typology, see John Schmalzbauer and Kathleen A. Mahoney, "Religion and Knowledge in the Post-Secular Academy," SSRC Working Papers, Social Science Research Council, February 2008, https://tif.ssrc.org/wp-content/uploads/2009/09/post-secular-academy.pdf; Schmalzbauer and Mahoney, "Religion and Knowledge." Other scholars have generated similar taxonomies. Douglas Jacobsen and Rhonda Hustedt Jacobsen have identified four "trail markers" for talking about religion and higher education: (1) spirituality (versus religion); (2) teaching about religion; (3) difficult dialogues; and (4) big questions. They also discuss six sites of engagement: (1) religious literacy; (2) interfaith etiquette; (3) framing knowledge; (4) civic engagement; (5) convictions; and (6) character and vocation. See Douglas Jacobsen and Rhonda Hustedt Jacobsen, *No Longer Invisible: Religion in University Education* (New York: Oxford University Press, 2012), 36–45.

91 Susan Barreto, "Religion and Science Centers Serve Both Public and Student Learning Needs," *Covalence*, April 2013. See the 2006 *Centers and Institutes Project* booklet, available from the Center for the Study of Religion and American Culture, Indiana University–Purdue University Indianapolis, https://web.archive.org/web/20130403143222/http://www.iupui.edu/~raac/CIP.html.

92 See Sam Hughes, "The Sages and the Spirit," *Trust*, Winter 2004, 2–9. Between 1997 and 2006, Pew awarded over $23 million in grants to the centers. For more on the mission of Pew's initiative, see "Centers of Excellence: Programs at a Glance," http://web.archive.org/web/20060220231717/http://www.pewtrusts.org/ideas/index.cfm?issue=17&misc_idea=2.

93 See the website of Princeton's Center for the Study of Religion, http://www.princeton.edu/csr/, and Justin Harmon, "Under-Studied Phenomenon: New Center for the Study of Religion to Promote Scholarship on Social, Cultural Practice," *Princeton Weekly Bulletin*, 22 March 1999.

94 C. P. Snow, *The Two Cultures and the Scientific Revolution* (Cambridge, MA: Cambridge University Press, 1959); Ann Taves, "'Religion' in the Humanities," *Journal of the American Academy of Religion* 79 (2): 305, 289, 293 (2011). For an extensive list of journals, centers, and associations, see the website of the International Association for the Cognitive Science of Religion, http://www.iacsr.com/.

95 Warren Nord, *Religion and American Education: Rethinking a National Dilemma* (Chapel Hill: University of North Carolina Press, 1995), 377. See also Nord, *Does God Make a Difference? Taking Religion Seriously in Our Schools and Universities* (New York: Oxford University Press, 2010).

96 A text of the *Wingspread Declaration on Religion and Public Life* (including a list of signatories) is available at http://www.svhe.org/wingspread.html.

97 Stephen Prothero, *Religious Literacy: What Every American Should Know and Doesn't* (San Francisco: HarperSanFrancisco, 2007); Pew Research Center's U.S. Religious Knowledge Survey, http://www.pewforum.org/; William A. Graham, "Why Study Religion in the Twenty-First Century?" *Harvard Divinity Bulletin*, Summer/Autumn 2012; Scott Atran, "God and the Ivory Tower: What We Don't Understand about Religion Just Might Kill Us," *Foreign Policy*, 6 August 2012. Albright is quoted in Nathan Schneider, "Why the World Needs Religious Studies," *Religion Dispatches*, 20 November 2011.

98 *Preliminary Report: Task Force on General Education*, Harvard University Faculty of Arts and Sciences, October 2006, https://web.archive.org/web/20070118232733/http://www.fas.harvard.edu/curriculum-review/Gen_Ed_Prelim_Report.pdf. Menand is quoted in Lisa Miller, "BeliefWatch: Ivy League," *Newsweek*, 22 January 2007. See *Report of the Task Force on General Education*, Harvard University Faculty of Arts and Sciences, 2007, http://projects.iq.harvard.edu/files/gened/files/genedtaskforcereport.pdf?m=1448033208; *General Education in a Free Society: Report of the Harvard Committee* (Cambridge, MA: Harvard University Press, 1945).

99 Associate Justice Tom Clark's opinion in *School District of Abington Township, Pennsylvania v. Schempp*, 374 U.S. 203, as well as Justice Goldberg's opinion, can be found at the website of the Legal Information Institute, http://www.law.cornell.edu/. In a recent article, Sarah Imhoff points out that *Schempp* did not cause the birth of religious studies but became part of its creation story later on. See Imhoff, "The Creation Story."

100 See Imhoff, "The Creation Story." Schmalzbauer, "Fifty Years of Non-sectarian Study of Religion." On the objectivity debate, see Peter Novick, *That Noble Dream: The 'Objectivity Question' and the American Historical Profession* (Cambridge: Cambridge University Press, 1988), 299; Robert Michaelsen, "Constitutions, Courts, and the Study of Religion," *Journal of the American Academy of Religion* 45 (3): 295–96 (1977); Allen, "Is Nothing Sacred?" 30–40; Martin E. Marty, "Half a Life in Religious Studies," in *The Craft of Religious Studies*, ed. Jon R. Stone (New York: St. Martin's, 1998); Stephen Prothero, "Belief Unbracketed: A Case for the Religion Scholar to Reveal More of Where He or She Is Coming From," *Harvard Divinity Bulletin* 32 (2): 10–11 (2004).

101 For an overview of these discussions, see Hent deVries, ed., *Religion: Beyond a Concept* (New York: Fordham University Pres, 2008). See also Talal Asad, *Genealogies of Religion: Discipline and Reasons of Power in Christianity and Islam* (Baltimore: Johns Hopkins University Press, 1993). The *Journal of the American Academy of Religion*'s call for papers appeared in the AAR's February 2009 *E-Bulletin*. Information on the 2007 Syracuse University conference from http://archive.aacu.org/ocww/volume35_2/opportunities.cfm.

102 Robert Orsi, "When 2 + 2 = 5," *American Scholar* 76 (2): 3–43 (2007). See "Finding the Presence in Mormon History: An Interview with Susanna Morrill, Richard Lyman

Bushman, and Robert Orsi," *Dialogue* 44 (2): 174–87 (2011); Ann Taves, "Negotiating the Boundaries in Theological and Religious Studies," public lecture delivered on September 21, 2005, to the Graduate Theological Union, Berkeley, California, available on the UC Santa Barbara Religious Studies website, http://www.religion.ucsb.edu. Not everyone agrees with Orsi's project. Asked about his approach, historian Amanda Porterfield replied, "I disagree with the direction he would like to take the study of religion." Randall Stephens, "Religious History and the Historian's Craft: An Interview with Amanda Porterfield," *Historically Speaking: The Bulletin of the Historical Society*, June 2009, 40. This paragraph draws on Schmalzbauer, "Fifty Years of Non-Sectarian Study of Religion."

103 Marsden, *The Soul of the American University*; Carolyn J. Mooney, "Devout Professors on the Offensive," *Chronicle of Higher Education*, 4 May 1994; Marsden, "Religious Professors Are the Last Taboo," *Wall Street Journal*, 22 December 1993; Marsden, "Church, State, and Campus," *New York Times*, 26 April 1994. Many scholars disagreed with Marsden's critique of higher education. While Alan Wolfe criticized Marsden for emphasizing the victimization of white male Protestants, Robert Orsi saw no evidence of discrimination, noting that "there's no lack of respect for evangelical historians in the academy." See Alan Wolfe, "Religion and American Higher Education: Rethinking a National Dilemma," *Current*, July 1996, 33; Randall Stephens, "Beyond the Niebuhrs: A Conversation with Robert Orsi on Recent Trends in American Religious History," *Harvard Divinity Bulletin*, July/August 2006; Leo Ribuffo, "God and Man at Harvard, Yale, Princeton, Berkeley, etc." *Reviews in American History* 23 (1): 173 (1995).

104 On Kuyper's impact on contemporary evangelical scholars, see George M. Marsden, "The State of Evangelical Christian Scholarship," *Reformed Journal* 37 (9): 12–16 (1987); James Turner, "Something to Be Reckoned With: The Evangelical Mind Reawakens," *Commonweal*, 15 January 1999, 11. On the parallels between Kuyper and Kuhn, see Nicholas Wolterstorff, "The Grace That Shaped My Life," in Clark, ed., *Philosophers Who Believe*, 259–75. See also Alvin Plantinga, "A Christian Life Partly Lived," in Clark, ed., *Philosophers Who Believe*, 45–82.

105 For evangelical alternatives to Kuyperian approaches, see Douglas Jacobsen and Rhonda Hustedt Jacobsen, "More than the 'Integration' of Faith and Learning," in *Scholarship and Christian Faith: Enlarging the Conversation*, ed. Douglas Jacobsen and Rhonda Hustedt Jacobsen (New York: Oxford University Press, 2004), 28; James K. A. Smith, *Desiring the Kingdom: Worship, Worldview, and Cultural Formation* (Grand Rapids, MI: Baker Academic, 2009); Todd C. Ream, Jerry Pattengale, and David L. Riggs, *Beyond Integration? Inter/Disciplinary Possibilities for the Future of Christian Higher Education* (Abilene, TX: ACU Press, 2012). While popular among Reformed evangelicals, Kuyperian thought has not won over the wider academy. In *Apostles of Reason: The Crisis of Authority in American Evangelicalism*, historian Molly Worthen criticized the "presuppositionalists' artful dodge." Observing that conservative Protestants shift back and forth between empirical evidence and unverifiable presuppositions, she noted that "evangelicals attempt to obey multiple authorities at the same time." See Molly Worthen, *Apostles of Reason: The Crisis of Authority in American Evangelicalism* (New York: Oxford University Press, 2014), 252, 258.

106 For the mission and membership of the Lilly Seminar, see https://web.archive.org/web/20090302010653/http://www.nd.edu/~lillysem/.

107 William Ringenberg estimates that there are about fifty religious scholarly associations in *The Christian College*, 215.

108 Alan Wolfe, "The Opening of the Evangelical Mind," *Atlantic Monthly*, October 2000, 55–76. For more on the Emerging Evangelical Intelligentsia Project, see http://www

.bu.edu/cura/projects/evangelicalculture/. See Michael Lindsay, *Faith in the Halls of Power: How Evangelicals Joined the American Elite* (New York: Oxford University Press, 2007); Janet L. Kroll and Rebecca A. Cornejo, "Onward, Christian Scholars," *In Trust*, May 2003, http://web.archive.org/web/20031214171231/http://pewtrusts.com/return_results.cfm?content_item_id=1597&page=rr1. Survey reported in Neil Gross and Solon Simmons, "How Religious Are America's College and University Professors?" Social Science Research Council Web forum on "The Religious Engagements of American Undergraduates," 6 February 2007, http://religion.ssrc.org/reforum/Gross_Simmons.pdf. Elaine Howard Ecklund's 2014 study found that 17 percent of American scientists identified as evangelical Protestants. See Ecklund, "Religious Communities, Science, Scientists, and Perceptions: A Comprehensive Survey," paper prepared for the Annual Meeting of the American Association for the Advancement of Science, 16 February 2014, 10, available on the AAAS website, http://www.aaas.org/.

109 There is no evangelical equivalent to Notre Dame, Georgetown, and Boston College. The closest parallel is Baylor University, an institution which is attempting to increase its endowment. Chapter titles are taken from Nick Salvatore, ed., *Faith and the Historian: Catholic Perspectives* (Urbana: University of Illinois Press, 2007). See also John McGreevy, "Faith Histories," in Sterk, *Religion, Scholarship, and Higher Education*, 63–75; Christopher Shannon, "From Histories to Tradition: A New Paradigm of Pluralism in the Study of the Past," *Historically Speaking*, January 2011. The Society of Catholic Social Scientists emphasizes loyalty to the Magisterium. See the organization's website, http://www.catholicsocialscientists.org/membership.html.

110 "Parker Palmer," *Character Clearinghouse*, 29 October 2001, https://web.archive.org/web/20080530155408/http://www.collegevalues.org/Spirit.cfm?id=606&a=1. The 1997 survey was reported in "Who's Who: Higher Education's Senior Leadership," *Change* 30 (1): 14–18, 20 (January/February 1998).

111 Parker Palmer, *To Know as We Are Known: Education as a Spiritual Journey* (San Francisco: HarperSanFrancisco, 1993); Palmer, *The Courage to Teach: Exploring the Inner Landscape of a Teacher's Life* (San Francisco: Jossey-Bass, 1997); Palmer, *A Hidden Wholeness: The Journey toward an Undivided Life* (San Francisco: Jossey-Bass, 2004); Parker Palmer and Arthur Zajonc with Megan Scribner, *The Heart of Higher Education: A Call to Renewal* (San Francisco: Jossey-Bass, 2010); Parker Palmer, *Healing the Heart of Democracy: The Courage to Create a Politics Worthy of the Human Spirit* (San Francisco: Jossey-Bass, 2014).

112 The quotation and figure of 800 attendees comes from the Education as Transformation Project website, https://web.archive.org/web/20081013150918/http://www.wellesley.edu/RelLife/transformation/edu-ngoverview.html. The book series is described at http://www.wellesley.edu/religiouslife/resources/east/publication/bookseries. See the website of the "Going Public with Spirituality in Work and Higher Education" conference, http://www.umass.edu/spiritual_conf/.

113 Scott quote on majors from Ali Crolius, "Unsequestered Spirits," *UMASS Magazine Online*, Winter 2000, http://www.umass.edu/; Eric Goldscheider, "Religion Journal; Seeking a Role for Religion on Campus," *New York Times*, 2 February 2002, B6. For more on the integrative university, see the collection of essays at David Scott's website, http://www.umass.edu/pastchancellors/scott/. See also G. Jeffrey MacDonald, "Search for Meaning on Campus: Schools Respond to Students' Quest for Spirituality," *Boston Globe*, 12 June 2005; Diana Chapman Walsh quoted in Peter Laurence, "Can Religion and Spirituality Find a Place in Higher Education?" *About Campus*, November/December 1999.

114 The Fall 2001 issue of *Liberal Education* focused on religion and higher education, as did the January/February 2006 issue of *Academe*. Susan VanZanten Gallagher explored the place of religion on campus in "Speaking of Vocation in an Age of Spirituality," *Change*, May–June 2007. See also American Academy of Religion, "The Religious Studies Major and Liberal Education," *Liberal Education*, Spring 2009.

115 The "Spirituality and Learning: Redefining Meaning, Values, and Inclusion in Higher Education" Conference was held April 18–20, 2002, in San Francisco. A 1990 study found that Astin was the most-cited researcher in the higher education field. See John M. Budd, "Higher Education Literature: Characteristics of Citation Patterns," *Research in Higher Education* 61 (1): 93, 94 (1990). Twenty years later, Astin was still at the top of the list. See John M. Budd and Lauren Magnuson, "Higher Education Literature Revisited: Citation Patterns Examined," *Research in Higher Education* 51 (3): 302 (2010).

116 Astin and Astin, *Meaning and Spirituality*, 1.

117 "A Position Statement from The Initiative for Authenticity and Spirituality in Higher Education," *Character Clearinghouse*, 23 August 2002, https://web.archive.org/web/20080530155432/http://www.collegevalues.org/Spirit.cfm?id=982&a=1.

118 See *The Spiritual Life of College Students: A National Study of College Students' Search for Meaning and Purpose* (Los Angeles: Higher Education Research Institute, UCLA, 2004); Alexander W. Astin, Helen S. Astin, and Jennifer A. Lindholm, *Cultivating the Spirit: How College Can Enhance Students' Inner Lives* (San Francisco: Jossey-Bass, 2011); Alyssa N. Bryant and Leslie M. Schwartz, *National Institute on Spirituality: Integrating Spirituality into the Campus Curriculum and Co-Curriculum* (Los Angeles: Higher Education Research Institute, 2006).

119 "Biography: Sir John Templeton," https://web.archive.org/web/20080103003633/http://www.templetonpress.org/SirJohn/biography.asp.

120 For information on John Fetzer, see the John E. Fetzer Memorial Trust website, http://www.fetzertrust.org/. See Astin and Astin, *Meaning and Spirituality*.

121 Astin and Astin, *Meaning and Spirituality*, 1.

122 This tripartite division of American religion can be found in Catherine L. Albanese, *A Republic of Mind and Spirit: A Cultural History of American Metaphysical Religion* (New Haven, CT: Yale University Press, 2007), 4.

123 See the website of the California Institute of Integral Studies, http://www.ciis.edu/. Conference attendance figure reported at the Center for Contemplative Mind website, http://www.contemplativemind.org/.

124 For more on Templeton's character education projects, see http://www.collegeandcharacter.org/ and http://www.templeton.org/what-we-fund/grant-search/results/taxonomy%3A7; Arthur Schwartz, "It's Not Too Late to Teach College Students about Values," *Chronicle of Higher Education*, 9 June 2000, A68; *The Templeton Guide: Colleges That Encourage Character Development*, https://www.templetonpress.org/content/colleges-encourage-character-development.

125 For a discussion of the "moral revival," see Alan Wolfe, "Moral Inquiry in Social Science," in *The Nature of Moral Inquiry in the Social Sciences: Occasional Papers of the Erasmus Institute* (Notre Dame, IN: Erasmus Institute, 1999), 1–20; Alan Wolfe, "The Revival of Moral Inquiry in the Social Sciences," *Chronicle of Higher Education*, 3 September 1999, B4.

126 This account of the rediscovery of morality in the 1960s draws heavily on Julie A. Reuben, "The University and Its Discontents," *Hedgehog Review* 2 (3): 72–91 (2000).

127 For an account of the upsurge in ethics courses during the 1970s (including statistics), see Emilie Tavel Livezey, "The Revival of Teaching Ethics," *Christian Science Monitor*, 4

September 1980, B10. On the rediscovery of ethics and character in the wake of Watergate and Vietnam, see Harvard Chaplain Peter Gomes' *The Good Life: Truths That Last in Times of Need* (San Francisco: HarperSanFrancisco, 2003); and Derek Bok, "Universities and the Decline of Civic Responsibility," *Journal of College and Character* 2 (9): 1–7 (2001).

128 On the early dominance of theology, see Daniel Callahan, "The Social Sciences and the Task of Bioethics," *Daedalus* 128 (4): 275 (1999); Carla M. Messikomer, Renee C. Fox, and Judith P. Swazey, "The Presence and Influence of Religion in American Bioethics," *Perspectives in Biology and Medicine* 44 (4): 485–508 (2001). On the secularization of bioethics, see John H. Evans, *Playing God? Human Genetic Engineering and the Rationalization of Public Bioethical Debate* (Chicago: University of Chicago Press, 2002).

129 This list comes from Wolfe, "Moral Inquiry in Social Science."

130 Amitai Etzioni, ed., *The Essential Communitarian Reader* (Lanham, MD: Rowman and Littlefield, 1998). On "social science as public philosophy," see Robert Bellah, Richard Madsen, William M. Sullivan, Ann Swidler, and Steven M. Tipton, *Habits of the Heart: Individualism and Commitment in American Life* (Berkeley: University of California, 1985), 297–307; Gans, "Best-Sellers by Sociologists: An Exploratory Study."

131 Robert D. Putnam, *Bowling Alone: The Collapse and Revival of American Community* (New York: Simon and Schuster, 2000). For a list of participants in the Saguaro Seminar, see http://www.hks.harvard.edu/saguaro/participants.htm.

132 Sandel's course is available at http://www.justiceharvard.org/. On its enrollment and global reach, see Thomas Friedman, "Justice Goes Global," *New York Times*, 14 June 2011.

133 Ernest Boyer, *College: The Undergraduate Experience in America* (New York: Harper and Row, 1987), 69, 4. This interpretation of Boyer and the quote from his widow are taken from Douglas Jacobsen, "Theology as Public Performance: Reflections on the Christian Convictions of Ernest L. Boyer," Messiah College Presidential Scholar's Lecture, 17 February 2000, 10, 12, https://web.archive.org/web/20040204082212/http://www.boyercenter.org/resources/boyertheology.pdf.

134 Anne Colby, Thomas Ehrlich, Elizabeth Beaumont, and Jason Stephens, *Educating Citizens: Preparing America's Undergraduates for Lives of Moral and Civic Responsibility* (San Francisco: Jossey-Bass, 2003).

135 Derek Bok, *Our Underachieving Colleges: A Candid Look at How Much Students Learn and Why They Should Be Learning More* (Princeton, NJ: Princeton University Press, 2006); Anthony Kronman, *Education's End: Why Our Colleges and Universities Have Given Up on the Meaning of Life* (New Haven, CT: Yale University Press, 2007), 238, 244; Andrew Delbanco, *College: What It Was, Is, and Should Be* (Princeton, NJ: Princeton University Press, 2012), 175, 66.

136 Robert McClory, "Campus Compact Urges Student Service," *National Catholic Reporter*, 6 October 1995, 13. For the Campus Compact mission and statistics, see http://www.compact.org; *Three Decades of Institutionalizing Change: 2014 Annual Member Survey* (Boston: Campus Compact, 2015), 3, 4.

137 The quotation is from Campus Compact's mission statement, http://compact.org/. On the separation of knowledge and morality, see Reuben, "The University and Its Discontents," 90.

138 Rebecca Chopp, "Living Lives of Integrity and Truth," *Journal of College and Character* 7 (6): 5 (2006).

139 Arthur Schwartz, "It's Not Too Late to Teach College Students about Values," *Chronicle of Higher Education*, 9 June 9, 2000, A68.

140 For more on the Pluralism Project's goals and mission, as well as Eck's definition of pluralism, see the Project's website, http://www.pluralism.org/. Diana Eck, *A New Religious America: How a "Christian Country" Has Become the World's Most Religiously Diverse Nation* (San Francisco: HarperSanFrancisco, 2001). For more on the interfaith study, see *America's Interfaith Infrastructure: A Pilot Study* (Cambridge, MA: Pluralism Project, 2011).

141 Recipients of fellowships listed at http://www.contemplativemind.org/archives and http://www.contemplativemind.org/archives/fellowships. The quotation on integrating contemplative practice into academic life can be found at https://web.archive.org/web/20040302084105/http://www.contemplativemind.org/programs/academic/overview.html. Statistics from Barbara A. Craig, *Contemplative Practice in Higher Education: An Assessment of the Contemplative Practice Fellowship Program, 1997–2009* (Amherst, MA: Center for Contemplative Mind in Society, 2011), 2. On the law program in contemplative practice, see http://www.contemplativemind.org/archives/law.

142 On the tension between secular and Buddhist influences, see the FAQ page of the Center as it existed in May of 2003, http://web.archive.org/web/20020504050139/http://www.contemplativemind.org/about/faq.html.

143 For more on the Association for Contemplative Mind in Higher Education, see http://www.contemplativemind.org/programs/acmhe; Shauna L. Shapiro, Kirk Warren Brown, and John A. Astin, "Toward the Integration of Meditation into Higher Education: A Review of Research," Center for Contemplative Mind in Society, October 2008, https://web.archive.org/web/20140124013831/http://www.colorado.edu/ftep/events/eventdocs/documents/ShapiroResearchReport.pdf.

144 See the Sikh Foundation website, http://www.sikhfoundation.org/. See also I. J. Singh and Hakam Singh, "Chairs in Sikh Studies in America: Problems and Solutions," *Sikh Review*, May 1996, 43–51; "Buddhist Studies Chair Named," *Harvard Gazette*, 20 September 2001; "Thinking Differently: T. S. Rukmani Holds the First Chair of Hindu Studies in North America," *Hinduism Today*, July/August 2000.

145 Meg Sullivan, "Building a Case for Buddhist Studies at UCLA," *UCLA College Report*, Fall 2003–Winter 2004.

146 "Harvard Receives $20M Gift for Islamic Studies," *Harvard Gazette*, 12 December 2005; Gitika Ahuja, "Saudi Prince Donates $40 Million to Harvard, Georgetown Universities," ABC News, 13 December 2005, http://abcnews.go.com/. For information about the North American Association of Islamic and Muslim Studies, see https://naaims.org/Home.html. For more information on the Institute, see http://www.iiit.org/. On the history of the journal, see https://naaims.org/Journals.html. On the International Qur'anic Studies Association, see https://iqsaweb.wordpress.com/about/.

147 These figures come from Daniel Jeremy Silver, "The American University and Jewish Learning," *Judaism* 25 (3): 285 (1976).

148 Robert Eisen, "Jewish Studies and the Academic Teaching of Religion," *Liberal Education*, Fall 2001, 14; Silver, "The American University and Jewish Learning," 286; Amy L. Sales and Leonard Saxe, "Engaging the Intellect: Jewish Studies on the College Campus," *Contact*, Winter 2005, 5–6.

149 Membership of Association for Jewish Studies available at http://www.ajsnet.org/. See also Silver, "The American University and Jewish Learning," 286; Sales and Saxe, "Engaging the Intellect," 6. A list of Posen courses is available at https://web.archive.org/web/20120717071149/http://www.posenfoundation.com/coursedescriptions.html. For more information on Posen's programs on cultural Judaism and Jewish secularism, see http://www.posenfoundation.co.il/en/. The Yale University Press description of the Posen

Library of Jewish Culture and Civilization can be found at http://yalepress.yale.edu/book.asp?isbn=9780300135534. See also Evan R. Goldstein, "A Feast of Jewish Culture, in 10 Volumes," *Chronicle of Higher Education*, 19 November 2012. For more on the Tikvah Fund, see http://tikvahfund.org/. David Biale is quoted in the Goldstein article.

150 On Arab studies at Columbia, see Chris Hedges, "Public Lives: Casting Mideast Violence in Another Light," *New York Times*, 20 April 2004. On the Israel studies chair, see Liel Lebovitz, "Battle of the Chairs," *Moment Magazine*, February 2006.

151 John S. Hawley, "Hinduism Here," in "Spotlight on Teaching," ed. Cynthia Humes, *Religious Studies News*, October 2006, iii, vii; Ellen Barry, "Indian Publisher Withdraws Book, Stoking Fears of Nationalist Pressure," *New York Times*, 13 February 2014; Wendy Doniger, *The Hindus: An Alternative History* (New York: Penguin, 2009), 17. On domestic criticism of Doniger, see Amy M. Braverman, "The Interpretation of Gods: Do Leading Religious Scholars Err in Their Analysis of Hindu Texts?" *University of Chicago Magazine*, December 2004.

152 Information on the programs was retrieved from https://web.archive.org/web/20070828164354/http://www.fordfound.org/news/more/dialogues/index.cfm. See the website of the Difficult Dialogues Program, https://web.archive.org/web/20130427133150/http://www.difficultdialogues.org/?.

153 See Matthew L. Kaplan, "Getting Religion in the Public Research University," *Academe*, July/August 2006. See also Janet R. Jakobsen, "Campus Religious Conflict Should Go Public," *Academe*, July/August 2006.

154 *Spirituality and the Professoriate: A National Study of Faculty Beliefs, Attitudes, and Values* (Los Angeles: Higher Education Research Institute, UCLA, 2006), 1.

155 AHA data from Townsend, "AHA Membership on the Rise Again in 2011." The 2010 American Psychological Association division memberships can be found at the APA website, http://www.apa.org/. Division 36 has a membership of 974, 1.4 percent of the APA's 67,000 division memberships. The American Philosophical Association had 9,007 members in 2016. See https://c.ymcdn.com/sites/apaonline.site-ym.com/resource/resmgr/data_on_profession/Member_Demo_Chart_FY2016_rev.pdf. The membership of the Society of Christian Philosophers has hovered around 1,000. See Barry Hankins, *American Evangelicals: A Contemporary History of a Mainstream Religious Movement* (Lanham, MD: Rowman and Littlefield, 2008), 178. In 2014, 605 of the 13,000 ASA's members belonged to the religion section (4.7 percent). In political science, the figure was 433 out of 15,000 members (2.9 percent). The 2015 membership of the American Sociological Association's sections (including Sociology of Religion) can be found at http://www.asanet.org/sections/CountsLastFiveYears.cfm. The August 2014 membership counts for the APSA's sections were retrieved at http://www.apsanet.org/sectioncounts.cfm. Journal data reported in Steven Kettell, "Has Political Science Ignored Religion?" *PS: Political Science and Politics* 45 (1): 93–100 (2012). See also Wald and Wilcox, "Getting Religion," 525.

156 Smilde and May, "The Emerging Strong Program."

157 Orsi in Stephens, "Beyond the Niebuhrs"; Orsi, *Between Heaven and Earth*, 7, 188. Jon Butler's remarks at the First Biennial Conference on Religion and American Culture (2009) in Indianapolis are available at http://raac.iupui.edu/files/9213/6724/5498/Proceedings2009.pdf. See also David Hollinger, "Enough Already: Universities Do Not Need More Christianity," in Sterk, *Religion, Scholarship, and Higher Education*, 41, 49. Quotation on the history of Christianity from Hollinger, "The 'Secularization' Question and the United States in the Twentieth Century," 136. The last quotation is from

Darren E. Sherkat, "Christian Sociology—It's the Opposite of the Sociology of Religion," May 30, 2012, http://iranianredneck.wordpress.com/2012/05/30/christian-sociology-its-the-opposite-of-the-sociology-of-religion/.

158 William Dembski, *Intelligent Design: The Bridge between Science and Theology* (Downers Grove, IL: InterVarsity Press, 1999), 121.

159 The survey is reported in Elaine Howard Ecklund, *Science vs. Religion: What Scientists Really Think* (New York: Oxford University Press, 2010). It found zero support for intelligent design. The story of ID is deeply ironic. An effort to bridge the worlds of science and religion has led to greater conflict.

160 Lawrence Krauss, "An Article of Faith: Science and Religion Don't Mix," *Chronicle of Higher Education*, 26 November 1999, A88.

161 Richard Sloan's "garbage research" quote and the "Beyond Belief" conference were reported in George Johnson, "A Free-for-All on Science and Religion," *New York Times*, 21 November 2006. See also Sloan, *Blind Faith*. For more on "Beyond Belief," see http://thescience network.org/programs/beyond-belief-science-religion-reason-and-survival.

162 Marilynne Robinson, "Hysterical Scientism: The Ecstasy of Richard Dawkins," *Harper's*, November 2006, 86; Terry Eagleton, "Lunging, Flailing, Mispunching," *London Review of Books*, 19 October 2006. See also Eagleton, *Reason, Faith, and Revolution: Reflections on the God Debate* (New Haven, CT: Yale University Press, 2009).

163 Jackson Lears, "Same Old New Atheism: On Sam Harris," *Nation*, 16 May 2011.

164 David Van Biema, "God vs. Science," *Time*, 5 November 2006. See also Francis Collins, *The Language of God: A Scientist Presents Evidence for Belief* (New York: Free Press, 2006).

165 The mission of the BioLogos Foundation can be found at http://biologos.org/about. Sam Harris, "Science Is in the Details," *New York Times*, 26 July 2009. For more recent criticism of Collins, see Eric Reitan, "Does NIH Head Francis Collins Believe in Intelligent Design?" *Religion Dispatches*, 4 February 2014. The budget of the NIH can be found at http://www.nih.gov/about/budget.htm.

166 The first survey data cited are from Neil Gross and Solon Simmons, "How Religious Are America's College and University Professors?" Social Science Research Council Web forum on "The Religious Engagements of American Undergraduates," February 6, 2007, http://religion.ssrc.org/reforum/Gross_Simmons.pdf. The statistic on "not spiritual and not religious" faculty is from Jennifer A. Lindholm, *The Quest for Meaning and Wholeness: Spiritual and Religious Connections in the Lives of College Faculty* (San Francisco: Jossey-Bass, 2014), 50. The finding on institutional prestige is reported in Neil Gross and Solon Simmons, "The Religiosity of American College and University Professors," *Sociology of Religion* 70 (2): 110 (2009). Data on elite scientists from Ecklund, *Science vs. Religion*, 15, 16, 33.

167 Elaine Howard Ecklund, "Religion and Spirituality among University Scientists," Social Science Research Council Web forum on "The Religious Engagements of American Undergraduates," 5 February 2007, http://religion.ssrc.org/reforum/Ecklund.pdf. See also Adelle M. Banks, "The Spiritual Lives of Atheist Scientists," *Huffington Post*, 6 May 2011, http://www.huffingtonpost.com/; Lindholm, *The Quest for Meaning and Wholeness*, 40.

168 The figures on the use of the term "post-secular" in dissertations, books, and conferences are from Boy, "What We Talk about when We Talk about the Postsecular." Google Scholar results retrieved on April 16, 2018. On the replacement of secular reason with theology, see Milbank, *Theology and Social Theory*. See also Simon During in Nathan Schneider, "Endgame Capitalism: An Interview with Simon During," Immanent Frame, 10 December 2010, http://blogs.ssrc.org/; Maczynska, "Toward a Postsecular Literary Criticism," 76.

The first Jürgen Habermas quotation is from Habermas, "Faith and Knowledge," speech to the German Book Trade, 15 October 2001, http://www.friedenspreis-des-deutschen-buchhandels.de/. The second is from Habermas, *Europe: The Faltering Project* (Malden, MA: Polity Press, 2009), 74. See also McLennan, "The Postsecular Turn."

169 The term "odd combinations" is from Robert Jay Lifton, *The Protean Self: Human Resilience in an Age of Fragmentation* (Chicago: University of Chicago Press, 1999), 5; Slavoj Žižek, *The Puppet and the Dwarf: The Perverse Core of Christianity* (Cambridge, MA: MIT Press, 2003); John Caputo, "Jacques Derrida (1930–2004)," *CrossCurrents* 55 (4) (2006); Mark Lewis Taylor, 21 December 2010, http://blogs.ssrc.org/tif/wp-content/uploads/2011/07/TaylorInterview.pdf; Fish, "One University under God?"; Gianni Vattimo and Richard Rorty, *The Future of Religion* (New York: Columbia University Press, 2005). On the prevalence of theology among contemporary cultural theorists, see James Wood, "God in the Quad," *New Yorker*, 31 August 2009.

170 Ray Hart, "Religious and Theological Studies in American Higher Education: A Pilot Study," *Journal of the American Academy of Religion* 59 (4): 715–827 (1991).

171 The study was conducted by Barbara Walvoord of the University of Notre Dame. The results were reported in Scott Jaschik, "The 'Great Divide' in Religious Studies," *Inside Higher Ed*, 20 November 2006. See Barbara Walvoord, *Teaching and Learning in College Introductory Religion Courses* (Malden, MA: Wiley-Blackwell, 2007).

172 *Spirituality and the Professoriate*, 9.

173 Data from the Walvoord study, reported in Jaschik, "The 'Great Divide' in Religious Studies."

174 See *The Spiritual Life of College Students*.

175 Survey of religion classes reported in Conrad Cherry, Betty A. DeBerg, and Amanda Porterfield, *Religion on Campus* (Chapel Hill: University of North Carolina Press, 2001).

176 Data from the 2005 AAR survey reported in "AAR Undergraduate Departments Survey Shows Increases in Religious Studies," *Religious Studies News*, May 2008, 11. Religiously affiliated institutions made up about half of the graduate programs in the 2002 AAR Graduate Survey, https://www.aarweb.org/programs-services/aar-graduate-survey-2002; Terrence Tilley, "The AAR Survey of Graduate Education in Religion and Theology," 2003 American Academy of Religion Annual Meeting, https://www.aarweb.org/.

177 Cherry, DeBerg, and Porterfield, *Religion on Campus*, 11–81. See especially DeBerg's case study of West University; Paul Bramadat, *The Church on the World's Turf: An Evangelical Christian Group at a Secular University* (New York: Oxford University Press, 2000).

Chapter 3

1 Relationships between colleges and churches, or colleges and religious bodies, vary. In this chapter, the phrases "church-related college," "religious college," and "denominational college" are used interchangeably to designate colleges connected with a Christian religious body. While some evangelical colleges identify as nondenominational, the vast majority are affiliated with a church or denomination (see http://cccu.org/). The same is true of most mainline Protestant and all Roman Catholic institutions. Douglas Jacobsen and Rhonda Hustedt Jacobsen reported that a total of 768 out of 2,345 colleges and universities (32.7 percent) had a religious affiliation in "The Ideals and Diversity of Church-Related Higher Education," in *The American University in a Postsecular Age*, ed. Douglas Jacobsen and Rhonda Hustedt Jacobsen (New York: Oxford University Press, 2008), 64.

2 Barbara Dunlap-Berg, "Church Schools among 'Best Colleges,'" United Methodist Church General Board of Higher Education and Ministry, 2010, available at the UMC Higher Education and Ministry website, http://www.gbhem.org/. Lists of Presbyterian and Lutheran colleges can be found at the Association of Presbyterian Colleges and Universities website, http://www.presbyteriancolleges.org/, and the Lutheran Educational Conference of North America website, http://www.lutherancolleges.org/.

3 Statistics on the number of Catholic colleges and universities can be found at the Association of Catholic Colleges and Universities website, http://www.accunet.org/.

4 The number of Jesuit institutions can be found at the Association of Jesuit Colleges and Universities website, http://www.ajcunet.edu/. The Jewish community's strategies in higher education are described in Paul Ritterband and Harold S. Wechsler, *Jewish Learning in American Universities: The First Century* (Bloomington: Indiana University Press, 1994); Marvin Fox, "Jewishness and Judaism at Brandeis," *CrossCurrents* 43 (4): 464–69 (1993). See also Tanya Storch, "Buddhist Universities in the United States of America," *International Journal of Dharma Studies* 1 (4): 1–16 (2013); Scott Korb, *Light without Fire: The Making of America's First Muslim College* (Boston: Beacon Press, 2013); Kimberly Winston, "Zaytuna College Recognized as First Accredited Muslim College in the US," Religion News Service, 18 March 2015.

5 Enrollment in religiously affiliated institutions of postsecondary education was 1,006,173 in 1980 (8.3 percent of all students) and 1,889,502 in 2012 (9.2 percent of all students). Statistics from *Digest of Education Statistics* (Washington, DC: National Center for Education Statistics, 2013). On church-related higher education, see William Ringenberg, *The Christian College: A History of Protestant Higher Education in America* (Grand Rapids, MI: Baker, 2006); Paul Dovre, ed., *The Future of Religious Colleges* (Grand Rapids, MI: Eerdmans, 2002); Robert Benne, *Quality with Soul: How Six Premier Colleges and Universities Kept Faith with Their Religious Traditions* (Grand Rapids, MI: Eerdmans, 2001).

6 Merrimon Cuninggim, *Uneasy Partners: The College and the Church* (Nashville, TN: Abingdon Press, 1994). For a lengthy, sometimes unbalanced account, see James T. Burtchaell, *The Dying of the Light: The Disengagement of Colleges and Universities from Their Christian Churches* (Grand Rapids, MI: Eerdmans, 1998).

7 This chapter will also discuss recent developments at some evangelical Protestant schools, including those affiliated with the Council for Christian Colleges and Universities. However, because this chapter looks at the strengthening of religious identity in church-affiliated higher education, our major focus is on mainline and Catholic colleges and universities. At most evangelical colleges, there is less emphasis on strengthening mission and identity because religious identity has usually been central. Of course, many evangelical colleges and universities have become more intentional about remaining connected to their sponsoring denominations. For such schools, the temptation in the past has been to assume a generic evangelical identity shorn of denominational particularities. See Melinda Bollar Wagner, "Generic Conservative Christianity: The Demise of Denominationalism in Christian Schools," *Journal for the Scientific Study of Religion* 36 (1): 13–24 (1997).

8 See John R. Thelin's "Rudolph Rediscovered: An Introductory Essay," and his supplemental bibliography in Frederick Rudolph, *The American College and University: A History*, 2nd ed. (Athens: University of Georgia Press, 1990), ix–xxiv; Roger L. Geiger, ed., *The American College in the Nineteenth Century* (Nashville, TN: Vanderbilt University Press, 2000).

9 According to one scholar, only one in ten Methodist institutions has survived. See F. Thomas Trotter, foreword to Cuninggim, *Uneasy Partners*, 10. On Catholic mortality rates,

see Roger L. Geiger, "The Era of Multipurpose Colleges in American Higher Education," in Geiger, *The American College*, 139.

10 Geiger, "Era of Multipurpose Colleges," 132; David Potts, "'College Enthusiasm!' as Public Response," *Harvard Educational Review* 47 (1): 28–42 (1977).

11 Geiger, "Era of Multipurpose Colleges," 143.

12 "Echoes of Faith: Church Roots Run Deep among Numerous HBCUs," *Diverse*, 19 July 2012, 14–15.

13 The fundraising pamphlet *New England's First Fruits* is reprinted in Samuel Eliot Morison, *The Founding of Harvard College* (Cambridge, MA: Harvard University Press, 1963), 432. Colonial colleges trained "divines" in great numbers: a substantial majority of college graduates during the colonial period became clergymen. See Bruce A. Kimball, *The "True Professional Ideal" in America: A History* (Cambridge, MA: Blackwell, 1992), appendix 2.

14 For brief histories of Calvin and Seattle Pacific, see James D. Bratt and Ronald A. Wells, "Piety and Progress: A History of Calvin College," in *Models for Christian Higher Education: Strategies for Success in the Twenty-First Century*, ed. Richard T. Hughes and William B. Adrian (Grand Rapids, MI: Eerdmans, 1997), 141–62; Steven Moore and William Woodward, "Clarity through Ambiguity: Transforming Tensions at Seattle Pacific University," in Hughes and Adrian, *Models for Christian Higher Education*, 284–309.

15 Philip Gleason, "The Main Sheet Anchor: John Carroll and Catholic Higher Education," *Review of Politics* 38 (4): 584 (1976).

16 Rudolph, *The American College and University*; Marsden, *The Soul of the American University: From Protestant Establishment to Established Nonbelief* (New York: Oxford University Press, 1994). For an example of a Catholic institution, see Anthony J. Kuzniewski, *Thy Honored Name: A History of the College of the Holy Cross, 1843–1994* (Washington, DC: Catholic University of America, 1999).

17 DePauw quote from James Findlay, "Agency, Denominations, and the Western Colleges, 1830–1860," in *The American College in the Nineteenth Century*, ed. Roger L. Geiger (Nashville, TN: Vanderbilt University Press, 2000), 118.

18 Roger L. Geiger, *The History of American Higher Education: Learning and Culture from the Founding to World War II* (Princeton, NJ: Princeton University Press, 2015), 244.

19 Philip Gleason, *Contending with Modernity: Catholic Higher Education in the Twentieth Century* (New York: Oxford University Press, 1995); Tracy Schier and Cynthia Russett, eds., *Catholic Women's Colleges in America* (Baltimore: Johns Hopkins University Press, 2002).

20 Merrimon Cuninggim examines the relationship between nineteenth-century colleges and churches in *Uneasy Partners*.

21 Lawrence Veysey, *The Emergence of the American University* (Chicago: University of Chicago Press, 1965); Rudolph, *American College and University*; Edward Shils, "The Order of Learning in the United States from 1865 to 1920: The Ascendancy of the Universities," in *The Order of Learning: Essays on the Contemporary University*, ed. and with an introduction by Philip G. Altbach (New Brunswick, NJ: Transaction, 1997); Christopher Jencks and David Riesman, *The Academic Revolution* (Garden City, NY: Doubleday, 1968), 30.

22 Richard J. Storr, *Harper's University: The Beginnings* (Chicago: University of Chicago Press, 1966).

23 Hugh Hawkins, "The University-Builders Observe the Colleges," *History of Education Quarterly* 11 (4): 353–62 (1971).

24 David Hollinger, *Science, Jews, and Secular Culture: Studies in Mid-Twentieth Century American Intellectual History* (Princeton, NJ: Princeton University Press, 1998). For an

example of the conflation of nonsectarianism with the social vision of liberal Protestantism in a state university, see George M. Marsden, "Liberal Protestantism at Michigan: New England Intentions with Jeffersonian Results," in Marsden, *The Soul of the American University*.

25 The two most comprehensive works on the secularization of the academy are Marsden, *The Soul of the American University*, and Julie A. Reuben, *The Making of the Modern University: Intellectual Transformation and the Marginalization of Morality* (Chicago: University of Chicago Press, 1996). The concept of de-Christianization is employed by Hollinger in *Science, Jews, and Secular Culture*. See also Douglas Jacobsen and Rhonda Hustedt Jacobsen, *No Longer Invisible: Religion in University Education* (New York: Oxford University Press, 2012).

26 Geiger, "Era of Multipurpose Colleges," 141.

27 Christian Smith, "Introduction: Rethinking the Secularization of American Public Life," in *The Secular Revolution: Power, Interests, and Conflict in the Secularization of American Life*, ed. Christian Smith (Berkeley: University of California Press, 2003), 73–78.

28 On the loss of control in Protestant colleges, see Dorothy C. Bass, "Ministry on the Margins: Protestants and Education," in *Between the Times: The Travail of the Protestant Establishment, 1900–1960*, ed. William R. Hutchison (Cambridge: Cambridge University Press, 1989), 50; unidentified Jesuit quoted in William J. McGucken, *Jesuits and Education: The Society's Teaching Principles and Practice* (Milwaukee: Bruce, 1932), 143. On the Jesuits' responses to the rise of the new academic order, see Kathleen A. Mahoney, *Catholic Higher Education in Protestant America: The Jesuits and Harvard in the Age of the University* (Baltimore: Johns Hopkins University Press, 2003).

29 Manning M. Pattillo Jr. and Donald M. Mackenzie, *Church-Sponsored Higher Education in the United States: Report of the Danforth Commission* (Washington, DC: American Council on Education, 1966), 17.

30 Walter P. Metzger, *Academic Freedom in the Age of the University* (New York: Columbia University Pres, 1955).

31 Marsden, *The Soul of the American University*, 281–82; Bass, "Ministry on the Margins," 52.

32 Peter J. Harrington, "Civil and Canon Law Issues Affecting American Catholic Higher Education, 1948–1998: An Overview and the ACCU Perspective," *Journal of College and University Law*, 26 (1): 67–105 (1999); Robert Wood Lynn, "'The Survival of Recognizably Protestant Colleges': Reflections on Old-Line Protestantism, 1950–1990," in *The Secularization of the Academy*, ed. George M. Marsden and Bradley J. Longfield (New York: Oxford University Press, 1992), 190; F. Thomas Trotter, "The College as the Church's Gift," *Christian Century*, 30 November 1988, 1098.

33 For an excellent account see Reuben, *The Making of the Modern University*.

34 David Riesman, *Constraint and Variety in American Education* (Garden City, NY: Doubleday, 1956), 14. The Shaw quote is from Theodore M. Hesburgh, *The Challenge and Promise of a Catholic University* (Notre Dame, IN: University of Notre Dame Press, 1994), 105.

35 Alexander W. Astin and Calvin Lee, *The Invisible Colleges: A Profile of Small, Private Colleges with Limited Resources* (New York: McGraw-Hill, 1972), 13.

36 Paul C. Kemeny, *Princeton in the Nation's Service: Religious Ideal and Educational Practice, 1868–1928* (New York: Oxford University Press, 1998); Marsden and Longfield, eds., *The Secularization of the Academy*.

37 Marion Lena Starkey, *The Congregational Way: The Role of the Pilgrims and Their Heirs in Shaping America* (New York: Doubleday, 1966). Carleton abolished mandatory chapel in 1964. See "Our History," http://apps.carleton.edu/about/history/. For a time Carleton

was also affiliated with the Northern Baptist Convention and the Episcopal Church. See Mark A. Greene, "The Baptist Fundamentalists' Case against Carleton, 1926–1928," *Minnesota History* 52 (1): 16–29 (1990). On Presbyterians and region, see William J. Weston, "The American Presbyterian College," in *Called to Teach: The Vocation of the Presbyterian Educator,* ed. Duncan S. Ferguson and William J. Weston (Louisville, KY: Geneva Press, 2003), 61–73. In 1940, Valparaiso president O. P. Kretzmann articulated a sweeping vision of the institution's mission in "The Destiny of a Christian University," republished in Paul J. Contino and David Morgan, eds., *The Lutheran Reader* (Valparaiso, IN: Valparaiso University, 1999), 109–16. The St. Olaf Self Study Committee produced *Integration in the Christian Liberal Arts College* (Northfield, MN: St. Olaf College Press, 1956). The quotation about Lutheran colleges is from Pattillo and Mackenzie, *Church-Sponsored Higher Education,* 52.

38 On Sewanee's status as "the stronghold of the Southern aristocracy," see Samuel S. Hill, *Religion in the Southern States: A Historical Study* (Macon, GA: Mercer University Press, 1983), 303. On Bard's postwar public intellectuals, see "About Bard," http://www.bard.edu/about/history/. On Quaker higher education in America, see the essays in John W. Oliver Jr., Charles L. Cherry, and Caroline L. Cherry, eds., *Founded by Friends: The Quaker Heritage of Fifteen American Colleges and Universities* (Lanham, MD: Scarecrow Press, 2007).The quote is from "Address by Daniel C. Gilman, President of the Johns Hopkins University," in *Addresses at the Inauguration of Bryn Mawr College,* ed. James M. Evans and Daniel Coit Gilman (Philadelphia: Sherman, 1886), 24.

39 The paragraph draws heavily on Gleason, *Contending with Modernity,* and Philip Gleason, *Keeping the Faith: American Catholicism, Past and Present* (Notre Dame, IN: University of Notre Dame Press, 1989). Gleason discusses fascination with the "mythic Middle Ages." The statistic is from Thomas J. Harte, "Catholics as Sociologists," *American Catholic Sociological Review* 13 (1): 8 (1952). See also John Tracy Ellis, *American Catholics and the Intellectual Life* (Chicago: Heritage Foundation, 1956); Kenneth L. Woodward, "The Abiding Presence of the Place," *Notre Dame Magazine* online, Summer 2007, http://magazine.nd.edu/.

40 David J. O'Brien, "The Land O'Lakes Statement," *Boston College Magazine,* Winter 1998; David O'Brien, *From the Heart of the American Church: Catholic Higher Education and American Culture* (Maryknoll, NY: Orbis, 1995). For the text of the Land O'Lakes Statement, see http://archives.nd.edu/episodes/visitors/lol/idea.htm. The Hesburgh quote is from Theodore M. Hesburgh, *God, Country, Notre Dame* (New York: Doubleday, 1990), 175.

41 Ringenberg, *The Christian College;* Joel A. Carpenter, *Revive Us Again: The Reawakening of American Fundamentalism* (New York: Oxford University Press, 1997); Mark Noll, *The Scandal of the Evangelical Mind* (Grand Rapids, MI: Eerdmans, 1994).

42 Molly Worthen discusses the pressures on Mennonite, Pentecostal, and Wesleyan schools in *Apostles of Reason: The Crisis of Authority in American Evangelicalism* (New York: Oxford University Press, 2013). On transdenominational evangelicalism, see George M. Marsden, "The Evangelical Denomination," in *Evangelicalism in Modern America,* ed. George M. Marsden (Grand Rapids, MI: Eerdmans, 1984), xiv. See Wagner, "Generic Conservative Christianity."

43 The "ministry on the margins" metaphor is from Bass, "Ministry on the Margins"; Hunter B. Blakely, "A Time for Decision: Presbyterians Look to the Future," in *Church and Campus: Presbyterians Look to the Future from Their Historic Role in Christian Higher Education,* ed. DeWitt Carter Reddick (Richmond, VA: John Knox Press, 1956), 165; Merrimon

Cuninggim, *The Protestant Stake in Higher Education* (New York: Council of Protestant Colleges and Universities, 1961), quoted in Lynn, "The Survival of Recognizably Protestant Colleges," 181. Also see Douglas Sloan, *Faith and Knowledge: Mainline Protestantism and American Higher Education* (Louisville, KY: Westminster John Knox Press, 1994), 97–101; "Education: College Building Church," *Time*, 3 February 1961.

44 In the 1960s, the Association of Catholic Colleges and Universities was part of the National Catholic Educational Association; it was known as the College Department.

45 Pattillo and Mackenzie, *Church-Sponsored Higher Education*, vii, 153.

46 Pattillo and Mackenzie, *Church-Sponsored Higher Education*, 171.

47 C. Robert Pace, *Education and Evangelism: A Profile of Protestant Colleges* (New York: McGraw-Hill, 1972). For more recent typologies, see William Weston and Dale Soden, "The American Presbyterian College," in Ferguson and Weston, *Called to Teach*, 65; William Weston and Dale Soden, "The Presbyterian College Ideal: A Proposal," unpublished paper prepared for the Association of Presbyterian Colleges and Universities Consultation on the Vocation of the Presbyterian Teacher, 10–13, August 2000, http://web.archive.org/web/20041101102003/www.apcu.net/thirtywho/beau/beau-paper.pdf.

48 Merrimon Cuninggim, "Categories of Church-Relatedness," in *Church-Related Higher Education*, ed. Robert Rue Parsonage (Valley Forge, PA: Judson Press, 1978), 42; Richard E. Anderson, *Strategic Policy Changes at Private Colleges* (New York: Teachers College Press, 1977). For an overview of assessments of religiosity see Cuninggim, *Uneasy Partners*, especially chap. 2.

49 Martin E. Marty, "Future Church-Culture Relations and Their Impact on Church-Related Higher Education—The Student Nexus," in *Church Related Higher Education*, ed. Robert Rue Parsonage (Valley Forge, PA: Judson Press, 1978), 311; Robert Rue Parsonage, "An Overview of Current Denominational Policies and Studies in Higher Education," in *Church Related Higher Education*, 218, 255, 239, 262. The "endangered species" quote is Parsonage's paraphrase of the UCC document.

50 On this new soul-searching, see Michael S. Hamilton, "Generation X and the Waynesburg Experiment," *A Point of View Online* 10 (2): 1–8 (2000); Peter Steinfels, *A People Adrift: The Crisis of the Roman Catholic Church in America* (New York: Simon and Schuster, 2003), 142.

51 Peter Steinfels, "Catholic Identity: Emerging Consensus," *Occasional Papers on Catholic Higher Education* 1 (1): 11–19 (1995). On the heightened attention of Protestant colleges to such matters, see Paul Dovre, "Lutheran Colleges: Past and Prologue," *Intersections* (30): 20 (Fall 2009).

52 Richard G. Hutcheson Jr., "Are Church-Related Colleges Also Christian Colleges?" *Christian Century*, 28 September 1998, 839.

53 Joel Gregory quoted in Michael Beaty and Larry Lyon, *Religion and Higher Education: A Case Study of Baylor University; A Preliminary Report Prepared for Lilly Endowment, Inc.* (Waco, TX: Baylor University, 1995). Beaty and Lyon's report gives further evidence of a sense of crisis in church-related higher education.

54 "A Statement of the Association of Presbyterian Colleges and Universities," 25 March 1990, quoted in Bradley J. Longfield and George M. Marsden, "Presbyterian Colleges in Twentieth-Century America," in *The Pluralistic Vision: Presbyterians and Mainstream Protestant Education and Leadership*, ed. Milton J. Coalter, John M. Mulder, and Louis B. Weeks (Louisville, KY: Westminster John Knox Press, 1992), 99; Lynn, "The Survival of Recognizably Protestant Colleges," 171.

55 Marsden, *The Soul of the American University*; Gleason, *Contending with Modernity*, 320; Burtchaell, *The Dying of the Light*. Scholars debated the declension narratives found in Marsden, Burtchaell, and Gleason. Though they may have exaggerated the threat of secularization, such works made colleges pay attention to religious identity.

56 Paul A. Keim, "The Ethos of Anabaptist-Mennonite Colleges," in Dovre, *The Future of Religious Colleges*, 264. See Ferguson and Weston, *Called to Teach*; Weston and Soden, "The Presbyterian College Ideal," 1–2. According to Weston and Soden's paper, "Since 1992, when historians Bradley Longfield and George Marsden wrote about the pattern of secularization among the nation's Presbyterian colleges, scholars have paid increasing attention to the fragile ecology of Presbyterian Church–related higher education." They are referring to Longfield and Marsden, "Presbyterian Colleges in Twentieth-Century America."

57 Cuninggim, *Uneasy Partners*, 23–39; Jacobsen and Jacobsen, "The Ideals and Diversity," 65–66.

58 Data on the percentage of Americans who identify as Presbyterian from the American Religious Identification Survey of 2001, https://web.archive.org/web/20051101020006/http://www.gc.cuny.edu/faculty/research_briefs/aris/key_findings.htm. Data on Presbyterian enrollment at Presbyterian institutions from the Association of Presbyterian Colleges and Universities, *A Ministry of Nurture: The Spiritual Life at Educational Institutions Affiliated with the Presbyterian Church (U.S.A.)* (Louisville, KY: Association of Presbyterian Colleges and Universities, 1998). It is summarized in Weston and Soden, "The American Presbyterian College," 66.

59 General Board of Higher Education and Ministry (GBHEM), "Strategic Plan for 2003–2008" (August 15, 2003, updated October 28, 2004), *Preparing a New Generation of Christian Leaders*, 6, 16, https://web.archive.org/web/20060426225851/http://gbhem.org/STRATPLAN.PDF.

60 Survey of church-related schools reported in Stephen Haynes, "Teaching Religion at a Church-Related College: Reflections on Professional Identity and Institutional Loyalty," *Religious Studies News*, February 1997, 18. Also see Judith A. Dwyer and Charles E. Zech, "ACCU Survey of Catholic Colleges and Universities: Report on Faculty Development and Curriculum," *Current Issues in Catholic Higher Education* 16 (2): 5–24 (1996); Charles Zech, "The Faculty and Catholic Institutional Identity," *America*, 22 May 1999, 11; James L. Heft, S.M., and Fred P. Pestello, "Hiring Practices in Catholic Colleges and Universities," *Current Issues in Catholic Higher Education* 20 (1): 89–97 (1999).

61 GBHEM, "Strategic Plan for 2003–2008," 6. The pipeline metaphor was also used by Robert Lynn in "The Survival of Recognizably Protestant Colleges," 170–94.

62 Steinfels, *A People Adrift*, 145–46. On efforts toward inclusivity, see O'Brien, *From the Heart of the American Church*, 130. Also see Florence Amamoto, "Diversity, Integrity, and Lutheran Colleges," *Intersections*, 16–22 (Winter 2000).

63 Jencks and Riesman, *The Academic Revolution*, 330.

64 Robert Wuthnow, *The Restructuring of American Religion: Society and Faith Since World War II* (Princeton, NJ: Princeton University Press, 1988), 71–99.

65 Robert Benne, "Augsburg College—Assessing Its Quality and Soul," 4, 15. Document retrieved from http://www.augsburg.edu; no longer available on the Augsburg College website. See also Christy Moran Craft and Alyssa Bryant Rockenbach, "Conceptualizations of Spirituality, Religion, and Faith: Comparing Biblical Notions with the Perspectives of Protestant Christian Students at a Lutheran College," *Christian Higher Education* 10: 444–63 (2011).

66 Bill J. Leonard, "Fostering Dissent in the Postmodern Academy," in *The Future of Baptist Higher Education*, ed. Donald D. Schmeltekopf and Dianna M. Vianza (Waco, TX: Baylor University Press, 2006), 67.

67 William D'Antonio, James V. Davidson, Dean R. Hoge, and Ruth A. Wallace, *Laity: American and Catholic* (Franklin, WI: Sheed and Ward, 1996), 88. Also see Peter Steinfels, "Passing on the Faith," in *A People Adrift*, 203–52; Christian Smith, Kyle Longest, Jonathan Hill, and Kari Christoffersen, *Young Catholic America: Emerging Adults In, Out of, and Gone from the Church* (New York: Oxford University Press, 2014).

68 Center for Applied Research in the Apostolate, "Frequently Requested Statistics," http://cara.georgetown.edu/frequently-requested-church-statistics/. Also see Patricia Wittberg, *The Rise and Decline of Catholic Religious Orders: A Social Movement Perspective* (Albany: State University of New York Press, 1994), 59.

69 Figure on lay presidents derived from statistics in Alexandra Bradley, "Catholic College and University Presidents: Trends Since 2000," *Update*, Summer 2015, 12; John Piderit and Melanie Morey, *Catholic Higher Education: A Culture in Crisis* (New York: Oxford University Press, 2006). Also see Charles L. Currie, "Where We Are and Where We Are Going in Jesuit Higher Education: Sunset or Sunrise," *America*, 20 May 2000, 7–8.

70 David M. O'Connell, C.M., J.C.D., "Address by The Very Rev. David M. O›Connell, C.M., J.C.D. on the occasion of his inauguration as 14th President of The Catholic University of America, 19 November 1998, Basilica of the National Shrine of the Immaculate Conception," Catholic University of America—Office of Public Affairs, http://publicaffairs.cua.edu/speeches/inauguralspeech98.htm.

71 William J. Weston, "The Dying Light and Glowing Embers of Presbyterian Higher Education," in Ferguson and Weston, *Called to Teach*, 3; Duncan J. Ferguson, "The Dawning of the Light," in Ferguson and Weston, *Called to Teach*, 167–68; Margaret O'Brien Steinfels, *The Catholic Intellectual Tradition*, Occasional Papers on Catholic Higher Education (Washington, DC: Association of Catholic Colleges and Universities, 1995).

72 James M. Jasper, *The Art of Moral Protest: Culture, Biography, and Social Movements* (Chicago: University of Chicago Press, 1997). Jasper discusses "perceived threats" and social movements.

73 Weston and Soden, "The Presbyterian College Ideal," 20.

74 Mark R. Schwehn, "Lutheran Higher Education in the Twenty-First Century," in Dovre, *The Future of Religious Colleges*, 215.

75 Roger G. Baldwin, "The Case of the Disappearing Liberal Arts College," *Inside Higher Ed*, 9 July 2009; David W. Breneman, *Liberal Arts Colleges: Thriving, Surviving, or Endangered?* (Washington, DC: Brookings Institution Press, 1994), 21; David W. Breneman, "Are We Losing Our Liberal Arts Colleges?" *AAHE Bulletin*, October 1990, 3–6; Loren Pope, *Colleges That Change Lives: 40 Schools That Will Change the Way You Think about Colleges* (New York: Penguin Books, 2006). Samuel Schuman argues that "small is different" in *Old Main: Small Colleges in Twenty-First Century America* (Baltimore: Johns Hopkins University Press, 2005). See Schuman, *Seeing the Light: Religious Colleges in the Twenty-First Century* (Baltimore: Johns Hopkins University Press, 2010).

76 Steinfels, *A People Adrift*, 146.

77 Alan Wolfe, "Catholic Universities Can Be the Salvation of Pluralism on American Campuses," *Chronicle of Higher Education*, 26 February 1999, B7. See an expanded form of this article in "The Potential for Pluralism: Religious Responses to the Triumph of Theory and Method in American Academic Life," in *Religion, Scholarship, and Higher*

Education: Perspectives, Models, and Future Prospects, ed. Andrea Sterk (Notre Dame, IN: University of Notre Dame Press, 2002), 22–39.

78 Schwehn, "Lutheran Higher Education in the Twenty-First Century," 215.

79 Edward Malloy, "Keepers of the Faith," *Notre Dame Magazine* 28 (3): 33 (Autumn 1999); Keim, "The Ethos of Anabaptist-Mennonite Colleges," 280.

80 Julie A. Reuben, "The University and Its Discontents," *Hedgehog Review* 2: 72–91 (2000). Also see her major historical study *The Making of the Modern University*. A sample of criticism of the contemporary university may be found in James Engell and Anthony Dangerfield, "Forum: The Market-Model University: Humanities in the Age of Money," *Harvard Magazine*, May/June 1998; Eyal Press and Jennifer Washburn, "The Kept University," *Atlantic*, March 2000; William Deresiewicz, *Excellent Sheep: The Miseducation of the American Elite and the Way to a Meaningful Life* (New York: Free Press, 2014).

81 Mark R. Schwehn, *Exiles from Eden: Religion and the Academic Vocation in America* (New York: Oxford University Press, 1992). Also see Storm Bailey, "Uneasy Partners? Religion and Academics," *Academe*, January–February 2001, 27–30.

82 Elizabeth Redden, "Spiritual Accountability," *Inside Higher Ed*, 1 February 2007. Lutheran college assessment data can be found at the Lutheran Educational Conference of North America (LECNA) website, http://lutherancolleges.org/. The CCCU results are reported in Charles E. Stoke and Mark D. Regnerus, *The CCCU and Spiritual Development of Their Students: A Review of Research*, January 2010 (Washington, DC: Council for Christian Colleges and Universities, 2010). The National Catholic College Admission Association studies from 2006 and 2012 are summarized at http://www.catholiccollegesonline.org/members/resources/values-that-matter.html.

83 Statistics from the survey from "Comparative Alumni Research 2011 Update Overall Comparision: Lutheran Colleges to Flagship Public Universities," December 2011, available on the LECNA website, http://lutherancolleges.org/our-research/. The brochure is entitled *The Lutheran College Advantage: Values-Based Communities of Learning.*

84 Jerry Filteau, "Study Finds Alumni Value Catholic College Experience," Catholic News Service, 5 February 2007; "National Catholic Colleges Week 2007 Observed February 18–24, 2007," press release, National Catholic College Admission Association, 25 January 2007.

85 Task Force Report of the Implementation Committee for Overture 00-71, *Reclaiming the Vision: A Mission Strategy to Strengthen the Partnership between the Presbyterian Church (USA) and Its Related Schools, Colleges, and Universities*, 215th General Assembly, 2003, Denver, Colorado, 6, available on the PCUSA UKirk website, https://ukirk.pcusa.org/site_media/media/uploads/ukirk/reclaiming_the_vision.pdf. A 2010 PCUSA resolution noted that higher education is the oldest Presbyterian mission "beyond the congregation." See Overture 102, "On Reestablishing an Office of Collegiate Ministries as a Vital Part of Ministry and Mission," available on the PC-Biz website, http://www.pc-biz.org/. See the ELCA, *A Social Statement on: Our Calling in Education*, from the 2007 Churchwide Assembly, http://download.elca.org/ELCA%20Resource%20Repository/EducationSS.pdf.

86 Hesburgh quoted in Woodward, "The Abiding Presence of the Place." David Jeffrey quoted in Randall Balmer, "2012: A School Odyssey," *Christianity Today*, 18 November 2002; Noll, *The Scandal of the Evangelical Mind*.

87 The survey was mailed to 1,124 program participants in 1999–2000. Thirty-two surveys did not reach the recipients because of incorrect addresses. Thus the total number of surveys sent was 1,092. A total of 680 surveys were eventually returned, yielding a response rate of 62 percent.

88 This paragraph draws on data reported in John Schmalzbauer, "Marsden and Secularization," in *American Evangelicalism: George Marsden and the State of American Religious History* (Notre Dame, IN: University of Notre Dame Press, 2014), 299. The statistics originally appeared in Kathleen A. Mahoney, John Schmalzbauer, and James Youniss, "Revitalizing Religion in the Academy: An Evaluation of Lilly Endowment's Initiative on Religion and Higher Education," unpublished report to Lilly Endowment, 7 August 2000. A summary is available online: *Revitalizing Religion in the Academy: Summary of the Evaluation of Lilly Endowment's Initiative on Religion and Higher Education* (Chestnut Hill, MA: Boston College, 2000), 10, http://www.resourcingchristianity.org/sites/default/files/transcripts/research_article/Mahoney_Schmalzbauer_Youniss_Revitalizing_Religion_Essay.pdf. Since then the list of publications has grown. See Benne, *Quality with Soul*; Susan VanZanten, *Joining the Mission: A Guide for (Mainly) New College Faculty* (Grand Rapids, MI: Eerdmans, 2011).

89 Quotation from "Integrated Strategic Plan" of Seaver College of Pepperdine University, https://web.archive.org/web/20130613104051/http://seaver.pepperdine.edu/dean/documentsandpolicies/isp.htm.

90 "The 2006 University of Dayton Strategic Plan," https://web.archive.org/web/20100609214459/http://provost.udayton.edu/Strategic%20Plan/UDStrategic%20Plan_2006.pdf.

91 The text of Baylor 2012 can be found at https://web.archive.org/web/20040213230646/http://www.baylor.edu/vision/pdf/vision_full.pdf. For more on Baylor 2012, see Balmer, "2012: A School Odyssey"; Robert Benne, "Crisis of Identity," *Christian Century*, 27 January 2004, 26. For an overview of developments at Baylor, see Barry G. Hankins and Donald D. Schmeltekopf, eds., *The Baylor Project: "Can a Protestant University Be a First-Class Research Institution and Preserve Its Soul?"* (South Bend, IN: St. Augustine's Press, 2007).

92 Heft and Pestello, "Hiring Practices in Catholic Colleges and Universities," 90.

93 The 1987 statement can be found at https://www.stolaf.edu/catalog/0304/academiclife/. See the 2016 mission statement, https://wp.stolaf.edu/about/mission/. It also foregrounds the college's Lutheran identity.

94 Robert Benne, "A College Recovers Its Christian Identity," *Christian Century*, 18 April 2001, 12–15, http://www.religion-online.org/showarticle.asp?title=2095. See http://roanoke.edu/about/purpose_and_principles/statement_of_purpose.

95 Kentucky Wesleyan College, https://kwc.edu/about-wesleyan/.

96 James K. Dittmar, "Against All Odds: An Investigation into the Transformation of Waynesburg College," *Christian Higher Education* 8 (2): 91 (2009). See the Maryville College Faith and Learning Statement, http://www.maryvillecollege.edu/about/mission-vision/faith/statement/. The last quote is from Hamilton, "Generation X and the Waynesburg Experiment."

97 See Schier and Russett, *Catholic Women's Colleges in America*, especially chapters 4 and 9. The quote is from a series of interviews with college administrators, part of the authors' evaluation work for Lilly Endowment, Inc. on its religion and higher education initiative, 1999–2000.

98 Columba Mullaly, *Trinity College, Washington, D.C.: The First Eighty Years, 1897–1977* (Westminster, MD: Christian Classics, 1987). The Seven Sisters colleges were Mount Holyoke, Vassar, Smith, Wellesley, Bryn Mawr, Barnard, and Radcliffe. The last two are no longer single-sex institutions. See https://www.mtholyoke.edu/about/history/seven_sisters.

99 Dorothy M. Brown and Carol Hurd Green, "Making It: Stories of Persistence and Success," in *Catholic Women's Colleges in America*, ed. Tracy Schier and Cynthia Russett (Baltimore: Johns Hopkins University Press, 2002), 243–45. Alumna quoted in Patricia A. McGuire, "Civic Virtue Starts at Home: Faith and Freedom for Institutional Transformation," *Cresset*, March 2014, 17.

100 Patricia A. McGuire, "Trinity College: Strategic Planning as the Roadmap to Renaissance," *Current Issues in Catholic Higher Education*, Winter 2003. On Trinity's recent successes, see its website, http://www.trinitydc.edu.

101 The demography of the Trinity student body is reported in McGuire, "Civic Virtue Starts at Home," 22–23. Information on the athletic center and capital campaign from McGuire, "Trinity College."

102 For a list of member institutions in the Hispanic Association of Colleges and Universities, see http://www.hacu.net/. For information on Our Lady of the Lake University, see the university's website on "Points of Pride" and "Mission, Vision, and Values," http://www.ollusa.edu/s/1190/hybrid/default-hybrid-ollu.aspx?sid=1190&gid=1&sitebuilder=1&pgid=7934; Mary Christine Morkovsky, *Living in God's Providence: History of the Congregation of Divine Providence* (San Antonio: Congregation of Divine Providence, 2009).

103 "Office for Mission Effectiveness Annual Report 2000–2001," https://web.archive.org/web/20040723202313/http://www3.villanova.edu/mission/mecommittees/reports/ome00-01.doc. In 2009, Villanova's Special Assistant to the President for Mission became the university's first Vice President for Mission and Ministry. Benne, "A College Recovers Its Christian Identity," 12–15.

104 Dennis H. Holtschneider and Melanie M. Morey, "Relationship Revisited: Catholic Institutions and Their Founding Congregations," *Occasional Paper of the Association of Governing Boards of Universities* (Washington, DC: Association of Governing Boards of Universities and Colleges, 2000), 8; Sandra M. Estanek, Michael J. James, and Daniel A. Norton, "Assessing Catholic Identity: A Study of Mission Statements of Catholic Colleges and Universities," *Catholic Education: A Journal of Inquiry and Practice* 10 (2): 204 (2013); Michael Galligan-Stierle, *A Mission Officer Handbook: Advancing Catholic Identity and University Mission*, vol. 1 (Washington, DC: Association of Catholic Colleges and Universities, 2014). The number of Catholic institutions with a mission and identity officer taken from "Strengthening Catholic Identity," Association of Catholic Colleges and Universities website, http://www.accunet.org/.

105 See Dale E. Soden and Arlin Migliazzo, "Whitworth College: Evangelical in the Reformed Tradition," in *Models for Christian Higher Education: Strategies for Success in the Twenty-First Century*, ed. Richard T. Hughes and William B. Adrian (Grand Rapids, MI: Eerdmans, 1997), 180. Whitworth College in Spokane, Washington, has a Dean of the Chapel position, which was created in the 1990s. So do Ferrum, Hood, Hope, and Roanoke.

106 Articles include R. Passon, "Hiring for Mission: An Overview," *Conversation on Jesuit Higher Education* 12: 5–13 (1997); Nancy Miller, "Hiring for Mission," *Perspectives: A Journal of Reformed Thought* 14 (8): 16–17 (1999); Don Briel, "Mission and Identity: The Role of Faculty," *Journal of Catholic Higher Education* 31 (2): 169–79 (2012).

107 On critical mass, see Benne, *Quality with Soul*, 96.

108 "St. Olaf College Recruitment Statement," available on the university website, http://wp.stolaf.edu/doc/files/2014/01/St.OlafRecruitmentStatement.pdf.

109 Loyola Marymount University, "Moving beyond Traditional Recruitment Strategies: Recruiting and Hiring for Mission," August 2008, available on the university website, http://www.lmu.edu/Assets/Academic+Affairs+Division/Intercultural+Affairs/

Moving+Beyond+Traditional+Recruitment+Strategies.pdf; Heft and Pestello, "Hiring Practices in Catholic Colleges and Universities."

110 Benne, *Quality with Soul*, 124; Margaret Fosmoe, "ND Seeks More Catholic Faculty and Scholars," *South Bend Tribune*, 21 October 2006. A brochure on Notre Dame's Mission Hire Database can be found at http://identifyyourself.nd.edu/assets/48643/ors.pdf. See also http://supporting.nd.edu/recognition-societies/presidents-circle/impact/.

111 Our 2000 evaluation of Lilly Endowment's religion and higher education initiative examined the websites at church-related institutions participating in five faculty and staff development programs.

112 Mahoney, Schmalzbauer, and Youniss, *Revitalizing Religion in the Academy*, 10.

113 "Advancing Knowledge and Mission," *Update: The Newsletter of the Association of Catholic Colleges and Universities*, Winter 2011, https://web.archive.org/web/20151016233647/http://www.accunet.org/files/public/Update/Winter2011b.pdf. Figure of 1,000 centers taken from https://web.archive.org/web/20170301075745/http://www.accunet.org/i4a/pages/index.cfm?pageid=3795. A list of Catholic studies programs can be found on the Association of Catholic Colleges and Universities website, http://www.accunet.org/.

114 See Institute for Faith and Learning, http://www.baylor.edu/ifl/; "Purpose," About the Center for Faith and Learning, http://www.pepperdine.edu/centerforfaithandlearning/purpose/. The figure of seventy-five faculty comes from Richard Hughes, "The Idea of a Christian University," public lecture delivered on September 19, 2000, and reprinted by the Center for Faith and Learning (Malibu, CA: Pepperdine University, 2000).

115 On the Wesley Center at Hamline, see the Center's website, http://www.hamline.edu/wesleycenter/.

116 Spiritual Formation Task Force Document, 1993, quoted in Moore and Woodward, "Clarity through Ambiguity," 303.

117 On Loyola University, see Rob Moll, "Engaged Education," Faith and Leadership, 14 September 2010, http://www.faithandleadership.com/features/articles/engaged-education. Loyola University's "Transformative Education in the Jesuit Tradition" is available at http://www.luc.edu/media/lucedu/mission/pdfs/Transformative%20Education%20document.pdf. For more information on St. Louis University's video and discussion series, see http://www.slu.edu/x25882.xml. See "Faculty Development Grant from the Bush Foundation," Augustana College, November 2002–November 2005, https://web.archive.org/web/20151222064941/http://www.augie.edu/pub/bush/Opportunity_6a.html.

118 For more on Pepperdine's Center for Faith and Learning, see https://community.pepperdine.edu/cfl/faculty-staff-programs/summerseminars.htm.

119 Caroline Simon et al., *Mentoring for Mission: Nurturing New Faculty at Church-Related Colleges* (Grand Rapids, MI: Eerdmans, 2003). A list of mentoring programs supported by the Lilly Fellows Program is available at http://www.lillyfellows.org/GrantsPrizes/MentoringPrograms.aspx.

120 Emmanuel Renner and Hilary Thimmesh, "The College of St. Benedict and St. John's University," in *Models for Christian Higher Education: Strategies for Success in the Twenty-First Century*, ed. Richard T. Hughes and William B. Adrian (Grand Rapids, MI: Eerdmans, 1997), 42. On the activities of the Benedictine Institute, see http://www.csbsju.edu/benedictine-institute.

121 For more on the Holy Cross Ignatian Pilgrimage, see https://www.holycross.edu/faith-service/mcfarland-center-religion-ethics-and-culture/ignatian-pilgrimage.

122 Quotations from the Lilly Fellows Program website, http://www.lillyfellows.org/about/about-us/.

123 Figures on Collegium from http://www.collegium.org/about.html. See the website of the Association for Student Affairs at Catholic Colleges and Universities, http://www.asaccu.org.

124 "About the Institute," Institute for Administrators in Catholic Higher Education, https://www.bc.edu/bc-web/schools/lsoe/sites/iache/about.html.

125 "AJCU Sponsors Trustee Program for Boards of Catholic Colleges and Universities," Association of Jesuit Colleges and Universities, 13 February 2003, http://office.ajcunet.edu/areas/news/press/detail.asp?itemID=19.

126 Paul DiMaggio and Walter Powell, "The Iron Cage Revisited: Institutional Isomorphism and Collective Rationality," in *The New Institutionalism in Organizational Analysis*, ed. Walter Powell and Paul DiMaggio (Chicago: University of Chicago Press, 1991), 63–82. Nancy Ammerman has noted this tendency in the organizational field of American congregations. See her *Pillars of Faith: American Congregations and Their Partners* (Berkeley: University of California Press, 2005). Robert Wuthnow and D. Michael Lindsay discuss similar kinds of isomorphism in "Financing Faith: Religion and Strategic Philanthropy," *Journal for the Scientific Study of Religion* 49 (1): 87–111 (2010). Eric Childers discusses institutional isomorphism at church-related institutions in *College Identity Sagas*, 197–99. Childers argues that isomorphism can both strengthen and weaken religious identity, depending on the context.

127 John Wilcox and Irene King, eds., *Enhancing Religious Identity: Best Practices from Catholic Campuses* (Washington, DC: Georgetown University Press, 2000); Karen E. Eifler and Thomas M. Landy, *Becoming Beholders: Cultivating Sacramental Imagination and Actions in College Classrooms* (Collegeville, MN: Liturgical Press, 2014).

128 Tracy Schier, "Mark Schwehn: On the Heightened Profile of Religion and Vocation within Higher Education," available on the Resources for American Christianity website, http://www.resourcingchristianity.org/.

129 See "History," About PTEV, https://web.archive.org/web/20160315011445/http://www.ptev.org/history.aspx. Lilly's summary of the program is available at http://lillyendowment.org/religion_ptev.html. The $225 million figure comes from Tim Clydesdale, *The Purposeful Graduate: Why Colleges Must Talk to Students about Vocation* (Chicago: University of Chicago Press, 2015), 46. Clydesdale also reports the number of follow-up grants.

130 For information on Messiah's PTEV grant, see https://web.archive.org/web/20130512130441/http://www.messiah.edu/christian_vocation/vision.html. A discussion of the Lutheran and non-Lutheran dimensions of the Gustavus program can be found in Darrell Jodock's essay "Vocational Discernment—A Comprehensive College Program," paper delivered at ELCA Conference on the Vocation of a Lutheran College, 3 August 2001, https://gustavus.edu/faith/pdf/vocation.pdf.

131 For syllabi for Lilly vocation courses, see https://web.archive.org/web/20090101061134/http://www.ptev.org:80/cdSyllabi.aspx?iid=9.

132 William Placher, ed., *Callings: Twenty Centuries of Christian Wisdom on Vocation* (Grand Rapids, MI: Eerdmans, 2005); Mark R. Schwehn and Dorothy C. Bass, eds., *Leading Lives That Matter: What We Should Do and Who We Should Be* (Grand Rapids, MI: Eerdmans, 2006); Kaethe Schwehn and L. DeAne Lagerquist, *Claiming Our Callings: Toward a New Understanding of Vocation in the Liberal Arts* (New York: Oxford University Press, 2014).

133 Craig Dykstra, "What Now Do We Mean by the Theological Exploration?" address delivered to participants at the Final PTEV Conference, 8 February 2007, https://web.archive

.org/web/20160314075623/http://www.ptev.org/news.aspx?iid=63; Marcia J. Bunge, "'Our Calling in Education': Working Together to Generate a Strong Social Statement on Public Schools, Lutheran Schools and Colleges, and the Faith Formation of Children and Young People," *Intersections* 23 (Summer 2006), 10; Gary Luhr, "Collegians Answer the Call of God," *Presbyterian Outlook*, 2 May 2013; Tom Gillem, "What Happens after Graduation?" *Interpreter*, March/April 2013.

134 Mahoney, Schmalzbauer, and Youniss, *Revitalizing Religion in the Academy*, 10.

135 Clydesdale, *The Purposeful Graduate*, 133, 134, 103.

136 For more information on the Network for Vocation in Undergraduate Education (NetVUE), see https://www.cic.edu/programs/NetVUE. See also Shirley Roels, "An Education for Life Abundant," *Liberal Education*, Winter 2014.

137 For more on the ACCU's activities, see http://www.accunet.org/. The conference on Jesuit higher education's future is described in Charles L. Currie, "Training the University Mission: The Specificity of the Jesuit Identity and Its Development on the Leadership and Academic Styles That It Promotes," http://issuu.com/ausjal/docs/charles_currie_ajcu. On the Association of Presbyterian Colleges and University gathering, see Ferguson and Weston, *Called to Teach*, 4.

138 For more on the Lutheran Academy of Scholars, https://web.archive.org/web/20121408044500/http://www.cord.edu/lutheranscholars/index.php.

139 For more on "The Future of Baptist Higher Education" conference, see the official website, https://web.archive.org/web/20100725163933/http://www.baylor.edu/fbhe/. Information on the Young Scholars in the Baptist Academy can be found https://www.georgetowncollege.edu/young-scholars-baptist-academy. Two volumes have been produced by the project. See Roger Ward and David Gushee, eds., *The Scholarly Vocation and the Baptist Academy* (Macon, GA: Mercer University Press, 2008); Roger Ward and Philip Thompson, *Tradition and the Baptist Academy* (Eugene, OR: Wipf and Stock, 2011).

140 On the increasing membership and influence of the CCCU, see Ringenberg, *The Christian College*, 211. Current statistics on the CCCU available at http://cccu.org/about.

141 For more on the "homogeneous model," see Jacobsen and Jacobsen, *No Longer Invisible*, 87; Noll, *The Scandal of the Evangelical Mind*, 3.

142 The first quote and information on scholarly productivity are from Susan VanZanten, "Christian Scholarship: Opportunities, Realities, and Challenges," in *The Christian College Phenomenon: Inside America's Fastest Growing Institutions of Higher Learning*, ed. Samuel Joeckel and Thomas Chesnes (Abilene, TX: ACU Press, 2012), 46, 50. The survey results and second quote appear in Samuel Joeckel and Thomas Chesnes, "A Slippery Slope to Secularization? The Worthwhile Risk of Christian Higher Education," in Joeckel and Chesnes, *The Christian College Phenomenon*, 43, 36.

143 See Hughes and Adrian, *Models for Christian Higher Education*. Information on the HarperCollins series can be found at http://www.harpercollins.com/. Books on Christian scholarship published by CCCU faculty include Harry Lee Poe, *Christianity in the Academy: Teaching at the Intersection of Faith and Learning* (Grand Rapids, MI: Baker Academic, 2004); Douglas Jacobsen and Rhonda Hustedt Jacobsen, eds., *Scholarship and Christian Faith: Enlarging the Conversation* (New York: Oxford University Press, 2004); and Todd Ream, Jerry Pattengale, and David Riggs, *Beyond Integration: Inter/Disciplinary Possibilities for the Future of Christian Higher Education* (Abilene, TX: ACU Press, 2012).

144 On Lutheran efforts, see Paul J. Contino and David Morgan, eds., *The Lutheran Reader* (Valparaiso, IN: Valparaiso University, 1999); Ernest J. Simmons, *Lutheran Higher Education: An Introduction for Faculty* (Minneapolis: Augsburg Fortress, 1998); Pamela

Schwandt, Gary DeKrey, and L. DeAne Lagerquist, eds., *Called to Serve: St. Olaf and the Vocation of a Church College* (Northfield, MN: St. Olaf College, 1999). See also Tom Christenson, *The Gift and Task of Lutheran Higher Education* (Minneapolis: Augsburg Fortress, 2004); and Tom Christenson, *Who Needs a Lutheran College? Values Vision Vocation* (Minneapolis, MN: Lutheran University Press, 2011). On Mennonite colleges, see Keith Graber Miller, *Teaching to Transform: Perspectives on Mennonite Higher Education* (Goshen, IN: Pinchpenny Press, 2000).

145 Wilcox and King, *Enhancing Religious Identity*; Thomas M. Landy, ed., *As Leaven in the World: Catholic Perspectives on Faith, Vocation, and the Intellectual Life* (Franklin, WI: Sheed and Ward, 2001); John Wilcox, Jennifer Anne Lindholm, and Suzanne Dale Wilcox, eds., *Revisioning Mission: The Future of Catholic Higher Education* (North Charleston, SC: CreateSpace, 2014); Oliver, Cherry, and Cherry, *Founded by Friends*.

146 On the doxological aspect of the Lutheran tradition, see Simmons, *Lutheran Higher Education*, 84. On Lutheran distinctiveness, see Marcia J. Bunge, "Introduction to Valaparaiso University in the Context of Lutheran Higher Education," in Contino and Morgan, *The Lutheran Reader*, 2. On the quintessential Lutheran themes of paradox and tension, see Simmons, *Lutheran Higher Education*; Contino and Morgan, *The Lutheran Reader*, and Schwandt, DeKrey, and Lagerquist, *Called to Serve*. See Hughes and Adrian, *Models for Christian Higher Education*; Richard T. Hughes, *The Vocation of the Christian Scholar: How Christian Faith Can Sustain the Life of the Mind* (Grand Rapids, MI: Eerdmans, 2005). On Mennonite higher education, see Miller, *Teaching to Transform*.

147 Jencks and Riesman, *The Academic Revolution*, 330.

148 Benne, "Augsburg College—Assessing Its Quality and Soul," 13.

149 In *The Dying of the Light*, James Burtchaell traces the "disengagement of the colleges from their Christian churches" while virtually ignoring the disengagement of churches from their colleges. See also Merrimon Cuninggim's *Uneasy Partners*.

150 Michael D. Wiese, Gideon Project, Phase I, Summary Report, 1997, 1.

151 The goals from the 2006–2012 General Board of Higher Education and Ministry strategic plan can be found at http://web.archive.org/web/20090130061632/http://www.gbhem.org/site/c.lsKSL3POLvF/b.3554121/k.C11E/Goal_I.htm.

152 On the forty-eight hearings leading up to the ELCA's social statement, see Melissa Ramirez Cooper, "ELCA Task Force Reviews Responses on Draft of Social Statement on Education," ELCA News Service, 26 October 2006, http://www.elca.org/. See Evangelical Lutheran Church in America, *A Social Statement on: Our Calling in Education*, January 2007, available on the ELCA website, http://download.elca.org/.

153 Task Force Report of the Implementation Committee for Overture 00-71, *Reclaiming the Vision: A Mission Strategy to Strengthen the Partnership between the Presbyterian Church (USA) and Its Related Schools, Colleges, and Universities*, 215th General Assembly, 2003, Denver, Colorado, 10, available on the PCUSA UKirk website, https://ukirk.pcusa.org/site_media/media/uploads/ukirk/reclaiming_the_vision.pdf; Janet Tuck, "220th GA Approves Recommendation for Development of Clear Definition for Affiliated Schools," *Presbyterian Outlook*, 7 July 2012; John Williams, "'PC(USA)-Related College'—What's That?" *Presbyterian Outlook*, 8 May 2014.

154 Elizabeth Hunter, "Grade-A College," *Lutheran*, November 1999. The *Here I Study* brochure is available at https://web.archive.org/web/20130720104943/http://www.elca.org/Growing-In-Faith/Education/Colleges-and-Universities/Resources/Here-I-Study.aspx. The video is available at http://www.youtube.com/watch?v=rDzLSLS-C0g.

155 Carrie Madren, "A Higher Calling for Higher Education," *Interpreter*, March/April 2013, 13; Jack Haberer, "Outlook College Partnership Award Goes to . . ." *Presbyterian Outlook*, 3 July 2013.

156 See "Covenant of Understanding between Waynesburg College and the Synod of the Trinity," https://web.archive.org/web/20081026031450/http://www.waynesburg.edu/index.php?q=About_Waynesburg/Covenant_of_Understanding.

157 "New Covenant Strengthens Church-School Connection," United Methodist News Service, 6 May 2000; Linda Green, "Church, Colleges Burning to Strengthen Connectional Ties," United Methodist News Service, 16 June 2004.

158 "Religious Life at Birmingham College," www.bsc.edu/campus/religious/religious-life-policies.pdf.

159 See Mahoney, Schmalzbauer, and Youniss, *Revitalizing Religion in the Academy*.

160 The $225 million figure comes from Clydesdale, *The Purposeful Graduate*, 46. For information on the Network for Vocation in Education, see http://www.cic.edu/Programs-and-Services/Programs/NetVUE/Pages/default.aspx.

161 On Collegium, see http://www.collegium.org/. Association for Student Affairs at Catholic Colleges and Universities numbers from Tom Gallagher, "The Making of a Catholic Campus," *National Catholic Reporter*, 19 March 2010.

162 For a discussion of the pipelines, see Lynn, "'The Survival of Recognizably Protestant Colleges," 170–94. On the elimination of the Higher Education Program Area, see Gerald W. Gibson, "Beyond Wistful Concern," *Presbyterian Outlook*, 26 October 2008. On the merger of the Presbyterian Church (USA) Collegiate Ministries Office with youth ministries, see Gary Luhr, "Keeping College Students Connected," *Presbyterian Outlook*, 28 June 200. On the reestablishment of the Collegiate Ministries unit and the denomination's campus strategy, see "Collegiate Ministries Task Force Named, Will Meet This Fall," Presbyterian News Service, 16 March 2011, https://www.pcusa.org/news/2011/3/16/collegiate-ministries-task-force-named-will-meet-f and https://ukirk.pcusa.org/page/about/.

163 On the elimination of the Division for Higher Education and Schools, see David L. Miller, "What's at Stake?" *Lutheran*, May 2004. The 2005 ELCA resolution creating the Vocation and Education unit is available at https://web.archive.org/web/20051110135149/http://www.elca.org/vocationeducation/resolution.html. The 2011 restructuring of the ELCA is discussed in "Redesign for 2011 Brings Staff Cuts," *Lutheran*, November 2010.

164 On the role of the Baptist college association as a substitute for the Southern Baptist Education Commission, see Tim Fields, "Agee to Retire as College Association's Executive Director," *Baptist Press*, 13 February 2007.

165 On the disaffiliation of Baptist colleges from the state Baptist conventions, see Alan Finder, "Feeling Strains, Baptist Colleges Cut Church Ties," *New York Times*, 22 July 2006; "Last 5 Colleges Linked to Baptists Prepare for Split," Associated Press, 24 March 2007, specifically discusses North Carolina Baptist institutions; Adelle Banks, "Baptist University Loses Third of Faculty over Lifestyle Statement," *Christianity Today*, 22 May 2010; Bob Allen, "Prof: Shorter Limiting Academic Freedom," *ABPNews*, 24 May 2012; Thomas Kidd, "Calvinist Controversy at Louisiana College," *Patheos*, 26 February 2013; Peter Smith, "Campbellsville University Draws Scrutiny of Southern Baptist Convention," *Louisville Courier-Journal*, 25 April 2013; Nancy H. McLaughlin, "Baptist Colleges Trade Funding for Freedom," *News and Record*, 14 November 2007; Colby Sledge, "Belmont, Baptists Part on Good Terms," *Tennessean*, 14 November 2007. Quotation from Marv Knox, "Baptist Colleges Face Crisis, Godsey Says," *Baptist Standard*, 7 July 2006.

166 This account draws on Michael Beaty, "Baptist Models: Past and Present," in Dovre, *The Future of Religious Colleges*, 116–40; Balmer, "2012: A School Odyssey"; Marv Knox, "Baylor 'Family Dialogue' Resembled Family Feud," *Baptist Standard*, 21 July 2003; Brian Garr, "Dueling Ads Reflect Division over Sloan Presidency," *Waco Tribune*, 29 August 2003; H. Rhea Gray, "Healing Baylor's Rift," *Waco Tribune*, 21 February 2004; "Baylor's Sloan Steps Down to Chancellor," *Christian Century*, 22 February 2005. For an overview of this entire period in Baylor's history, see Hankins and Schmeltekopf, *The Baylor Project*. The last quotation is from *Pro Futuris: A Strategic Vision for Baylor University* (Waco, TX: Baylor University, 2012). Baylor reaffirmed the vision of *Pro Futuris* in May of 2014 with a statement of the university's goals for 2014–2018, http://www.baylor.edu/profuturis/index.php?id=863691. On Baylor's recent challenges, see Eric Kelderman and Robin Wilson, "'Fundamental Failure' on Sexual Assaults Brings Sweeping Change at Baylor," *Chronicle of Higher Education*, 27 May 2016; "Baylor University Board of Regents Announces Leadership Changes and Extensive Corrective Actions Following Findings of External Investigation," Baylor University Media Communications, 26 May 2016, http://www.baylor.edu/mediacommunications/news.php?action=story&story=170207; Bobby Ross Jr., "Baylor's First Woman President Brings Fresh Start to Baptist University," Religion News Service, 27 June 2017.

167 Mahoney, Schmalzbauer, and Youniss, *Revitalizing Religion in the Academy*, 15. The gender report of an unidentified department at the University of Notre Dame is available as part of the handbook prepared by ND Watch, "an independent collective to inform, mentor, and support women faculty at the University of Notre Dame." See chapter 3 of ND Watch's "Best Practices for Women: Negotiating the University of Notre Dame," https://web.archive.org/web/20160311233546/http://www.nd.edu/~watch/chap3.htm. For another critique of the male bias of the mission and identity conversation, see Nancy Haegel, "Whose Catholic Identity? Let's Look to the Future, Not the Past," *Commonweal*, 10 April 1998.

168 Jon Nilson, "The Impending Death of Catholic Higher Education," *America*, 28 May 2001, 10–13; Richard McBrien, "Theologians at Risk? Ex Corde and Catholic Colleges," *Academe*, January/February 2001.

169 Pope Benedict XVI's address to Catholic educators during his 2008 visit to the United States is available at https://zenit.org/articles/benedict-xvi-s-address-to-catholic-educators/. See also Beth McMurtrie, "Catholic-College Leaders Welcome New Pope as Scholar and Advocate," *Chronicle of Higher Education*, 13 March 2013.

170 Piderit and Morey, *Catholic Higher Education*, 312. Also see Leslie Woodcock Tentler, "Identity Crisis," *Commonweal*, 22 September 2006, 29–30.

171 The Boston College and Notre Dame data come from a Baylor University survey. See Larry Lyon, Michael Beaty, and Stephanie Litizzette Mixon, "Making Sense of a 'Religious' University: Faculty Adaptations and Opinions at Brigham Young, Baylor, Notre Dame, and Boston College," *Review of Religious Research* 43 (4): 335 (2002).

172 Robert Andringa, appendix A in William C. Ringenberg, *The Christian College: A History of Protestant Higher Education in America* (Grand Rapids, MI: Baker, 2006), 249.

173 The quotation is from Douglas Jacobsen and Rhonda Hustedt Jacobsen, "More than the 'Integration of Faith and Learning,'" in Jacobsen and Jacobsen, *Scholarship and Christian Faith*, 6, in which they paraphrase Craig Dykstra. For several years, Macalester has appeared on a list of the least religious student bodies in the United States. For more information on Macalester's Lilly Project for Vocation and Ethical Leadership, see https://web.archive.org/web/20100830083325/http://www.macalester.edu/lilly/About.html.

The statistic is from Martha Sawyer Allen, "Searching, Learning, Faithful," *Minneapolis Star Tribune* 26 January 2002; Eily Marlow, "Lilly Pad: From First Year Agnostic to Associate Chaplain," *Mac Weekly*, 6 December 2002; Jan Shaw-Flamm, "Are There Religious Students at Macalester? Is the Pope German?" *Macalester Today*, 6 January 2005; Jeanne Halgren Kilde, *Nature and Revelation: A History of Macalester College* (Minneapolis: University of Minnesota Press, 2010), 12.

174 The quotation from Haverford is from Diana Franzusoff Peterson, "Haverford College," in Oliver, Cherry, and Cherry, *Founded by Friends*, 17. For information on Grinnell's Lilly grant, see the website of the Lilly Program on the Liberal Arts and Vocation, https://web.archive.org/web/20100528181425/http://www.grinnell.edu/offices/cfgrelations/campus/lillyfront; "White Paper: Teagle Working Group on Secularity and the Liberal Arts: Bucknell University, Macalester College, Vassar College, and Williams College," September 2008, http://projects.vassar.edu/secularity/docs/secularity_whitepaper.pdf.

175 L. DeAne Lagerquist, "'Lest We Become Beasts Who Devour Each Other': A Lutheran Calling to Higher Education in Multi-Religious Settings," *Dialog: A Journal of Theology* 50 (2): 174–85 (2011); L. DeAne Lagerquist, "Secularization—A Bad Thing? A View from St. Olaf College," unpublished paper presented at the annual meeting of the American Academy of Religion, 2006; David Gonnerman, "Hindu Scholar Rambachan to Address World Council of Churches," *St. Olaf College News*, 7 February 2005. Statistics from https://wp.stolaf.edu/. Quotation from St. Olaf's president from David Anderson, "Summit on the Hill Address," 21 September 2013, http://wp.stolaf.edu/president/public-remarks/summit-on-the-hill-address/. A list of Religion Department faculty can be found at http://wp.stolaf.edu/religion/contact-us/.

176 For information on Georgetown's Office of Mission and Ministry, see https://missionandministry.georgetown.edu/.

177 At non-Catholic religious institutions, 68 percent of faculty agreed that their institutions should facilitate the spiritual development of students. The figure was 62 percent for professors at Catholic colleges and universities. See Jennifer A. Lindholm, Helen S. Astin, and Alexander W. Astin, *Spirituality and the Professoriate* (Los Angeles: Higher Education Research Institute, 2006), 9, http://spirituality.ucla.edu/docs/results/faculty/spirit_professoriate.pdf.

178 Lyon, Beaty, and Mixon, "Making Sense of a 'Religious' University," 344.

179 Jennifer A. Lindholm, "The Role of Faculty in Students' Spiritual Development," Keynote Address presented at the 14th Annual Institute on College Student Values, 7 February 2004, Tallahassee, Florida, https://web.archive.org/web/20080313122926/http://www.collegevalues.org/proceedings.cfm?y=2004. See also Neil Gross and Solon Simmons, "How Religious Are America's College and University Professors?" SSRC Web Forum on the Religious Engagements of American Undergraduates, 6 February 2007, http://religion.ssrc.org/reforum/Gross_Simmons.pdf. According to Gross and Simmons, almost one-third of professors at religious colleges and universities identify as born again, compared to just 1 percent of faculty at elite doctoral institutions.

180 "CCCU Reports Surging Enrollment for Christian Higher Education," press release, Council for Christian Colleges and Universities, 10 October 2005, https://web.archive.org/web/20160429191010/http://www.cccu.org/news/articles/2005/cccu_reports_surging_enrollment_for_christian_higher_education. Catholic university enrollment figures for the 1990s from the Association of Catholic Colleges and Universities, http://web.archive.org/web/20050828231459/http://www.accunet.org:80/display.asp?Category=6.

More recent enrollment figures for Catholic institutions from *Digest of Education Statistics* (Washington, DC: National Center for Education Statistics, 2016).

181 For a sober view of evangelical higher education with data on SAT scores and finances, see Allen Guelzo, "Course Corrections: Whither the Evangelical College?" *Touchstone*, May/June 2011; Guelzo, "Cracks in the Tower: A Closer Look at the Christian College Boom," *Books and Culture*, July/August 2005.

182 As noted earlier, George Marsden, author of the influential *Soul of the American University*, also believes that there is no longer reason to believe that church-related higher education will "continue along the slippery slope toward secularism." Marsden was quoted in Beth McMurtrie, "Future of Religious Colleges Is Bright, Say Scholars and Officials," *Chronicle of Higher Education*, 20 October 2000, A41. See also George M. Marsden, "A Renaissance of Christian Higher Education in the United States," in *Christian Higher Education: A Global Reconnaissance* (Grand Rapids, MI: Eerdmans, 2014), 257–76.

Chapter 4

1 Large portions of this chapter were originally published in John Schmalzbauer, "Campus Religious Life in America: Revitalization and Renewal," *Society* 50 (2): 115–31 (2013); and John Schmalzbauer, "Campus Ministry: A Statistical Portrait," SSRC Web Forum on the Religious Engagements of American Undergraduates, 6 February 2007, http://religion.ssrc.org/reforum/Schmalzbauer.pdf. Statistics have been updated to reflect changing membership rolls, as well as shifts in American denominations and campus religious organizations.

2 Philip E. Wentworth, "What College Did to My Religion," *Atlantic Monthly*, June 1932; J. Budziszewski, *How to Stay Christian in College* (Colorado Springs, CO: NavPress, 2004). For historical treatments of student religion, see George M. Marsden, *The Soul of the American University: From Protestant Establishment to Established Nonbelief* (New York: Oxford University Press, 1994); Douglas Sloan, *Faith and Knowledge: Mainline Protestantism and American Higher Education* (Louisville, KY: Westminster John Knox Press, 1994); Dorothy C. Bass, "Ministry on the Margins: Protestants and Education," in *Between the Times: The Travail of the Protestant Establishment in America, 1900–1960*, ed. William R. Hutchison (Cambridge: Cambridge University Press, 1989), 48–71.

3 On the decline in student religiosity during this period, see Dean R. Hoge, *Commitment on Campus: Changes in Religion and Values over Five Decades* (Philadelphia: Westminster Press, 1974). Christian Smith cites several older studies showing a correlation between college attendance and religious disaffiliation in *Souls in Transition: The Religious and Spiritual Lives of Emerging Adults* (New York: Oxford University Press, 2009). 248. For more on this pattern, see Kirk Hadaway and Wade Clark Roof, "Apostasy in American Churches: Evidence from National Survey Data," in *Falling from the Faith: Causes and Consequences of Religious Apostasy*, ed. David Bromley (Beverly Hills, CA: Sage, 1988), 29–46; David Caplovitz and Fred Sherrow, *The Religious Drop-Outs: Apostasy among College Graduates* (Beverly Hills, CA: Sage, 1977). On student affairs in the 1980s, see James R. Collins, James C. Hurst, and Judith K. Jacobson, "The Blind Spot Extended: Spirituality," *Journal of College Student Personnel* 28 (3): 274–76 (1987).

4 On the "spiritual vacuum" left by the decline of the ecumenical student movement, see Alice Hageman, "Reflections on the Student Christian Movement of the 1960's and Its Effect on My Life," *Journal of Ecumenical Studies* 32 (3): 379 (1995). Information on the founding of the Muslim Students' Association can be found at http://msanational.org/about-us/.

The number of MSA chapters is reported in Altaf Husain, "Envisioning a Continent Wide Student Organization," *MSA Link*, Fall/Winter 2008, 8–9. The term "spiritual marketplace" comes from Wade Clark Roof, *Spiritual Marketplace: Baby Boomers and the Remaking of American Religion* (Princeton, NJ: Princeton University Press, 2001). Smith discusses recent studies documenting a positive correlation between higher education and religiosity in *Souls in Transition*, 248–49.

5 As Roger Finke and Rodney Stark note, the decline of particular denominations "is not a decline in religion, but only a decline in the fortunes of specific religious organizations as they give way to new ones." See Finke and Stark, *The Churching of America, 1776–2005: Winners and Losers in Our Religious Economy* (New Brunswick, NJ: Rutgers University Press, 2005), 46; Finke, "Innovative Returns to Tradition: Using Core Teachings as the Foundation for Innovative Accommodation," *Journal for the Scientific Study of Religion* 43 (1): 19–34 (2004). See also Robert D. Putnam and David E. Campbell, *American Grace: How Religion Unites and Divides Us* (New York: Simon and Schuster, 2010), 82; this does not mean that religious decline is not a possibility in American society. See chapter 6 for a lengthy discussion of this topic.

6 On colleges and cycles of student activism, see Arthur Levine, *When Hope and Fear Collide: A Portrait of Today's College Student* (San Francisco: Jossey-Bass, 1998).

7 Among the works that have shaped our general understanding of the cycles of student religion are Clarence P. Shedd, *A Century of Christian Student Initiative* (New York: Association Press, 1945); Clarence P. Shedd, *Two Centuries of Student Christian Movements: Their Origin and Intercollegiate Life* (New York: Association Press, 1934); Clarence P. Shedd, *Religion in the State University* (New Haven, CT: Edward W. Hazen Foundation, 1947); Marsden, *The Soul of the American University*; Sloan, *Faith and Knowledge*; Dorothy C. Bass, "The Independent Sector and the Educational Strategies of Mainstream Protestantism, 1900–1980," in *Religion, The Independent Sector, and American Culture*, ed. Conrad Cherry and Rowland A. Sherrill (Atlanta: Scholars Press, 1992), 51–72; Keith Hunt and Gladys Hunt, *The Story of InterVarsity Christian Fellowship, 1940–1990* (Downers Grove, IL: InterVarsity Press, 1991).

8 On the protean quality of campus religion, see Conrad Cherry, Betty DeBerg, and Amanda Porterfield, *Religion on Campus* (Chapel Hill: University of North Carolina Press, 2001), 5.

9 Bruce A. Kimball, *The "True Professional Ideal" in America: A History* (Cambridge, MA: Blackwell, 1992), 78; Marsden, *The Soul of the American University*, 41–42.

10 Marsden, *The Soul of the American University*, 55. Harvard student quoted in Frederick Rudolph, *The American College and University: A History* (Cambridge, MA: Blackwell, 1962), 79; Shedd, *Two Centuries of Student Christian Movements*, 37, 48.

11 Clarence P. Shedd, a midcentury chronicler of campus religion, believed that the "best times for religion and religious movements have generally been those times when its assumptions, practices, and sanctions have been most vigorously challenged." See Shedd, *Two Centuries of Student Christian Movements*, 37. On Princeton, see Mark Noll, *Princeton and the Republic, 1768–1822: The Search for a Christian Enlightenment in the Era of Samuel Stanhope Smith* (Princeton, NJ: Princeton University Press, 1989), 105. The last statistic is from Shedd, *Two Centuries of Student Christian Movements*, 69.

12 The first statistic is from Marsden, *The Soul of the American University*, 81; James Angell, "Religious Life in Our State Universities," *Andover Review* 13: 365–72 (April 1890). The Angell study is reported in Marsden, *The Soul of the American University*, 171, who also discusses faculty religious activities. For a discussion of state university chapel services, see Clarence P. Shedd, *Religion in the State University* (New Haven, CT: Hazen Foundation, 1947).

13 Founded in London in 1844, the YMCA came to the United States in 1851. The U.S. YWCA chapter began in 1858. Though initially an urban ministry, it had some of its greatest influence on American colleges and universities. On the YMCA and colleges, see David P. Setran, *The College "Y": Student Religion in the Era of Secularization* (New York: Palgrave Macmillan, 2007); Shedd, *Two Centuries of Student Christian Movements*; Hopkins, *History of the YMCA in North America*; William H. Morgan, *Student Religion during Fifty Years: Programs and Policies of the Intercollegiate YMCA* (New York: Association Press, 1935). On the YWCA, see Mary Sophia Stevens Sims, *The Natural History of a Social Institution: The Young Women's Christian Association* (New York: Woman's Press, 1936).

14 The statistic of 85 percent comes from Keith Hunt and Gladys Hunt, *For Christ and the University: The Story of InterVarsity Christian Fellowship* (Downers Grove, IL: InterVarsity Press, 1992), 36. Shedd attributes the rapid growth of the Y to the "free religious atmosphere" of state universities, "together with the greater sense of responsibility that rested upon the individual Christian student for the propagation of his faith." See Shedd, *Student Christian Movements*, 112, 104. On the first collegiate YWCA and the organization's subsequent growth, see Donald G. Shockley, *Campus Ministry: The Church Beyond Itself* (Louisville, KY: Westminster John Knox Press, 1989), 18. On the YWCA's autonomy and use of female college graduates, see Johanna Solles, "The Role of Women in the Formation of the World Student Christian Federation," *International Bulletin of Missionary Research* 30 (4): 189–94 (2006).

15 Morgan, *Student Religion during Fifty Years*, 54, 98. The statistics on student decisions were collected as part of an evangelism campaign at a major state university.

16 Morgan, *Student Religion during Fifty Years*, 104, 105.

17 Shedd, *Two Centuries of Student Christian Movements*, 161–62.

18 C. Howard Hopkins, *History of the YMCA in North America* (New York: Association Press, 1951), 626.

19 William A. Scott, "The Religious Situation in State Universities," *Biblical World* 26: 25, cf. 20–24 (July 1905), reported in Marsden, *The Soul of the American University*, 269, 343. Figures from 1921 in Marsden originally reported in Hopkins, *History of the YMCA in North America*, 628, 645–46. On the collegiate Y's many functions, see Julie A. Reuben, *The Making of the Modern University: Intellectual Transformation and the Marginalization of Morality* (Chicago: University of Chicago Press, 1996), 129–30; Setran, *The College "Y"*; Morgan, *Student Religion during Fifty Years*; John Butler, "An Overview of Religion on Campus," in *Religion on Campus*, ed. John Butler (San Francisco: Jossey-Bass, 1989), 3–16.

20 Michael Parker, *The Kingdom of Character: The Student Volunteer Movement for Foreign Missions (1886–1926)* (Lanham, MD: University Press of America, 1998), 11, 12, 14. See also Solles, "The Role of Women," 192, 193. The 30 percent statistic is from Solles.

21 Hunt and Hunt, *For Christ and the University*, 42–43.

22 Parker, *Kingdom of Character*, 33.

23 Shedd, *Two Centuries of Student Christian Movements*, 338, 371–72. On the YWCA and women's missionary organizations, see Solles, "The Role of Women."

24 William R. Hutchison, "Protestantism as Establishment," in Hutchison, *Between the Times*, 7–8; Shedd, *A Century of Christian Student Initiative*, 13. See also E. Digby Baltzell, *The Protestant Establishment: Aristocracy and Caste in America* (New York: Random House, 1964).

25 Nathan Hatch, *The Democratization of American Christianity* (New Haven, CT: Yale University Press, 1991). This definition of "parachurch" is a paraphrase of Richard

Hutcheson taken from his *Mainline Churches and the Evangelicals: A Challenging Crisis?* (Atlanta: John Knox Press, 1981), 63. On the parallels between parachurch groups and religious orders, see Arthur Glasser, "Discovering Mission," paper presented at Mission Consultation, Presbyterian Church, U.S., January 1978, reported in Hutcheson, *Mainline Churches*, 63.

26 Marsden, *The Soul of the American Universities.*

27 On the displacement of the YMCA by the field of Student Affairs, see Hopkins, *History of the YMCA in North America*, 655; Reuben, *The Making of the Modern University.* On the YMCA's changing function, see Setran, *The College "Y."*

28 Figures from Hopkins, *History of the YMCA in North America*, 646. See also Hunt and Hunt, *For Christ and the University*; Morgan, *Student Religion during Fifty Years.*

29 Hunt and Hunt, *For Christ and the University*, 45.

30 On the "Christian Student" statue and the shifts in the YMCA, see Setran, *The College "Y"*, 182–83. See also Parker, *The Kingdom of Character*; Morgan, *Student Religion during Fifty Years*, 149–50; Hopkins, *History of the YMCA in North America*, 635–36, 642–45. On the YWCA, see Nancy Marie Robertson, *Christian Sisterhood, Race Relations, and the YWCA, 1906–46* (Champaign: University of Illinois Press, 2007).

31 Dorothy Bass discusses the role of the YMCA/YWCA as a precursor to 1960s student radicalism in "Revolutions, Quiet and Otherwise: Protestants and Higher Education in the 1960s," in *Caring for the Commonweal: Education for Religious and Public Life*, ed. Parker J. Palmer, Barbara G. Wheeler, and James W. Fowler (Macon, GA: Mercer University Press, 1990), 207–26.

32 Such institutional mimicry is discussed in Paul DiMaggio and Walter Powell, "The Iron Cage Revisited: Institutional Isomorphism and Collective Rationality," in *The New Institutionalism in Organizational Analysis*, ed. Walter Powell and Paul DiMaggio (Chicago: University of Chicago Press, 1991), 63–82. Nancy Ammerman discusses institutional isomorphism in the field of American congregations. See her *Pillars of Faith: American Congregations and Their Partners* (Berkeley: University of California Press, 2005). For statistics on the decline of the Y in the 1920s, see Morgan, *Student Religion during Fifty Years*, 172–76.

33 On the rise of the university and implications for denominational colleges, see Roger L. Geiger, "The Era of Multipurpose Colleges in American Higher Education, 1850–1890," in *The American College in the Nineteenth Century*, ed. Roger L. Geiger (Nashville, TN: Vanderbilt University Press, 2000); and Kathleen A. Mahoney, *Catholic Higher Education in Protestant America: The Jesuits and Harvard in the Age of the University* (Baltimore: Johns Hopkins University Press, 2003). Clarence P. Shedd discusses the worries of denominational leaders in *The Church Follows Its Students* (New Haven: CT: Yale University Press, 1938).

34 Shedd, *The Church Follows Its Students*, 11, 25, 27; Hart, *The University Gets Religion*, 76. On the Bible Chair movement, see Ronald Flowers, "The Bible Chair Movement in the Disciples of Christ Tradition: Attempts to Teach Religion in State Universities" (Ph.D. diss., University of Iowa, School of Religion, 1967).

35 Earlier figures from Shedd, *The Church Follows Its Students*, 32, 63. Figures from 1933 reported in Hart, *The University Gets Religion*, 97.

36 John Whitney Evans, *The Newman Movement: Roman Catholics in American Higher Education, 1883–1971* (Notre Dame, IN: University of Notre Dame Press, 1980), 18, 21.

37 Evans, *The Newman Movement*, 27, 31.

38 Evans, *The Newman Movement*, 55.

39 Figures from Shedd, *The Church Follows Its Students*, 61; Evans, *The Newman Movement*.

40 Discussion of Harvard anti-Semitism and 1926 *Yale Daily News* from Edward S. Shapiro, "The Friendly University: Jews in Academia since World War II," *Judaism: A Quarterly Journal of Jewish Life and Thought* 46 (3): 365–75 (1997). See also James O. Freedman, "Ghosts of the Past: Anti-Semitism at Elite Colleges," *Chronicle of Higher Education*, 1 December 2000; Dan A. Oren, *Joining the Club: A History of Jews and Yale* (New Haven, CT: Yale University Press, 2001); Harold S. Wechsler, *The Qualified Student: A History of Selective College Admission in America* (New York: Wiley, 1977).

41 Alfred Jospe, "The Jew on the College Campus," *Judaism* 25 (3): 275 (1976).

42 Marianne R. Sanua, "Jewish College Fraternities in the United States, 1895–1968: An Overview," *Journal of American Ethnic History* 19 (2): 3–41 (2000).

43 Jospe, "The Jew on the College Campus," 275–76. Quotation and statistics on 1938 Hillel from Shedd, *The Church Follows Its Students*, 107, 109, 110.

44 Shedd, *The Church Follows Its Students*, 86, 137. On the "religious depression" of the 1930s, see Robert Handy, *Christian America: Protestant Hopes and Historical Realities* (New York: Oxford University Press, 1984).

45 See A. Roy Eckardt, *The Surge of Piety in America: An Appraisal* (New York: Association Press, 1958); Putnam and Campbell, *American Grace*, 84; Shedd, *The Church Follows Its Students*, 137; Hoge, *Commitment on Campus*. Statistics on postwar campus ministry from Sam Portaro and Gary Peluso, *Inquiring and Discerning Hearts: Vocation and Ministry with Young Adults on Campus* (Atlanta: Scholars Press, 1993), 14, 13, 34, 38, 39.

46 Evans, *The Newman Movement*, 99, 131.

47 Catholic chaplain quoted in Evans, *The Newman Movement*, 100.

48 Maurice B. Pekarsky, "The Future of Hillel—From the Perspective of the Hillel Director," in *Changing Patterns of Jewish Life on the Campus*, ed. Alfred Jospe (Washington, DC: B'nai B'rith Hillel Foundation, 1961), 86.

49 Figure of seventy-seven Hillel Foundations from Alfred Jospe, *Jewish Students and Services at American Universities* (Washington, DC: B'nai B'rith Hillel Foundation, 1963), 29, http://www.hillel.org/docs/default-source/historical/1963_jewish_students.pdf?sfvrsn=0.

50 Statistics on Jewish learning from Jospe, *Jewish Students and Services*, 33–34. See also Benjamin M. Kahn, "Changing Patterns of Jewish Life on the Campus Today," in Jospe, *Changing Patterns of Jewish Life*, 16–17.

51 On the growing attention to campus religion in postwar America and the survey of college and university religious life, see Merrimon Cuninggim, *The College Seeks Religion* (New Haven, CT: Yale University Press, 1947), 301.

52 Seymour A. Smith, *The American College Chaplaincy* (New York: Association Press, 1954), 10, 21, 11.

53 Cuninggim, *The College Seeks Religion*, 1.

54 Quote from "Aspire Nobly, Adventure Daringly, Serve Humbly," KU History, University of Kansas, available on the KU History website, http://kuhistory.com/; "Graduates Remember Danforth Chapels' Origins on College Campuses," *East Valley Tribune*, 19 October 2007; Margaret M. Grubiak, "The Danforth Chapel Program on the Public American Campus," *Buildings and Landscapes* 19 (2): 77–96 (2012).

55 Sloan, *Faith and Knowledge*, 40–41; Bass, "Revolutions, Quiet and Otherwise," 210. Berger's *The Noise of Solemn Assemblies* (New York: Doubleday, 1961) and Cox's *The Secular City* (New York: Macmillan, 1965) were commissioned by the National Student Christian Federation.

56 On the "social dimensions" of faith and "structural evangelism," see Sloan, *Faith and Knowledge*, 76–77; Sara M. Evans, "Introduction," in *Journeys That Opened Up the World: Women, Student Christian Movements, and Social Justice, 1955–1975*, ed. Sara M. Evans (New Brunswick, NJ: Rutgers University Press, 2003), 5–6, 1.

57 Shedd, *A Century of Christian Student Initiative*, 46.

58 This paragraph relies heavily on Sloan, *Faith and Knowledge*, 77; Alexander Schmemann, *For the Life of the World* (New York: National Student Christian Federation, 1963).

59 Sloan, *Faith and Knowledge*, 79; Portaro and Peluso, *Inquiring and Discerning Hearts*, 59; Bass, "Revolutions, Quiet and Otherwise"; see also Robert Mills and Martha Lund Smalley, "Guide to the Archives of United Ministries in Higher Education," Yale University Library, Divinity Library Special Collections, August 2003, http://webtext.library.yale.edu/xml2html/divinity.104a.con.html. For more information, see Guide to the United Ministries in Higher Education Records, RG 104, available on the Yale University Library website, http://drs.library.yale.edu/. This paragraph relies heavily on Sloan, *Faith and Knowledge*.

60 The circulation of *motive* is from David Hollinger, *After Cloven Tongues of Fire: Protestant Liberalism in Modern American History* (Princeton, NJ: Princeton University Press, 2013), 39. See also Sloan, *Faith and Knowledge*, 83. The figure of 1,300 campus ministers comes from Phillip Hammond, *The Campus Clergyman* (New York: Basic Books, 1966), xiii, 5. The 3,000 figure comes from Kenneth Underwood, *The Church, the University, and Social Policy: The Danforth Study of Campus Ministries*, vol. 1 (Middletown, CT: Wesleyan University Press, 1969), 75. On the *motive* controversy, see David Hollinger, "After Cloven Tongues of Fire: Ecumenical Protestantism and the Modern American Encounter with Diversity," *Journal of American History* 98 (1): 21–48 (2011). The final issues of *motive* can be found on the website of the Lesbian, Gay, Bisexual, and Transgender Religious Archives Network, http://www.lgbtran.org/.

61 See Hammond, *The Campus Clergyman*, 10–11, for a discussion of the ambiguous role of the campus minister. On the upheaval of the sixties and campus ministry, see Sloan, *Faith and Knowledge*; Bass, "Revolutions, Quiet and Otherwise"; Cox, *The Secular City*; Berger, *The Noise of Solemn Assemblies*. On student Christian movement alumnae and 1970s feminism, see Evans, *Journeys That Opened Up the World*.

62 My account of the UCM's demise relies heavily on Sloan, *Faith and Knowledge*; Bass, "Revolutions, Quiet and Otherwise"; and two special issues of the *Journal of Ecumenical Studies*, 32 (3): 1995 and 32 (4): 1995.

63 Hoge, *Commitment on Campus*, 69–70; Dean Kelley, *Why Conservative Churches Are Growing* (New York: Harper and Row, 1972); Wade Clark Roof and William McKinney, *American Mainline Religion: Its Changing Shape and Future* (New Brunswick, NJ: Rutgers University Press, 1987).

64 Portaro and Peluso, *Inquiring and Discerning Hearts*, 60, 108, 110. The statistic is reported in Bass, "Revolutions, Quiet and Otherwise," 214. It comes from Daniel E. Statello and William M. Shinto, *Planning for Ministry in Higher Education* (New York: United Ministries in Higher Education, n.d. [1970s]), 25.

65 Portaro and Peluso, *Inquiring and Discerning Hearts*, 121; Kelley, *Why Conservative Churches Are Growing*; Roof and McKinney, *American Mainline Religion*. On the weakening pipelines in mainline Protestantism, see Robert Wood Lynn, "'The Survival of Recognizably Protestant Colleges': Reflections on Old-Line Protestantism, 1950–1990," in Marsden and Longfield, *The Secularization of the Academy*, 170–94.

66 F. Thomas Trotter, "Campus Ministry in the Last Decade of the Century," paper delivered at national meeting of United Methodist chaplains and campus ministers, Fairbanks, AK, 1993, available on the Religion Online website, http://www.religion-online.org/.

67 On the temporary increase in funding, see Portaro and Peluso, *Inquiring and Discerning Hearts*, 142–44. On the renewed cuts, see "Campus Ministries Face Tough Financial Times," *Christian Century*, 1 November 1995.

68 Timothy J. Hallett, "Eating the Seed Corn: The Abandonment of Campus Ministry," in *Disorganized Religion: The Evangelization of Youth and Young Adults*, ed. Sheryl Kujawa (Cambridge, MA: Cowley Publications, 1998), 167.

69 Harold V. Hartley III, "Commentary: Will the UM Church Abandon Its Students?" *United Methodist Reporter*, 19 November 2002, http://web.archive.org/web/20030202051233fw_/http://www.reporterinteractive.org/archives.htm. For a discussion of more recent budget cuts, see Kelsey Rice Bogdan, *A Time to Build: Opportunities and Challenges for New England Presbyterian Campus Ministry*, Report of the New England Presbyterian Campus Initiative, 25 April 2009, available at http://fpcnh.org/MC/NEPCIreport.pdf. See also Steven J. Rye, "Budget Cuts Really Do Hurt,"*Lutheran*, November 2006; Creighton Alexander, "An Interview with Luther Felder," College Union, 1 February 2007, http://collegeunion.org/.

70 Finke and Stark, *The Churching of America*.

71 Figures for evangelical groups from the website of Cru's publicist, https://web.archive.org/web/20160401173916/http://demoss.com/newsrooms/cru/background/cru-overview; InterVarsity Christian Fellowship's website, https://intervarsity.org/about-us/ministry-impact?action, the Fellowship of Christian Athletes 2013 ministry report, http://2013.fca.org/; Young Life's website, https://www.younglife.org/ResourceLibrary/Documents/Facts-at-Your-Fingertips-2017.pdf; and the 2001 Ivy Jungle report on *The State of College and University Ministry*, https://web.archive.org/web/20020611062458/http://www.ivyjungle.org/HTML/survey/index.html. According to Ivy Jungle's 2001 report, there were 3,232 students involved in Great Commission Ministries (1998 data), 5,000 students in the Navigators (2001 data), 2,280 in Victory Campus Ministry (1997 data), and 10,000 in Reformed University Fellowship. In 2011 CCO (formerly the Coalition for Christian Outreach) employed 224 staff on ninety campuses in 2011. See http://ccojubilee.org/am-site/media/cco-history.pdf. In 2014, Reformed University Fellowship employed 140 campus ministers, up from 50 in 1999 (no information is available on the number of student participants in 2014). For more information, see http://www.ruf.org/about/front. Figures on conservative Protestant denominational ministries from Southern Baptist, Assemblies of God, Missouri Synod Lutheran, and Ivy Jungle statistics (Reformed University Fellowship is the official campus ministry of the Presbyterian Church in America). On Baptist college groups, see John Hall, "Student Ministries Survive by Coping with Cultural, Denominational Changes," *Associated Baptist Press News*, 9 October 2003. On Assemblies of God campus ministries, see https://chialpha.com/about/our-story/#why-we-exist. Data on Missouri Synod Lutherans can be found at https://in.lcms.org/other-campus-ministries/.

72 Hageman, "Reflections on the Student Christian Movement," 379.

73 Hunt and Hunt, *For Christ and the University*, 397; Richard Quebedeaux, *I Found It! The Story of Bill Bright and Campus Crusade* (New York: Harper and Row, 1979), 21. Figure of 1,300 campus ministers from Hammond, *The Campus Clergyman*, xiii, 5; Cox, *The Secular City*, 224, 223.

74 Hunt and Hunt, *For Christ and the University*, 66, 87; David Goodhew, "The Rise of the Cambridge Inter-Collegiate Union, 1910–1971," *Journal of Ecclesiastical History* 54 (1): 62–89 (2003); Steve Bruce, *Firm in the Faith* (Brookfield, VT: Gower, 1984).

75 Hunt and Hunt, *For Christ and the University*, 84, 78, 89.

76 Figures from Hunt and Hunt, *For Christ and the University*, 385–412. For number of students and faculty, see https://intervarsity.org/about-us/ministry-impact?action. For figures on chapters, see https://web.archive.org/web/20170317081834/http://intervarsity.org/about/our/vital-statistics.

77 Hunt and Hunt, *For Christ and the University*, 127, 414. The comparison to the SVM is from Parker, *Kingdom of Character*, 190. Figures on the 1976 meeting from David Howard, *Student Power in World Missions* (Downers Grove, IL: InterVarsity Press, 1979), 122. See also Richard Pierard, "*Pax Americana* and the Evangelical Missionary Advance," in *Earthen Vessels: American Evangelicals and Foreign Missions, 1880–1980*, ed. Joel A. Carpenter and Wilbert Shenk (Grand Rapids, MI: Eerdmans, 1990), 155–79. Attendance figures for Urbana 2006 can be found at https://web.archive.org/web/20081012060217/http://www.intervarsity.org/gfm/news/open-for-business-report. The 300,000 figure is from https://urbana.org/about-urbana.

78 Charles Troutman quoted in Hunt and Hunt, *For Christ and the University*, 79–80. On the lineage of InterVarsity, see Parker, *Kingdom of Character*; Goodhew, "The Rise of the Cambridge Inter-Collegiate Union."

79 Hunt and Hunt, *For Christ and the University*; Bruce, *Firm in the Faith*. See also Goodhew, "The Rise of the Cambridge Inter-Collegiate Union."

80 Hunt and Hunt, *For Christ and the University*; Goodhew, "The Rise of the Cambridge Inter-Collegiate Union"; Bruce, *Firm in the Faith*. In David Howard's *Student Power in World Evangelism* (Downers Grove, IL: InterVarsity Press, 1970), InterVarsity is described as the organizational successor to the YMCA and the SVM.

81 Hunt and Hunt, *For Christ and the University*, 81.

82 The "liberal morass" quote is from A. Donald MacLeod, *C. Stacey Woods and the Evangelical Rediscovery of the University* (Downers Grove, IL: InterVarsity Press, 2007), 19. The comparison of IVCF to the ecumenical movement is from sociologist Steve Bruce in *Firm in the Faith*, 81, 91. Roger Finke argues that a return to core teachings leads to vitality in Finke, "Innovative Returns to Tradition."

83 Figures from the 2001 Ivy Jungle report on *The State of College and University Ministry*. According to Ivy Jungle, there were 6,900 students involved in Great Commission Ministries (2001 data), 5,000 students in the Navigators (2001 data), and 2,280 in Every Nation Campus Ministry (2001 data). In addition, the group Campus Ambassadors has 48 campus groups (2001 data). Although the Fellowship of Christian Athletes does not release data on the number of college students involved in its ministries, 450,000 high school and college students took part in FCA in 2013. Data from 2013 on FCA can be found at http://2013.fca.org/. Figures on Navigators' campus presence from https://www.navigators.org/ministry/college/. Information on CCO is available at http://ccojubilee.org/am-site/media/cco-history.pdf. Figures on Young Life from https://www.younglife.org/ResourceLibrary/Documents/Facts-at-Your-Fingertips-2017.pdf.

84 Ivy Jungle reported that between 10,000 and 12,000 students participating in Reformed University Fellowship (2001 data). According to the 2017 RUF website, the group is active on over 140 campuses, up from 65 in 2001. That information is available at http://www.ruf.org/about/front. Chi Alpha data can be found at https://chialpha.com/about/our-story/. The 2003 Chi Alpha figure is from the 2003–2004 Chi Alpha Census Summary,

Assemblies of God. Data on student participation in Missouri Synod campus centers can be found at http://in.lcms.org/other-campus-ministries/. Southern Baptist Convention data and quotation from official can be found in John Hall, "Student Ministries Survive by Coping with Cultural, Denominational Changes," *Christian Post*, 10 October 2003. The national Baptist Collegiate Ministries database is available at http://bcmlife.net/ministry-directory/.

85 Bill Bright quotation from John G. Turner, *Bill Bright and Campus Crusade for Christ: The Renewal of Evangelicalism in Postwar America* (Chapel Hill: University of North Carolina Press, 2008), 43. The statistics from 1960 are reported in Quebedeaux, *I Found It!*, 21.

86 On Bright's pietism and pragmatism, see Quebedeaux, *I Found It!*, 79–108. For a discussion of pragmatism among evangelicals, see Grant Wacker, *Heaven Below: Early Pentecostals and American Culture* (Cambridge, MA: Harvard University Press, 2001). On business and marketing, see Wendy Zoba, "Bill Bright's Wonderful Plan for the World," *Christianity Today*, 14 July 1997. J. I. Packer compares Bright to Ford in the same piece. See also Beth McMurtrie, "Crusading for Christ, amid Keg Parties and Secularism," *Chronicle of Higher Education*, 18 May 2001, A42.

87 On nineteenth- and early twentieth-century ministry statistics, see Morgan, *Student Religion during Fifty Years*, and Parker, *Kingdom of Character*. On Campus Crusade's ministry statistics, see https://web.archive.org/web/20120722104447/http://campuscrusadeforchrist.com/about-us/facts-and-statistics.

88 This paragraph draws on Quebedeaux, *I Found It!* For Bright's restatement of the Student Volunteer Movement watchword, see 168 and 170. On Bright's use of the language of "penetration" and "saturation," see 126–27. For a contemporary example of this language, see Jim Sylvester, *Building Movements on a Staffed Campus* (Orlando, FL: CruPress, 2010). On the use of the revised SVM motto, see Rick James, *The Role of Revivals in the Great Commission* (Orlando, FL: CruPress, 2010).

89 Statistics from 1995–1996 and 2015–2016 available at https://web.archive.org/web/19990203144419/http://www.uscm.org/aboutus/stats.html and https://web.archive.org/web/20160401173916/http://demoss.com/newsrooms/cru/background/cru-overview. The 1990 statistic is from McMurtrie, "Crusading for Christ," A42.

90 On Campus Crusade's slump and revival, see Turner, *Bill Bright and Campus Crusade for Christ*, 218.

91 Statistics on the growth of Asian IVCF from Rebecca Y. Kim, "Second-Generation Korean American Evangelicals: Ethnic, Multiethnic, or White Campus Ministries," *Sociology of Religion* 65 (1): 21 (2004). The 80 percent figure is cited in Kim. It is originally from C. Chang, "Amen. Pass the Kimchee: Why Are Asian-Americans in College Converting to Christianity in Droves?" *Monolid: An Asian American Magazine for Those Who Aren't Blinking* 1: 1–9 (2000). For more on Korea Campus Crusade for Christ in the United States, see https://www.gcx.org/kcccusa/. The discussion of kimchi and prayer draws on Rebecca Y. Kim, *God's New Whiz Kids? Korean American Evangelicals on Campus* (New York: New York University Press, 2006).

92 On Campus Crusade's ImpactMovement, see http://www.impactmovement.com/articles_view.asp?articleid=9095&columnid=1445. The figure of 15,000 attendees comes from "Making an Impact!" *Gospel Today*, 27 March 2011. On InterVarsity's Black Campus Ministries, see http://bcm.intervarsity.org/campus. The 41 percent figure comes from the IVCF Ministry Overview at https://intervarsity.org/about-us/ministry-impact?action. On the increase of minority staff at InterVarsity, see "One Lord, One Faith, Many Ethnicities: How to Become a Diverse Organization and Keep Your Sanity," *Christianity*

Today, January 2004, 52. Figures on 2015–2016 staff from https://web.archive.org/web/20170317081834/http://intervarsity.org/about/our/vital-statistics.

93 See John Schmalzbauer, "Whose Social Justice? Which Evangelicalism? Social Engagement in a Campus Ministry," in *The New Evangelical Social Engagement*, ed. Brian Steensland and Philip Goff (New York: Oxford University Press, 2014), 50–72. Quebedeaux, *I Found It!* 31–35. This paragraph is indebted to Richard Quebedeaux, *The Young Evangelicals* (New York: Harper and Row, 90–98). The material about InterVarsity appears on page 93.

94 On InterVarsity's programs in this area, see www.intervarsity.org. On the YMCA and "social evangelism," see Morgan, *Student Religion during Fifty Years*. The Cru Inner City website can be found at http://www.hlic.org/pages/page.asp?page_id=203055. The quotation is from the organization's old website, https://web.archive.org/web/20090419131833/http://www.hlic.org/aboutvalues.htm.

95 For more on the AME group at Virginia Tech, see https://web.archive.org/web/20130313193351/http://gobblerconnect.vt.edu/organization/stpaulamebburg/about. A description of the Hallelujah Church at Princeton can be found at http://religiouslife.princeton.edu/programs-events/interfaith/hallelujah. See also Frederick Houk Borsch, *Keeping Faith at Princeton: A Brief History of Religious Pluralism at Princeton and Other Universities* (Princeton, NJ: Princeton University Press, 2012), 206. Figure on choirs from Terrell L. Strayhorn, "Singing in a Foreign Land: An Exploratory Study of Gospel Choir Participation among African American Undergraduates at a Predominantly White Institution," *Journal of College Student Development* 52 (2): 137–53 (2011). Strayhorn discusses the role of choirs in building ethnic community. Survey data from Smith, *Souls in Transition*, 131.

96 Data on InterVarsity's Greek ministry from https://intervarsity.org/about-us/ministry-impact?action. See Cru's Greek website, http://greekmovement.com/. Data from 2013 on FCA available at http://2013.fca.org/. Information on Athletes in Action available at https://goaia.org/. On evangelicalism and athletics, see Betty DeBerg, "Athletes and Religion on Campus," *PeerReview*, Summer 2002, 10–12.

97 The phrase "influence the influencers" comes from a profile of Christian Union by G. Jeffrey MacDonald, *Layman*, 8 July 2009. The Princeton statistic is from Michael Lindsay, *Faith in the Halls of Power: How Evangelicals Joined the American Elite* (New York: Oxford University Press, 2007), 91. On Harvard's Campus Crusade chapter, see Stephanie Garlow, "Harvard Christians on the Rise," *Harvard Crimson*, 2 May 2006. For information on Brown and Yale, see Audrey Barrick, "Ivy League Schools See Rise in Evangelical Students," *Christian Post*, 27 December 2005, http://www.christianpost.com/news/ivy-league-schools-see-rise-in-evangelical-students-7809/. For more information on Christian Union, see http://www.christianunion.org/. The quotation on Ivy League schools is from Christian Union's sponsorship brochure, available on the Christian Union website, http://involve.christian-union.org/site/DocServer/CU_Sponsorship_Brochure_sml.pdf?docID=2901.

98 The quotation is from Youth Transition Network's college brochure, originally retrieved from the Network's website, http://www.youthtransitionnetwork.org/. Statistic of 70 percent from https://web.archive.org/web/20160313041345/http://ytn.org/. It is based on a LifeWay Christian Ministries study reported in Cathy Lynn Grossman, "Young Adults Aren't Sticking with Church," *USA Today*, 6 August 2007. For more on the LifeWay study, see Thom S. Rainer and Sam S. Rainer III, *Essential Church? Reclaiming a Generation of Dropouts* (Nashville, TN: B&H, 2008), 88.

99 Rainer and Rainer, *Essential Church?* 88, 89. See Jeremy E. Uecker, Mark D. Regnerus, and Margaret L. Vaaler, "Losing My Religion: The Social Sources of Religious Decline in Early Adulthood," *Social Forces* 85 (4): 1667–92 (2007). The authors find that college makes it less likely for respondents to lose their religion. The statistic on conservative Protestant campus ministry participation can be found in Christian Smith with Patricia Snell, *Souls in Transition: The Religious and Spiritual Lives of Emerging Adults* (New York: Oxford University Press, 2009), 131. Information on the 2011 study can be found in David Briggs, "Religion and Higher Education: The Effect on Faith of Being Smarter than a Fifth Grader," ARDA Working Paper Series, 12 August 2011, available on the ARDA website, http://blogs.thearda.com/.

100 Christian Smith, "Evangelicals Behaving Badly with Statistics," *Books and Culture*, January/February 2007.

101 The figure of 2,200 Catholic campus ministers and the number of collegiate Catholics from the website of the Catholic Campus Ministry Association. About one-third belong to the CCMA. See http://www.ccmanetwork.org/history/. The survey was conducted by UCLA's Higher Education Research Institute as part of the College Student Survey. It was reported in Patrick J. Reilly, "Are Catholic Colleges Leading Students Astray?" *Catholic World Report*, March 2003, 42. The National Study of Youth and Religion asked eighteen- to twenty-four-year-olds about participation in campus-based religious groups. See Smith, *Souls in Transition*, 131.

102 Evans, *The Newman Movement*, 167, xiii.

103 United States Conference of Catholic Bishops, *Empowered by the Spirit: Campus Ministry Faces the Future*, 15 November 1985, available on the Conference website, http://www.usccb.org/.

104 Father Edward Beutner quoted in Bill Kurtz, "Campus Newman Centers Minister to Students," *Catholic Herald*, 18 April 2002.

105 Patricia Rice, "University's Catholic Center Is Flourishing; Popularity Here Reflects Growing Interest in Religion among Students Nationwide," *St. Louis Post-Dispatch*, 9 October 1994, 1D.

106 Arthur Jones, "Campus Ministry Fills Need as Funds Shrink," *National Catholic Reporter*, 15 March 1996, 10.

107 Data on ordinations from Peter Steinfels, *A People Adrift: The Crisis of the Roman Catholic Church in America* (New York: Simon and Schuster, 2003), 316. Data from Catholic Campus Ministry Association, reported in Susan Hogan-Albach, "Campus Ministry Crunch," *Minneapolis Star Tribune*, 1 August 1998, 5B. The 1970s figure is from Evans, *The Newman Movement*, 167.

108 Jones, "Campus Ministry Fills Need as Funds Shrink," 10. The 15 percent figure comes from Gill Donovan, "Catholic Campus Ministers Urged to Step Up Staffing," *National Catholic Reporter*, 2 May 2003. The $75 million figure comes from "New Center for Catholics Opens," *Yale Daily News*, 4 December 2006. For more on the St. Thomas More Catholic Chapel and Center at Yale, see http://www.yale.edu/stm/development/. See the Petrus website, http://www.petrusdevelopment.com/. For information on CCMA development training, see http://www.ccmanet.org/ccma.nsf/resources-fundraising?OpenPage.

109 Information on the St. Thomas More Catholic Campus Center and Yale's Catholic student population comes from http://stm.yale.edu/stm-history. Easha Anand, "Church to Expand with New Center," *Yale Daily News*, 11 October 2004; Lawrence Gipson, "A 'Golden' Age for Catholic Center," *Yale Daily News*, 25 February 2009.

110 For more on the St. Lawrence Catholic Campus Center at the University of Kansas, see https://www.kucatholic.org/. Information on Ohio State and Duke available at https://web.archive.org/web/20110516212759/http://www.petrusdevelopment.com/clients.

111 Mark M. Gray and Mary Bendyna, *Catholic Campus Ministry: A Report of Findings from CARA's Catholic Campus Ministry Inventory* (Washington, DC: Center for Applied Research in the Apostolate, September 2003), 30, 25.

112 Betty DeBerg with John Schmalzbauer and Sarah Ehlinger, *National Study of Campus Ministries: A Report to Lilly Endowment, Inc.* (Cedar Falls, IA: National Study of Campus Ministries, 2008), 119.

113 Dean R. Hoge, William D. Dinges, Mary Johnson, and Juan L. Gonzalez, *Young Adult Catholics: Religion in the Culture of Choice* (Notre Dame, IN: University of Notre Dame Press, 2001); Smith, *Souls in Transition*. On the impact of college education on religiosity, see Uecker, Regnerus, and Vaaler, "Losing My Religion"; Michael J. McFarland, Bradley R. E. Wright, and David L. Weakliem, "Educational Attainment and Religiosity: Exploring Variations by Religious Tradition," *Sociology of Religion* 72 (2): 166–88 (2010). McFarland, Wright, and Weakliem found that more education actually led to greater religiosity among Roman Catholics.

114 Paul Perl and Bryan Froehle, *Exploring the Impact of Campus Ministry on Catholics in the United States* (Washington, DC: Center for Applied Research in the Apostolate, 2002), 1, 14, 18.

115 Kris Berggren, "Minnesota Newman Center Shut Down," *National Catholic Reporter*, 3 July 1998; Teresa Malcolm, "Protesters Attack Newman Center," *National Catholic Reporter*, 14 June 1996.

116 FOCUS refers to Pope John Paul II and the "new evangelization" on its website. The figure of twenty-four students is from Kimberly Jansen, "Catholic College Students 'Focus' on the Faith," *National Catholic Register*, 3 February 2002. The 2016 statistics are from FOCUS, *On One Foundation: Fiscal Year 2016 Annual Report*, https://www.focus.org/about/annual-reports. The SEEK2017 statistics are from FOCUS, *Fiscal Year 2017 Annual Report*. On eucharistic adoration, see Anthony Flott, "Sharp Focus: University Catholic Outreach Marks 10 Years," *National Catholic Register*, 23 December 2007–5 January 2005, http://www.ncregister.com/site/print_article/7606/. The personal relationship quotation is from Amy Smith, "Back to School: The Fellowship of Catholic University Students," *St. Anthony Messenger*, September 2008, 37. Information on the FOCUS board can be found at http://www.focus.org/about/annual-reports.html. See also Teresa Hartnett, "Campus Crusade for Catholicism," *Crisis*, September 2001; Patricia Lefevere, "Evangelizers Aim to Build Students' Faith," *National Catholic Reporter*, 29 October 2004.

117 On the Opus Dei presence in the Ivy League, see James Martin, "Opus Dei in the United States," *America*, 25 February 1995; Neir Eshel, "Spotted History Aside, Opus Dei Forges Close Links to Princeton," *Daily Princetonian*, 22 March 2005; Maurice Timothy Reidy, "Catholicism on Campus: How Faith Is Presented at Secular Universities," *Commonweal*, 5 April 2006; George Weigel, "A Catholic Renaissance at Princeton," *Catholic Difference*, 9 November 2005.

118 In *The New Faithful: Why Young Adults are Embracing Christian Orthodoxy* (Chicago: Loyola Press, 2002), the journalist Colleen Carroll notes that Catholic ministries "are realizing that in order to attract—and keep—young Catholics in the church, they must imitate the boldness of evangelical fellowships while emphasizing what makes Catholicism distinctive."

119 Figure of 77 Hillel Foundations from Jospe, *Jewish Students and Services*, 29. Figure of 110 Hillel Foundations from Jennifer Jacobson, "The New Hillel: It's Not Just about Praying Anymore," *Chronicle of Higher Education*, 27 April 2001, A49. Figure of 550 campuses from http://hillel.org/about/hillels-around-the-world.

120 Chabad Houses statistic from http://www.chabad.edu/templates/articlecco_cdo/aid/387553/jewish/About.htm. See also Josh Nathan-Kazis, "Chabad Houses Proliferating on Campus," *Forward*, 9 April 2010. Dinner statistic from Chabad's 2011 annual report, http://chabad.edu/media/pdf/618/WYkc6185728.pdf.

121 On Hillel's struggles in the 1960s, see Mark I. Rosen, "The Remaking of Hillel: A Case Study on Leadership and Organizational Transformation," January 2006, http://bir.brandeis.edu/handle/10192/22948?show=full. On the marginalization of Hillel, see Jay L. Rubin, "Re-engineering the Jewish Organization," https://web.archive.org/web/20110101135151/http://www.hillel.org/NR/rdonlyres/2D8B7513-18F6-45FF-8CB0-8B3DC53B4CF0/0/HillelReengineering.pdf. It originally appeared in the Summer 2000 issue of the *Journal of Jewish Communal Service*. On funding cuts, see Jack Wertheimer, "Jewish Education in the United States: Recent Trends and Issues," *American Jewish Year Book*, ed. David Singer (New York: American Jewish Committee, 1999).

122 This paragraph draws heavily on Rosen, "The Remaking of Hillel"; Rubin, "Re-engineering the Jewish Organization"; and Wertheimer, "Jewish Education in the United States." The $37 million figure comes from Wertheimer.

123 This motto can be found in "Hillel's New Strategy: Open Doors to Non-Jews, Focus on Wider Campus," *JTA*, 1 April 2008. For more on Hillel's approach during this period, see Rubin, "Re-engineering the Jewish Organization."

124 Statistics on Hillel's Campus Entrepreneurs Initiative and Peer Network Engagement Internship can be found in the organization's 2010 annual report, available on the Hillel website, http://www.hillel.org/.

125 Jacobson, "The New Hillel," A49. The figure of thirty-seven new buildings is from "Hillel Building Boom Enhances Jewish Life on College Campuses," *Hillel News and Views*, 3 October 2005; "Hillel Buildings Sprout All Over," *Hillel News and Views*, 7 April 2011; Bruce Fellman, "A Home of One's Own," *Yale Alumni Magazine*, November 1995. For information on the Princeton University Center for Jewish Life, see http://hillel.princeton.edu/.

126 See Gabrielle Birkner, "Trends 101: The New Jewish Life on Campus," *Reform Judaism*, Fall 2006. Figures from Alpha Epsilon Phi are available on the sorority's website at http://www.aephi.org/aephi_story/aephi_today/. Information from Alpha Epsilon Pi can be found at https://www.aepi.org/about/. On the revitalization of AEP, as well as its emphasis on Jewish identity, see http://www.weareaepi.org/smu/History.

127 Jewish leader quoted in Rachel Pomerance, "Chabad Expands on Campus," *Jewish Telegraphic Agency*, 3 January 2003.

128 See Maya Balakirsky Katz, *The Visual Culture of Chabad* (New York: Cambridge University Press, 2010).

129 Quotation and the early history of Chabad's campus outreach are from Sue Fishkoff, *The Rebbe's Army: Inside the World of Chabad-Lubavitch* (New York: Random House, 2009), 95, 96. Information on Chabad in the 1980s from the timeline in Chabad's 2010 annual report, http://chabad.edu/media/pdf/492/SBVf4921608.pdf.

130 Figures on Chabad houses from Nathan-Kazis, "Chabad Houses Proliferating on Campus."

131 Columnist David Brooks discusses Chabad in "The Haimish Line," *New York Times*, 29 August 2011. On Chabad's "home-like atmosphere," see Everett Rosenfeld, "Table

Tent Talmud," *Yale Daily News*, 15 October 2010. The gefilte fish statistic was reported in Chabad's 2008 annual report, http://chabad.edu/media/pdf/245/swbo2459780.pdf. On the home-like atmosphere, see Barry Chazan and David Bryfman, "Home away from Home: A Research Study of the Shabbos Experience on Five University Campuses," August 2006, 4, http://www.chabad.edu/media/pdf/125/bByP1251438.pdf.

132 Wertheimer, "Jewish Education in the United States."

133 On Chabad's access to two-thirds of Jewish college students, see the organization's 2008 annual report, http://www.chabad.edu/media/pdf/245/swbo2459780.pdf. On Hillel's being accessible to 400,000 Jewish students, see Jerry Silverman, "Keeping a Jewish Flame Alive on Campus," 20 January 2017, https://jewishfederations.org/from-our-ceo/keeping-a-jewish-flame-alive-on-campus-219835. Silverman is president and CEO of the Jewish Federations of North America.

134 On participation in Hillel and Chabad, see Amy L. Sales and Leonard Saxe, "Particularism in the University: Realities and Opportunities for Jewish Life on Campus," Maurice and Marilyn Cohen Center for Modern Jewish Studies, Brandeis University, January 2006, available on the Brandeis Institutional Repository website, http://bir.brandeis.edu/. See also Ariela Keysar and Barry A. Kosmin, *"Eight Up": The College Years; The Jewish Engagement of Young Adults Raised in Conservative Synagogues, 1995–2003* (New York: Jewish Theological Seminary, 2004).

135 Data on the nonobservant tendencies of Jewish emerging adults can be found in Smith, *Souls in Transition*. On the growth of secular Jews, see Lynn Davidman, "The New Voluntarism and the Case of Unsynagogued Jews," in *Everyday Religion: Observing Modern Religious Lives* (New York: Oxford University Press, 2007), 51–67.

136 The 75,000 statistic was reported in Holly Lebowitz Rossi, "Filling a Hole in Campus Communities: Program Aims to Train Muslim Chaplains to Help University Students," *Washington Post*, 25 May 2002, B9.

137 Diana Eck, *A New Religious America: How a "Christian" Country Has Become the World's Most Religiously Diverse Nation* (San Francisco: HarperSanFrancisco, 2001). The Eck quote is from the September–October 1996 issue of *Harvard Magazine*. The article is quoted at http://www.wellesley.edu/religiouslife/resources/east/consultation/concept.

138 Quote and information on the Education as Transformation Project can be found at https://web.archive.org/web/20081013150918/http://www.wellesley.edu/RelLife/transformation/edu-ngoverview.html.

139 Beth McMurtrie, "Pluralism and Prayer under One Roof," *Chronicle of Higher Education*, 3 December 1999, A48. The Education as Transformation project handbook, *Beyond Tolerance: A Campus Religious Diversity Kit*, was published by NASPA. Its contents are now available online at http://www.wellesley.edu/religiouslife/resources/east/publication/diversitykit. On the chapel renovation, see http://www.wellesley.edu/religiouslife/houghton#pOlAG2kIKU3xIUG5.97.

140 McMurtrie, "Pluralism and Prayer under One Roof"; Dan Adler, "Multifaith Retreat Explores Different Visions of Change," *Yale Daily News*, 10 November 2003.

141 The university alumni magazine used the phrase "religious laboratory" in Diane Krieger, "Leap of Faiths," *Trojan Family Magazine*, Summer 2004; Krieger, "The Un-Chaplain," *USC Trojan Family*, Summer 2011. Figures on the number of student religious groups at USC in 2017 from http://orl.usc.edu/organizations/.

142 According to National Public Radio, chaplains are becoming "more like interfaith cruise directors than traditional pastors." See Monique Parsons, "Interfaith Chaplains Revitalize an Old Role on College Campuses," National Public Radio, 16 October 2014, http://www

.npr.org/. ACURA's "Principles of Religious Life" are available at http://acura-online.org/principles/. A list of institutions served by NACUC members can be found at http://www.nacuc.net/institutions. The NACUC quotation is from http://www.nacuc.net/. The survey data are reported in Peter Laurence, "Can Religion and Spirituality Find a Place in Higher Education?" *About Campus*, November–December 1999.

143 For more information on the Princeton gathering, see Belda Chan, "'Coming Together' Sparks Interfaith Dialogue on Campus," *Daily Princetonian*, 18 February 2005. The attendance figures are from *Coming Together: College Multi-Faith Councils (2005)*, research report by the Pluralism Project at Harvard University, http://pluralism.org/reports/view/85. See also Ellen Shakespear, "Princeton University Hosts 'Coming Together' Interfaith Conference for Students from 30 Colleges," *Times of Trenton*, 22 February 2011.

144 For more information on Interfaith Youth Core, see http://www.ifyc.org. See also "Interfaith Cooperation and American Higher Education: Recommendations, Best Practices, and Case Studies," Interfaith Youth Core, 2010; Eboo Patel and Cassie Meyer, "The Civic Relevance of Interfaith Cooperation for Colleges and Universities," *Journal of College and Character* 12 (1) (2011); Eboo Patel and Cassie Meyer, "Introduction to 'Interfaith Cooperation on Campus': Interfaith Cooperation as an Institution-Wide Priority," *Journal of College and Character* 12 (2) (2011). President Obama is quoted in Adelle Banks, "Obama Taps Campuses for Interfaith Service Projects," Religion News Service, 18 March 2011. For information on the number of campuses participating, see Mara Vanderslice, "White House, Department of Education, Corporation for National and Community Service Continue the President's Interfaith and Community Service Campus Challenge," White House Office of Faith-Based and Neighborhood Parternships, 26 June 2012, available on the Obama White House Archives website, https://obamawhitehouse.archives.gov/. Data on student, faculty, staff, and community member participation from *The President's Interfaith and Community Service Campus Challenge Inaugural Report* (Washington, DC: Department of Education, September 2013), x. For information on participation in the Spiritual Climate Survey, see http://www.ifyc.org/content/campus-religious-and-spiritual-climate-survey. This survey was developed by Alyssa Rockenbach and Matthew Mayhew.

145 The 1974 statistic is from Jodi Wilgoren, "Muslims Make Gains at U.S. Universities," *New York Times*, 13 February 2001. Current data on Muslim students from Kevin Eagan, Ellen Bara Stolzenberg, Abigail K. Bates, Melissa C. Aragon, Maria Ramirez Suchard, and Cecilia Rios-Aguilar, *The American Freshman: National Norms, Fall 2016* (Los Angeles: Higher Education Research Institute, 2017), 42.

146 On the formation and current reach of the Muslim Students' Association, see Husain, "Envisioning a Continent Wide Student Organization"; Teresa Mendez, "The New Role of Muslim Chaplains," *Christian Science Monitor*, 18 January 2005.

147 Wilgoren, "Muslims Make Gains at U.S. Universities"; Kevin Eckstrom, "Colleges Adapting to Increased Muslim Student Presence," Beliefnet.com, 16 March 2000, http://www.beliefnet.com/. See website of the MSA, http://www.msanational.org/about. On Ramadan celebrations, see Shelvia Dancy, "Ramadan on College Campuses," Beliefnet.com, 21 November 2000. On management coursework for Muslim Students' Associations, see Omaira Alam, "The Evolution of COMPASS: MSA's National Training Program," *COMPASS*, March 2007, 3–4. List of topics retrieved from http://www.msanational.org/compass/files/pdf/AnnualReport2.pdf. See also Mendez, "The New Role of Muslim Chaplains."

148 "Georgetown Names a Muslim Chaplain," *Los Angeles Times*, 28 August 1999; Sarah Pease-Kerr, "U to Hire First Full-Time Hindu, Muslim Chaplains," *Daily Princetonian*, 1

April 200. For the number of prayer rooms, see Wilgoren, "Muslims Make Gains at U.S. Universities." Wilgoren's story appeared in February of 2001. It is likely that the number of prayer rooms has increased since that time.

149 Elizabeth Bell, "On the College Front; Muslim Student Organizations Say They're Misunderstood," *San Francisco Chronicle*, 30 December 2001, A6; Council on American-Islamic Relations, "Islamic Prayer Area Vandalized at AU in D.C.," press release, 13 September 2004, available on the Council on American-Islamic Relations website, http://www.cair.com/press-center/press-releases/949-islamic-prayer-area-vandalized-at-au-in-dc.html. See also "Some Students Groups under Scrutiny," Associated Press, 27 December 2001; Paul M. Barrett, "Idaho Arrest Puts Muslim Students under Scrutiny," *Wall Street Journal*, 28 May 2003; Beth McMurtrie, "For Many Muslims, College Is a Balancing Act," *Chronicle of Higher Education*, 9 November 2001, A55; Tara Bahrampour, "Hostility across U.S. Jars Muslim College Students," *Washington Post*, 27 August 2010, B1; Neil MacFarquhar, "For Muslim Students, a Debate on Inclusion," *New York Times*, 21 February 2008. The guiding principles of the MSA are available at http://msanational.org/us/who-we-are/. On the special challenges of Muslim women, see Shabana Mir, *Muslim American Women on Campus: Undergraduate Social Life and Identity* (Chapel Hill: University of North Carolina Press), 3.

150 Data on Hindu students from Eagan et al., *The American Freshman, 2016*, 42.

151 On the founding of HSC, see "Hindu Students Council Holds Its 22nd Annual Camp," *India Herald*, 13 June 2012. Statistics on HSC are from http://hindustudentscouncil.org/about-us/. Quotation and statistic on American-born Hindus from Harvard University's Pluralism Project: "Hindu Revival on Campus," Pluralism Project, http://pluralism.org/religion/hinduism/issues/campus. See also "Hindu Revival Stirs College Campuses," *Little India*, June 1994.

152 "Hindu Students Council to Host Global Dharma Conference to Commemorate 25th Anniversary," press release, Religion News Service, 7 April 2015.

153 Twain quote from the website of the North Carolina State University HSC, https://clubs.ncsu.edu/hsc/hsc/About_Us.html.

154 Pease-Kerr, "U to Hire First Full-Time Hindu, Muslim Chaplains"; Marsha A. Green, "Abdullah Antelpi, Duke's First Muslim Chaplain," *Duke Today*, 27 June 2011.

155 Figure on Sikh organizations from http://www.sikhcoalition.org/stay-informed/sikh-coalition-advisories/478. For information on "Tie a Turban Day," see "Tie a Turban Day in San Antonio, TX," *San Antonio Express-News*, 24 January 2004. See the Hofstra University Sikh Studies website, http://www.hofstra.edu/academics/colleges/hclas/rel/sikh/. See also Arthur J. Pais, "Ann Arbor Gets a Sikh Chair," Rediff on the Net, June 1999, http://www.rediff.com/news/.

156 On the nineteenth-century rediscovery of Asian religions, see Robert C. Fuller, *Spiritual, but Not Religious: Understanding Unchurched America* (New York: Oxford University Press, 2001). On post-1965 religious pluralism, see Eck, *A New Religious America*.

157 Data on Buddhist students from Eagan et al., *The American Freshman, 2016*, 42. On the interest of white students in Buddhism, see David Cho, "Finding Each Other's Religions; As Asian Students Try Christianity, White Students Meditate," *Washington Post*, 4 May 2003, A1.

158 Steven C. Rockefeller, "Meditation, Social Change, and Undergraduate Education," paper delivered at the meeting of the Working Group, Center for Contemplative Mind in Society, Pocantico, New York, September 29–October 2, 1994, http://www.contemplativemind.org/files/rockefeller.pdf.

159 On the Rockefeller family and religion, see Conrad Cherry, *Hurrying toward Zion: Universities, Divinity Schools, and American Protestantism* (Bloomington: Indiana University Press, 1995).

160 Don Oldenburg, "Beyond the Mat: Yoga Stretches Out," *Washington Post*, 29 August, 2004, A1. Survey data from Rick A. LaCaille and Nicholas J. Kuvaas, "Coping Styles and Self-Regulation Predict Complementary and Alternative Medicine and Herbal Supplement Use among College Students," *Psychology, Health, and Medicine* 16 (3): 327 (2011). See also Amy L. Versnik Nowak and Steve M. Dorman, "Social-Cognitive Predictors of College Student Use of Complementary and Alternative Medicine," *American Journal of Health Education* 39 (2): 80–90 (2008); Susan K. Johnson and Anita Blanchard, "Alternative Medicine and Herbal Use among University Students," *Journal of American College Health* 55 (3): 163–68 (2006); Chwee Lye Chng, Kweethai Neill, and Peggy Fogle, "Predictors of College Students' Use of Complementary and Alternative Medicine," *American Journal of Health Education* 34 (5): 267–71 (2003); Christopher M. Adams and Ana Puig, "Incorporating Yoga into College Counseling," *Journal of Creativity in Mental Health* 3 (4): 357–72. Pew data reported in Candy Gunther Brown, "What Makes the Encinitas School Yoga Program Religious?" *Huffington Post*, 24 July 2012, http://www.huffingtonpost.com/. See also Andrea K. Jain, "The Malleability of Yoga: A Response to Christian and Hindu Opponents of the Popularization of Yoga," *Journal of Hindu-Christian Studies* 25 (4): 8 (2012).

161 Andrew Greeley, "There's a New-Time Religion on Campus," *New York Times Magazine*, 1 June 1969, retrieved from *New York Times* Historical.

162 See the Pagans on Campus site, http://www.sunspotdesigns.com/c/collpgn.html. Related websites include a site on College Pagan Groups, which lists groups on ninety-nine campuses. See http://www.angelfire.com/ia/Geoff/cgroups.html.

163 Figures on Institute of Religion participation from the Church of Jesus Christ of Latter-Day Saints, *Seminaries and Institutes of Religion Annual Report for 2013*, 3. On the Moscow, Idaho, Institute, see Leonard J. Arrington, "The Founding of the L.D.S. Institutes of Religion," *Dialogue: A Journal of Mormon Thought*, Summer 1967, 137–47. The quote appears on page 140. Figures for 1967 are found on page 137. The number of Institutes of Religion in 2007 is reported in David E. Edwards, "The Future Is Now," *New Era*, September 2007. The Institutes of Religion website reports a worldwide enrollment of 350,000 students at 2,700 locations. See https://www.lds.org/si/institute/about/faq?lang=eng.

164 Statistics, the quotation about growth, and a brief history of the OCF are available at http://www.ocf.net/about/. For more on the history of OCF, see earlier versions of the group's website, https://web.archive.org/web/20101209055750*/http://www.ocf.net/pages/about1.aspx. This paragraph draws heavily on the organization's website. Information on OCF board members can be found at http://www.ocf.net/about/board/. Former board member Mickey Hodges once worked for Campus Crusade.

165 Neil Shister, "Liberal Evangelists on Campus," *UU World*, September/October 2002.

166 Statistics from Donald Skinner, "UU Young Adult Population Grows in Number and Voice," *UU World*, June 2006. List and map from https://maps.google.com/. Information on UU campus ministry programs, as well as the campus organizers handbook, can be found on the UUA website, www.uua.org/religiouseducation/campusministry/index.shtml and http://www.uua.org/.

167 Gustav Niebuhr, "Religion Journal: Campus Skeptics Unite Against Aggressive Faith," *New York Times*, 28 September 1996, 12. A list and map of campus groups can be found

at http://www.centerforinquiry.net/oncampus/groups/. Posters are available at http://centerforinquiry.net/oncampus/posters.

168 The 1996 Campus Freethought Alliance Declaration of Necessity is available at http://www.skeptictank.org/files/newest/ft-ca.htm.

169 Steve Kolowich, "Humanist Chaplains," *Inside Higher Ed*, 12 November 2009.

170 Quote from https://secularstudents.org/sites/secularstudents.org/files/GRG.3rd.web.pdf. For more on the SSA, see Christopher Zara, "Atheism on the Rise, and It's Finally Paying Off," *International Business Times*, 1 December 2012. For a map and list of groups in the SSA, see https://www.secularstudents.org/affiliates. In July 2017, it listed 222 groups, including 23 based in high schools.

171 Smith, *Souls in Transition*, 131. Figure of 1,300 Presbyterian Church (USA) higher education ministries from the PCUSA Collegiate Ministries website, https://pma.pcusa.org/ministries/collegiate/about-pcusa-collegiateyoung-adult-ministries/. A 2006 report lists 1,152 Presbyterian campus ministries, including 738 congregation-based campus ministries, 352 campus-based collegiate ministries that report to a PCUSA body, and 62 chaplaincies at PCUSA related colleges. See *By the Numbers*, NMD Committee Report, 24 April 2006, https://web.archive.org/web/20111029094524/http://www.pachem.org. The comparison to Campus Crusade and InterVarsity is from *Renewing the Commitment: A Church-Wide Mission Strategy for Ministry in Higher Education by the Presbyterian Church (USA)*, submitted to the 213th General Assembly of the Presbyterian Church (USA) 2001, available on the PCUSA website, https://ukirk.pcusa.org/. Figure of 510 United Methodists campus ministries from http://findyourplace.herokuapp.com/#/universities. A list of Episcopal campus ministries can be found on the website of the church, http://www.episcopalchurch.org/page/campus-young-adult-ministries. Figure of 580 Evangelical Lutheran Church in America campus ministries (including 400 congregation-based campus ministries) from http://www.elca.org/en/Our-Work/Related-Ministries/Campus-Ministry. Figure of 140 Disciples of Christ campus ministries from http://disciples.org/higher-education/. A list of the 61 American Baptist Churches (USA) campus ministers can be found at https://web.archive.org/web/20150918225843/http://www.nationalministries.org/education/campus_ministers.cfm. Figure of 19 United Church of Christ campus ministries calculated from the UCC's website, http://www.ucc.org/higher-education_campus-ministry. Some of these campus ministries are at church-related colleges and universities. Others are housed in congregations or Ecumenical Campus Ministry Team sites.

172 In 2014, the Ecumenical Campus Ministry Team (ECMT) of the National Council of Churches listed 800 campus ministries affiliated with seven mainline denominations. See the ECMT website, https://web.archive.org/web/20140104041233/http://higheredmin.org/. Several other ecumenical ventures continue in higher education. Lutherans and Episcopalians maintain several jointly run campus ministries. The 2005 list of United-Methodist-Related Chaplains and Campus Ministers can be found at http://web.archive.org/web/20050825220601/http://www.gbhem.org/asp/campusMin.asp. The 2017 number is from http://findyourplace.herokuapp.com/#/universities. The first quotation is from Linda Green, "Campus Ministry Offers Church Presence at College," United Methodist News Service, 30 August 2007. The second quotation is from Roger Wharton, "Campus Ministry," a talk presented at the Silicon Valley Ministry Conference, 23 September 2000 (information updated for ECR Convention 2001), https://web.archive

.org/web/20040710232626/http://www.sjspirit.org/documents/stateofcampus.html. The third quotation is from Bogdan, "A Time to Build."

173 See Sloan, *Faith and Knowledge*, for an account of the 1969 collapse of the University Christian Movement. On the various "Celebrate" conferences, see Sarah Scherschligt and Martha Lund Smalley, "Guide to the Archives of the Ecumenical Student Christian Ministry," Yale University Library, Divinity Library Special Collections, June 2002, http://webtext.library.yale.edu/xml2html/divinity.107.con.html. For more information, see Guide to the Council for Ecumenical Student Christian Ministry Records, RG 107, available on the Yale University Library website, http://drs.library.yale.edu/. On the second "Celebrate" meeting, see Julian Shipp, "Ecumenical Student Conference Speakers Urge Spiritual Commitment, Activism," *PCUSA NEWS*, 12 January 1995. The 2,100 figure for Celebrate I comes from Portaro and Peluso, *Inquiring and Discerning Hearts*, 145. The attendance at Celebrate II was 1,800. See Julian Shipp, "Presbyterians Celebrate Christian Diversity at Student Conference," *PCUSA NEWS*, 5 May 1996. The attendance at Celebrate III was 1,300. See "Tutu Stresses Justice, Mercy, Humility in Remarks to Students," United Methodist News Service, 5 January 1999. The attendance at Celebrate IV was 1,100. This figure comes from "Students Celebrate Christian Diversity and Similarity," *Christian Post*, 15 January 2003. Celebrate V ("Celebrate at the River") drew 700 students to New Orleans. See Robyn Graves, "Young Adults Encouraged to Tell Their New Orleans Stories after Conference," *Disciples World*, 29 January 2007.

174 Philip Jenks, "Historic U.S. Student Christian Movement to Be Reborn 8–11 October at Morehouse," National Council of Churches USA, 21 July 2010, http://archive.wfn.org/2010/07/msg00197.html; Adelle M. Banks, "Students Seek to Revive Progressive Movement," Religion News Service, 25 July 2010. For more information on the Student Christian Movement–USA, see the organization's website, https://www.scm-usa.org/. The quotation can be found at https://www.scm-usa.org/affiliate. Information on SCM-USA chapters and chapter building from *World Student Christian Federation North America 2013 Annual Report*, https://wscfnadotorg.files.wordpress.com/2016/01/2013annualreportfinaldraftupdate10-6.pdf.

175 On Episcopal development efforts, see Gurdon Brewster, "Ministry on the Frontier: The Contribution of Episcopal Campus Ministry to the Present and Future Church," July 2000, http://web.archive.org/web/20030305031227/http://www.esmhe.org/ministryonthefrontier.htm. See also Leonard Freeman, "Campus Ministries Show Record of Success in Forming Leaders," *Living Church*, 10 September 2000. On current grant programs, see "Episcopal Church Grants Available for Campus Ministries," 15 February 2014, Episcopal Church, http://www.episcopalchurch.org/library/article/episcopal-church-grants-available-campus-ministries.

176 Information on University Presbyterian's campus ministry can be found in "A Model for Church-Based Campus Ministry: Real Life in Jesus Christ," University Presbyterian Church, Seattle, Washington, available on the PCUSA website, https://ukirk.pcusa.org/. For more information on the Ascent Network, see http://web.archive.org/web/20110319234455/http://www.upc.org/umin/Ascent.aspx. The figure of 700-plus Presbyterian Church (USA) congregations engaged in campus ministry comes from "By the Numbers."

177 The figure of 400 congregations comes from the Evangelical Lutheran Church in America campus ministry website, http://www.elca.org/Our-Work/Related-Ministries/Campus-Ministry.

178 "A New Theme for Dorms: God," *New York Times*, 30 July 2006; Jerry L. Van Marter, "Campus Ministry on the Rebound," *Presbyterians Today*, May 2001. See also Lizbeth Trotti, "A Spiritual Oasis at the University," *Presbyterians Today*, September 2007, 10; Tanya Schevitz, "Dorm with a Spiritual Dimension," *San Francisco Gate*, 24 August 2006. For more information on Presby Hall at the University of Illinois, see http://www.presbyhall.com/. See Kansas State's Wesley Foundation for information on its residential Christian community, http://kstatewesley.com/the-dorm/; Arian Campo-Flores, "Religious Dorms Sprout Up," *Wall Street Journal*, 3 September 2013. For more on the Newman Student Housing Fund, see http://newmanstudenthousing.com/.

179 *Renewing the Commitment*, 1.

180 Jerry L. Van Marter, "General Assembly Backgrounder: Campus Ministry," *PCUSANews*, 8 May 2001. On the elimination of the Collegiate Ministries office, see Gary Luhr, "Keeping College Students Connected," *Presbyterian Outlook*, 28 June 2009.

181 Lynn Hargrove, "GA 2010: GA Affirms the Work of PHEWA, Re-establishes Collegiate Ministries," *Presbyterian Outlook*, 10 July 2010. The 2010 Presbyterian Church (USA) General Assembly's overture on collegiate ministries is available on the PCUSA website, https://www.pcusa.org/. See also "Collegiate Ministries Task Force Named, Will Meet This Fall," Presbyterian News Service, 16 March 2011; Leslie Scanlon, "Panel Strives to Breathe New Life into Flagging Campus Ministries," *Presbyterian Outlook*, 15 November 2011. The Collegiate Ministries Task Force Report is available at https://web.archive.org/web/20150729185007/http://www.ukirk.org/files/Collegiate_Ministries_Task_Force_Report.doc. For more on UKirk, see http://www.ukirk.org/index.php/who-we-are/history/. Figures on UKirk sites and goals can be found in "UKirk Ministries Reclaiming Presbyterian Heritage of Integrating Faith and Service," *Presbyterian Outlook*, 16 June 2014.

182 See "Interview with Bishop Scott Jones," College Union, 29 November 2005, available at https://web.archive.org/web/20150908230920/http://www.collegeunion.org/. The most recent Refresh conference was held in 2014. For a discussion of the networks behind evangelical and liberal approaches to Methodist campus ministry, see Russell Richey, "'For the Good of the World,' Methodism's Ministry to the Campus," Occasional Papers, General Board of Higher Education and Ministry, April 2010, available on the UMC Higher Education and Ministry website, www.gbhem.org/.

183 The campus ministry portion of the "General Board of Higher Education and Ministry, Strategic Plan for 2009–2012" is available at https://web.archive.org/web/20130121100129/http://www.gbhem.org/site/c.lsKSL3POLvF/b.3554127/k.35FD/Strategic_Priority_3.htm. The proceedings of the 2009 conference are published in Bridgette D. Young and Henrik R. Pieterse, *The Promise of United Methodist Campus Ministry: Theological Explorations* (Nashville, TN: General Board of Higher Education and Ministry, 2010). The quotation is from Richey, "'For the Good of the World,'" 14. This paragraph draws heavily on the Richey paper.

184 Evangelical Lutheran Church in America, *A Social Statement on: Our Calling in Education*, 10 August 2007, 51, http://download.elca.org/ELCA%20Resource%20Repository/EducationSS.pdf.

185 "ELCA Council Recommends Budget Proposals through 2013," ELCA News Service, 10 April 2011, https://web.archive.org/web/20110413051712/http://www.elca.org/Who-We-Are/Our-Three-Expressions/Churchwide-Organization/Communication-Services/News/Releases.aspx?a=4739; "Lutheran Campus Ministry: Gutted Edition," Praying with Evagrius, 18 September 2011, https://web.archive.org/

web/20111228194032/http://prayingwithevagrius.wordpress.com/2011/09/18/lutheran-campus-ministry-gutted-edition/.

186 ELCA Division for Higher Education and Schools director Robert Sorensen quoted in Debra Illingworth Greene, "Changing with the Times," *Lutheran*, July 1997. The 2005 ELCA resolution creating the Vocation and Education unit is available at https://web.archive.org/web/20051110135149/http://www.elca.org/vocationeducation/resolution.html. The 2011 restructuring of the ELCA is discussed in "Redesign for 2011 Brings Staff Cuts," *Lutheran*, November 2010. On the ELCA's most recent program director for campus ministry, see "Welcome the Rev. Don Romsa as Program Director for Campus Ministry in the ELCA," 26 March 2014, https://lcmnet.wildapricot.org/.

187 Reuben, *The Making of the Modern University*, 129–30; Hopkins, *History of the YMCA in North America*; Morgan, *Student Religion during Fifty Years*; Butler, "An Overview of Religion on Campus."

188 American Council for Education, *The Student Personnel Point of View* (Washington, DC: American Council for Education, 1949), 1, as cited in Leah Temkin and Nancy J. Evans, "Religion on Campus: Suggestions for Cooperation between Student Affairs and Campus-Based Religious Organizations," *NASPA Journal* 36 (1): 61 (1998). See also David A. Hoffman, "Reflections on the 2000 ACPA Spiritual Maturation Institute," Character Clearinghouse, 11 February 2001, http://web.archive.org/web/20080530155332/http://www.collegevalues.org/Spirit.cfm?id=435&a=1.

189 See James R. Collins, James C. Hurst, and Judith K. Jacobson, "The Blind Spot Extended: Spirituality," *Journal of College Student Personnel* 28 (3): 274–76 (1987); Patrick Love and Donna Talbot, "Defining Spiritual Development: A Missing Consideration for Student Affairs," *NASPA Journal* 37 (1): 361–75 (1999).

190 George W. Jones, *The Public University and Religious Practice: An Inquiry into University Provision for Campus Religious Life* (Muncie, IN: Ball State University, 1973); Seymour A. Smith, *Religious Cooperation in State Universities: An Historical Sketch* (Ann Arbor: University of Michigan, 1957).

191 Collins, Hurst, and Jacobson, "The Blind Spot Extended," 274–76. Quotations come from pages 276 and 274.

192 John Butler, "Building New Relationships for the Future," in *Religion on Campus*, ed. John Butler (San Francisco: Jossey-Bass, 1989), 79, 80.

193 Greer and Lot, "Spirituality in the Counseling Process: An Ethical Issue," paper presented at the 1990 American College Personnel Association national conference; Alan Cureton, Larry Ebbers, and John Bole, "Spiritual Development Theory and Practice: Emerging Models and Research," paper presented at the 1991 National Association of Student Personnel Administrators conference; Emil Spees, "Have You Spoken to a Buddhist Lately?" paper presented at the 1992 American College Personnel Association national conference; David Hoffman and Karen Boyd DeNicola, "Taking Responsibility for Student Spiritual Development," paper presented at the 1993 National Association of Student Personnel Administrators conference; Char Kopchick and Lisa Kirkpatrick, "A Spiritual Awakening: Giving Students Permission to Explore Their Spiritual Wellness," paper presented at the 1994 American College Personnel Association national conference; Patrick Love and Anne Jannarone, "The Spiritual Development of Lesbian Gay Students," paper presented at the 1999 National Association of Student Personnel Administrators conference.

194 Temkin and Evans, "Religion on Campus," 61.

195 Patrick Love, "Spirituality and Student Development: Spiritual Connections," in *The Implications of Student Spirituality for Student Affairs Practice*, ed. Margaret A. Jablonski (San Francisco: Jossey-Bass, 2001), 7.

196 Hoffman, "Reflections on the 2000 ACPA Spiritual Maturation Institute." See Sharon Daloz Parks, *Big Questions, Worthy Dreams: Mentoring Young Adults in Their Search for Meaning* (San Francisco: Jossey-Bass, 1999); Sharon Daloz Parks, *Common Fire: Leading Lives of Commitment in a Complex World* (Boston: Beacon Press, 1997). For more on the NASPA event, see Gwendolyn J. Dungy, "From the Executive Director: Spirituality in Higher Education," *Forum Enewsletter*, 4 December 2003. On NASPA's Spirituality and Religion in Higher Education knowledge community, see https://www.naspa.org/constituent-groups/kcs/spirituality-and-religion-in-higher-education. For more on ACPA's Commission for Spirituality, Faith, Religion and Meaning, see http://www.acpa.nche.edu/commsfrm.

197 See the website of the Institute, http://studentvalues.fsu.edu/.

198 Alexander W. Astin, Helen S. Astin, and Jennifer A. Lindholm, *Cultivating the Spirit: How College Can Enhance Students' Inner Lives* (San Francisco: Jossey-Bass, 2011); Jennifer A. Lindholm, Melissa L. Millora, Leslie M. Schwartz, and Hanna Song Spinosa, *A Guidebook of Promising Practices: Facilitating College Students' Spiritual Development* (Los Angeles: Regents of the University of California, 2011).

199 Jon Dalton, "Supporting Students' Spiritual Growth in College: Recommendations for Student Affairs Practitioners," *Journal of College and Character* 5 (10) (2004). Others have made a similar case. In a 2000 piece, higher education specialist Carney Strange wrote that public universities should integrate spirituality into most of their student development programs. See Carney Strange, "Spirituality at State: Private Journeys and Public Visions," *Journal of College and Character* 1 (3) (2000).

200 William Campbell and Megan Lane, "Better Together: Student Interfaith Leadership and Social Change," *Journal of College and Character* 15 (3): 195–202 (2014); John A. Mueller and Shannon O'Reilly, "Faitheist: How an Atheist Found Common Ground with the Religious," *Journal of College and Character* 15 (3): 203–6 (2014); Ryan T. Cragun, Patrick Henry, and Russell Krebs, "Chapel Use on College and University Campuses," *Journal of College and Character* 15 (2): 103–18 (2014).

201 For more information on the religious groups at Penn State University's Pasquerilla Spiritual Center and the Center for Spiritual and Ethical Development, see the Penn State Student Affairs website, http://studentaffairs.psu.edu/; Lindholm et al., *A Guidebook of Promising Practices*, 70–71.

202 Patrick Love, "Differentiating Spirituality from Religion," Character Clearinghouse, 12 December 2000, http://www.collegevalues.org under "Spirituality on Campus"; Strange, "Spirituality at State."

203 The UCLA study of spirituality and higher education found that one-third of college juniors scored high on a Spiritual Quest scale. See Astin, Astin, and Lindholm, *Cultivating the Spirit*, 31. The first study is Barry A. Kosmin and Ariela Keysar, *Religious, Spiritual and Secular: The Emergence of Three Distinct Worldviews among American College Students* (Hartford, CT: Trinity College, 2013), 8. The second study is *The Spiritual Life of College Students: A National Study of College Students' Search for Meaning and Purpose* (Los Angeles: Higher Education Research Institute, UCLA, 2004), 5. On the "quest culture," see Roof, *Spiritual Marketplace*; Wade Clark Roof, *A Generation of Seekers: The Spiritual Journeys of the Baby Boom Generation* (San Francisco: HarperSanFrancisco, 1993).

204 Maricia Kennard Kiessling, "Spirituality as a Component of Holistic Student Development: Perspectives and Practices of Student Affairs Professionals," *Journal of College and Character* 11 (3) (2010); Judy L. Rogers and Patrick Love, "Graduate Student Constructions of Spirituality in Preparation Programs," *Journal of College and Character* 48 (6): 689–705 (2007).

205 The National Study of Youth and Religion data are reported in Smith, *Souls in Transition*, 131. Religious service attendance data from Ray Franke, Sylvia Ruiz, Jessica Sharkness, Linda DeAngelo, and John Pryor, *Findings from the 2009 Administration of the College Senior Survey (CSS): National Aggregates* (Los Angeles: Higher Education Research Institute, 2010), 64.

206 Figures from the 1921 YMCA/YWCA are from Marsden, *The Soul of the American University*, 343, but were originally reported in Hopkins, *History of the YMCA in North America*, 628, 645–46. According to Marsden, 90,000 out of the 600,000 college students in 1921 were enrolled in the YMCA/YWCA. There were about 300 Protestant, Catholic, and Jewish denominational organizations on campus in the 1920s. Assuming each of these attracted an average of 100 students, that would mean an additional 30,000 students involved in campus religious groups. For figures for Protestants, Catholics, and Jews, see Shedd, *The Church Follows Its Students* (New Haven: CT: Yale University Press, 1938), 63, 109; Evans, *The Newman Movement*, 55. Jospe, "The Jew on the College Campus," 275–76. Shedd states that were 128 Protestant university pastors in 1923. Evans lists 134 Newman Clubs in 1926. Jospe writes that there were 50 chapters of the Menorah Society in 1930. Shedd notes the existence of at least 8 Hillel Foundations prior to 1929. By arguing that involvement in campus religious groups has not dramatically declined, we do not mean to suggest that student religiosity has always remained the same. In *Commitment on Campus*, Dean Hoge found a decrease in student religiosity in the wake of the 1960s. In a later study, Hoge and his colleagues found that students in the 1980s were more sympathetic to traditional religion and more religiously involved. See Dean R. Hoge, Jann L. Hoge, and Janet Wittenberg, "The Return of the Fifties: Trends in College Students' Values between 1952 and 1984," *Sociological Forum* 2 (3): 500–519 (1987).

207 Uecker, Regnerus, and Vaaler, "Losing My Religion." See also Jonathan Hill, "Faith and Understanding: Specifying the Impact of Higher Education on Religious Belief," *Journal for the Scientific Study of Religion* 50 (3): 533–51 (2011).

208 Philip Schwadel, "The Effects of Education on Americans' Religious Practices, Beliefs, and Affiliations," *Review of Religious Research* 53:161–82 (2011). Study reported in Jim Kavanagh, "Study: More Educated Tend to Be More Religious, by Some Measures," *CNN Belief Blog*, 11 August 2011, religion.blogs.cnn.com/; Briggs, "Religion and Higher Education."

209 The 1971 figure is from Kevin Eagan, Ellen Bara Stolzenberg, Hilary B. Zimmerman, Melissa C. Aragon, Hannah Whang Sayson, and Cecilia Rios-Aguilar, *The American Freshman: National Norms, Fall 2014* (Los Angeles: Higher Education Research Institute, 2014), 9. The 2016 statistic is from Eagan et al., *The American Freshman, 2016*, 42.

210 Astin, Astin, and Lindholm, *Cultivating the Spirit*, 31; Jenny J. Lee, "Religion and College Attendance: Change among Students," *Review of Higher Education* 25 (4): 369–84 (2002).

211 Schwadel, "The Effects of Education," 161–82.

212 According to a 2009 UCLA survey, 78 percent of college seniors identify with a religious tradition. See Franke et al., *Findings from the 2009 Administration of the College Senior Survey*, 82. The theism and prayer statistics are from *The Spiritual Life of College Students*, 5.

213 Jospe, "The Jew on the College Campus," 276.

214 Pat McCloskey, "Campus Ministry Today: Not Your Mom and Dad's Newman Center," *St. Anthony Messenger*, March 2002.

215 Statistics on InterVarsity's graduate and faculty ministries are available at https://intervarsity.org/about-us/ministry-impact?action. Statistics from Campus Crusade's Faculty Commons can be found at http://www.cru.org/communities/ministries/faculty-and-graduates.html. The quotation is from Mark Noll, "The Evangelical Mind Today," *First Things*, October 2004, 34–39. The Veritas Forum website includes a list of the campuses where forums have been held. See http://www.veritas.org/. The statistic of 100,000 comes from Kelly Monroe, "Finding God at Harvard: Reaching the Post-Christian University," in *Telling the Truth: Evangelizing Postmoderns*, ed. D. A. Carson (Grand Rapids, MI: Zondervan, 2002), 304–5. Information on the Consortium of Christian Study Centers is available at https://studycentersonline.org/.

216 Lindholm, Millora, Schwartz, and Spinosa, *A Guidebook of Promising Practices*, 25–33.

217 Mimi Cooper, "Chabad vs. Hillel: The Friday Night Dinner Showdown," *Brandeis Hoot*, 17 November 2006; Turner, *Bill Bright and Campus Crusade for Christ*; Prema A. Kurien, "Being Young, Brown, and Hindu: The Identity Struggles of Second-Generation Indian Americans," *Journal of Contemporary Ethnography* 40 (5): 434–69 (2011).

218 Annysa Johnson, "Jewish, Muslim Students Clash at UWM," *Journal Sentinel*, 30 April 2010; Adelaide Blanchard, "Muslim Students Crash UWM's 'Israelpalooza,'" *Badger Herald*, 5 May 2010; "Jewish Student Sues UC Berkeley for Not Protecting Her," *Jerusalem Post*, 7 March 2011.

219 Francis C. Assisi, "How Christian Evangelists Target Hindu American Students," Hindu Mahasabha of America, 26 June 2015, http://www.hmsamerica.org/issues/us/; Stuart Federow, "Missionaries," in *Where We Stand: Jewish Consciousness on Campus*, ed. Allan L. Smith (New York: UAHC Press, 1997), 251–59; Allen Proctor, "Proclaiming the Gospel on the College Campus: Feed My Sheep," 8 August 2001, http://www.web.archive.org/web/20050124180027/http://www.campusministry.net/feedmysheep.htm.

220 Pam Chamberlain, "Conservative Campus Organzing: Growing Pains or Arrested Development," *Public Eye Magazine*, Fall 2005; R. J. Eskow, "The Evangelighouls: How the Christian Right Exploits War's Youngest Victims," *Huffington Post*, 3 June 2006, http://www.huffingtonpost.com/. On Campus Crusade founder Bill Bright's political activities, see Turner, *Bill Bright and Campus Crusade for Christ*. In Crusade's early days, Bright emphasized the struggle against communism in the university. Later Bright forged connections with many of the founders of the new Christian Right. While he claimed to separate the campus ministry from his political activities, they sometimes mixed.

221 See Michael Paulson, "Colleges and Evangelicals Collide on Bias Policy," *New York Times*, 9 June 2014; Burton Gollag, "Choosing Their Flock," *Chronicle of Higher Education*, 28 January 2005, 33; Andy Crouch, "Campus Collisions," *Christianity Today*, October 2003, 60–64; Thomas Bartlett, "Law School Can Deny Recognition to Christian Group That Bans Gay and Lesbian Students, Judge Rules," *Chronicle of Higher Education*, 5 May 2006, A46; Michael Cass, "Vanderbilt University Nondiscrimination Policy Called Unfair to Religious Groups," *Tennessean*, 27 September 2011; Brooke Metz, "Cal State Retracts Recognition for InterVarsity on All 23 Campsues," *USA Today*, 18 September 2014; Sarah Eekhoff Zylstra, "Will InterVarsity Losing Cal State Standoff Be Tipping Point for Campus Ministries Nationwide?" *Christianity Today*, 8 September 2014. On the reversal of Cal State's ban, see Jeremy Weber, "InterVarsity Regains Access to Cal State Campuses," *Christianity Today*, 19 June 2015.

222 Micah White, "Spirituality on America's Liberal Campuses: A Call for Dialogue," *Free Inquiry*, Fall 2001; Alwa A. Cooper, "Chabad vs. Hillel: How Two Jewish Students Groups Cooperate and Coexist," *Harvard Crimson*, 8 March 2006; Jared Sichel, "Sharing the Next Gen: How Chabad Is Changing Hillel—and Reshaping Campus Life," *Jewish Journal*, 24 October 2013; Lillian Kwon, "Christian Campus Groups Vow Not to Compete for Students," *Christian Post*, 17 February 2011. On previous meetings between InterVarsity and Campus Crusade, see Turner, *Bill Bright and Campus Crusade for Christ*.

223 Stephanie Keeler, "One Dinner, Two Traditions," MIT News Office, 1 October 2010; Reed Cooley, "Jewish and Muslim Communities Share a Dinner at Fifth Annual Iftar," *GW Hatchet*, 23 October 2006; Katie Walsh, "Interfaith Shabbat Draws Jewish, Muslim Students," *Daily Princetonian*, 3 March 2008; Zeke Pariser and Ibaad Sadiq, "Students Should Work for Better Understanding," *Daily Targum*, 6 September 2011.

224 The "ethical framework" of the University of Southern California Office of Religious Life is available at https://orl.usc.edu/organizations/ethical/.

225 Michael M. Kocet and Dafina Lazarus Stewart, "The Role of Student Affairs in Promoting Religious and Secular Pluralism and Interfaith Cooperation," *Journal of College and Character* 12 (1) (2011). For more information on the University of Delaware's University Religious Leaders Organization, see http://www.udel.edu/spirituallife/. On the University of Kentucky's Interfaith Dialogue Organization, see http://erb.unaoc.org/interfaith-dialogue-organization-university-of-kentucky/. The Penn State Center for Spiritual and Ethical Development posts its code of ethics at https://studentaffairs.psu.edu/spiritual/mission-vision.

226 Survey on InterVarsity reported in Schmalzbauer, "Whose Social Justice?"; John Schmalzbauer, "Social Engagement in an Evangelical Campus Ministry: The Case of Urbana 2006," *Journal of College and Character* 11 (1) (2011); Gerald R. McDermott, *Can Evangelicals Learn from World Religions?* (Downers Grove, IL: InterVarsity Press, 2000); Turner, *Bill Bright and Campus Crusade for Christ*. On Crusade's new name, see https://web.archive.org/web/20120206062430/http://www.ccci.org/about-us/donor-relations/our-new-name/qanda.htm.

227 See Martin E. Marty, "From the Centripetal to the Centrifugal in Culture and Religion," *Theology Today* 51 (1): 5–16 (1994). On the religious center, see Catherine L. Albanese, *America: Religions and Religion* (Belmont, CA: Wadsworth, 1999).

Chapter 5

1 The first section of this chapter is adapted from John Schmalzbauer and Kathleen A. Mahoney, "Religion and Knowledge in the Post-Secular Academy," in *The Post-Secular in Question*, ed. Philip Gorski, David Kyuman Kim, and Jonathan VanAntwerpen (New York: New York University Press, 2012), 234–35.

2 Diane Winston, "Campuses Are a Bellwether for Society's Religious Revival," *Chronicle of Higher Education*, 16 January 1998, A60.

3 A fuller account of campus religion would discuss its influence on American congregations, the nonprofit sector, and the world of work. See chapter 4 for a discussion of the role of church-related colleges in fostering a sense of vocation.

4 Bill Bishop, *The Big Sort: Why the Clustering of Like-Minded Americans Is Tearing Us Apart* (New York: Mariner Books, 2009); Mark Brewer and Jeffrey Stonecash, *Split: Class and Cultural Divides in American Politics* (Washington, DC: CQ Press, 2007). On generational differences, see Paul Taylor, *The Next America: Boomers, Millennials, and*

the Looming Generational Showdown (New York: PublicAffairs, 2014). Diana Eck, *A New Religious America: How a "Christian" Country Has Become the World's Most Religiously Diverse Nation* (New York: HarperSanFrancisco, 2001).

5 John Danforth, *Faith and Politics: How the "Moral Values" Debate Divides America and How to Move Forward Together* (New York: Penguin, 2006). For more information on the mission statement, advisory board, and programs of the Danforth Center, see http://rap.wustl.edu/. See also Tim Townsend, "Danforth Center Unveils Online Magazine 'Religion and Politics,'" *St. Louis Post-Dispatch*, 5 May 2012. The last quote is from R. Marie Griffith, "Letter from the Center Director," *2016–2017 Annual Report*, John C. Danforth Center on Religion and Politics, Washington University in St. Louis, 5. While avoiding partisan rhetoric, Griffith has not hesitated to speak out against racism and white supremacy, as she did following an attack on an antiracist protest in Charlottesville, Virginia. See Griffith, "White Christians Must Condemn White Supremacy," *Religion and Politics*, 15 August 2017.

6 As we noted in chapter 2, Stephen Prothero makes a case for religious studies in *Religious Literacy: What Every American Should Know and Doesn't* (San Francisco: HarperSanFrancisco, 2007). Findings are reported in *U.S. Religious Knowledge Survey* (Pew Forum on Religion and Public Life, Washington, DC, 2010), 37–38.

7 This paragraph draws on Schmalzbauer and Mahoney, "Religion and Knowledge," 234–35. On the professions, see Magali Sarfatti Larson, *The Rise of Professionalism: Sociological Analysis* (Berkeley: University of California Press, 1977), 74. On religion in law and medicine, see Winnifred Fallers Sullivan, "Judging Religion," *Marquette Law Review* 81 (2): 441–60 (1998); Wendy Cadge, "Becoming a Spiritual Generalist? What Physicians Know about Religion and Spirituality," *Huffington Post*, 31 July 2012, http://www.huffingtonpost.com/.

8 Douglas Johnston and Cynthia Sampson, eds., *Religion, The Missing Dimension of Statecraft* (New York: Oxford University Press, 1994). Quotations from Shaun Casey and John Kerry are from "Remarks at the Launch of the Office of Faith-Based Community Initiatives," U.S. Department of State, 7 August 2013, https://2009-2017.state.gov/secretary/remarks/2013/08/212781.htm.

9 Information on the Berkley Center is available at http://berkleycenter.georgetown.edu/.

10 Information on Yale's Faith and Globalization course is available at http://faith.yale.edu/legacy-projects/legacy-projects/faith-globalization/faith-globalization. The first quotation is from Tony Blair, "Education Is a Security Issue," Speech to the Counter-Terrorism Committee of the United Nations, 21 November 2013, https://web.archive.org/web/20160420060118/http://tonyblairfaithfoundation.org/foundation/news/education-security-issue; Claudia Parsons, "Blair to Launch Faith Foundation," Reuters, 29 May 2008. The second quotation is from Tony Blair, "Religious Difference, Not Ideology, Will Fuel This Century's Epic Battles," *Guardian*, 25 January 2014.

11 Edward E. Curtis IV, "Explaining Islam to the Public," Immanent Frame, 9 May 2011, http://blogs.ssrc.org/; Winnifred Fallers Sullivan, "The Extra-Territorial Establishment of Religion," Immanent Frame, 22 March 2010, http://blogs.ssrc.org/; Elizabeth Shakman Hurd, "What's Wrong with Promoting Religious Freedom?" *Foreign Policy*, 12 June 2013. See also Hurd, "International 'Religious Freedom' Agenda Will Only Embolden ISIS," *Religion Dispatches*, 10 November 14. For a response, see Daniel Philpott, "Religious Freedom Advocates Resemble ISIS? Really?" Arc of the Universe: Religion and Global Justice, http://arcoftheuniverse.info/. For a range of responses to the State Department's new Office of Religious Engagement, see "Engaging Religion at the State Department,"

Immanent Frame, 30 July 2013, http://blogs.ssrc.org/. For a defense of the office, see Mark Silk, "A Cheer for the State Department's New Faith Office," Religion News Service, 19 August 2013.

12 Max Weber, *Max Weber: Collected Methodological Writings* (New York: Routledge, 2012); Clifford Geertz, "'From the Native's Point of View': On the Nature of Anthropological Understanding," *Bulletin of the American Academy of Arts and Sciences* 28 (1): 26–45 (1974); T. M. Luhrmann, *When God Talks Back: Understanding the American Evangelical Relationship with God* (New York: Knopf, 2012); R. Marie Griffith, *God's Daughters: Evangelical Women and the Power of Submission* (Berkeley: University of California Press, 1997); Robert Orsi, "Snakes Alive: Resituating the Moral in the Study of Religion," in *In the Face of the Facts: Moral Inquiry in American Scholarship*, ed. Richard Wightman Fox and Robert I. Westbrook (Cambridge: Cambridge University Press, 2002), 213, 226.

13 *Engaging Worldview: A Snapshot of Religious and Spiritual Campus Climate* (Chicago: Interfaith Youth Core, 2014), 22–24. This survey was conducted by Alyssa Rockenbach and Matthew J. Mayhew. Findings on ecumenical worldview and pluralistic orientation reported in Bryant and Mayhew, "How Institutional Contexts and College Experiences Shape Ecumenical Worldview Development," in *Spirituality in College Students' Lives: Translating Research Into Practice*, ed. Alyssa Bryant Rockenbach and Matthew J. Mayhew (New York: Routledge, 2013), 88–104; Alyssa N. Bryant, "The Impact of Campus Context, College Encounters, and Religious/Spiritual Struggle on Ecumenical Worldview Development," *Research in Higher Education* 52 (5): 441–59 (2011). See also William A. Graham, "Why Study Religion in the Twenty-First Century?" *Harvard Divinity Bulletin*, Summer/Autumn 2012; American Academy of Religion, "The Religious Studies Major and Liberal Education," *Liberal Education*, Spring 2009. Information on Harvard Religious Literacy Project is available at http://rlp.hds.harvard.edu/home.

14 The phrase "crypto-theological" comes from Donald Wiebe, *The Politics of Religious Studies: The Continuing Conflict with Theology in the Academy* (New York: Palgrave Macmillan, 1999); Stanley Fish, "Will the Humanities Save Us?" *New York Times* Opinionator Blog, 6 January 2006, http://opinionator.blogs.nytimes.com/; Stanley Fish, *Save the World on Your Own Time* (New York: Oxford University Press, 2008); Stanley Fish, "Academic Virtue," *Lapham's Quarterly*, Fall 2008. See also Russell McCutcheon, "A Default of Critical Intelligence? The Scholar of Religion as Public Intellectual," *Journal of the American Academy of Religion* 65 (2): 443–68 (1997).

15 Eboo Patel, "Is Your Campus Diverse? It's a Question of Faith," *Chronicle of Higher Education*, 17 September 2012. The quotation on campuses as models is from the website of Interfaith Youth Core, https://web.archive.org/web/20170317063528/http://www.ifyc.org/campuses-as-models. See also Robert Nash, *How to Talk about Hot Topics on Campus: From Polarization to Moral Conversation* (San Francisco: John Wiley and Sons, 2008); Robert Nash, "A Clash of Opposing Worldviews: How One Professor Teaches the Intelligent Design / Evolution Controversy," *Religion and Education* 33 (3): 90 (2006).

16 See Cass Sunstein, *Going to Extremes: How Like Minds Unite and Divide* (New York: Oxford University Press, 2009), 4; Eboo Patel, *Sacred Ground: Pluralism, Prejudice, and the Promise of America* (Boston: Beacon Press, 2012); Bryant, "The Impact of Campus Context," 454.

17 On the influence of diverse networks, see Robert Wuthnow, *America and the Challenges of Religious Diversity* (Princeton, NJ: Princeton University Press, 2005), 137–39; Sunstein, *Going to Extremes*; Cass Sunstein, "The Architecture of Serendipity," *Harvard Crimson*, 4 June 2008.

18 Susan Harding, *The Book of Jerry Falwell: Fundamentalist Language and Politics* (Princeton, NJ: Princeton University Press, 2000); Hanna Rosin, *God's Harvard: A Christian College on a Mission to Save America* (Orlando, FL: Harcourt, 2007); "Liberty University Election Poll," *Liberty Champion*, 1 November 2016. For a sample of Liberty University student reactions to Trump, see https://twitter.com/CahnEmily/status/689120714415304709. Tim Mak, "Trump Campaign Bombs in Virginia, Again," *Daily Beast*, 27 August 2016. Quotation about Liberty from Adam Laats, "Why So Many Evangelicals Voted for Trump? Adam Laats Responds," *The Way of Improvement Leads Home*, 8 December 2016, https://thewayofimprovement.com/. For a rebuttal to Laats with voting returns from other evangelical colleges, see Chris Gehrz, "How Did Evangelical College Students Vote in the Presidential Election?" *Pietist Schoolman*, 7 December 2016. See also Samuel Smith, "Hillary Clinton Wins Wheaton College Student Poll," *Christian Post*, 8 November 2016. The second part of this paragraph is adapted from Schmalzbauer and Mahoney, "Religion and Knowledge," 235. On evangelical moderates and progressives, see David Swartz, *Moral Minority: The Evangelical Left in an Age of Conservativism* (Philadelphia: University of Pennsylvania Press, 2012); Robert Wuthnow, *The Struggle for America's Soul: Evangelicals, Liberals, and Secularism* (Grand Rapids, MI: Eerdmans, 1989); Craig Detwiler, *A Purple State of Mind: Finding Middle Ground in a Divided Culture* (Eugene, OR: Harvest House, 2008).

19 Jamie Birdwell, "Professors Debate Israeli-Palestinian Conflict," *Oklahoma Daily*, 4 February 2009; Sophie Dasinger, "New Tufts Chaplaincy Series Seeks Civil Dialogue on Israeli-Palestinian Conflict," *Tufts Daily*, 8 October 2014. See also Debra Nussbaum Cohen, "Muslim-Jewish Dialogue at U.S. Colleges Proves Hard to Sustain," *Haaretz*, 27 February 2014; Chris Bone, "Israel-Palestine Discussions Lack Civility," *Heights*, 7 December 2006; Sarah Burns, "Three Pepper-Sprayed South of UC Berkeley Campus Following Protests," *Daily Californian*, 25 February 2012; "The Statement Magazine: A Polarized Debate," *Michigan Daily*, 14 October 2014.

20 Bonnie Miller, "Lutheran College Opens the Door to Same-Sex Wedding," *Chicago Tribune*, 14 January 2013; Cat Zakrzewski, "Catholic Colleges Respond to Demand for LGBTQ Resources," *USA Today*, 5 September 2013; Kyle Spencer, "A Rainbow over Catholic Colleges," *New York Times*, 30 July 2013. On evangelicals and LGBT students, see Amy Green, "An Unlikely Gay-Straight Alliance," *Christianity Today*, 13 January 2009. Quotations about Eastern Mennonite University from Martha Greene Eads, "Campus Conversations about Sexuality and the Church," *Cresset* 78 (2) (2014). On the limits of such conversations, see Dawne Moon, "Difficult Dialogues: The Technologies and Limits of Reconciliation," in *Religion on the Edge: De-centering and Re-centering the Sociology of Religion*, ed. Courtney Bender, Wendy Cadge, Peggy Levitt, and David Smilde (New York: Oxford University Press, 2012), 179–99. The number of LGBT groups at evangelical colleges was reported in Philip Francis and Mark Longhurst, "How LGBT Students Are Changing Christian Colleges," *Atlantic*, 23 July 2014. For a discussion of the legal issues faced by some religious colleges, see Scott Jaschik, "The Supreme Court Ruling and Christian Colleges," *Inside Higher Ed*, 29 June 2015; Julia K. Stronks, "After Obergefell," *Inside Higher Ed*, 7 July 2015. On Goshen and Eastern Mennonite, see Scott Jaschik, "To Avoid Split on Gay Marriage, 2 Colleges Quit Christian Group," *Inside Higher Ed*, 22 September 2015.

21 Douglas Jacobsen and Rhonda Hustedt Jacobsen, *No Longer Invisible: Religion in University Education* (New York: Oxford University Press, 2012), 83; Libby A. Nelson, "Catholic College, Interfaith Identity," *Inside Higher Ed*, 16 August 2012. Quotation from DePaul

from Office of Religious Diversity website, https://offices.depaul.edu/student-affairs/about/departments/Pages/ord.aspx. Statistic on Catholic Interfaith Youth Core campuses from Kerry Weber, "The Talking Cure," *America*, 13 September 2010. On interfaith activities at Lutheran institutions, see Jason A. Mahn, "Why Interfaith Understanding Is Integral to the Lutheran Tradition," *Intersections*, Fall 2014, 7–16; Eboo Patel, "What It Means to Build the Bridge: Identity and Diversity at ELCA Colleges," *Intersections*, Fall 2014, 23. On evangelicals and interfaith dialogue, see Chris Norton, "Christian Colleges Part of White House Interfaith Service Push," *Christianity Today*, 8 August 2011.

22 According to former InterVarsity Christian Fellowship's president Alec Hill, most institutions include a religious exemption in their nondiscrimination policies. See Hill, "Pluralism at Risk: The University as a Case Study," in *Principled Pluralism: Report of the Inclusive America Project* (Washington, DC: Aspen Institute, 2013), 65–68. Derecognized by the twenty-three-institution California State University system for maintaining a faith test for officers, InterVarsity chose to operate off campus. See Kimberly Winston, "Intervarsity, College Christian Group, 'De-Recognized' at California State University Campuses," *Huffington Post*, 9 September 2014, http://www.huffingtonpost.com/. On the reversal of Cal State's ban, see Jeremy Weber, "InterVarsity Regains Access to Cal State Campuses," *Christianity Today*, 19 June 2015. In 2016, InterVarsity urged staff members who disagreed with the organization's position on homosexuality to resign, provoking a heated debate. See Kate Shelnutt, "InterVarsity Asks Staff to Choose a Stance on Sexuality," *Christianity Today*, 7 October 2016.

23 Sociologist Prema A. Kurien discusses the influence of Hindu nationalism on the Hindu Students Councils in "Being Young, Brown, and Hindu: The Identity Struggles of Second-Generation Indian Americans," *Journal of Contemporary Ethnography* 40 (5): 434–69 (2011). For more on religious diversity in HSC chapters, see the website of the Hindu Students Council, http://hindustudentscouncil.org/about-us/reflections-of-diversity-and-plurality-in-hsc/. For more on the inclusive membership policies of the Cal State Long Beach chapter of the MSA, see Sabrina Stambride, "Christian Group Calls CSU Inclusionary Policy Discriminatory," *Los Angeles Times*, 28 October 2014. On campus Muslims and evangelicals, see Michael De Groote, "Religious Clubs Face Hurdles on Campuses," *Deseret News*, 13 April 2013. On the Ohio State University, see "Victory for Religious Freedom at Ohio State," press release, Foundation for Individual Rights in Education, 4 October 2004, http://www.thefire.org/victory-for-religious-freedom-at-ohio-state/. For contrasting views on this issue, see Tom Krattenmaker, "Christian Should Lead Christians," *USA Today*, 10 November 2014; Mark Joseph Stern, "Christian Groups Beg Public Universities to Subsidize Their Anti-Gay Discrimination," *Slate*, 11 September 2014, http://www.slate.com/.

24 Adam Bell, "Duke University Reverses Decision, Will Not Allow Muslim Call to Prayer at Its Chapel," *Charlotte News-Observer*, 15 January 2015; Eboo Patel, "An Old Bias Found a New Target at Duke U." *Chronicle of Higher Education*, 20 January 2015; Sam Hodges, "Chapels Can Be Battlegrounds, but Trend Is toward Use by All," United Methodist News Service, 2 February 2015, http://www.umc.org/news-and-media/chapels-can-be-battlegrounds-but-trend-is-toward-use-by-all; Tiffany L. Steinwart, "A Legacy of Holiness: Toward a Wesleyan Praxis of Interreligious Engagement in Higher Education," https://oimts.files.wordpress.com/2013/09/2013-6-steinwert.pdf. See also Shabana Mir, *Muslim American Women on Campus: Undergraduate Social Life and Identity* (Chapel Hill: University of North Carolina Press, 2014), 4.

25 On variety among institutions, see Sunstein, *Going to Extremes*, 149–50. The quote is from Nathan Hatch, "Hope and Challenge in the Middle Ground," Keynote Address, Symposium on Religion and the Liberal Aims of Higher Education, Boston College, 8 November 2012, 3–5, available on the Boston College website, http://www.bc.edu/.

26 Ethan Bronner, "A Flood of Suits Fights Coverage of Birth Control," *New York Times*, 26 January 2013; Winnifred Fallers Sullivan, "The Impossibility of Religious Freedom," Immanent Frame, 8 July 2014, http://blogs.ssrc.org/; Beckie Supiano, "Obama Offers New Policy on Contraceptive Insurance at Religious Colleges," *Chronicle of Higher Education*, 10 February 2012; Manya Brachear Pashman, "Wheaton College Ends Coverage amid Fight against Birth Control Mandate," *Chicago Tribune*, 29 July 2015. A 2016 ruling by the U.S. Supreme Court directed lower courts to develop a compromise that religious nonprofits could live with. See David G. Savage, "Supreme Court Ruling Should Clear the Way to Free Birth Control for Women with Religious Employers," *Los Angeles Times*, 16 May 2016. On the Trump administration, see Richard Wolf, "Trump Administration Reversing Obamacare's Birth Control Mandate," *USA Today*, 31 May 2017.

27 On Secretary Sebelius at Georgetown, see Judy Cabassa Tart, "Kathleen Gilligan Sebelius: Advancing the Health of the Nation," *Trinity Magazine*, 2011; Kevin Carey, "The Trinity Sisters," *Washington Monthly*, July/August 2011. For conservative critiques of Sebelius and Pelosi, see Joan Frawley Desmond, "Sebelius Speaks at Georgetown Despite Protests," *National Catholic Register*, 18 May 2012; "Catholic University Extols Pro-Abortion Alumnus Nancy Pelosi," *LifeSiteNews*, 30 January 2008, http://www.lifesitenews.com/. For the text of Sebelius' speech, see Kathleen Sebelius, "HHS Secretary Kathleen Sebelius' Full Remarks to Georgetown University's Public Policy Institute," *Washington Post*, 18 May 2012. The quotation on Ryan is from Laurie Goodstein, "Georgetown Faculty Latest to Chide Ryan," *New York Times*, 24 April 2012; Dan Merica, "In Culture War Skirmishes, Georgetown Becomes Political Football," CNN Belief Blog, 18 May 2012, http://religion.blogs.cnn.com/; David Gibson, "Controversial Koch Brothers Give Big (Again) to Catholic University," Religion News Service, 30 January 2015.

28 The Wolfe quotation is from Elias Crim, "Culture without the War," *American Conservative*, 9 August 2012. The "spanning the gap" quotation is from https://www.facebook.com/ImageJournal/videos/10150269215845525/. The other Wolfe quotation is from Crim, "Culture without the War." Discussion of Ofili from "A Conversation with Charles Pickstone," *Image* (69), https://imagejournal.org/. In April 2018 *Image* terminated founding editor Gregory Wolfe, after an investigation revealed accusations of harassment and a hostile work environment. The journal's future is uncertain.

29 On the artistic contributions of congregations, see Mark Chaves, *Congregations in America* (Cambridge, MA: Harvard University Press, 2004), 183, 179; Robert Wuthnow, *All in Sync: How Music and Art Are Revitalizing American Congregations* (Berkeley: University of California Press, 2003). See also Robert Wuthnow, *Creative Spirituality: The Way of the Artist* (Berkeley: University of California Press, 2001); Matthew Milliner, "The Return of the Religious in Contemporary Art," *Huffington Post*, 6 January 2011, http://www.huffingtonpost.com/.

30 According to Martin Marty, "There is a large enough critical mass of creative energy and people to appreciate it in the Lutheran colleges and universities of the greater Midwest that some sort of tradition has been born: of galleries, choirs, musical compositions, and artistry." See Marty, "Creativity and Creation: A Lutheran Context for the Arts," *Cresset* 47 (4): 5–7. On the role of Lutheran colleges in disseminating a capella choral music, see Paul Benson, "A Cappella Choirs in the Scandinavian-American Lutheran Colleges,"

Norwegian American Studies 32:221–46 (1989); Amy Gage, "St. Olaf Is Deepest, Broadest Source in 'Land of 10,000 Choirs,'" *St. Olaf College News*, 29 July 2002; Gretchen Buggeln, "The Shape of a New Era: Valparaiso's Chapel of the Resurrection in Historical Context," *Cresset* 73 (3): 6–14 (2010); Scott Carlson, "Marcel Breuer at St. John's," *Chronicle of Higher Education*, 7 March 2008; Hilary Thimmesh, "Saint John's University and Minnesota Public Radio," *Headwaters*, 2007, 17.

31 On the Society for the Arts, Religion and Contemporary Culture and other postwar developments, see John Dillenberger, *The Visual Arts and Christianity in America: From the Colonial Period to the Present* (New York: Crossroad, 1989); Betty H. Meyer, *The ARC Story: A Narrative History of the Society for the Arts, Religion, and Contemporary Culture* (New York: CrossCurrents Press, 2003). ARC founder Marvin Halverson was a graduate of Augustana College in South Dakota, a church-related college with deep roots in Norwegian Lutheranism. See also the Society's website, http://www.sarcc.org/index.htm. For a discussion of *motive* and the Methodist student gathering featuring Odetta and Dave Brubeck, see Wilson Yates, "*Motive* Magazine, the Student Movement, and the Arts," *Journal of Ecumenical Studies* 32 (4): 555–73 (1995). The circulation of *motive* is from David Hollinger, *After Cloven Tongues of Fire: Protestant Liberalism in Modern American History* (Princeton, NJ: Princeton University Press, 2013), 39. On the Catholic literary revival, see Paul Elie, *The Life You Save May Be Your Own: An American Pilgrimage* (New York: Farrar, Straus and Giroux, 2003); Arnold Sparr, *To Promote, Defend, and Redeem: The Catholic Literary Revival and the Cultural Transformation of American Catholics, 1920–1960* (Westport, CT: Greenwood Press, 1990).

32 Cynthia L. Haven, "A Public Catholic: An Interview with 2010 Laetare Medalist Dana Gioia," *Commonweal*, 13 May 2010. See also Dana Gioia, "Catholic Sensibility, American Culture, and Public Life," Spring 2000 Joint Consultation, Commonweal Foundation and Faith and Reason Institute, June 2000, http://web.archive.org/web/20060523005646/http://www.catholicsinpublicsquare.org/papers/spring2000joint/jointpanel/jointpanel1.htm. Quotation on ecosystem from the brochure for an *Image* seminar at Laity Lodge, https://web.archive.org/web/20120427125947/http://imagejournal.org/page/events/the-image-seminars/the-image-seminars-texas/program. See also Christine A. Scheller, "Connoisseur for Christ: Roberta Green Ahmanson," *Christianity Today*, 19 January 2011; Eric Gorski, "Evangelicals Start Push in the Arts," Associated Press, 26 July 2007.

33 For more on Christians in the Visual Arts, see http://civa.org/. CIVA statistics from the Council for Christian Colleges and Universities website, http://www.cccu.org/. On the Calvin event, see Agnieszka Tennant, "Electing to Be Open, a Christian Writing Festival Invites Non-believers, Too," *Wall Street Journal*, 16 May 2008; Yvonne Zipp, "Festival of Faith and Writing: The Conference That Brought John Updike, Salman Rushdie to Western Michigan," *Christian Science Monitor*, 23 April 2012.

34 On Baylor's Art and Soul conferences, see https://www.baylor.edu/ifl/index.php?id=935065.

35 The Wolfe quotation is from "Catholic Sensibility, American Culture, and Public Life," Spring 2000 Joint Consultation, Commonweal Foundation and Faith and Reason Institute, June 2000, http://web.archive.org/web/20060523005646/http://www.catholicsinpublicsquare.org/papers/spring2000joint/jointpanel/jointpanel1.htm. The first quotation from Yale Institute for Sacred Music appeared in "Yale Institute of Sacred Music Announces International Fellowship," *Yale News*, 13 July 2009. See also "Christian Wiman Joins Yale Faculty," Institute for Sacred Music, Yale University, available on the Beinecke Rare Book and Manuscript Library website, http://beinecke.library.yale.edu/

about/blogs/poetry-beinecke-library/2013/01/11/beinecke-welcomes-christian-wiman; Christian Wiman, *My Bright Abyss: Meditation of a Modern Believer* (New York: Farrar, Straus and Giroux, 2013); Marcia Z. Nelson, "Poets Can Learn from Theologians: PW Talks with Christian Wiman," *Publishers Weekly*, 8 February 2013; Thomas Gardner, "Marilynne Robinson: Narrative Calvinist," *Christianity Today*, February 2010, 32. The last quotation is from Marilynne Robinson, "2011 Principal Address," College of the Holy Cross Commencement, available on the Holy Cross website, http://www.holycross.edu/commencement/commencement-archives/2011principal-address.

36 The "creative ecosystem" phrase is from the Laity Lodge brochure. On the St. Louis University gallery, see "The Best University Art Museums in America," *Architectural Digest*, 2 May 2017. See also http://www.slu.edu/mocra and http://www.slu.edu/mocra/mocra-past-exhibitions. On Regis University's Faith in Art Program, see https://static1.squarespace.com/static/55d1dd88e4b0dee65a6594f0/t/5604369ee4b01128f1904c21/1443116702380/Regis-Art+at+Regis.pdf. The first statistic and quotations about CCCU art programs are from *2010 National Status Report of Art and Design Programs* (Wenham, MA: Christians in the Visual Arts, 2010), 8, 9. Statistics on new programs in the arts from G. Jeffrey MacDonald, "From Word to Image: Christian Colleges Expand Visual Art Programs," Religion News Service, 17 May 2017.

37 For more on the Buechner Institute, see https://www.buechnerinstitute.com/about/. The Walker Percy Center's website can be found at http://www.loyno.edu/wpc/. Molly Worthen describes the awakening of the evangelical imagination in *Apostles of Reason: The Crisis of Authority in American Evangelicalism* (New York: Oxford University Press, 2013). Though the Inklings have been invoked in the culture wars, their following extends far beyond the religious Right. For more on the Georgetown Faith and Culture lecture series, see https://president.georgetown.edu/initiatives/faith-and-culture.html.

38 For more on Spirit and Place, see http://www.spiritandplace.org/. Information on USC's spirituality and arts program can be found at https://orl.usc.edu/programs/arts/. See the website of the Architecture, Culture, and Spirituality Forum, http://www.acsforum.org/index.htm.

39 For a description of the Luce Foundation's activities in this area, see http://www.hluce.org/archives_news.aspx?page=americanart&year=2001. The quotation on research is from *Crossroads: Art and Religion in American Life*, Proceedings from the Grantmakers in the Arts Conference, November 5–7, 2001, available on the Grantmakers in the Arts website, http://www.giarts.org/sites/; Wuthnow, *Creative Spirituality*; Wuthnow, *All in Sync*; Sally Promey, "The 'Return' of Religion in the Scholarship on American Art," *Art Bulletin* 85 (3): 581–603 (2003); Sally Promey and David Morgan, eds., *The Visual Culture of American Religions* (Berkeley: University of California Press, 2001); David Morgan, *Visual Piety: A History and Theory of Popular Religious Images* (Berkeley: University of California Press, 1999); David Morgan, *The Sacred Gaze: Religious Visual Culture in Theory and Practice* (Berkeley: University of California Press, 2005); Colleen McDannell, *Material Christianity: Religion and Popular Culture in America* (New Haven, CT: Yale University Press, 1995); Colleen McDannell, *Picturing Faith: Photography and the Great Depression* (New Haven, CT: Yale University Press, 2004). For a list of the AAR's program units, see http://papers.aarweb.org/program_units.

40 Survey data on higher education and art reported in Paul DiMaggio, "Arts Participation and Cultural Capital in the United States, 1982–2002," *Poetics* 32: 169–94 (2004). Data on Lutheran colleges from "Comparative Alumni Research: What Matters in College after College," Lutheran Educational Conference of North America, available on the

Lutheran Colleges website, http://lutherancolleges.ncgbeta.com/files/. For the 2006 data on Catholic colleges and the fine arts, see the website of the National Catholic College Admission Association, http://www.catholiccollegesonline.org/resources/pdfs/values-that-matter-2006-hardwick-day.pdf.

41 On the architectural history of campus chapels, see Margaret M. Grubiak, *White Elephants on Campus: The Decline of the University Chapel in America, 1920–1960* (Notre Dame, IN: University of Notre Dame Press, 2014). The quotation from Eero Saarinen appears on page 112. See Kevin M. Schultz, *Tri-Faith America: How Catholics and Jews Held Postwar America to Its Protestant Promise* (New York: Oxford University Press, 2011). On the new diversity, see Eck, *A New Religious America*. On new sacred spaces, see "The 50 Best Campus Meditation Spaces," Best Counseling Schools, http://www.bestcounseling-schools.org/; "10 Colleges with Impressive Meditation Spaces," The Best Colleges, http://www.thebestcolleges.org/; Michael Crosbie, "A New Kind of Sacred Space on Campus," Religion News Service, 21 April 2017.

42 On the impact of campus ministries and the Jesus movement on congregational music, see Larry Eskridge, *God's Forever Family: The Jesus People Movement in America* (New York: Oxford University Press, 2013). For a critique of such music, see Thomas Bergler, *The Juvenilization of American Christianity* (Grand Rapids, MI: Eerdmans, 2012). On Inter-Varsity's National Arts Ministry and local arts communities, see http://arts.intervarsity.org/. Statistic from https://intervarsity.org/about-us/ministry-impact?action. On Catholic colleges and liturgy, see Melanie Morey and John Piderit, *Catholic Higher Education: A Culture in Crisis* (New York: Oxford University Press, 2006), 367. According to Morey and Piderit, "Conventional wisdom in Catholic colleges and universities is that as a result of excellent liturgical experiences on campus, students after graduation often become disenchanted with what parishes have to offer them and frequently disengage from parish life." The "gourmet liturgy" quotation is from Christian Smith in Naomi Schaefer Riley, "College's 'Religious Cliff,'" *Intercollegiate Review*, Fall 2014. Statistics on undergraduate participation in campus religious groups can be found in Smith, *Souls in Transition*, 131.

43 Borrowing from Lawrence Cremin and Robert Wood Lynn, this section considers the ecology of religious institutions to include congregations, youth organizations, campus ministries, and other organizations. The ecology of religious intellectual life is sustained by magazines, colleges and universities, seminaries, and divinity schools. See Dorothy C. Bass and Glenn Miller, "Robert W. Lynn," Protestant Educators, Talbot School of Theology, http://www.talbot.edu/ce20/educators/protestant/robert_lynn/. Historian Matthew Hedstrom charts the emergence of liberal Protestant book culture and spirituality in *The Rise of Liberal Religion: Book Culture and American Spirituality in the Twentieth Century* (New York: Oxford University Press, 2013). On the role of magazines, see Elesha Coffman, *The Christian Century and the Rise of Mainline Protestantism* (New York: Oxford University Press, 2013), 31, 68. Peter Steinfels quoted in Kenneth L. Woodward, "The U.S. Church: Unify Us," *Newsweek*, 8 October 1979. The second part of this paragraph draws on the analysis in John Schmalzbauer, "Editors More Important than Bishops," Call and Response Blog, Duke Divinity School, 21 January 2010, http://www.faithandleadership.com/. Quotation and 40 percent statistic from "Support *Commonweal's* College Subscription Program," *Commonweal*, 6 August 2012, https://web.archive.org/web/20150910065212/http://www.commonwealmagazine.org/support-commonweals-college-subscription-program. Figure of 1,500 students from http://www.commonwealmagazine.org/support-college-program.

44 This paragraph draws on John Schmalzbauer, "The Grand Rapids Intellectuals," *Comment*, 28 March 2012. See also James D. Bratt and Ronald A. Wells, eds., *The Best of "The Reformed Journal"* (Grand Rapids, MI: Eerdmans, 2011). For more on Baker, Eerdmans, Kregel, and Zondervan, see James Bratt and Christopher Meehan, *Gathered at the River: Grand Rapids, Michigan and Its People of Faith* (Grand Rapids, MI: Eerdmans, 1993), 122–23. *Books and Culture* marketing data from http://web.archive.org/web/20100329083041/http://www.ctiadvertising.com/print/books-culture/audience/; Noll, *The Scandal of the Evangelical Mind*, 219. On the Inter-Varsity Press–UK and intellectual renewal, see "IVP Academic Publishing Rationale," Summer 1994, http://www.gospelcom.net/ivpress/academic/rationale.php. Figures on IVP's sales from "Our History," https://www.ivpress.com/about/our-history. Though the stable of IVP authors pales in comparison to the SCM backlist (the SCM Classics line includes such luminaries as Dietrich Bonhoeffer, Jürgen Moltmann, and Wolfhart Pannenberg), InterVarsity has increased the theological literacy of the evangelical public.

45 On Naropa's history, see http://www.naropa.edu/about-naropa/history/index.php. See the website of the Jack Kerouac School of Disembodied Poetics, http://www.naropa.edu/academics/jks/. The quotation and information on Ginsberg's ties to Naropa are from "The Poet That Changed America: Allen Ginsberg—Beat Poet, Activist, Queer American, Buddhist Co-founder of Naropa's Kerouac School," *Elephant*, Autumn 2006, 45–47. The quote appears on page 45.

46 Edward Queen and Stephen Prothero, "Islam," in *Encyclopedia of American Religious History*, ed. Edward Queen and Stephen Prothero (New York: Facts on File, 2009), 521; Gutbi Mahdi Ahmed, "Muslim Organizations in the United States," in *The Muslims of America*, ed. Yvonne Yazbeck Haddad (New York: Oxford University Press, 1991), 16; Osman Bakar, "The Intellectual Impact of American Muslim Scholars on the Muslim World," in *Muslims in the United States: Demography, Beliefs, Institutions*, ed. Philippa Strum and Danielle Tarantolo, Conference Proceedings (Washington, DC: Woodrow Wilson International Center for Scholars, 2003), 151. On Zaytuna College, see Mark Oppenheimer, "A Muslim College Mixes Subjects to Achieve an American Feel," *New York Times*, 12 April 2013. The quote is from Eboo Patel, Panel on "Dyamic Tensions," Proceedings of Symposium on Religion and the Liberal Aims of Higher Education, Boston College, November 9, 2013, 22, available on the Boston College website, http://www.bc.edu/. See also Scott Korb, *Light without Fire: The Making of America's First Muslim College* (Boston: Beacon Press, 2013). On *Renovatio*, see https://renovatio.zaytuna.edu/article/renovatio-a-new-muslim-publication.

47 Charles Kadushin, *The American Intellectual Elite* (New Brunswick, NJ: Transaction, 2006), 15, 20, 24. Jews made up about half of Kadushin's 1970 sample, followed by Protestants and Catholics. On the New York intellectuals, see Joseph Dorman, *Arguing the World: The New York Intellectuals in Their Own Words* (Chicago: University of Chicago Press, 2001). On the growth of Jewish studies, see Robert Eisen, "Jewish Studies and the Academic Teaching of Religion," *Liberal Education*, Fall 2001. On the ecology of Jewish cultural life, see Gary A. Tobin, *A Study of Jewish Culture in the Bay Area* (San Francisco: Institute for Jewish and Community Research, 2002), 53, 20, http://jewishresearch.org/PDFs/Culture_Report_web.pdf. On the *Jewish Review of Books*, see Jordan Michael Smith, "A Jewish Journal of Ideas Is Born," *Haaretz*, 14 February 2010. For more on the 92nd Street Y, see https://www.92y.org/about.aspx.

48 Trinity College's Leonard E. Greenberg Center for the Study of Religion in Public Life was the home of the Pew Program on Religion and the News Media and Lilly

Endowment's Program on Religion by Region. In 2003, the Pew Charitable Trusts established the Center on Religion and the Professions at the University of Missouri. Sponsoring one of the nation's premier journalism programs, Missouri is also the home of the Religion News Association (formerly the Religion Newswriters Association). RNA's Religion Stylebook can be found at http://religionstylebook.com/. The online resource Religion Link is available at http://www.religionlink.com/.

49 See "Web Fills the Void of Shrinking Religion Coverage in Print Media," *Insights into Religion*, http://religioninsights.org/articles/web-fills-void-shrinking-religion-coverage-print-media. The quotation is from Nathan Schneider, *The New Landscape of the Religion Blogosphere* (New York: Social Science Research Council, 2010), 3, 6. This paragraph draws on John Schmalzbauer, "The New Landscape of the Religion Blogosphere," Immanent Frame, 2 March 2010, http://blogs.ssrc.org/. For more on the Luce Foundation's grant to the SSRC, see http://www.hluce.org/rel_intaffgrant.aspx. Christopher D. Cantwell and Hussein Rashid, *Religion, Media, and the Digital Turn: A Report for the Religion and Public Sphere Program* (New York: Social Science Research Council, 2015), 29.

50 *U.S. Religious Knowledge Survey*, 75, 37; Bryant, "The Impact of Campus Context," 441–59. Data on Lutheran colleges from "Comparative Alumni Research."

Chapter 6

1 Quentin Smith, "The Metaphilosophy of Naturalism," *Philo* 4 (2) (2001), www.philoonline.org/library/smith_4_2.htm; Robert B. Townsend, "AHA Membership Grows Modestly, as History of Religion Surpasses Culture," *AHA Today*, 30 June 2009; Alexander W. Astin, Helen S. Astin, and Jennifer A. Lindholm, *Cultivating the Spirit: How College Can Enhance Students' Inner Lives* (San Francisco: Jossey-Bass, 2011).

2 The declension story was told in works such as James T. Burtchaell, *The Dying of the Light: The Disengagement of Colleges and Universities from Their Christian Churches* (Grand Rapids, MI: Eerdmans, 1998); Philip Gleason, *Contending with Modernity: Catholic Higher Education in the Twentieth Century* (New York: Oxford University Press: 1995).

3 Philip Schwadel, "The Effects of Education on Americans' Religious Practices, Beliefs, and Affiliations," *Review of Religious Research* 53:161–82 (2011); Jeremy E. Uecker, Mark D. Regnerus, and Margaret L. Vaaler, "Losing My Religion: The Social Sources of Religious Decline in Early Adulthood," *Social Forces* 85 (4): 1667–92 (2007); Jonathan Hill, "Faith and Understanding: Specifying the Impact of Higher Education on Religious Belief," *Journal for the Scientific Study of Religion* 50 (3): 533–51 (2011).

4 On the peak in religious philanthropy, see Robert Wuthnow and D. Michael Lindsay, "Financing Faith: Religion and Strategic Philanthropy," *Journal for the Scientific Study of Religion* 49 (1): 87–111 (2010). See also Robert Wuthnow and D. Michael Lindsay, "The Role of Foundations in American Religion," in *American Foundations: Roles and Contributions*, ed. Helmut K. Anheier and David C. Hammack (Washington, DC: Brookings Institution Press, 2010), 305–27.

5 Wuthnow and Lindsay, "Financing Faith," 106. With the exception of the Danforth Center, the Danforth family has stayed out of this area for decades.

6 Lilly Endowment's annual reports are available at http://www.lillyendowment.org/annualreports.html. The endowment's Religion Division awarded $141 million in 2000, $135 million in 2001, and $237 million in 2002. On the drop in Lilly's assets (which began before the Great Recession), see "Lilly Endowment's 2008 Losses Continuation of Eight-Year Decline in Assets," *Philanthropy News Digest*, 25 May 2009. According to

this report, Lilly's portfolio declined from $15.6 billion in 2000 to $5.7 billion at the end of 2008. See also "Slow Economy Impacts Lilly Endowment," *Inside Indiana Business*, 18 May 2010; Brad A. Greenberg, "Perfect Storm for Charities: Contributions Go Down and Requests Go Up," *Jewish Journal*, 19 November 2008; Kathy L. Gilbert, "Church Giving, Membership Decline in Recession," United Methodist News Service, 8 March 2010.

7 "Starr's Vision, 2012 and Beyond," *Baylor Lariat*, 23 August 2010.

8 Alexander W. Astin and Calvin Lee, *The Invisible Colleges: A Profile of Small, Private Colleges with Limited Resources* (New York: McGraw-Hill, 1972). See "ELCA-Affiliated Dana College Shuts Down," *Lutheran*, 1 July 2010; Scott Jaschik, "The Sale of Waldorf," *Inside Higher Ed*, 6 May 2009; Christopher S. Pineo, "Marian Court College to Close at End of June," *Pilot*, 26 June 2015; Lawrence Biemiller, "Iowa's Small Colleges Scrap for Students and Survival," *Chronicle of Higher Education*, 29 May 2011; Martin Van Der Werf, "The Precarious Balancing Act at Small Liberal-Arts Colleges," *Chronicle of Higher Education*, 30 July 1999. See also Kim Clark, "Why Black Colleges Might Be the Best Bargains," *US News*, 9 February 2009; Ken Camp, "Christian Colleges Not Spared from Recession's Impact," *Associated Baptist Press*, 27 August 2010. On the closing of the Institute for the Study of American Evangelicals, see Michael S. Hamilton, "Philanthropic Funding, the ISAE, and Evangelical Scholarship," *Evangelical Studies Bulletin*, Fall 2014, 6–8.

9 Niraj Chokshi, "The Economy's Bouncing Back. But Higher Education Funding Isn't," *Washington Post*, 13 May 2015; "The Academic Study of Religion in the Face of Budget Cuts," *Religious Studies News*, October 2009, 25–26. For more information on Miami University's budget cuts, see the February 2, 2010, issue of the *Miami Student*. Arizona State University's cuts were discussed in "ASU Announces Budget Reduction Plan," *ASU News*, 18 August 2008. Jessica Jimenez, "UC Berkeley Discontinues Religious Studies Program," *Daily Californian*, 5 March 2017. AAR data from Scott Jaschik, "Praying for Jobs," *Inside Higher Ed*, 13 November 201. Michael Kisielewski with John Curtis, "Faculty Position Opportunities in Sociology Appear to Hold Steady: Position Postings from the 2013 ASA Job Bank," *Data Brief*, August 2014, 7. The same ASA report found that religion ranked seventeenth out of seventy in a list of graduate student specializations, suggesting a mismatch between openings and student interests.

10 Robert D. Putnam, *Bowling Alone: The Collapse and Revival of American Community* (New York: Simon and Schuster, 2000); "Number of Americans Who Read Print Newspapers Continues to Decline," Pew Research Center, 11 October 2012, http://www.pewresearch.org/; "Beyond Borders: American Bookshops in Decline," *Economist*, 21 March 2011; Philip Kennicott, "America's Orchestras Are in Crisis," *New Republic*, 25 August 2013; David Carr, "Wondering How Far Magazines Must Fall," *New York Times*, 12 August 2012. For a comparison of the newspaper business and American denominations, see Anthony B. Robinson, "Articles of Faith: Newspapers, Protestants Share Sad Realities," *Seattle Post-Intelligencer*, 30 January 2009.

11 Robert T. Handy, "The American Religious Depression, 1925–1935," *Church History* 29 (1): 3–16 (1960); Pew Forum on Religion and Public Life, *"Nones" on the Rise: One-in-Five Adults Have No Religious Affiliation* (Washington, DC: Pew Research Center, 2012). Figures on giving and church construction from Ben Leubsdorf, "Decline in Church-Building Reflects Changed Tastes and Times," *Wall Street Journal*, 4 December 2014. See also Katherine Burgess, "Report: Church Giving Reaches Depression-Era Record Lows," Religion News Service, 24 October 2013; Michael Hout and Claude Fischer, "Why More Americans Have No Religious Preference: Politics and Generations," *American Sociological Review* 67: 165–90 (2002); Frank Newport, "Most Americans Say Religion

Is Losing Influence in U.S." Gallup, 29 May 2013. On Europe and America, see Mark Chaves, "The Decline of American Religon?" ARDA Guiding Papers Series, 2011, 1, http://www.thearda.com/. Chaves also discusses the softening of church attendance.

12 Kathryn Lofton discussed the "hysteria of some colleagues about the end of the university" and the "claims that religion will end" in her remarks at the Third Biennial Conference on Religion and American Culture. See Lofton, "The Future of the Study of American Religion," in *Proceedings: Third Biennial Conference on Religion and American Culture*, Center for the Study of Religion and American Culture, Indiana University–Purdue University Indianapolis, June 2013.

13 Kevin Carey, *The End of College: Creating the Future of Learning and the University of Everywhere* (New York: Riverhead Books, 2015); Ryan Craig, *College Disrupted: The Great Unbundling of Higher Education* (New York: Palgrave Macmillan, 2015); Goldie Blumenstyk, *American Higher Education in Crisis? What Everyone Needs to Know* (New York: Oxford University Press, 2015); "Clayton Christensen Talks Venture Capital, Crowd Funding, and How to Measure Your Life," *Tech Crunch*, 6 April 2013; Clayton M. Christensen and Henry J. Eyring, *The Innovative University: Changing the DNA of Higher Education* (San Francisco: John Wiley and Sons, 2011); Nathan Harden, "The End of the University as We Know It," *American Interest*, January/February 2013; "Higher Ed: An Obituary," *New Criterion*, January 2013; Jon Marcus, "Higher Education Is Headed for a Shakeout," *Hechinger Report*, 3 September 2013; Michael Kinsley, "How the Internet Will Disrupt Higher Education's Most Valuable Asset: Prestige," *Washington Post*, 5 Februrary 2016. See also NPR Staff, "Debate: In an Online World, Are Brick and Mortar Colleges Obsolete?" National Public Radio, 9 April 2014, http://www.npr.org/. Along the same lines, the cover of the September 2014 issue of the *Atlantic* asked the question "Is College Doomed?" See Graeme Wood, "The Future of College?" *Atlantic*, September 2014.

14 The statistic on the increased cost of higher education appeared in "Cost of College Degree in U.S. Soars 12 Fold: Chart of the Day," *Bloomberg*, 15 August 2012. Statistics on public institutions from Scott Thurm, "Who Can Still Afford State U?" *Wall Street Journal*, 14 December 2012. See also Ruth Simon, "Public-University Costs Soar," *Wall Street Journal*, 6 March 2013. The 2013 survey from Moody's Investor Services appeared in Andrew Martin, "Colleges Expect Lower Enrollment," *New York Times*, 10 January 2013. See also Jeffrey J. Selingo, *College (Un)Bound: The Future of Higher Education and What It Means for Students* (Boston: New Harvest, 2013). See also "Moody's: US Higher Education Sector Outlook Revised to Negative as Revenue Growth Prospects Soften," Moody's Investor Services, 5 December 2017, https://www.moodys.com/.

15 Verlyn Klinkenborg, "The Decline and Fall of the English Major," *New York Times*, 22 June 2013; Francesca Donner, "Are Humanities Degrees Doomed? Experts Weigh In," At Work, *Wall Street Journal*, 6 June 2013, http://blogs.wsj.com/atwork/2013/06/06/whats-a-college-student-to-study-experts-weigh-in/; David Silbey, "A Crisis in the Humanities?" Edge of the American West blog, *Chronicle of Higher Education*, 10 June 2013, http://chronicle.com/; Diane Sheets, "The Crisis in the Humanities: Why Today's Educational and Cultural Experts Can't and Won't Resolve the Failings of the Liberal Arts," *Huffington Post*, 15 June 2013, http://www.huffingtonpost.com/. See *The Teaching of the Arts and Humanities at Harvard College: Mapping the Future* (Cambridge, MA: Harvard University, 2013); *The Heart of the Matter: The Humanities and Social Sciences* (Cambridge, MA: American Academy of Arts and Sciences, 2013); David Brooks, "The Humanist Vocation," *New York Times*, 20 June 2013.Alan Brinkley, "The Landscape of Humanities Research

and Funding," Humanities Indicator Project (Cambridge, MA: American Academy of Arts and Sciences, 2009).

16 On neoliberalism and higher education, see Tarak Barkawi, "The Neoliberal Assault on Academia," *Al Jazeera*, 25 April 2013. See also Clayton M. Christensen, Michael B. Horn, Louis Soares, and Louis Caldera, *Disrupting College: How Disruptive Innovation Can Deliver Quality and Affordability to Postsecondary Education* (Washington, DC: Center for American Progress, 2011); Christensen and Eyring, *The Innovative University*; T. Vance McMahan and Mario Loyola, *College 2.0: Transforming Higher Education through Greater Innovation and Smarter Regulation* (Washington, DC: U.S. Chamber of Commerce, 2011); Robert Kuttner, "Higher Education: The Coming Shakeout," *Huffington Post*, 26 May 2013, http://www.huffingtonpost.com/; Byron G. Auguste, Adam Cota, Kartik Jayaram, and Martha C. A. Laboissiere, *Winning by Degrees: The Strategies of Highly Productive Higher-Education Institutions* (New York: McKinsey, 2010). Education researcher Arthur Levine compares higher education to the book industry and newspapers in Levine, "Essay on the Nature of Change in Education and the Media," *Inside Higher Ed*, 21 October 2014. See also Craig, *College Disrupted*.

17 Steve Forbes, "Dinosaur U." *Forbes*, 9 February 2011; Michael Horn, "Disruptive Innovation and Education," *Forbes*, 2 July 2014; Nick Morrison, "Blended Learning: The Future of Higher Education," *Forbes*, 29 January 2016, http://www.forbes.com; Dinesh Paliwal, "Engineering Is the New Liberal Arts," *Forbes*, 24 February 2016.

18 William J. Bennett and David Wilezol, *Is College Worth It?* (Nashville, TN: Thomas Nelson, 2013), 92. On Bennett's shift, see Andrew Hartman, "How Austerity Killed the Humanities," *In These Times*, 19 May 2015.

19 Scott Jaschik, "Florida GOP vs. Social Science," *Inside Higher Ed*, 12 October 2011.

20 Katie Billotte, "Conservatives Killed the Liberal Arts," *Salon*, 14 September 2012, http://www.salon.com. For examples of progressive advocates of online education and disruptive innovation, see Thomas Friedman, "Revolution Hits the Universities," *New York Times*, 26 January 2013; Kuttner, "Higher Education: The Coming Shakeout"; Aamer Madhani, "Obama Apologizes for Joking About Art History Majors," *USA Today*, 19 February 2014. Comment on online learning from Barack Obama, "Remarks by the President in Working Mothers Town Hall," 15 April 2015, available on the Obama White House Archives website, https://obamawhitehouse.archives.gov/.

21 Out of the 884 courses available on edX in early 2017, only 34 included the words "religion" or "religious." Religion is also neglected in the for-profit sector. Still the largest player in online learning (despite recent drops in enrollment), the University of Phoenix offers just four undergraduate religious studies courses. Information on edX courses retrieved from https://www.edx.org/. For course listings, see www.phoenix.edu.

22 Stacy Rapacon, "10 Worst College Majors for a Lucrative Career," *Kiplinger*, 7 September 2017, http://www.kiplinger.com/; Derek Thompson, "Fear of a College-Educated Barista: Is There Really a Millennial Underemployment Crisis? Yes, but Only among Liberal-Arts Majors," *Atlantic*, 20 September 2016; Douglas Belkin, "Liberal Arts Colleges, in Fight for Survival, Focus on Job Skills," *Wall Street Journal*, 24 April 2017. Figures on majors from the Humanities Indicators project of the American Academy of Arts and Sciences. For data on religion degrees, see http://www.humanitiesindicators.org/content/indicator doc.aspx?i=10996. Data on the proportion of degrees awarded to humanities majors reported in Scott Jaschik, "Study Shows 8.7% Decline in Humanities Bachelor's Degrees in 2 Years," *Inside Higher Ed*, 14 March 2016; Steven Pearlstein, "Meet the Parents Who

Won't Let Their Children Study Literature," *Washington Post,* 2 September 2016; Kellie Woodhouse, "Arts and Sciences Deficits," *Inside Higher Ed,* 4 June 2015.

23 Kellie Woodhouse, "Closure Concerns and Financial Strategies: A Survey of College Business Officers," *Inside Higher Ed,* 17 July 2015; "Moody's: One Third of US Colleges Facing Falling or Stagnant Tuition Revenues," Moody's Investors Service, 10 January 2013, https://www.moodys.com/; Dawn Lyken-Segosebe and Justin Cole Shepherd, "Learning from Closed Institutions: Indicators of Risk for Small Private Colleges and Universities," Higher Education Leadership and Policy Studies, Vanderbilt University, July 2013, available on the Tennessee Independent Colleges and Universities Association website, http://www.ticua.org/public_policy/sm_files/Learning%20from%20Closed%20 Institutions.pdf. On the CCCU, see Chris Gehrz, "How Financially Sustainable Are Christian Colleges?" *Pietist Schoolman,* 27 June 2013. Forbes ratings available at Matt Schifrin, "Is Your College Going Broke? The Most and Least Financially Fit Schools in America," *Forbes,* 24 July 2013. See also Paul Blezien and Polly Graham, "The Voice of Experience: A Phenomenological Study of Institutional Budgeting and Prioritization at Faith-Based Higher Education Institutions," in *Funding the Future: Preparing University Leaders to Navigate the Coming Change,* ed. Stephen T. Beers, Timothy W. Herrman, and Paul Blezien (Abilene, TX: ACU Press, 2012), 21. The quotation is from Anderson, "Summit on the Hill Address," 21 September 2013, http://wp.stolaf.edu/president/public-remarks/summit-on-the-hill-address/.

24 Richard Vedder, "The Perfect Storm: A Coming Revolution?" *Chronicle of Higher Education,* 30 October 2010. See also Steve Cohen, "A Perfect Storm Is Heading toward Higher Education," *Time,* 25 February 2015.

25 See Goldie Blumenstyk, "One-Third of Colleges Are on Financially 'Unsustainable' Path, Bain Study Finds," *Chronicle of Higher Education,* 23 July 2012. Quotation on stereotypes from Council of Independent Colleges Campaign for the Liberal Arts website, https://www.cic.edu/programs/liberal-arts-campaign. See also Beckie Supiano, "Now Defending the Liberal Arts on Twitter: A Couple of Cartoons," *Chronicle of Higher Education,* 20 August 2014; Libby and Art's tweets can be found at https://twitter.com/SmartColleges. Employer data reported in Hart Research Associates, *It Takes More than a Major: Employer Priorities for College Learning and Student Success,* 10 April 2013, 2, 7, http://www.aacu.org/leap/documeNts/2013_employersurvey.pdf.

26 Quotation from Silbey, "A Crisis in the Humanities?" See also Jeffrey Brainard, "Are the Humanities on the Ropes? Maybe Not," *Chronicle of Higher Education,* 28 February 2010. Data on philosophy and religious studies majors from "Change in Number of Bachelor's Degrees Awarded by Field of Study, 1991–2011," *Almanac of Higher Education 2013* (Washington, DC: Chronicle of Higher Education, 2013). For 1987 and 2014 data on religion degrees, see "Degree Completions in the Academic Study of Religion," http://www.humanitiesindicators.org/. For more on salaries in various majors, see "2016–2017 PayScale College Salary Report," PayScale, http://www.payscale.com/. Data on majors that "change the world" from "2016–2017 PayScale College Salary Report," PayScale, http://www.payscale.com/college-salary-report/most-meaningful-majors?page=22. See also Debra Humphreys and Patrick Kelly, *How Liberal Arts and Sciences Majors Fare in Employment: A Report on Earnings and Long-Term Career Paths* (Washington, DC: Association of American Colleges and Universities, 2014). Data comparing midcareer salaries from Melissa Korn, "Liberal Arts Salaries Are a Marathon, Not a Sprint," *Wall Street Journal,* 22 January 2014.

27 I. Elaine Allen and Jeff Seaman, *Distance Education Enrollment Report 2017* (Babson Park, MA: Babson Survey Research Group, 2017), 4. Survey data on presidents from Scott Jaschik, "MOOC Skeptics at the Top," *Inside Higher Ed*, 2 May 2013. Other quotations are from Ghanashyam Sharma, "A MOOC Delusion: Why Visions to Educate the World Are Absurd," *Chronicle of Higher Education*, 15 July 2013; Will Oremus, "Forget MOOCS," *Slate*, September 2013, http://www.slate.com/; Judith Shulevitz, "Don't You Dare Say 'Disruptive,'" *New Republic*, 15 August 2013. Patricia McGuire is quoted in Scott Carlson and Goldie Blumenstyk, "For Whom Is Higher Education Being Disrupted?" *Chronicle of Higher Education*, 17 December 2012.

28 On physical copresence, see Louis Betty, "The End of the University?" *Inside Higher Ed*, 1 February 2013. The quote about the obsolescence of residential colleges is from Nathan Harden, "The End of the University as We Know It," The American Interest, January/February 2013. For a different view of place, see Matthew J. Milliner, "Ghosts of Princeton Past," *Books and Culture*, September/October 2013, ; Gretchen Buggeln, "Campus Places and Placemaking: Tradition and Innovation in the Architecture of American Higher Education," *Cresset* 74 (4): 6–16 (2011). Darryl Tippens advocates blended approaches in Douglas Belkin, "Can MOOCs and Universities Co-exist?" *Wall Street Journal*, 11 May 2014. See also Tippens, "Technology Has Its Place: Behind a Caring Teacher," *Chronicle of Higher Education*, 6 August 2012.

29 Kathryn Masterson, *Online Education: Heading toward the Future* (Washington, DC: Chronicle of Higher Education, 2017), 10, 4. Information on edX courses from https://www.edx.org/. On the edX Bible course, see Yasmine Hafix, "Harvard Bible edX Course 'Early Christianity: The Letters of Paul' Draws 22,000 Students from 180 Countries—and Counting," *Huffington Post* 21 January 2014, http://www.huffingtonpost.com/; "As Harvard Hosts the World's Largest Bible Course, Pat Robertson's Regent Launches MOOC," *Christianity Today*, 24 January 2014.

30 On Arizona State University's ventures in online higher education, see Michael M. Crow and William B. Dabars, *Designing the New American University* (Baltimore: Johns Hopkins University Press, 2015). For more on ASU Online's religious studies major, see http://asuonline.asu.edu/online-degree-programs/undergraduate/bachelor-arts-religious-studies. Quotation from Ellen Posman and Reid B. Locklin, "Translating Religion Courses to an Online Format," *Religious Studies News*, May 2013, http://rsnonline.org/.

31 Enrollment figures for Grand Canyon University and Liberty University from Allen and Seaman, *Distance Education Enrollment Report 2017*, 28. Clifford quoted in Paul Glader, "Online Christian Higher Ed Skyrockets," *Christianity Today*, October 2014. Mary Beth Marklein, "Jerry Falwell's Legacy: A Thriving Liberty University," Religion News Service, 23 September 2013. On Liberty's status as the largest private nonprofit institution, see Nick Anderson, "Virginia's Liberty Transforms into Evangelical Mega-University," *Washington Post*, 4 March 2013. Data on Liberty's growth from "Fastest-Growing Campuses: 2001–11," *Almanac of Higher Education*. See also Sean Coughlan, "Google Reveals Most Searched-for Universities," *BBC News*, 23 September 2014; Jack Stripling, "An Online Kingdom Come," *Chronicle of Higher Education*, 23 February 2015; Danielle Douglas-Gabriel, "These 20 Schools Are Responsible for a Fifth of All Graduate School Debt," *Washington Post*, 9 July 2015. The $800 million figure is from Tobin Grant, "Liberty University, a Hub of Conservative Politics, Owes Rapid Growth to Federal Student Loans," *Washington Post*, 15 July 2015.

32 Indiana Wesleyan 2017 enrollment figures from https://www.indwes.edu/about/quick-facts and https://www.indwes.edu/adult-graduate/online/. See also Byron G.

Auguste, Adam Cota, Kartik Jayaram, and Martha C. A. Laboissiere, *Winning by Degrees: The Strategies of Highly Productive Higher-Education Institutions* (New York: McKinsey, 2010). The 2015 enrollment of BYU-Idaho is from Allen and Seaman, *Distance Education Enrollment Report 2017,* 28.

33 L. Gregory Jones, "Traditioned Innovation," *Faith and Leadership,* 20 January 2009; Mary Jacobs, "Learning Swerve—UMC Institutions Enter Online Education World," *United Methodist Reporter,* 8 October 2012. Project DAVID quotations from Eric Childers and Ann Hill Duin, "Project DAVID: A Framework for Vocation and Reinvention in Liberal Arts Colleges" and "Moving Forward," in *Project DAVID: Vocation and Reinvention in Liberal Arts Colleges,* ed. Eric Childers and Ann Hill Duin (2014), 15, 157, http://conservancy.umn.edu/handle/11299/162339.

34 For a list of edX partners, see https://www.edx.org/schools. See NotreDameX on edX's website, https://www.edx.org/school/notredamex. Along with "Math in Sports," Notre Dame has offered "Jesus in Scripture and Tradition." Jackson Sveen, "Davidson Joins Online Learning Consortion edX," *Weekly Herald,* 31 May 2013. For a list of edX courses, see https://www.edx.org/.

35 Libby A. Nelson, "A Global Jesuit University?" *Inside Higher Ed,* 27 March 2013; Peter Tormey, "Jesuit Commons: Higher Education at the Margins," *Gonzaga,* 2012. See also https://www.jwl.org/en/home.

36 On the confused purposes of higher education, see John Thelin, "Success and Excess: The Contours and Character of American Higher Education," *Society,* April 2013, 106–14. On corporatization and neoliberalism, see Nicolaus Mills, "The Corporatization of Higher Education," *Dissent,* Fall 2012; Victoria Harper, "Henry A. Giroux: Neoliberalism, Democracy, and the University as Public Sphere," *Truthout,* 22 April 2014. Gaye Tuchman is quoted in "Exchange: What the Economy Holds for Higher Education," *Contexts* 14: 15 (2009). The "hedge against utilitarian values" quote is from Andrew Delbanco, *College: What It Was, Is, and Should Be* (Princeton, NJ: Princeton University Press, 2012), 32. The quotation about disruption is from Jill Lepore, "The Disruption Machine," *New Yorker,* 23 June 2014.

37 For more on these trends, see Robert D. Putnam and David E. Campbell, *American Grace: How Religion Divides and Unites Us* (New York: Simon and Schuster, 2010); Mark Chaves, *American Religion: Contemporary Trends* (Princeton, NJ: Princeton University Press, 2011); George Gallup and Michael Lindsay, *Survey the Religious Landscape: Trends in U.S. Beliefs* (Harrisburg, PA: Morehouse, 2000); Dean Kelly, *Why Conservative Churches Are Growing* (New York: Harper and Row, 1972); Eck, *A New Religious America*; Wade Clark Roof, *Spiritual Marketplace: Baby Boomers and the Remaking of American Religion* (Princeton, NJ: Princeton University Press, 1999); "Religion in the Aftermath of September 11: A Question and Answer Session with George Gallup, Jr. and Frank Newport," Gallup News Service, 21 December 2001.

38 On the softening of church attendance, see Chaves, *American Religion,* 42–54. On the shifting patterns of religious involvement across generations, see Putnam and Campbell, *American Grace,* 82–133. On the decline in the Christian share of the American population and statistics on the "nones," see Pew Research Center, *America's Changing Religious Landscape* (Washington, DC: Pew Research Center, 2015), 3, 11. See also Pew Forum on Religion and Public Life, *"Nones" on the Rise.*

39 The first quote is from Gary Laderman, "The Rise of Religious 'Nones' Indicates the End of Religion as We Know It," *Huffington Post,* 20 March 2013, http://www.huffingtonpost.com. See also Roger Finke and Rodney Stark, *The Churching of America, 1776–2005:*

Winners and Losers in Our Religious Economy (New Brunswick, NJ: Rutgers University Press, 2005). On the end of the evangelical boom, see Putnam and Campbell, *American Grace*, 105. On religion's changing influence, see Cathy Lynn Grossman, "American's Confidence in Religion Hits New Low," Religion News Service, 17 June 2015. The 77 percent figure is from "Most Americans Say Religion Is Losing Its Influence," Gallup News Service, 29 May 2013; Chaves, "The Decline of American Religion?" 1; Robert P. Jones, *The End of White Christian America* (New York: Simon and Schuster, 2016). See also Luis Lugo, "The Decline of Institutional Religion," Faith Angle Forum, 18 March 2013, available at http://www.washingtonpost.com/r/2010-2019/WashingtonPost/2013/03/25/Editorial-Opinion/Graphics/Pew-Decline-of-Institutional-Religion.pdf.

40 On the connections between the "nones" and the growth of religious publishing, see Matthew Hedstrom, "A History of the Unaffiliated: How the 'Spiritual Not Religious' Gospel Has Spread," *Religion Dispatches*, 24 October 2012. On Barnes and Noble as synagogue, see Robert C. Fuller, *Spiritual, but Not Religious: Understanding Unchurched America* (New York: Oxford University Press, 2001), 153–74. On the influence of religious studies on new spiritualities, see Amanda Porterfield, *The Transformation of American Religion* (New York: Oxford University Press, 2001), 210, 203. Gary Laderman discusses the search for religious meaning in popular culture in "The Rise of Religious 'Nones.'"

41 Pew Forum on Religion and Public Life, *"Nones" on the Rise*, 22, 24, 10, 22.

42 Survey data reported in Penny Long Marler, "'Being Religious' or 'Being Spiritual' in America: A Zero-Sum Proposition?" *Journal for the Scientific Study of Religion* 41 (2): 289–300 (2002). See also Nancy T. Ammerman, "Spiritual but Not Religious? Beyond Binary Choices in the Study of Religion," *Journal for the Scientific Study of Religion* 52 (2): 267 (2013); Sean McCloud, "Nones, Somes, and the Combinativeness of American Religious Practices," *Huffington Post*, 28 February 2013, http://www.huffingtonpost.com/.

43 This discussion of Harvard and alternative spirituality draws on Courtney Bender's *The New Metaphysicals: Spirituality and the American Religious Imagination* (Chicago: University of Chicago Press, 2010), 23. See also Louis Menand, *The Metaphysical Club: A Story of Ideas in America* (New York: Farrar, Straus and Giroux, 2001); William James, *The Varieties of Religious Experience: A Study in Human Nature* (New York: Modern Library, 1902); Don Lattin, *The Harvard Psychedelic Club: How Timothy Leary, Ram Dass, Huston Smith, and Andrew Weil Killed the Fifties and Ushered in a New Age for America* (San Francisco: HarperOne, 2010); Harvey Cox, *Turning East: Why Americans Look to the Orient for Spirituality—And What That Search Can Mean to the West* (New York: Simon and Schuster, 1977).

44 Barry A. Kosmin and Ariela Keysar, *Religious, Spiritual and Secular: The Emergence of Three Distinct Worldviews among American College Students* (Hartford, CT: Trinity College, 2013), 8, 9, 18, 20. The 2016 figure is from Kevin Eagan, Ellen Bara Stolzenberg, Abigail K. Bates, Melissa C. Aragon, Maria Ramirez Suchard, and Cecilia Rios-Aguilar, *The American Freshman: National Norms, Fall 2016* (Los Angeles: Higher Education Research Institute, 2017), 42, https://www.heri.ucla.edu/monographs/TheAmericanFreshman2016.pdf. The 1971 religious affiliation figure and data on self-rated spirituality are from Kevin Eagan, Ellen Bara Stolzenberg, Hilary B. Zimmerman, Melissa C. Aragon, Hannah Whang Sayson, and Cecilia Rios-Aguilar, *The American Freshman: National Norms, Fall 2014* (Los Angeles: Higher Education Research Institute, 2014), 9, 10, https://www.heri.ucla.edu/monographs/TheAmericanFreshman2014.pdf. On the decline of religiosity before college, see Jean M. Twenge, Julie J. Exline, Joshua B. Grubbs, Ramya Sastry, and W. Keith Campbell, "Generational and Time Period Differences in American Adolescents'

Religious Orientation, 1966–2014," PLOS One, 11 May 2015, 11. See also Tobin Grant, "College Freshmen Less Religious than Ever—Just Like Their Parents," Religion News Service, 17 March 2015. Data on increased interest in spirituality reported in Alexander W. Astin, Helen S. Astin, and Jennifer A. Lindholm, *Cultivating the Spirit: How College Can Enhance Students' Inner Lives* (San Francisco: Jossey-Bass, 2011). The last statistic is from *The Spiritual Life of College Students: A National Study of College Students' Search for Meaning and Purpose* (Los Angeles: Higher Education Research Institute, UCLA, 2004), 4.

45 On the appeal of religious colleges to spiritual seekers, see Beth McMurtrie, "Catholic Colleges Greet an Unchurched Generation," *Chronicle of Higher Education*, 13 October 2014.

46 Peter Berger, "The Desecularization of the World: A Global Overview," *The Desecularization of the World: Resurgent Religion and World Politics*, ed. Peter Berger (Grand Rapids, MI: Eerdmans, 1999), 2; *Religious Adherents Globally on the Rise* (Tony Blair Faith Foundation, 2014), https://web.archive.org/web/20160420055338/http://tonyblairfaithfoundation.org/religion-geopolitics/reports-analysis/report/religious-adherents-globally-rise. The Blair Foundation cites Brian J. Grim et al., *Yearbook of International Religious Demography* (Leiden: Brill, 2014). See also Pew Forum on Religion and Public Life, *The Global Religious Landscape: A Report on the Size and Distribution of the World's Major Religious Groups as of 2010* (Pew Research Center: Washington DC, 2010). On global religious demographics in 2050, see "The Future of World Religions: Population Growth Projections, 2010–2050," Pew Research Center, 2 April 2015, http://www.pewforum.org/; Sarah Pulliam Bailey, "The World Is Expected to Become More Religious," *Washington Post*, 24 April 2015. On the shift of Christianity's "center of gravity," see Philip Jenkins, *The Next Christendom: The Coming of Global Christianity* (New York: Oxford University Press, 2011), 1.

47 Pew Forum on Religion and Public Life, *The Future of the Global Muslim Population: Projections for 2010–2030* (Washington, DC: Pew Research Center, 2011); Linda Learman, ed., *Buddhist Missionaries in the Era of Globalization* (University of Hawai'i Press, 2005); Steven Vertovec, *The Hindu Diaspora: Comparative Patterns* (New York: Routledge, 2000).

48 On the internationalization of the field, see Gregory Alles, "Afterword: Toward a Global Vision of Religious Studies," in *Religious Studies: A Global View*, ed. Gregory Alles (New York: Routledge, 2008), 301–22; David John Frank and Jay Gabler, *Reconstructing the University: Worldwide Shifts in Academia in the 20th Century* (Stanford, CA: Stanford University Press, 2006), 89–116.

49 See Gregory Alles, "The Study of Religions: The Last 50 Years," in *The Routledge Companion to the Study of Religion*, ed. John R. Hinnells (New York: Routledge, 2010), 39–55. On the IAHR, see http://www.iahr.dk/.

50 Rick Ostrander, "In the Developing World, a Renaissance in Christian Higher Education," *Chronicle of Higher Education*, 10 October 2013; Joel A. Carpenter, "Universities on the Mission Field? Part I: New Evangelical Universities: Cogs in a World System, or Players in a New Game," *International Journal of Frontier Missions* 20 (2): 55–65 (2003); Joel A. Carpenter, "Universities on the Mission Field? Part II: New Evangelical Universities: Cogs in a World System, or Players in a New Game," *International Journal of Frontier Missions* 20 (3): 95–102 (2003); Perry L. Glanzer, "Dispersing the Light: The Status of Christian Higher Education around the Globe," *Christian Scholars Review* 43 (4): 321–43 (2013); Joel A. Carpenter, Perry L. Glanzer, and Nicholas Lantinga, eds., *Christian Higher Education: A Global Reconnaissance* (Grand Rapids, MI: Eerdmans, 2014). Statistics from Perry L. Glanzer, Joel A. Carpenter, and Nick Lantinga, "Looking for God in the University:

Examining Trends in Christian Higher Education," *Higher Education* 61 (6): 728, 729 (2011). Rick Ostrander, "The Next Revolution," *Books and Culture*, May/June 2014, 31.

51 Megan Lindow and Joseph Krauss, "Islamic Universities Spread through Africa," *Chronicle of Higher Education*, 6 July 2007, A33–A37. Global statistics on Muslim institutions from James Arthur, *Faith and Secularisation in Religious Colleges and Universities* (New York: Routledge, 2006), 3.

52 Quotation from the International Association of Buddhist Universities from http://www.iabu.org/About and http://www.iabu.org/Members/Universities-List. Information on the International Association of Theravada Buddhist Universities from http://atbu.org/. A master list of participants in the association's 2007 conference is available at http://atbu.org/Members. The mission of Banares Hindu University can be found at http://www.bhu.ac.in/aboutus/obj.php.

53 Statistics from Clarence P. Shedd, *Two Centuries of Student Christian Movements: Their Origin and Intercollegiate Life* (New York: Association Press, 1934), 372. See also Dana Robert, *Christian Mission: How Christianity Became a World Religion* (West Sussex, UK: Wiley-Blackwell, 2009), 60. See also David P. Setran, *The College "Y": Student Religion in the Era of Secularization* (New York: Palgrave Macmillan, 2007; Clarence P. Shedd, *A Century of Christian Student Initiative* (New York: Association Press, 1945); Robin Boyd, "The Witness of the Student Christian Movement," *International Bulletin of Missionary Research* 31 (3): 3–8 (2007).

54 Robert Woodberry commented on the influence of the YMCA on the Young Men's Muslim Association, Young Men's Hebrew Association, and Young Men's Buddhist Association at "Religion and the Open Society Symposium: Session Three: Religion, Innovation and Economic Progress," Council on Foreign Relations, 25 March 2008, available on the Council on Foreign Relations website, https://www.cfr.org/. See also Torkel Brekke, *Prophecy and Protest in the Age of Globalization* (Cambridge: Cambridge University Press, 2012), 57. On the Young Men's Buddhist Association in Ceylon, see Mark Frost, "'Wider Opportunities': Religious Revival, Nationalist Awakening, and the Global Dimension in Colombo, 1870–1920," *Modern Asian Studies* 36 (4): 963, 944 (2002). For information on the Young Men's Hindu Association, the Young Men's Sikh Association, and the Young Men's Jain Association in colonial India, see Susan Billington Harper, *In the Shadow of the Mahatma: Bishop V. S. Azariah and the Travails of Christianity in British India* (Grand Rapids, MI: Eerdmans, 2000), 50–51. On the Young Men's Muslim Association and the Palestinian revolt, see Israel Gershoni, "The Muslim Brothers and the Arab Revolt in Palestine, 1936–39," *Middle Eastern Studies* 22 (3): 367–97 (1986). On the YMMA and the Muslim Brotherhood, see Peter Mandaville, *Global Political Islam* (New York: Routledge, 2007), 69. See also Elizabeth Fuller Collins, "Islam and the Habits of Democracy: Islamic Organizations in Post–New Order South Sumatra," *Indonesia* 78: 93–120 (2004). On the YMBA in contemporary Sri Lanka, see the Colombo chapter's website, http://www.ymba-colombo.org/. On Islamic Student Associations in the United Kingdom, see Miri Song, "Part of the British Mainstream? British Muslim Students and Islamic Student Associations," *Journal of Youth Studies* 15 (2): 143–60 (2012).

55 Information on the contemporary reach of the WSCF from http://www.wscfglobal.org/. For an account of its history, see Risto Lehtonen, *Story of a Storm: The Ecumenical Student Movement in the Turmoil of Revolution* (Grand Rapids, MI: Eerdmans, 1998); John B. Lindner, Alva I. Cox Jr., and Linda-Marie Delloff, *By Faith: Christian Students among the Cloud of Witnesses* (New York: Friendship Press, 1991). See also Christine Ledger,

"Historical Sketch of the WSCF," https://web.archive.org/web/20170403195045/http://www.wscfap.org/globalmovement/history.html.

56 Current statistics from IFES can be found at https://ifesworld.org/en/about. On its history, see Pete Lowman, *The Day of His Power: A History of the International Fellowship of Evangelical Students* (Leicester, UK: Inter-Varsity Press, 1983); Donald W. B. Robinson, "Fifty Years of the International Fellowship of Evangelical Students," *Lucas* 23, 24: 111–20 (1997–1998). For more on Cru, see John G. Turner, *Bill Bright and Campus Crusade for Christ: The Renewal of Evangelicalism in Postwar America* (Chapel Hill: University of North Carolina Press, 2008). Statistics on Cru's presence on international campuses from http://demoss.com/newsrooms/cru/background/fact-sheet-campus.

57 For more on Korea Campus Crusade (SOON Movement), see Rebecca Y. Kim, *God's New Whiz Kids? Korean American Evangelicals on Campus* (New York: New York University Press, 2006).

58 Jeffrey Mehlman, *Émigré New York: French Intellectuals in Wartime Manhattan, 1940–1944* (Baltimore: Johns Hopkins University Press, 2000); Lewis Coser, *Refugee Scholars in America: Their Impact and Their Experiences* (New Haven, CT: Yale University Press, 1984). Statistics from Dongbin Kim, Lisa Wolf-Wendel, and Susan Twombly, "International Faculty: Experiences of Academic Life and Productivity in U.S. Universities," *Journal of Higher Education* 82 (6): 720–21 (2011).

59 A list of AAR presidents can be found at https://www.aarweb.org/about/past-presidents; Kwo Pui-lan, "2011 Presidential Address: Empire and the Study of Religion," *Journal of the American Academy of Religion* 80 (2): 285–303 (2012). Other AAR presidents have addressed global themes. See Diana Eck, "Prospects for Pluralism: Voice and Vision in the Study of Religion," *Journal of the American Academy of Religion* 75 (4): 743–76 (2007); Mark Juergensmeyer, "2009 Presidential Address: Beyond Words and War; The Global Future of Religion," *Journal of the American Academy of Religion* 78 (4): 882–95 (2010); Ninian Smart, "2000 Presidential Address: The Future of the Academy," *Journal of the American Academy of Religion* 69 (3): 549 (2001). SBL numbers from John Dart, "Scholars and Believers," *Christian Century*, 5 April 2011, 38. See the website of the International Connections Committee, https://www.aarweb.org/about/international-connections-committee.

60 Statistics on American undergraduates studying abroad from *Opendoors "Fast Facts"* (Boston: Institute of International Education, 2016). First quotation on study abroad from https://eap.ucsb.edu/academics/Religious-Studies. Second quotation from https://religiousstudies.artsci.wustl.edu/programs/study_abroad.

61 Data on international student enrollment from "International Student Enrollment and U.S. Higher Education Enrollment, 1948/49–2015/16," Institute of International Education, available on the Institute website, https://www.iie.org/. Data on countries of origin from Neil G. Ruiz, *The Geography of Foreign Students in U.S. Higher Education: Origins and Destinations*, Brookings Institution Report, 29 August 2014, available on the Brookings website, http://www.brookings.edu/research/interactives/2014/geography-of-foreign-students#/M10420. Data on second-generation students from Sandra Staklis and Laura Hern, *New Americans in Postsecondary Education: A Profile of Immigrant and Second-Generation American Undergraduates* (Washington, DC: National Center for Education Statistics, 2012), 5. On responses to the Trump presidency, see Elizabeth Redden, "Will International Students Stay Away?" *Inside Higher Ed*, 13 March 2017; Elizabeth Redden, "'Serious Times' for International Education," *Inside Higher Ed*, 1 June 2017.

62 On the Berkeley Young Men's Buddhist Association, see http://www.berkeleysangha.org/hi/history1.htm. On the early Muslim Students' Association, see Altaf Husain, "Envisioning a Continent Wide Student Organization," *MSA Link*, Fall/Winter 2008, 8–9, https://web.archive.org/web/20120326160426/www.msanational.org/MSA_Content/Projects/msa_link/link_fall_winter2008.pdf. The 2006 figures for Korea Campus Crusade were reported in Kim, *God's New Whiz Kids?* 31. See also Rebecca Y. Kim, *The Spirit Moves West: Korean Missionaries in America* (New York: Oxford University Press, 2015); Gina A. Bellofatto and Todd M. Johnson, "Key Findings of Christianity in Its Global Context, 1970–2020," *International Bulletin of Missionary Research* 37 (3): 161 (2013); Steve Sang-Cheol Moon, "The Protestant Missionary Movement in Korea: Current Growth and Development," *International Bulletin of Missionary Research* 32 (2): 59 (2008). The ten largest missionary agencies in Korea include University Bible Fellowship (1,463 members), Campus Mission International (561 members), and Youth with a Mission (386 members).

63 Data on specific institutions from "International Students: Leading Institutions by Institutional Type," Institute of International Education, available on the Institute website, https://www.iie.org/.

64 On support systems for undocumented immigrants at Catholic institutions, see Libby A. Nelson, "Documenting the Undocumented," *Inside Higher Ed*, 26 February 2013. "Statement of AJCU Presidents on Undocumented Students," press release, 30 November 2016, available on the Association of Jesuit Colleges and Universities website, http://www.ajcunet.edu/. Statistics on Latinos at American colleges and universities from "Hispanic-Serving Institutions (HSIs): 2012–13," http://www.edexcelencia.org/research/hsis-2012-13.

65 Joseph Shaw, *Dear Old Hill: The Story of Manitou Heights, the Campus of St. Olaf College* (Northfield, MN: St. Olaf College, 1992); James D. Bratt, *Dutch Calvinism in Modern America: A History of a Conservative Subculture* (Grand Rapids, MI: Eerdmans, 1984); Jay Dolan, *The Irish Americans: A History* (New York: Bloomsbury Press, 2008). On the "Fighting Irish," see Murray A. Sperber, *Shake Down the Thunder: The Creation of Notre Dame Football* (Bloomington: Indiana University Press, 2002). On the "Flying Dutch," see the website of the athletic department of Hope College, http://athletics.hope.edu/landing/index.

66 On immigration and religious vitality, see Peter Berger, Grace Davie, and Effie Fokas, *Religious America, Secular Europe? A Theme and Variations* (Burlington, VT: Ashgate, 2008), 30. On cultural pluralism and American religion, see R. Stephen Warner, "Work in Progress toward a New Paradigm for the Sociological Study of Religion in the United States," *American Journal of Sociology* 98 (5): 1058 (1993).

67 On the decline of America's largest evangelical denomination, see Molly Worthen, "Did the Southern Baptist 'Conservative Resurgence' Fail?" *Daily Beast*, 1 June 2014, https://www.thedailybeast.com/. On immigrants and church growth, see Wesley Granberg-Michaelsen, "The Hidden Immigration Impact on American Churches," Religion News Service, 23 September 2013. See also Lekan Oguntoyinbo, "Reaching Out to Hispanic Students May Be Key for Some Colleges' Survival," *Diverse*, 8 October 2013; Eric Hoover, "Minority Applicants to Colleges Will Rise Significantly by 2020," *Chronicle of Higher Education*, 10 January 2013; John Lauerman, "Enrollment in U.S. Colleges Declines for a Second Year," *Bloomberg*, 24 September 2014; Mark Hugo Lopez and Richard Fry, "Among Recent High School Grads, Hispanic College Enrollment Rate Surpasses That of Whites," Pew Research Center Fact Tank, 4 September 2013, http://www.pewresearch.org/; Jeanne Kim, "This Fall, Minorities Will Outnumber White Students in U.S. Schools," *Atlantic*,

20 August 2014; Ronald Roach, "Report: National Pool of High School Graduates to Shrink, Grow More Diverse," *Diverse*, 17 January 2013.

68 On the "softening" of church attendance, see Chaves, *American Religion*. On the postwar revival, see A. Roy Eckardt, *The Surge of Piety in America: An Appraisal* (New York: Association Press, 1958); Douglas Sloan, *Faith and Knowledge: Mainline Protestantism and American Higher Education* (Louisville, KY: Westminster John Knox Press, 1994). The reference to today's resurgence is from Lisa Miller, "Religious Studies Revival," *Newsweek Education*, 12 September 2010.

69 The "new depression" quote can be found in M. A. Farber, "College Financial Crisis Found in Carnegie Study," *New York Times*, 4 December 1970. The list of institutions that were classified as financially troubled or "headed for trouble" is from M. A. Farber, "Universities: They Face 'Greatest Financial Crisis Ever,'" *New York Times*, 6 December 1970; Douglas Martin, "Earl Cheit: Prescient Educator, Dies at 87," *New York Times*, 13 August 2014; Peter Monaghan, "Boston College Mourns a Former Leader Who Helped Bring It Prominence," *Chronicle of Higher Education*, 20 February 2011. Boston College 2017–2018 endowment from https://www.bc.edu/bc-web/about/bc-facts.html.

70 On the survival of most colleges and universities, see Judith Shulevitz, "The Future of College Is Not as Bleak as You Think," *New Republic*, 21 August 2014. Thelin is quoted in "Interview with John Thelin," *Figure/Ground*, 25 March 2013, http://figureground.org. Levine's comments appear in Arthur Levine, "Why Higher Education Cannot Resist Disruptive Change," *Forbes*, 16 July 2014.

71 On the possible decline of American religion, see Chaves, *American Religion*; Chaves, "The Decline of American Religion?"; Philip Jenkins, "A Secular Latin America?" *Christian Century*, 12 March 2013; Tobin Grant, "The Great Decline: 61 Years of Religiosity in One Graph, 2013 Hits a New Low," Religion News Service, 5 August 2014; Philip Zuckerman, *Society without God: What the Least-Religious Nations Can Tell Us about Contentment* (New York: New York University Press, 2008), 2.

72 Chaves, "The Decline of American Religion?" 10; Emma Green, "American Religion Is Complicated, Not Dead," *Atlantic*, 13 May 2015. Figures on church membership from Finke and Stark, *The Churching of America*, 23. Comparative data are available in Peter B. Andersen, Peter Gundelach, and Peter Lüchau, "Religion in Europe and the United States: Assumptions, Survey Evidence, and Some Suggestions," *Nordic Journal of Religion and Society* 21 (1): 61–74 (2008). On the persistence of religious studies in a secularizing Europe, see Michael Stausberg, "The Study of Religion(s) in Western Europe (II): Institutional Developments after World War II," *Religion* 38 (4): 305, 311 (2008). On student piety in Britain, see Mathew Guest, Kristine Aune, Sonya Sharma, and Rob Warner, *Christianity and the University Experience: Understanding Student Faith* (London: Bloomsbury, 2013), 214, 137, 98. The quotation from *Times Higher Education* appeared in the introduction to Gerald Pillay, "Christianity and the University Experience: Understanding Student Faith, by Mathew Guest, Kristin Aune, Sonya Sharma and Rob Warner," *Times Higher Education*, 12 September 2013. According to Guest and his colleagues, "Christian students include a larger proportion of active, institutionally committed individuals than the Christian population in the broader national context." See Guest et al., *Christianity and the University Experience*, 98. On alternative spiritualties in Britain, see Linda Woodhead, "Mind, Body, Spirit: It's the De-Formation of Religion," *Guardian*, 7 May 2012.

73 Versions of these scenarios are discussed in Ostrander, "In the Developing World"; Michaelsen, "The Hidden Immigration Impact."

74 The percentage of nonaffiliated persons in the world is reported in Pew Research Center, "Religiously Unaffiliated," 18 December 2012, http://www.pewforum.org/. Statistics on Brazil and Uruguay from Jenkins, "A Secular Latin America?" Statistics on religiously unaffiliated Latinos from Kimberly Winston, "Hispanics Increasingly Identify as 'Nones,'" Religion News Service, 17 October 2013. On Asian American "nones," see Stephen Prothero, "My Take: Asian Immigration Is Making the U.S. Less Religious," *CNN Belief Blog*, 20 June 2012. On ex-Muslims in Western countries, see Darren E. Sherkat, "Losing Their Religion: When Muslim Immigrants Leave Islam," *Foreign Affairs*, 22 June 2015.

75 On the secularization of non-Western church-related universities and colleges, see Joel A. Carpenter, "Introduction," in *Christian Higher Education: A Global Reconnaissance*, ed. Joel A. Carpenter and Perry Glanzer (Grand Rapids, MI: Eerdmans, 2014), 3; Kuk-Won Shin, "Korean Christian Higher Education: History, Tasks, and Vision," in Carpenter and Glanzer, *Christian Higher Education*, 97. On Latin America, see José Ramón Alcántara Mejía, "Christian Higher Education in Mexico," in Carpenter and Glanzer, *Christian Higher Education*, 191–205; Alexandre Brasil Fonseca and Cristiane Candido Santos, "Christian Higher Education in Brazil and Its Challenges," in Carpenter and Glanzer, *Christian Higher Education*, 207–29. Quotation on Buddhist higher education from Izumi Ogura, "To Attract Students, Universities Stay Buddhist in All but Name," *Asahi Shimbun*, 1 September 2007, http://www.buddhistchannel.tv/. On the narrowly vocational and technical focus on church-related higher education, see the contributors to Carpenter and Glanzer, *Christian Higher Education*. On the global crisis of the humanities, see Philip Altbach, "Dangerous Neglect of the Humanities," *Education World*, September 2008; Matthew Reisz, "World Crisis in Humanities, Not Many Hurt," *Times Higher Education*, 21 October 2010; Ella Delany, "Humanities Studies under Strain Around the Globe," *New York Times*, 1 December 2013.

76 "Religious Hostilities Reach Six-Year High," Pew Research Center, 14 January 2014, http://www.pewforum.org/; "The New Wars of Religion," *Economist*, 1 November 2007.

77 Kevin McDonald, "ISIS Jihadis Aren't Medieval—They Are Shaped by Modern Western Philosophy," *Guardian*, 9 September 2014; Giles Fraser, "It's Not the Religion That Creates Terrorists, It's the Politics," *Guardian*, 27 June 2015; Arun Kundnani, *A Decade Lost: Rethinking Radicalisation and Extremism* (London: Claystone, 2015); Elizabeth Shakman Hurd, "A Suspension of (Dis)Belief: The Secular-Religious Binary and the Study of International Relations," in *Rethinking Secularism*, ed. Craig Calhoun, Mark Juergensmeyer and Jonathan Van Antwerpen (New York: Oxford University Press, 2011), 171.

78 Philip Schwadel, "Birth Cohort Changes in the Association between College Education and Religious Non-affiliation," *Social Forces*, 1 August 2014, 24; Christian Smith with Patricia Snell, *Souls in Transition: The Religious and Spiritual Lives of Emerging Adults* (New York: Oxford University Press, 2009), 249–50.

79 Lofton, "The Future of the Study of American Religion," https://raac.iupui.edu/wp-content/uploads/2017/09/Proceedings2013.pdf.

INDEX